Cambridge Studies in Ethnomusicology

General Editor: John Blacking

Khyāl

This book is a study of *khyāl*, the genre of North Indian classical music which has dominated in performances by highly trained vocalists for at least the past 150 years. It is also a study of cultural history. Spanning as it does a good portion of the periods of the British raj in India, the struggle for independence, and the flourishing of India as a republic, the history of *khyāl* and of *khyāl* singers is a story of generous patronage by native princes, of the loss of this patronage when courts were dissolved, and of the resilience of musicians in adjusting to the vicissitudes of contemporary artistic life.

In performing *khyāl*, the singer presents a brief composition, and then improvises from twenty to forty minutes according to certain guidelines. One chapter of this book describes the compositions, the modal and metric materials, and the improvisational guidelines utilized by *khyāl* singers. Descriptions are illustrated with musical examples in transcription (in Western notation and also in a modified Indian notation) and on an accompanying cassette.

Because *khyāl* was developed by musicians employed at courts scattered throughout North India, the manner of performing it varies among different groups of musicians (*gharānā*s). Bonnie Wade considers six major group traditions – Gwalior, Agra, Sahaswan/Rampur, Alladiya Khan, Kirana, and Patiala – tracing the personal histories of singers (both members of lineages and other disciples), presenting the statements made in Indian sources about their musical styles, and considering those statements through analysis of recorded performances by leading musicians of recent decades. Since individual artistic achievement is so important among musicians in the Hindustani tradition, and in the development and performance of *khyāl*, this perspective is also considered.

The book contains an extensive bibliography and discography, as well as illustrations of *khyāl* in performance, genealogical charts, and maps.

Cambridge Studies in Ethnomusicology

General Editor: John Blacking

Ethnomusicological research has shown that there are many different ingredients in musical systems. The core of this series will therefore be studies of the logics of different musics, analysed in the contexts of the societies in which they were composed and performed. The books will address specific problems related to potential musical ability and practice, such as how music is integrated with dance, theatre and the visual arts, how children develop musical perception and skills in different cultures and how musical activities affect the acquisition of other skills. Musical transcriptions will be included, sometimes introducing indigenous systems of notation. Cassettes will accompany most books.

forthcoming volumes:

Peter Cooke, *The Fiddle Tradition of the Shetland Isles*
Regula Burckhardt Qureshi, *Sound, Context and Meaning in the Qawwali*

To singers of *khyāl*: past, present, and future

Khyāl

Creativity within
North India's classical music tradition

Bonnie C. Wade

Professor of Music
University of California at Berkeley

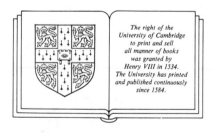

The right of the
University of Cambridge
to print and sell
all manner of books
was granted by
Henry VIII in 1534.
The University has printed
and published continuously
since 1584.

Cambridge University Press

Cambridge
London   New York   New Rochelle
Melbourne   Sydney

Published by the Press Syndicate of the University of Cambridge
The Pitt Building, Trumpington Street, Cambridge CB2 1RP
32 East 57th Street, New York, NY 10022, USA
296 Beaconsfield Parade, Middle Park, Melbourne 3206, Australia

© Cambridge University Press 1984

First published 1984

Printed in Great Britain at
the University Press, Cambridge

Library of Congress catalogue card number: 84–1755

British Library Cataloguing in Publication Data
Wade, Bonnie C.
Khyal – (Cambridge studies in ethnomusicology)
1. Music, Hindustani – History and criticism
I. Title
784′.0954   ML338
ISBN 0 521 25659 3

Contents

Illustrations

Plates

Maps

Preface

This is a monograph on a genre of Indian classical music, *khyāl*, which was cultivated in the princely states of Hindustan from about the mid eighteenth century and has been the predominant concert vocal genre since the early nineteenth century. Chapter 1 sets the scene, describing the Hindustani musical system briefly, sketching the political situation in which *khyal* has been cultivated, and initiating the discussion of musicians who have cultivated it. Chapter 2 delineates the three types of characteristics which distinguish *khyal* as a genre: (1) the particular melodic, metric, and compositional materials which can be utilized; (2) the selection of types of improvisation (*ālāp*, *tān*, *boltān*, *bolbāṇṭ*, *sargam*, and *nom-tom*) which are acceptable; and (3) the placement of all of those materials for the creation of a formally balanced and aesthetically pleasing performance. Because *khyal* is an improvisatory genre, this is not a study of a *repertoire* of vocal music; rather, it is a study of musical knowledge and choice.

While all *khyal* singers retain the generalized characteristics of the genre, there are also distinct ways of performing *khyal*; these distinct styles are termed *gharānā* traditions. In a clear instance of socio-musical contexts influencing performance practice, *gharana* traditions were spawned by the conditions in which *khyal* developed – the diverse vocal genres that preceded it, the different family musical traditions fostered within it, and patronage of the singers in courts of Hindustan as widely separated as Gwalior in present-day Madhya Pradesh and Patiala in the northwestern Punjab. Chapters 3, 4 and 5 are discussions of the Gwalior, Agra, and Sahaswan *gharana*s respectively, and Chapters 6, 7 and 8 are devoted to the Alladiya Khan, Kirana, and Patiala *gharana*s. Each of these chapters considers the context and the musicians of the *gharana* and their musical styles, and closes with a summary. In addition, Chapter 9 considers musicians who have attained prominence more as individuals than by association with the musical style of any single group. It has not been possible to discuss all *khyal* singers in each *gharana*, and so some choices had to be made. This was determined largely by the availability of both printed materials about an artist and his or her music, and sound recordings of an artist's performances. My intention was to consider those artists for whom I had at least four performances (but exceptions were made in a few cases).

Recorded performances which I have analyzed are from several sources. My own taped collection of about 150 performances, gathered in 1968–9, was the basic source; it is available at the University of California, Berkeley, and the University of California, Los Angeles, Ethnomusicology Archive. Several other recordings are in the UCLA archive collection proper, while others are owned by the Department of Music at Brown University and the Department of Music at the University of California, Berkeley. I owe personal thanks to my colleagues Brian Silver and Regula Burckhardt Qureshi who provided me with a selection of rare recorded items. For printed materials, I utilized the resources at the Nehru Memorial Library, the National Archives, and the Library of the Sangeet Natak Akademi in New

Delhi, the Library of the Department of Music at Delhi University, and the National Library in Calcutta. In the United States, I found the South Asia collection in the Regenstein Library at the University of Chicago most fruitful, and appreciated the courtesies extended to me there by Maureen Patterson and her staff.

Interviews with leading musicians of different *gharana*s were important; I was not permitted to record these, so I made it a practice to read my notes back for clarification, correction, or approval. In this respect, there are many musicians, archivists, scholars, technicians, critics, teachers, and others to whom I am indebted; they know who they are and deserve my thanks. I offer special thanks here to Yunus Husain Khan, Sumati Mutatkar, Dipali Nag, Lakshman Krishnarao Pandit, Vinay Chandra Maudgalya, Pran Nath, Nasir Ahmed Khan, Munnawar Ali Khan, Irene Roy Chowdhury, Dilip Chandra Vedi, and Amar Nath. For specific training in *khyal* I am particularly appreciative of instruction by Pran Nath (vocal: Kirana) and Sharda Sahai (*tablā*: Benares (Varanasi)).

The music examples in this study are given in two systems of notation. I transcribed from recordings in a *sargam* notation (indicating pitch by the Indian solfege syllables) which I 'created' to incorporate the Western notational system of showing pitch contour. I then transnotated the examples into Western staff notation. The principal incompatibility of Western notation in these examples is in the indications of rhythm. If carried out thoroughly, Western notation of rhythm gives the impression of greater precision than singers of *khyal* intend at some moments in their performances; when those moments arise in the examples included here, I have left off the stems and rhythm signs, placing the pitches relative to the *tabla* strokes. The key for the notational systems is on pp. x–xiv. I am grateful to Kate Sanderson, who accomplished the formidable task of copying my *sargam* notations, to Jane Imamura, who prepared the Western notations to coordinate with them, and to Janet Smith, who assisted us with numerous graphic details. I am also grateful to Sangeet Karyalaya, Music Publishers, Hathras, and to the Sangit Gaurava Granth Mala of Poona for permission to reproduce the compositions shown in Exx. 2–4a and 2–4b.

I wish to acknowledge the support which made this study possible: United States Educational Foundation, Fulbright, 1968–9; the American Institute of Indian Studies, Senior Research Fellowship, 1978; the University of California, Berkeley, Humanities Research Fellowship, 1981; and the University of California, Berkeley, research stipends, 1976–83.

In a more personal vein, I have benefitted by discussions of my research with Daniel Neuman, Regula Burckhardt Qureshi, Harriet Hurie, and graduate students at the University of California, Berkeley, especially Peter Maund and Myla Lyons. For assistance in assuring 'accuracy' in the Hindi song text translations, I thank my colleagues at the University of California, Berkeley, Department of South and Southeast Asia Studies – Usha Jain, Bruce Pray, Karine Schomer, and Rita Sahai. Preparation of the genealogical charts was ably completed by Yos Santasombat of the Department of Anthropology at the University of California, Berkeley. Preparation of the accompanying cassette was completed by Michael Gore.

Four other persons have been particularly helpful with the final preparations of this book. Ann Pescatello has been a good colleague in developing several facets of this study; Rosemary Dooley, of Cambridge University Press, has been an extremely supportive and knowledgeable editor; Judith Nagley, of Cambridge University Press, undertook with spirit, skill, and intelligence the daunting task of subediting this manuscript; and John Blacking, without whose foresight the book would not have reached this stage, has been a sympathetic colleague in ethnomusicology. I owe much to him in ways too numerous to mention, not the least of which has been our dialogue in ethnomusicology, which has led to this volume.

BONNIE C. WADE

University of California, Berkeley
September 1983

Note on music examples

All music examples are transcriptions by the author from recorded performances. Transcription decisions were made in terms of the form of *sargam* notation developed for this book; the examples were then transnotated into Western notation. The greatest difference between this *sargam* notation system and Hindustani systems is the inclusion here of melodic contour for increased readability (in terms of Western notation).

Key to *sargam* notation

Tāla and rhythm

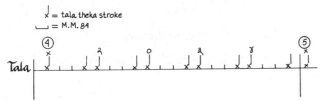

Read across for the *tala* line. A vertical line through the staff indicates end of *tala* cycle.

× ꓽ o ꓷ ꓩ	(count 1, 2nd *tali*, *khali*, 3rd *tali*, 4th *tali*) indicate beginning of *tala* subdivisions
④	Number of the *tala* cycle being performed
⌣	Unit of time, either a count or subdivision of a count
⌣ = M.M. 84	One unit performed at the metronome-speed indicated
⌿	*Tabla* stroke written on the *tala* line, indicating
	(*a*) start of a *tala* count, or
	(*b*) start of a *tala* subdivision, or
	(*c*) *tala theka* stroke, or
	(*d*) other *tabla* stroke

Subdivisions within a unit of time

R S̥ — 2 pitches of equal duration, e.g. ♩♪ or ♫ or ♬

G R̥ S̥ R — 4 pitches of equal duration, e.g. ♩♩♩♩ or ♬♬

G̲R̲ (with tie)	Rhythmic relationship of 3 + 1, e.g. ♪♩
G R (with tie)	Rhythmic relationship of 1 + 3, e.g. ♩♪
G R S (with tie)	Rhythmic relationship of 1 + 2 + 1, e.g. ♪♪♪
GRS / 3	3 equal durations, e.g. ♪♪♪ (³)
GRSRG / 5	5 equal durations, e.g. (⁵)
G R S	1/2 the unit subdivided into 2 equal durations, e.g. ♪♪♪
GRSRG	1/2 the unit subdivided into 4 equal durations, e.g.
G RS R / 3	1/2 the unit subdivided into 3 equal durations, e.g.
G R S / 3	3 equal durations within 2 units of time, e.g. ♩♩♩ (³)
D N S	When no rhythmic indication underlies multiple pitches in a unit, rhythm is indefinite.
,	Breath mark (*see* Articulation and dynamics below)
,—	Rest, after a breath (e.g. in first half of unit ,—s there is a rest: ⅞ ♪ or ⅞ ♪ or ⅞ ♪)
—	Sustained pitch (e.g. in S —S previous pitch is sustained through first half of unit: ♩ ♪)

Pitch

Entire pitch selection of the example is given in a vertical column at the beginning; thereafter the selection is for the line only.

Ġ⤍R Ṡ⤌N	Read top to bottom, left to right to left to right (etc.)
G̲	Underlining indicates lower form of the pitch; two forms of a pitch may be shown in either of two ways in the pitch selection column:
G/G̲	on same line (notated as E/E♭ in Western notation), or
G G̲	on two lines
M'	Short vertical line indicates raised form of Ma (F♯)
Ṣ	Dot below indicates low pitch register (of three) (low C)
Ṡ	Dot above indicates high pitch register (of three) (high C)
[S]	Brackets indicate unclear pitch on recording
(S)	Parentheses indicate grace note
[G̲RS]	Box indicates pitches played on *sāraṅgī*

Articulation and dynamics

◁═══	Increase in volume
G̀	Vocal stress
Ḡ	Marcato
G⌣	Pitch followed by slight 'dip' down and back
G̗	Pitch produced with a vocal 'dip'
͜S S̃	Pitch preceded by slide from below or above
(G) R⌐⌐	Repetition of grace-note-to-pitch pattern
G̃	Quick trill
∿∿∿	Tight vibrato
∿∿∿	Loose vibrato (oscillation)
S——◝	Pitch sustained, then downward slur
G⌒R	Slur (above pitches), or phrase mark
,	Breath mark (in music or text)

Other indications

‖	End of example
▐	End of performance
[ha-re]	Text unclear on recording
. . .	Non-notated music follows
ss	Sung by supporting singer

Key to Western notation

Tala and rhythm

④ Number of the *tala* cycle being performed.

Bar lines indicate end of a *tala* cycle.

In the *tala* cycle illustrated above there are 6 subdivisions; each mark x 0 2 3 4 above the line indicates the beginning of a subdivision.

Each count of the *tala* is notated as a quarter note (♩), no matter how slow or fast the performance speed.

In slow-speed performances when rhythmic values become ♫♫ or ♫♫ the beats are marked in either of two ways:

   (a) by a bracket above the melody line, e.g. ♪♪♫♫♪♪ or

   (b) by joining all units in a count by a single beam, e.g. ♪♪♫♫♩♫.

When rhythm is indefinite only note-heads are shown, e.g. ⁎•• ⁎•.

Approximate rhythmic placement of a pitch is shown in either of two ways:

(a) placement of the pitch relative to a drum stroke ♩, or

(b) placement of the pitch relative to bracket and beat subdivision marks ⌐ ı ı ı ¬.

Grace notes are shown by small notes: ♪.

Pitch

All transcriptions place Sa at middle C 𝄞 or 𝄢 See p. xiv for actual performance pitches for Sa.

No key signatures are used for *rāga*; accidentals are notated where needed.

Brackets indicate that the pitch is unclear in the recording.

Diamond-shaped notes in a box are performed on *sarangi*.

Articulation

⌢   Slur (or phrase) marks, above and below pitches
〰   Loose vibrato (oscillation)
〰   Tight vibrato
◁   Crescendo
▷   Decrescendo
,   Breath mark (in music or text)

For other signs, see Key to *sargam* notation, pp. x–xii.

Pitch at which Sa is transcribed in all examples

Pitches given below are the actual pitches at which Sa was performed.
Where there are two pitches given for an example, Sa was sung
somewhere between the two
(+) indicates a pitch slightly higher than notated
(−) indicates a pitch slightly lower than notated

Note on orthography

Since most Indian musicological sources are based on Sanskrit sources, and most of the older terms used by Indian musicians in general, and by scholars in particular, are of Sanskritic origin, the basic system for transliteration of Hindi and Sanskritic terms used in this book is that used by the international Sanskritists (see Basham 1954). Many words which in customary English spelling are spelled with 'ch' or 'sh' must, according to correct Sanskritic transliteration, be rendered as 'c' or 'ś' (or 's') respectively.

Certain general exceptions have been made. Except for words usually given Sanskritized pronunciation (e.g. *Nāṭya Śāstra*) the final short 'a' has usually been left off words where it is not pronounced in modern Hindi (e.g. *tān* rather than *tāna*). The short 'a' in between full consonants is not written unless it is pronounced: *jalsā*, not *jalasā*; *kīrtankār*, not *kīrtanakār*. The 'ṅ' before guttural stops has been retained. The retroflex consonants have been transliterated as 'd' and 'dh'. In some cases established customary spelling is substituted for Sanskritic forms, for example *padma bhushan*, not *padm bhuṣṇ*.

Due to the lack of absolute conformity between modern Hindi pronunciation and Sanskritic transliteration, there are particular difficulties in transliterating Perso-Arabic words. Many commonly used words of Perso-Arabic origin have been given English spellings which are in common usage although they may not accurately reflect the *devanagari* or Urdu spelling (e.g. *ghazal*, not *gazal*; *qawwali*, not *ḳavvālī*; *hookah*, not *huḳḳā*). Proper names have been spelled according to customary usage.

Transliterating song texts in the medieval Hindi dialect of Braj Bhasha is a difficult matter. In Braj Bhasha short or long vowels are optional and there can be discrepancies from modern Hindi. The nasal 'ṅ' is optional in Braj Bhasha, being more a matter of pronunciation than of transliteration. Since the final short 'a' is usually sung, it has been transliterated in the song texts: 'jana', not 'jan', 'gunavanta', not 'gunavant'.

In direct quotes from primary sources written in English, variant spellings may be observed.

Diacritical markings occur only on the first occurrence of musical terms, and on titles of publications and song texts. Names of *rāga*s, proper names, and words such as *nawab*, *sultan*, *maharaja* are not spelled with diacriticals. *Devanagari* for musical terms occurs in the Index.

Note on the genealogical and teaching charts

1	△	male
2	○	female
3	◇	sex unknown
4	=	marriage
5	|	descent
6	△ ○ △	siblings
7	△ ◇	possible siblings
8	△ △	twins
9	⇓	possible blood ties
10	− − − −	teaching ties
11	=:=:=:=	possible teaching ties
12	⬚	contradictory information

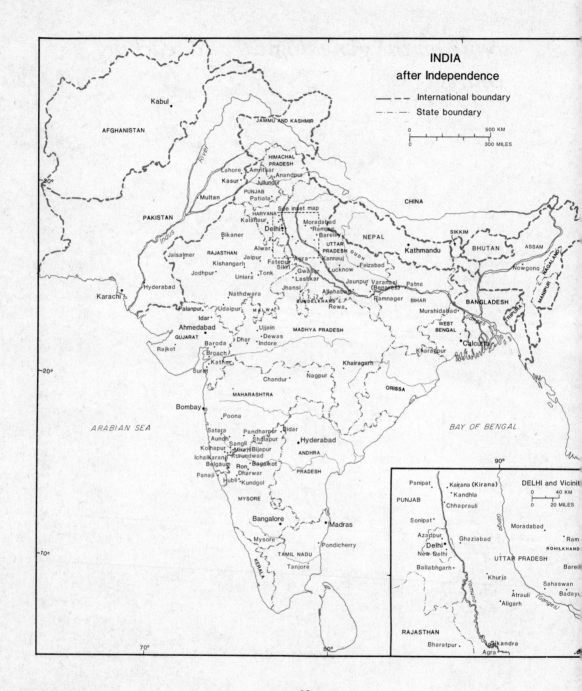

INDIA
after Independence

--- International boundary
-·- State boundary

0   500 KM
0   300 MILES

AFGHANISTAN

Kabul

30°

JAMMU AND KASHMIR

HIMACHAL
PRADESH

CHINA

PAKISTAN

Lahore Amritsar
Kasur Anandpur
Jullundur
Multan PUNJAB
Patiala
HARYANA
Kalanaur
Bikaner Delhi
See inset map
Moradabad
Rampur
Bareilly
UTTAR
PRADESH OUDH
Alwar Kannauj
Jaisalmer RAJASTHAN Jaipur
Fatepur
Sikri Agra
Kishangarh Gwalior Lucknow Faizabad
Jodhpur Lashkar
Uniara Tonk Jaunpur Varanasi
Jhansi (Benares)
Allahabad Ramnager
BUNDELKHAND
Rewa
Hyderabad
Karachi Nathdwara
Palanpur Udaipur MALWA
Idar
Ujjain MADHYA PRADESH
Ahmedabad
GUJARAT Dewas
Dhar Indore
Baroda
Rajkot
Broach
Kathor Khairagarh
Surat Chandur Nagpur

20°

NEPAL
Kathmandu

SIKKIM
BHUTAN ASSAM
Nowgong
NAGALAND
MANIPUR
TRIPURA
BANGLADESH
Patna
BIHAR
Murshidabad
WEST
BENGAL
Calcutta
Kharagpur

ORISSA

MAHARASHTRA

ARABIAN SEA

Bombay

Poona

Satara
Aundh Pandharpur Bidar
Kolhapur Sangli Sholapur
Mira Bijapur
Ichalkaranji Kurundwad
Belgaum Ron Bagalkot
Panaji Dharwar
Hubli Kundgol

MYSORE

Bangalore

Mysore

KERALA

TAMIL NADU
Tanjore

Hyderabad

ANDHRA

PRADESH

BAY OF BENGAL

Madras

Pondicherry

90°

DELHI and Vicinit

0   40 KM
0   20 MILES

Panipat
Kairana (Kirana)
Kandhla
Chhaprauli
PUNJAB

Sonipat
Azadpur
Delhi
New Delhi
Ballabhgarh

Ghaziabad

Moradabad

Ram
ROHILKHAND

UTTAR PRADESH
Bareil

Khurja

Sahaswan
Atrauli Badayu
Aligarh

RAJASTHAN
Bharatpur
Sikandra
Agra

10°

70°   80°

Map 1

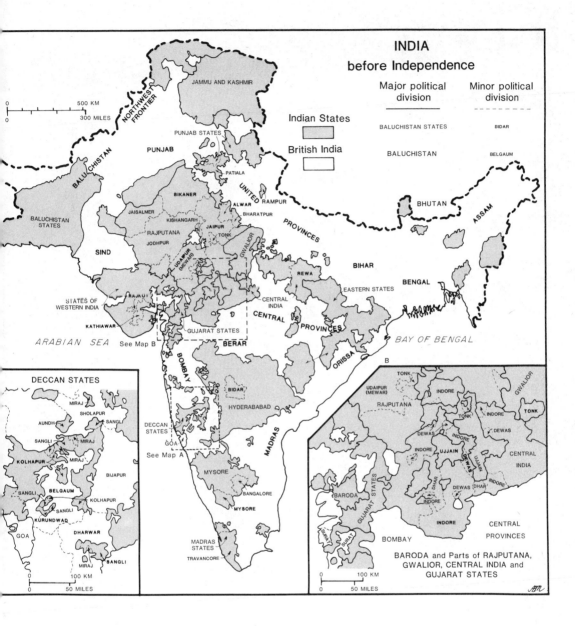

Map 2

1   *Historical and social contexts of khyāl*

Khyāl is the earliest art-music genre of North India for which contributions of individual musicians can be traced to any great extent. Legend, scattered commentary, and speculation suggest that the genre originated with the poet Amir Khusrau Dihlavi (Bandopadhyaya 1958: 71; Gangoly 1935: 38–40; Garg 1957: 90–3; Pandit 1969: 89; Popley 1966: 91; Sastri 1968). Khusrau (1251–1326), born in North India but raised in a Turki-Iranian ethnic environment, was a composer as well as a poet and, some say, a great musician (Mirza 1935: 29). He enjoyed importance at the courts of the Khalji rulers in Delhi, particularly Balban, and of the first Tughluq ruler, and certainly seems to have been a leading figure in the world of courtly arts. *Khyal*'s origin may have been attributed to Khusrau because there was a rapid fusion of the Perso-Arabic, Turki-Iranian, and Indic musical systems during his lifetime. It does seem that the name *khyal* ('lyric', 'imagination') was given to a particular mannerism and a particular song form in Khusrau's time.

After Khusrau, the next figures in the speculation about the history of *khyal* are *sultan*s of Jaunpur – Muhammad Sharqui (1401–40), and Hussain Sharqui, the last of the Jaunpur *sultan*s who ruled from 1458 to 1499 (contemporary with Babur, the first Mughal ruler in India). Jaunpur was an independent Muslim kingdom close to Varanasi and Kannauj, the old centers of Hindu culture (see Map 1). The precise role of the Sharqui *sultan*s with respect to *khyal* is unclear; some scholars recount the innovation of *khyal* by Hussain (Bandopadhyaya 1958: 70; Bali n. d.: 46; Fox Strangways, 1967: 287; Mathur and Mitra n. d.: 72; Popley 1966: 91; Willard 1965: 102); others suggest a patronage role for them. The uncertainties in the matter are well summarized by Prajnananda (1965: 204):

most of the scholars are of the opinion that neither Amir Khusrau nor Sharqui was the innovator of Khyal but it was an outcome of a gradual process of evolution that was at work during the reigns of any one of the Sultans like Ghiasuddin, Balban, Jalaluddin, Allauddin Khilji and Tughluq rulers supported by inventive geniuses of the Muslims and Indo-Persian musicians.

Whatever *khyal* was in fifteenth-century Jaunpur, Thakur Jaideva Singh suggests that it was ornate and romantic, and popular with musicians other than those who performed at the Hindu temples (1961: 132). This implies that while *khyal* was an attractive entertainment for the Muslim patrons at the Jaunpur court, it was not espoused by the Hindu musical establishment.

In the seventeenth century – over 100 years after the Sharqui *sultan*s – a list of musicians at the court of the Mughal ruler Shah Jahan (ruled 1627–58) was included in the book *Rāg Darpan* (*Mirror of Music*, 1666) by Faqir Ullah, one-time governor of Kashmir. In this list there were two mentions of *khyāliyā*s (*khyal* performers):

Ide Singh, grandson of Raja Ram Singh of Kharagpur, proficient in music of Amir Khusru and Sultan Sharqui, composed Khayal and Tarana very well.
Sheikh Bahauddin, an ascetic who composed khyāl, dhrupad, and tarana (Imam 1959a: 15–18).

I

From the *Rāg Darpan* there is a jump to the reign of the Mughal Muhammad Shah in the mid eighteenth century, at which point this account begins.

The history of *khyal*, as cultivated in the princely states of Hindustan from about the mid eighteenth century, began with hereditary musicians and musical knowledge fostered within the family, for these early *khyaliya*s were scions of families who specialized in music. They came particularly from families who specialized in two other types of vocal music – *dhrupad* (an earlier important improvisational genre of Hindustani art music) or *qawwali* (a genre of Indian Muslim religious culture). Since the political milieu in which *khyal* was spawned was primarily dominated by rulers of Muslim faith, the earliest *khyal* singers were, with few exceptions, Muslim. Through the nineteenth century *khyal* was gradually brought closer to the form in which we know it today. In the twentieth century, as the political structure and cultural milieu of India has changed, *khyal* too has continued to change, cultivated by a much broader spectrum of artists – families of *khyal* singers, members of families of *dhrupad* singers, families of musicians with diverse specializations, and also individual members of families who do not specialize in music.

The diverse precedents to *khyal*, its different family traditions, and its patronage in scattered courts of Hindustan nurtured a genre in which flexibility and latitude for creative imagination are prime elements. It won a place as the predominant vocal genre in the improvisatory system of North Indian music. A thorough explication of the musical characteristics that distinguish it from other performance genres in an improvisatory musical system is given in Chapter 2 and elsewhere. These characteristics form the tradition which all singers of *khyal* share.

Gharānā

Another heritage of the development of *khyal* from diverse sources, among several families of musicians and in different places, has been its distinct styles of performance, as sung by musicians of different *gharana*s – Gwalior, Agra, Sahaswan/Rampur, Alladiya Khan, Kirana, or Patiala (see Chapters 3–8). Thus it is necessary to understand *khyal* both on the generalized level of the performance genre and on the more particular level of *gharana* styles distinct from one another.

The term *gharana* carries multiple and diverse connotations. The most thorough discussion of the concept is found in Neuman (1980: Chapter 5, 'Gharanas: The Politics of Pedigree'). Neuman is concerned primarily with *gharana* as it is manifested in family structures and relationships, in families of accompanists as well as in families of soloists (whether vocal, instrumental, or both); he also discusses families of accompanists from which soloists have emerged. His definition of *gharana* is useful as a basis for considering *khyal gharana*s:

Although gharanas connote many things to many people, the concept may be said to include, minimally, a lineage of hereditary musicians, their disciples, and the particular musical style they represent . . . One has constantly to keep in mind that gharanas are essentially abstract categories . . . The closest analogues I can think of in the West are loosely structured European intellectual circles . . . They differ from gharanas in that their structural cores are non-familial institutions, whereas the structural core of a gharana is a lineage of hereditary musicians. What binds all such groups is style – formulated, shared, and represented by the membership (1980: 146).

Neuman's inclusion of 'a lineage of hereditary musicians' as a minimal criterion in the concept of *gharana* can be refined in the case of *khyal gharana*s. *Khyal gharana*s may consist of one lineage or of several lineages of hereditary musicians. The distinction can be made between a lineage which is the 'founding family' of the *khyal* style and a lineage which has become successor to the tradition. In the Gwalior *gharana*, the oldest of the *khyal gharana*s, the lineage of hereditary musicians who were the founding family of the *khyal* style is extinct; a different family of hereditary musicians (the Pandits) who were trained into the tradition by the founding family carries on the tradition of family transmission.

Furthermore, no lineage was involved in the 'founding' of the style of the Alladiya Khan *gharana*. Alladiya Khan himself was a member of a family of musicians, but no other members of his family contributed to the cultivation of his *khyal* style; two of his preeminent successors, however, are mother and daughter of a different family. Here a distinction must be made between a single musician who happens to be a member of a lineage and the actual involvement of a lineage in the musical style. The latter is applicable in the Alladiya Khan *gharana* more to the successors of the tradition than to Alladiya Khan himself.

For *khyal gharana*s it is also pertinent to distinguish between the *presence* (now or in the past) of members of a lineage of hereditary musicians in the tradition, and their *function*. The major implication of a lineage of hereditary musicians in the concept of *gharana* among soloists was, in the nineteenth century and into the twentieth, control of musical knowledge in their particular performance spheres. The existence of a continuing lineage of hereditary musicians in the Pandit family of the Gwalior *gharana* does not mean a vital lineage in traditional terms of control of musical knowledge, however, for 'membership' in the Gwalior *gharana* was greatly diffused early in the twentieth century. Even in the Pandit family, control of a portion of their family musical knowledge was relinquished when songs were taught in the 1910s to the musicologist Vishnu Narayan Bhatkhande, who notated and published them.

In my study, the membership of the leading *khyal gharana*s is traced from their inception to the present. A perspective is thereby provided on the changing implications of the presence or absence of lineages of hereditary musicians in the history of the performance genre, and the differences between the *gharana*s in that respect. In the discussion on the Agra *gharana* it will be demonstrated, for example, that diffusion of the tradition beyond the family has been minimal and that there really is a functioning lineage of hereditary musicians. In the Kirana *gharana*, however, the founding family displayed diverse musical specializations (including the playing of accompanying instruments), and the singing of *khyal* never emerged as the prime specialization of most members of the family.

The second criterion suggested by Neuman as a minimal component of the concept of *gharana* is that the lineage of hereditary musicians has disciples. In the case of *khyal gharana*s, it is accepted that a performance style can be considered a *gharana* style if it has endured through three generations of continuous cultivation (V. H. Deshpande 1973: 11). The first three generations in some *khyal gharana*s (Gwalior, Agra, Patiala, Sahaswan, for example) were within the lineage of hereditary musicians of the founding family of the style. In the Alladiya Khan *gharana*, however, the principal disciples of successive generations are not of Alladiya Khan's family. Thus, consideration of disciples in *gharana*s allows for the exploration of relationships between families of hereditary musicians and musicians not related by family ties. Non-family musicians have been prominent in the cultivation of *khyal*. Whether a disciple in a *khyal gharana* is a member of a lineage of hereditary musicians or is not related to the teacher by family ties, the implications of the discipleship can be the same if the teacher so chooses. From the teacher's point of view he is giving (or withholding) personal (or family or *gharana*) musical knowledge; the disciple reciprocates by committing himself or herself to respect and maintain that musical knowledge, thereby assuring continuity of the musical tradition.

Because transmission of the musical tradition is of such basic importance in the concept of *gharana*, the teaching lines within the leading *khyal gharana*s have also been traced in this study. Not all great *khyaliyas* have assumed the role of teacher; and in some *gharana*s the dedicated teachers have not been the best-known performers. In traditional terms, discipleship has been a one-to-one relationship with a teacher, and an extremely personal experience. The system of learning is now changing, however, and there are actually *khyal* performers associated with *gharana* styles who learned primarily from recorded performances rather than from a teacher. In such circumstances the only way in which artists can control the transmission of their musical knowledge is by refusing to make recordings, or by recording only items of general knowledge.

The third criterion of *gharana*s delineated by Neuman applies to *khyal gharana*s: 'What binds all such groups is style – formulated, shared, and represented by the membership' (1980: 146). Throughout the twentieth century, musicians in *khyal gharana*s have been related increasingly by shared musical traditions and decreasingly by family ties. Accordingly, explication of the musical style of the leading *khyal gharana*s forms the core of this study.

One of the prime purposes of this study has been to collect whatever information is available on the various styles adopted by the different *gharana*s for performing *khyal*, and to utilize it in presenting a cohesive account of the perceptions of *khyal gharana* styles, although the styles are usually described in the literature in analytical generalizations such as 'close to *dhrupad*', 'emphasis on melody or rhythm', and the like. The sources for studying *gharana* musical style are scattered, diverse in nature, uneven, and sometimes contradictory. Rather than take the role of critic or corrector of the information, I thought it more important at this point to present whatever information is available, including all contradictory versions. As John Blacking has asserted: 'all perceptions must be treated as valid data in finding out more about the musical process' (1981: 186). The most important sources for information about the music are the musicians themselves, whether my own interviews with them, or published interviews, or works published by them (Vilayat Hussain Khan, in particular). Biographies of musicians have been useful; of particular value is *Hamāre Saṅgīt Ratna*, edited by Garg.[1] Scholarly articles, usually on a single *gharana*, have been published in Indian music journals, and scholars and informed journalists have contributed newspaper articles and essays in Indian periodicals. Two Indian writers have enumerated style characteristics of the major *gharana*s: Vinay Agarwala (1966) in sketchy generalizations, and Vamanrao Deshpande (1973) in considerable depth. Music critics in North Indian newspapers occasionally speak of *gharana* style. Another source of increasing importance is pictorial material, useful for documenting changes in instruments, ensemble arrangement, and other more subtle details.

The most important evidence of *gharana* musical styles (as opposed to perceptions of them) is musical performance. For this study, published data and information obtained in interviews about each *gharana*'s style provide the basis for analysis of live and recorded performances. I have tried to make it clear when statements are a result of my own analysis.

[1] Of the 152 vocalists for which there are biographical sketches there, I found several for each *gharana* useful: Gwalior, 21; Agra, 3; Sahaswan/Rampur, 5; Alladiya Khan, 4; Kirana, 6; Patiala, 1; and various other individuals, 8.

After considering musicians as members of groups, and musical style as the product of performers from those groups, it is appropriate next to consider musicians as creative individuals, and musical style as style developed by individual musicians. A *khyal* singer must demonstrate in each performance that he or she understands and controls the generalized genre of *khyal*, and more particularly *khyal* in the style of his or her *gharana*, and that he or she can show the personal creativity, imagination, and skill that is demanded of every performance.

Even in the earliest history of *khyal*, contributions of individual musicians were consistently important and, indeed, frequently formed the basis of what has become associated with family or *gharana* style. This was so, for example, of Hassu and Haddu Khan of the Gwalior *gharana* (see Chapter 3), and in more recent times of Faiyaz Khan of the Agra *gharana* (see Chapter 4), of Bade Ghulam Ali Khan of Patiala (see Chapter 8), and of Alladiya Khan, for whom a *gharana* is named (see Chapter 6). Furthermore, the pressures on musicians in this respect have increased greatly in the last few decades, as public performance has heightened competition. Because of the importance of individual musicians, Indian sources are likely to describe *gharana* style through accounts of the styles of individuals in the *gharana*; therefore, I follow that format here.

Some characteristics of individual style, however, remain associated with the individual artist rather than being subsumed into group style. This is the third 'level' at which the music of *khyal* singers must be considered – the level of particularity of the individual musician. Although this sort of analysis can be attempted thoroughly only with very detailed case studies, the particularity of some individuals' styles has been suggested in the summaries of each chapter.

The last analytical chapter (Chapter 9) of this study considers musicians who have attained prominence more as individuals than by association with any single group's musical style. The great Amir Khan is discussed in this context (for it is too soon to know whether his style will form the basis of a group style), as well as Nasir Ahmed Khan of the Delhi *gharana* of musicians. Like those of the Kirana *gharana*, members of the Delhi family have pursued a variety of music specialities rather than concentrate on *khyal*. But, unlike Kirana, the musical styles of individual Delhi singers have not been subsumed and cultivated by a group of disciples so as to constitute a distinct *khyal gharana*.

It is too soon to know whether the viability of *gharana*s will outlast the twentieth century. It has already been demonstrated that not all *khyal gharana*s are consistently structured as lineages, and in extreme cases the discipleship aspect of *gharana* is eliminated. Shared musical style remains the underlying factor in the vitality of *gharana* in *khyal* singing. However, numerous young aspiring musicians are choosing and adding elements of style at will, preferring the freedom of individual style to the restrictions of group style. If the group-style aspect of *khyal* singing diminishes or disappears, then what will remain is individual maintenance of and contributions to *khyal* as a generalized performance genre, knowledge of which is shared by all singers of *khyal*. At that point, future developments in the genre become impossible to predict.

Patronage

Another focus of this study is patronage – both the patrons of *khyal* singers and the circumstances in which the artists functioned. Throughout most of its existence, *khyal* has been a music for elite patrons, specifically princes with political power; only in the twentieth century has any other group attained significance in support of *khyaliyas*. There have been a few instances – such as Muhammad Shah of Delhi – of individual patrons, but mostly it has been successive generations of a royal family that have underwritten the cultivation of *khyal*, so that the princely states are more frequently cited here than the princes themselves. Three *khyal gharana*s carry the names of the princely states in which they were originally fostered – Gwalior, Rampur (Sahaswan), and Patiala (others are designated by the ancestral home of the musicians or by the 'founding' musician himself).

The patronage of artists – musicians, dancers, poets – by rulers of Hindustan was an enduring tradition, in both Hindu and Muslim courts. For *khyal*, the first musical evidence of court support is noted at the Delhi *darbār* (court) of the eighteenth-century Mughal emperor Muhammad Shah (ruled 1720–48), where the musicians Sadarang (Nyamat Khan) and Adarang (Firoz Khan) composed songs that have been transmitted to the present time. The next significant settings of patronage were Lucknow and Gwalior: two families of Lucknow

Plate 1   The Mughal emperor Muhammad Shah Rangile (ruled 1720–48) viewing a garden from a palanquin (painting, c. 1730–40; courtesy, Museum of Fine Arts, Boston)

who competed as *khyaliya*s moved to the princely state of Gwalior where the first *gharana* of *khyal* singing developed in the nineteenth century. Political events in the subcontinent in the period between Muhammad Shah and nineteenth-century Gwalior shaped the context in which the first and subsequent *khyal gharana*s flourished.

Muhammad Shah was the last ruler in a dynasty of great patrons of the arts who could afford to maintain that family practice. His family dynasty was that of the Mughals, whose rule in South Asia began effectively with Babur, in 1526, and ended, *de facto*, with the exile to Burma of Bahadur Shah II in 1858. Muhammad Shah took the throne in 1720, at the age of eighteen. Pleasure-loving and genial, he reinstated at his court in Delhi the lavish patronage of his great Mughal ancestors. There was little money for grand buildings, but considerable sums for musicians, poets, and painters. Muhammad's reign witnessed the effective end of the Mughal Empire. In 1739 the Persian armies of Nadir Shah sacked Delhi and plundered the remaining riches of the Mughal treasury. On his departure from Delhi, Nadir Shah reinstated Muhammad Shah but carried back to Persia the Peacock Throne, symbol of Mughal sovereignty. The brief interregnum did little to alter Muhammad Shah's appreciation of the arts, and his patronage continued, albeit on a scale befitting an empty treasury, until his death in 1748.

At the time of Muhammad Shah, the strongest Muslim states in the subcontinent were Hyderabad to the south, under the Asaf Jahi dynasty, and to the east Faizabad, and Lucknow in Oudh which was to replace Delhi as the literary capital. By the mid-eighteenth century (the end of Muhammad Shah's reign, 1748), the Mughal Empire continued the post-Aurangzeb pattern of balkanization and the proliferation of independent hereditary kingdoms. New centers of political power arose quickly – Murshidabad in Bengal, to the east, and Poona in Maharashtra, to the west.

The would-be minor Mughals were challenged from two sources. One was the potent regional forces – Jats, Sikhs, and especially the Marathas who, since the period of leadership under the Peshwa Baji Rao (1720–40), had steadily expanded northward from present-day Maharashtra at the expense of the Mughal *subah*s (states) of central India. The other challenge issued from the political intrigues of Europe. Only the Portuguese, French, and British were seriously involved in South Asian affairs by the mid-eighteenth century, and the Portuguese had fairly confined themselves to pockets on India's west coast. The French and the British, both represented by their commercial East India companies since the early seventeenth century, vied for allies among the regional native powers.

India was of vital importance to the British. Hopes for an empire in the western hemisphere had fallen on excessive resistance by colonists in North America; thus, the British shifted their focus to South Asia. They were preoccupied with Calcutta in the east, Madras to the south, and Bombay in the west, spending little energy in the northern reaches which still were dominated by the Mughal presence. The gradual encroachment of British control soon shifted from a policy of alliance to one of sponsorship, that is, sustaining a ruler and influencing his policy by providing sufficient force to maintain him against internal and external enemies.

After 1761, with the effective removal of the powerful Marathas and rival French, the British began a concerted drive for more land, more spoils, more power. Until 1765, the East India Company had no sovereign status; it was only a trading organization with its own army, similar to a European feudal baron's organization. Government was under a governor formally authorized by the Mughal emperor. In 1765, the governor, Robert Clive, seized the opportunity provided by continuing confusion in Delhi to legalize the Company by coercing Emperor Shah Alam to name the Company as revenue collector in Bengal, that is, to receive the *divan* (authority). In return for the right to collect (and keep) revenue worth millions of English pounds, and to enjoy full freedom of trade throughout the vast eastern reaches of the subcontinent, the British agreed to maintain the emperor and to pay him the paltry annual sum of £260,000. It was only a matter of time before the vices of power began to squeeze the native rulers. The revenue collector eventually came to be perceived as, and to assume the role of *de facto* administrator. Native state after native state fell victim to this formula for usurpation of Empire.

The Company's charter expired in 1780 and was replaced in 1784 by the India Act, which was to define British India until 1857. This new measure, the penultimate step toward Raj, in effect gave the British government total control of policy without interfering with Company administration. The end of Cornwallis's tenure as governor-general in 1793 revealed a well-defined British Indian state, commonly called 'Company Bahadur' (or 'John Company Raj'), carefully constructed by more than two decades of unabashed corruption and plunder by Company officials.

By 1818, the outline of a distinct political entity had emerged. Consolidation of a British subcontinent and the scrambling for position in it by native rulers occupied the next four decades. Territories of native rulers, those potentially powerful who had been troublesome or uncooperative, were annexed as, for example, the former Maratha Confederacy and the Peshwa's lands, which became the Bombay Presidency. But a pattern of special relationships developed between the British and those who quickly accepted British hegemony. Hyderabad, in return for the Nizam's services, was enlarged through annexation of neighboring states. Many Rajput rulers were able to retain their lands, but as dependent chiefs. Scindia, in Gwalior, retained his identity as a neutral prince, but was relieved of his theretofore special influence in Rajput territories. Holkar, in Indore, was restored to power and granted subsidiary forces. This pattern of allegiance *qua* subsidy was to be followed even more exactly after 1857.

The process of formal anglicization was inexorable; some powerful British and Indians were for it, some against it. The final murmurs of resistance came in the amalgamation of events commonly referred to as the 'mutiny' of 1857. From 1818 until the rule of Dalhousie (1848–56), the Indic states had been left fairly autonomous in pursuit of their own cultural impetus. In tandem were the often abusive sinecures of office, a state of affairs that was unacceptable to Dalhousie. Using the twin excuses of alleged misgovernment and the lack of direct heirs, Dalhousie placed states under direct British rule. The first state to fall victim was Oudh, soon followed by a province in Hyderabad and other states such as Nagpur and Jhansi in central India. In addition, Dalhousie deprived several ex-sovereign families of their pensions and their titles. Among these were the *nawabs* of the Karnatak and Surat, the Raja of Tanjore, the ex-Peshwa Nana Sahib, head of the Maratha Confederacy, who lost both title and pension in 1853, and even the Mughal emperor, Bahadur Shah II, who was informed that the title would lapse upon his death.

Dalhousie's work was a prelude to 'mutiny', and it is not surprising that many of the states affected by his policies were involved in the final throes of resistance to Company Bahadur. Dalhousie left South Asia in 1856, believing he had completed a major service. Less than a year later, the subcontinent was engulfed in the fury of armed resistance, with a variety of insurrections, some savage, equally savagely put down by the British.

After 1857–8, the subcontinent came directly under British rule, the East India Company was deprived of its powers, and the Mughal Empire disbanded, its last emperor being banished to Burma. Those states which sided with the British during the 'mutiny' were amply rewarded and fitted into a system of special relationships. The British Raj was in place, and it was to last until 1947.

In all there were to be ten British provinces interlaced with 562 native princely states. The smallest states were numerous, frequently comprising but a few acres of territory. There were twenty or thirty that could be counted of particular significance with a population substantial enough to present a powerful presence to the British. When, later in their rule (1921), the British established a Chamber of Princes, 109 of the states were considered important enough to have individual representation. The major states and, coincidentally, those that had worked out special relationships with the British, were Jammu and Kashmir in the north; Patiala in Punjab; Jaipur and Jodhpur in Rajasthan; Gwalior, Indore, and Baroda in central and western India; and Mysore, Travancore, and Hyderabad, in central and southern India. Hyderabad, at 32,000 square miles the size of England and Scotland combined, and with a population of some 16 million, was the preeminent state.

British alliances with states crucial to the support of their Raj and, in particular, loyal, or perceived to be loyal to the British during the uprisings in 1857, were rewarded with subsidies and arms agreements. The subsidies and stipends enabled those rulers who wished to do so to entertain lavishly and otherwise spend their monies in whatever fashion they desired. Many adopted the interests of their overlords, acquiring a taste for horseracing, polo, and other European pastimes, while a few continued the great tradition of patronage of the arts that had been the Indic heritage.

Some *maharajas*, *rajas*, and *nawabs* provided employment for numerous artists – musicians, dancers, and poets. Others preferred (or could only afford) to maintain a few artists or to invite artists to visit on a temporary basis. Some patrons, such as the Gaekwads of Baroda, employed *khyaliyas* from more than one *gharana*, so that Baroda is not associated with any one style of performance. Others, such as the rulers of Gwalior and Rampur, preferred to patronize consistently and primarily musicians of one *gharana*, so that those courts are associated with one style of *khyal* singing. The situation in each princely state which patronized *khyal* musicians of importance to this study is discussed at the beginning of each chapter that deals with a *gharana*.

In the late nineteenth century wealthy urban citizens, who constituted another, growing elite group, joined the ranks of royal patrons in increasing numbers. By the early twentieth century, some *khyaliyas* were leading in efforts to initiate the general public in art-music traditions, thereby broadening the patronage base.

During that same period, but especially in the early twentieth century, two ideas gained currency that were to affect *khyaliyas* greatly, because they were to affect the process of study and transmission. One was the growing espousal of institutional teaching. Music schools were founded within the sphere of royal courts and in burgeoning urban centers, through royal dictum on the one hand and by musicians' instigation on the other. Choices of teaching methods and material had to be considered with a view to transmission on a much less restricted basis than formerly. Attitudes and responses in this process varied greatly.

The second idea was that systematization and generalization of the tradition was desirable. One should be able clearly to define and describe a *rāga* instead of having to say 'Ustad X sings it with komal Ni'; one should be able to say 'this is the song', instead of having to specify 'this is the way Pandit X sings the song'. One result of this idea was the notation of essentially non-notated musical material. Another was a wave of All-India Music Conferences which brought together theorists and performing musicians for discussion and, perhaps, decision on some general points. A leader in the dissemination of those two ideas – widespread education and systematization of tradition – was Vishnu Narayan Bhatkhande, whose activities are recounted to some extent in this volume (Chapters 3 and 5).

Independence of the subcontinent from Britain (1947) reinforced the necessity for change in the music culture, since the princely states important to the development of *khyal* were absorbed into two new nation-states, Pakistan and India. In considering *khyal* after Independence, this study follows the musicians and their traditions through the era when financial support shifted from hundreds of courts to one 'center' – the Government of India.

Among the 'unsettling circumstances' of these times was the tragedy of the strife between the Hindu and Muslim communities. Since singers of *khyal* were from both communities, the turmoil directly affected the history of *khyal*. Most musicians elected to remain aloof from the situation, while a few (primarily Hindu) decided to participate in political events. Musical activities such as theoretical study, publication of writings on music, and music notation began to be regarded in communal terms. The partition of the subcontinent into India and Pakistan also affected musicians directly, as musicians had to decide whether to remain in or leave their homes, basing their decision in part on the community to which they 'belonged'. *Khyal gharana*s were a source of relatively stable continuity in the unsettling circumstances created by the struggle for independence and the process of partition.

The history of *khyal*, then, is one facet of the social and political history of the subcontinent. Through changing systems of government, through economic times good and lean, the singers of *khyal* have persevered. In such circumstances they created and have developed a genre of music which remains vital, a genre through which they maintain the traditions they share, but which has always offered avenues for individual creativity.

2 *Khyal: definition of the genre*

Khyal is that vocal genre among all Hindustani vocal genres which allows its performers the greatest opportunity and also the greatest challenge to display the depth and breadth of their musical knowledge and skills. Because *khyal* is an improvisatory genre, a study of it is not a study of a *repertoire* of vocal music. Rather, it is a study of the manner in which artists take the characteristics that distinguish *khyal* as a genre, make those choices that lie within their group traditions, summon their own creative individuality, and create a unique *khyal* at each performance. In this chapter, the characteristics that distinguish *khyal* as a genre, and which are available to all *khyal* singers, will be discussed, while the remainder of the book is devoted to specific group traditions and to individual creativity.

The characteristics that distinguish *khyal* as a genre are of three types: (1) the particular musical materials that can be utilized, that is, the *raga* (melodic mode), the *tala* (meter), and the *cīz* (the composition itself); (2) the selection of types of improvisation which are acceptable for *khyal*, that is, *alap, tan, boltan, bolbant, sargam*, and *nom-tom*; and (3) the placement of all those materials for the creation of a formally balanced and aesthetically pleasing performance.

It is the complex combination of those three characteristics that distinguishes *khyal* as a genre among the various Hindustani improvisational genres. Other vocal genres utilize the particular materials of a *raga*, a *tala*, and a composition: the two predecessors of *khyal* – *alap-dhrupad* and *dhamār* – include them, for instance, as do two genres contemporary with *khyal* – the rhythmic *tarānā* and, in many cases, the lyrical *thumri*. However, placement of the *raga, tala*, and composition at the outset occurs in *tarana* and in *thumri*, but not in the majestic *alap-dhrupad*. Likewise, while other vocal genres include a selection of types of improvisation, only *khyal* includes the particular package consisting of *alap, tan, boltan, bolbant, sargam*, and *nom-tom*. *Alap, bolbant*, and *nom-tom*, for instance, are utilized in the genre *alap-dhrupad*, but not *tan, boltan*, or *sargam*.

Precisely because the number and the diverse nature of the types of improvisation included in *khyal* is greater than in any other single Hindustani vocal genre, *khyal* is considered a very imaginative genre. Indeed, the word *khyal*, from Arabic to Urdu, connotes fancy or imagination, feelings, and even an imaginative composition of verse as well as music.

Particular musical materials

1 *Raga*: the melodic mode

While some *raga*s seem to be more popular than others for *khyal* performances, *khyal* can be sung in hundreds of *raga*s. With a few exceptions such as Rag Khamaj and Rag Pilu (as pointed out in A. Ranade 1976b: 43), which are *raga*s associated with the light classical genres of Hindustani music, there seem to be few conceptualized restrictions on *raga*s appropriate for the genre as a whole. Rather, considerations about *raga* involve artistic preference – whether of a group of musicians (*gharana*) or of an individual – or the mood and texts of the composition, or the time of day of the peformance.

As to artistic preference, some *khyal* singers revel in a large repertoire of *raga*s, while others prefer to focus on a relatively small selection. Some of these singers who are reported to have a wide-ranging knowledge of *raga*s are best known, nevertheless, for a few in which they excel or which audiences demand that they sing. Since *raga*s themselves are so diverse in character, the range of choices for artists with particular skills or vocal qualities is practically unlimited. A singer with a higher-pitched voice can cultivate a repertoire of *raga*s which emphasize the upper register (*uttar-anga raga*s). A singer particularly secure in intonation can be comfortable with *raga*s which have melodic skips in them. Those singers with relatively heavy vocal quality can cultivate *raga*s that are ponderous in mood, while those with sweeter voices can choose others. Those artists (or groups of artists) who enjoy intellectual and musical challenge might choose *raga*s of a complex nature, while others prefer simpler ones.

It is considered important in *khyal* (and in other Hindustani vocal genres) for the mood of the *raga* and the mood of the text of a composition to be complementary. The mood of the words should match the mood of the music. Texts 1 and 2 given below, for example, are both from *ciz* in Rag Miyan ki Todi, a *raga* expressing 'delighted adoration in a gentle, loving sentiment' (Kaufmann 1968: 551).

TEXT 1

The path to the river is difficult to pass. The urchin [Krishna] does not allow me to fill my pitcher.
Oh *sakhī!* How can I accompany you to a desolate place [the bank of the River Yamuna] when that naughty boy is standing in the middle of the path? (Composed by Sadarang. Translated by B. D. Yadav)

DAIYĀ BAṬH DŪBHAR BHAĪ

दैयां बठ दूभर भई । मैं का लंगरवा भरन न देत गगरिया ॥
बिहान तोरे संग कैसे जाउं सजनी । बीच मांझ ठाडा सदारंग उचकैया ॥

TEXT 2

Oh my beloved, please come to us.
I have been your servant for many ages. You are my beloved, oh lovely and princely one. (Translated by B. D. Yadav)

DEU DARAS MORE PYĀRE

देउ दरस मोरे प्यारे ॥
हों तो दासी तोरी जनम जनम की । तुही हैं मोरा प्यारा प्रेम रसबा राजदुलारे ॥

On the other hand, Indian aesthetic theory recognizes that music is capable of expressing at the same moment both pain and comfort, vigor and happiness, peace and love, and the like. Consequently, one finds *ciz* in the same *raga* with contrasting topics and sentiments, as in Texts 3 and 4 of *ciz* in Rag Ramkali.

TEXT 3

There is comfort and happiness at the house of Pir Nizamuddin.
So we sang songs of blessings and goodness. (Translated by Bruce Pray)

ĀCHE RAṄGĪLA RE

आछे रंगील रे सानु रंग लगया हित करे बनत बनाईलारे
निज़ामुद्दीन पीर घर सुख आनंद सोहिल रा माई रे हे सन मंगल गाईला रे ।।

TEXT 4

I remained awake the whole night [waiting] but my handsome, intelligent, vigorous, young husband came in the morning.

Without a string of beads, Kajal on her lips, or putting koyal as a tilak on her forehead [without marrying], who is the lucky lady on whom my husband has sacrificed his body, mind, and wealth? (Composed by Harrang, Muhammad Ali Khan of Jaipur. Translated by B. D. Yadav)

SAGARĪ RAIN

सगरी रैन के जागे पागे । सुघर चतुर सुर जनवा बल्मा । भोर ही मेरे आये ।।
बिन गुण माल अधर पर अंजन । अंजन जावक तिलक लगाये । हररंग कवन सती बड़ा भागिनी ।।
तन मन धन नैछावर कराये ।।

Of the three musical elements of a *khyal* performance, the *raga* is clearly of greatest significance. In program announcements, for example, it is considered more essential to acknowledge the *raga* that a musician is singing than to acknowledge the particular composition. In newspaper reviews the *raga*s performed will always be mentioned, but the names of the compositions only inconsistently. The song is most likely to be mentioned by name if the artist is especially associated with it, having composed or popularized it. (The initial text-phrase of the composition becomes its 'name'.) In radio broadcasts, of *khyal*, the *raga* is announced, then the *tala* and names of the compositions, and even, perhaps, the complete text; but just as the artist is ready to begin, the announcer repeats the artist's name and the *raga* again, so that priorities are clear.

2 *Tala*: the meter

Seven *tala*s constitute the selection of *tala*s in which songs have usually been composed and are performed: *tilwāḍā*, *jhūmrā* and *rūpak*; *ektāl* and *jhaptāl*; *tīntāl*; and the rare *aḍacautāl*. Although little has been written or said about *tala*, the following principles seem to me to apply generally. *Tilwada tal* (sixteen counts; see Ex. 2–1b), *jhumra tal* (fourteen counts; see Ex. 2–2b) and *rupak tal* (six counts) seem always to have been used for relatively slow (*vilambit laya*) performance. (In the notated examples, unless otherwise indicated, a vertical line through the staff indicates the end of a cycle of the *tala*.) Performances of *rupak tal* compositions are relatively few in number. *Ektal* (twelve counts; see Ex. 2–1c) seems initially to have been for slow and relatively medium-speed (*madhya laya*) performances, but *ektal* is used increasingly for fast (*drut laya*) performances as well. Compositions in *jhaptal* (ten counts; see Ex. 2–2a) were formerly referred to as *sādra*, but these have now been absorbed into *khyal*; now, as formerly, *jhaptal* is usually featured in medium-speed performance, though it is also rendered at slow speed. *Tintal* (sixteen counts; see Ex. 2–4) seems to have been associated initially with relatively fast (particularly medium-speed) performances, and especially those that emphasize rhythmic play. *Tintal* has now become associated with all three speeds of performance – *vilambit*, *madhya*, and *drut laya*. *Adacautal* (fourteen counts; see Ex. 2–1a) is sung both slow and fast, but it is rarely encountered. Examples of some of these *tala*s can be heard on the cassette. Partly because they were used for all three levels of speed, *ektal* and *tintal* were the two most prevalent *tala*s in *khyal* performance during the 1960s and 1970s. It appears, on the whole, that association of *tala* with a particular level or levels of speed is no longer as vital a principle in *khyal* performance as it once was.

Artistic preference comes into play with *tala* as well as with *raga*. Some *khyaliya*s enjoy singing in a variety of *tala*s; other *khyaliya*s (or groups of *khyaliya*s) perform, for the most part, in only one *tala* (for instance, *tintal*) for all performance speeds; and some artists concentrate on only two *tala*s (for instance *ektal* and *tintal* or *jhumra tal* and *tintal*) for contrasting performance speeds. A few artists have used *tala*s other than these seven; such *tala*s are referred to as 'rare' *tala*s.

The relationship between the *tala* and the text of a *khyal* song is relatively flexible for the composer or performer because the texts are prose-poems rather than metered poetry. It can even happen that a song text is sung to different *tala*s by different performers (see Exx. 2–4 and 2–5 below, for a song notated in *tintal* but performed in *ektal*).

3 *Ciz*: the composition

The composition is generally termed *bandish*, but in *khyal* the term *ciz* is specifically used. *Khyal* compositions are songs in a *raga* and *tala*, usually in two sections called *sthaī* and *antarā*. (If there are three sections, the third will be an additional *antara* verse.) Each section is usually only one, two, or three cycles (*āvart*s) of the *tala*; thus a *ciz* is a short composition but, though short, it is an effective means for presenting all the musical materials for an improvised *khyal* performance.

Hindustani scholars and performing artists characterize the sections in *khyal* compositions in terms of three pitch registers (low, middle, and high): in these terms the *sthai* melody is said to be composed in the low register and bottom half of the middle register, while the *antara* melody is said to be composed in the upper-middle and high registers. This characterization of the *sthai* and *antara* is related to the most important performance structure in Hindustani classical music – *alap* (or *rāgālāp*), the structure for manifesting the melodic mode. *Ragalap* (in free rhythm, sung to vocables) is likely to be described in terms of sections – two of which are *sthai ke alap* (the *sthai* section of the *alap* structure) and *antara ke alap* (the *antara* section of the *alap* structure). *Sthai ke alap* (or *asthai*, as it seems to have been called by some *khyaliya*s) is considered to include improvisation in the lower octave (*mandra saptak*) and middle octave (*madhya saptak*) up to Ma (4th pitch) or Pa (5th pitch) or even Ni (7th pitch), depending on who is describing it. Singing *sthai ke alap* thus demands a wide vocal range, showing the greater part of a singer's theoretical three-octave range. *Antara ke alap* extends the pitch register and vocal range into the high octave (*tār saptak*). While theorists characterize the two sections of *khyal* compositions in terms of the *sthai* and *antara* of *ragalap*, in reality the pitch registers of these sections always overlap. Therefore, it is important to look for further significance of the sectioning.

The *sthai* of the *khyal* composition is considered the more important of the two sections.

The primary reason for this is melodic: the *sthai* is composed to present in a compact fashion the characteristics of a particular *raga*. That is, the melody includes the selection of pitches in the mode (or most of them); it also includes the distinctive melodic contours or pitch relationships in the mode, if any, as well as the pitch hierarchy of the *raga*, if there is one.

Rag Bageshri, for instance, utilizes the following pitch selection: Sa Re G̲a Ma Pa Dha N̲i (the line under the pitch syllable indicates the flattened form).

If a singer presented Rag Bageshri in all three pitch registers (or octaves) the pitch selection would be the same in all registers: Ṣa Ṛe G̲ạ Mạ Pạ Ḍhạ N̲ị Sa Re G̲a Ma Pa Dha N̲i Sȧ Rė G̲ȧ Mȧ Pȧ Dhȧ N̲i̇. (The form of Bageshri notated in Ex. 2–4 is a rare one, with natural Ni as well as flat Ni.) In Ex. 2–1 the *sthai* sections of three compositions in Rag Bageshri are shown in a modified form of Hindustani notation devised for this book and in Western staff notation. Ex. 2–1a includes the pitches D̲ N̲ S R G̲ M P; if these are arranged in one octave it becomes clear that all the seven pitches in the Bageshri pitch selection are included: S R G̲ M P D N̲. Because this is the *sthai* section of the composition, however, the pitches Dha and Ni are in the lower octave. Ex. 2–1b demonstrates the overlap of pitch registers in a *sthai* of a *khyal* composition: the pitches in that section are D̲ N̲ S R G̲ M P D N̲, encompassing the entire middle octave. Ex. 2–1c shows an extreme example of overlapping registers, beginning on *tar* Sa (high Sa, or Sȧ) and descending through the entire middle register, into the low register; the pitch selection, of course, is still that of Rag Bageshri.

An important characteristic of melodic motion in Rag Bageshri is the avoidance of direct step-by-step descent through an octave; rather than D P M G̲ R S it will be D M G̲ M G̲ R S, avoiding Pa and pivoting at Ma. It is permissible to descend through the lower tetrachord, however: M G̲ R S N̲ S. This pattern of descent shows off the intriguing relationship in Rag Bageshri between pitches Dha and Ga – the tritone which is resolved by a return to the important pitch Ma. As seen in Exx. 2–1b and 1c particularly, melodic motion in composi-

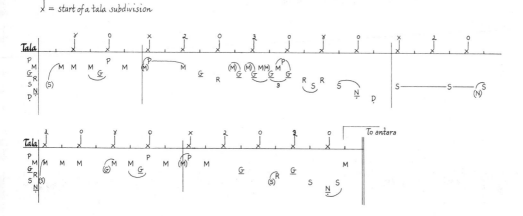

Composition Sthai in Rag Bageshri　　　　　　　　　　　　　**Example 2-1b**

KPM III: 472　Tilwada　Slow Speed

↓ = start of a tala subdivision

Composition Sthai in Rag Bageshri　　　　　　　　　　　　　**Example 2-1c**

KPM III: 468　Ektal　Slow Speed (See antara in Ex.2-2c below)

↓ = start of tala subdivision

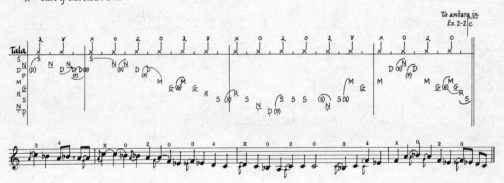

tions in Bageshri is likely to exploit that. In Rag Bageshri the important pitches are Ma and Sa, and the *ciz sthai* notated here demonstrate that clearly. In Ex. 2–1a especially, the melody gravitates between those two pitches.

After a brief *sthai* section has shown the pitch selection, melodic contours and important pitches of the *raga*, an *antara* section usually holds no surprises in musical material. While *antara*s do adhere to the *raga* of their respective compositions, those of compositions in different *raga*s have a similar contour: a direct (as direct as the *raga* permits) ascent from the mid-middle register to *tar* Sȧ declares their presence like an alarum. *Antara* sections from three different *raga*s are shown in Ex. 2–2a (Hamir), 2b (Bhupali) and 2c (Bageshri); the ascents to *tar* Sȧ occur within the initial beats in each case. After the ascent to Sȧ, the *antara* melody extends the range into the high register, then ends with a tuneful descent to *sthai* range.

Metrically, most *antara* are composed to meet the beginning of the *sthai* melody in smooth cyclic manner. The complete *khyal ciz* shown in Exx. 2–1c and 2–2c displays the cyclic nature of the composition: that *sthai* melody begins on count 9 of the twelve-count cycle in *ektal*, and ends on count 8. Likewise, the *antara* melody of Ex. 2–2c begins on count 9 and ends on count 8.

In addition, the text of the *sthai* and *antara* in many compositions are conceived to link early. In a stunning *khyal* in Rag Gaur Malhar, Narayan Rao Vyas used the initial words of the *ciz sthai* 'Sāvana kī' ('of Sāvana', the fifth month in the Hindu year) to tie in neatly with the initial statement of the *antara* 'Sāvana men' ('in Sāvana'); this is Selection 1 on the cassette, transcribed as Ex. 3–12 in Chapter 3. The melody of 'Sāvana kī' in the *ciz sthai* begins the example, then 'Sāvana kī' is sung to melody which is associated with an *antara* – the ascent to Sȧ. The composition *antara* is thus anticipated on *sthai* text; the *ciz antara* 'Sāvana men umage' comes in the eighth cycle of the example, again enunciating the melodic ascent to Sȧ. The following eight cycles of the *tala* present the entire *ciz antara*, tying neatly back into the *sthai* in the last transcribed cycle.

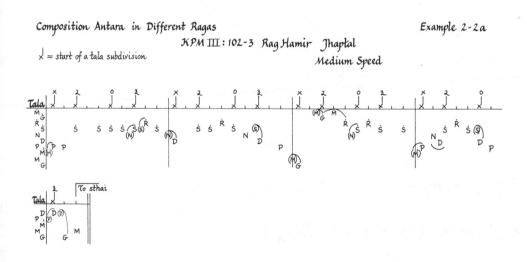

Composition Antara in Different Ragas   Example 2-2a
                    KPM III: 102-3 Rag Hamir   Jhaptal
✗ = start of a tala subdivision   Medium Speed

Composition Antara in Different Ragas   Example 2-2b

x = start of a tala subdivision

KPM III : 50-1 Rag Bhupali Jhumra

Slow Speed

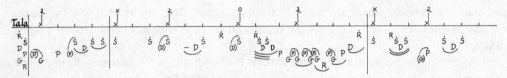

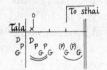

Composition Antara   Example 2-2c

x = start of a tala subdivision

KPM III : 468-9 Rag Bageshri Ektal

Slow Speed

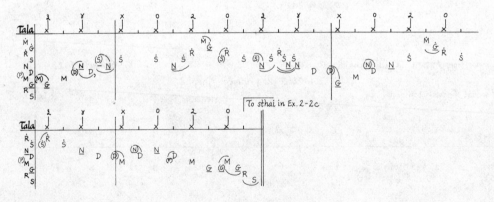

Another distinction between *ciz sthai* and *ciz antara* is textual density. *Antara* texts are likely to have more syllables than *sthai* texts; as a result, in melodies of equal-length *sthai* and *antara*, the text setting of the *antara* is more syllabic. The song 'Rain kā sapanā' in Rag Lalit, transcribed in Ex. 2–3 from a performance, demonstrates this. (The *antara* ascent to Sȧ from count 13 (3) to count 1 (x) is made twice as performed here.)

"Rain kā sapanā"   Rag Lalit   Example 2-3
                         Slow Speed Tintal

♩ = start of a tala subdivision

TEXT 5

Sthai: O *sakhī*! To whom shall I tell my dream of the night?

Antara: All of a sudden I got up from a deep sleep and saw no husband in my bed. (Translated by B. D. Yadav. Rag Lalit, *vilambit laya*, performed by Bhimsen Joshi)

RAIN KĀ SAPANĀ

रैन का सपना री मैं कासे कहूं री ॥
सोवत सोवत आंख खुली जब कोई न पायो अपना ॥

In Hindustani classical vocal music, text carries the implication of rhythm, if not meter, and the implication of the more syllabic *antara* text is that the *antara* is more rhythm-oriented than the *sthai*. This is borne out in the improvised performance, as emphasis on rhythm becomes a major factor only after the *raga* has been adequately emphasized as in the *sthai*. Thus, the *ciz* is a microcosmic glimpse of the performance in a second way.

The *ciz*, then, presents the basic musical elements – *raga* and *tala* – of the particular performance, and it provides a text as well. It is also a microcosmic view of the structural principles of the performance to come, first emphasizing the *raga* (*sthai*) through pitch-register extension (*sthai* to *antara*), then emphasizing the rhythm (*antara*).

Many *khyal* singers have composed *ciz*, though few compositions are attributable to anyone. It is possible to recognize the composer – who is also usually the lyricist – when he has included his *mudrā* (pen name, 'signature') in the text, although it has been known for a *mudra* of a respected person to be inserted into songs he did not write. This is possibly the case with some of the numerous *ciz* said to have been composed by Sadarang (Nyamat Khan) and Adarang (Firoz Khan), the two great singers at the court of the Mughal emperor Muhammad Shah (ruled 1720–48). The Agra *gharana* of *khyal* singers spawned numerous composers whose *mudra*s ended in '-rang', such as Sarasrang (Dayam Khan), Shyamrang (Qayam Khan), and Rasrang (Anwar Husain Khan), while other Agra composers chose different *mudra*s such as Rangile (Ramzan Khan), Pran Piya (Vilayat Hussain Khan), Prem Piya (Faiyaz Khan), and Darpan (Yunus Husain Khan). From Jaipur came Manrang (Mahawat Khan) and Harrang (Muhammad Ali Khan). From Khurja were Khusrang (Aslam Husain Khan) and Ramdas (Zahoor Khan). Jagannath Buwa Purohit of Agra chose Gunidas as his *mudra*.

The *mudra* may be worked into the text in different ways. In 'Daiyā baṭṭh dubhar bhaī' (Rag Miyan ki Todi), cited above (Text 1), the name of Sadarang occurs next to 'uchkaiya', ('naughty boy'). Similarly, in 'Kaise ke dharū' (Rag Jaunpuri), Harrang appears next to 'piyā' ('husband'), as if taking on the identity of that person in the text (Text 6).

TEXT 6

Sthai: Oh my husband, how can I be patient when my heart is impatient?
Antara: My days and nights pass restlessly waiting for you. Oh, my husband Harrang, come and meet me. (Translated by B. D. Yadav)

KAISE KE DHARŪ

कैसे के धरुं धीर पिया मोरा न माने जीयरंवा मोरा ॥
रात दिन मोहे तरफत बीती । आब मिलो हररंग पिया मोरा ॥

In some songs the composer gives advice or commentary, as Daras does in Text 7 and Adarang in Text 8 below. Since the *mudra* normally appears in the *antara* text, Text 8 is an exception.

TEXT 7

Sthai: Don't touch the feet of a person who doesn't listen to the advice of wise men.
Antara: He will pay lip service, then go away. Don't go near such a person. Daras says 'Always be wary of him'. (Translated by Vasant Thakur)

PARĪYE PĀYA NA VĀKE

परीये पाय न वाके सजनी जो न माने गुनियन की सीख ॥
हाथ जोर फोर न्यारो होवे । ऐसे नर के पास न जाये । दरस कहे वासों नित डारीये ॥

For the most part, then, the lyricists for *khyal ciz* have been musicians rather than poets. Only one Hindi poet of classical love-lyrics, Ghananand, who was also an excellent musician and singer, contributed to the repertoire of song texts. At the court of Muhammad Shah with Sadarang, Ghananand composed 1,057 texts specifically for *dhrupad* and *khyal* and indicated the *raga* in which he meant each to be sung. His texts are extant in the voluminous collection of song texts compiled by Krishnananda Vyasadeva, the *Sangit Rāga Kalpadrūma* (1842–9), but they are not performed today.

Khyal ciz texts speak to numerous topics. They might express views on life or religious devotion; many concern Lord Krishna; patrons are praised, and seasons are described (for examples see Van der Meer 1980). Love receives lavish attention – whether divine love or human, whether sorrow of absence from or joy of union with a lover. They are also rich in symbolism and imagery. In 'Sānchī kahat hai', for instance (Text 8), Adarang expresses his view that in life we are related to the world like a boat is related to the river – sometimes being completely together, sometimes only partially so.

TEXT 8

Sthai: Adarang speaks the truth. Life is like a boat and a river meeting.
Antara: Who comes and who goes to anyone's house: You will eat and drink whenever it is in your fortune to do so. Everyone says so. (Translated by Puran Acharya)

SĀNCHĪ KAHAT HAI

सांची कहत है । अदारंग यह । नदी नाव संजोग ॥
कौन किसी के आवे जावे । दाना पानी किस्मत लान । यही कहत सबलोग ॥

In a more pragmatic vein, one *khyāl* singer used song to entreat his patron for support (Text 9).

TEXT 9

Sthai: I run to the court and come back with milk, sons, honor and many kinds of wealth.
Antara: O mighty Mu'inuddin [Chishti], cause of the world's deliverance; today I offer my prayer at your feet. O wise one, protect my honor; I present my petition. (Translated by Bruce Pray)

DARBĀR DHĀŪN PĀŪN

दरबार धाऊं पाऊं दूध पूत और आन धन बहु विध । विधि रचकर आऊं ॥
मैइनुद्दीं परबीन जगतारन कारन । मुकत चरन चित लाउं आज ।
सुजान मान रख लीजे बिनती सुनाऊं ॥

The largest number of *khyal* texts concern Lord Krishna; Krishna appears as a boy (sometimes mischievous as in Text 1), as a man, as a lover. The Krishna in 'Bhalī bajāī' (Text 10) is a familiar characterization of the deity in Indian culture.

TEXT 10

Sthai: You have played your flute very well, Krishna.
Antara: With the many-colored melodies you have played, you have charmed all the women of Brij. (Translated by Gulzar Singh Sandhu)

BHALĪ BAJĀĪ

भली बजाई रे तु ने बांसुरियां बनवारी ॥
अने का रंग गतरंग उप जावत मोहलाई री सब बिजनारी ॥

In *khyal* texts the devotional theme of the relationship of Radha to Krishna, symbolizing the soul's search for God and devotion to God, is often transformed to evocations of human love, as in 'Mhārā rasiyā' (Text 11).

TEXT 11

Sthai and *Antara*: O my handsome husband! I wish you to be a King. I have been your servant since many previous births. You are my lord/master. (Translated by B. D. Yadav)

MHĀRĀ RASIYĀ

म्हारा रसिया बाल्मा थाने चाहै हो राज
दासी थारी जनम जनम रो । थै तो म्हाका सिरताज ॥

'Piyā milana kī' (Text 12) expresses, as many *khyal* texts do, the anticipation of the return of a mate or lover.

TEXT 12

Sthai: I have a chance to meet my beloved, o *sakhī*! I would sacrifice my life for you if you would tell me how to love him.
Antara: My beloved has come after a long time. O *sakhī*s, please sing the blessing songs. (Translated by B. D. Yadav)

PIYĀ MILANA KĪ

पिया मिलन की बारी अरिए री । सखी जतन कछु बता मैं तोरी बलिहारी वारी ॥
बहुत दिनन पछ्ठे पिया मोरे आये । मंगल गावो सखियां सारि ॥

Such texts of expectation frequently include reference to the ankle-bells worn by women; the jingling of the bells (onomatopoetically sung as 'jhanananana' or 'chanananana') expresses the tinkling of joy as in Text 13 below, or it can give away to the watchful ears of the women of a household an attempt to sneak away to a tryst.

TEXT 13

Sthai: Oh my mother, my anklets are jingling, so I know that my husband has come.
Antara: It has been four days since he came; all my heart's sadness has gone. (Translated by
Bruce Pray)

CHON CHANANA

छों छननन बिछुवा बाजे मोरी मा । यातें मैं जानूं पी को आगम भई ॥

चार दिनन ते आगम भईलवा । मेरे तो जिया के सब दुख गईला ॥

What might seem a woman's song text may in *khyal* be sung by a man or woman. Likewise,
what seems a specifically Hindu text is just as likely to be sung by a Muslim artist. In 'Allāh
sāheb jamāl' (Text 14 below) the synthesis of religious cultures that marks North Indian
music can be seen: God is addressed as an Indian Muslim would address him – 'Allāh sāheb' –
but the reference to 'the beauty of the supreme lord' is Hindu.

TEXT 14

Sthai: *Allāh sāheb*, the all-graceful God, is sitting on his throne.
Antara: One feels wonderful to behold the beauty of the Supreme Lord. (Translated by B. D.
Yadav)

ALLĀH SĀHEB JAMĀL

अल्लाह साहेब जमाल तखत बैठे कमाल ॥

साहे आजम पी को छवि निरखत । जब तब होवे कमाल ॥

In performance, the text of a *khyal ciz* is usually treated as a vehicle for music rather than as
a meaningful entity to be exploited as such (as is the text in *thumri*, for instance). Thus, when
singers learn a *ciz* with a text in a language not their own – or even when they do know the
language – there does not seem to be much effort exerted toward the text. The result can be
incorrect grammar, the mixing of dialects, or words (apart from vocables) which do not seem
to mean anything.

There are two other indications of an attitude of 'flexibility' toward the texts. One is the fact
that the mood of a text does not seem to make all performers feel compelled to render the song
in one speed or another. Secondly, *ciz* may have more than one version of the text; it is
possible to find the same composition (*raga*, *tala*, and melody) printed in various *ciz* notation
sources with different versions of the text, or one text version may be printed and a different
one sung.

In fact, *khyal* is characterized by an attitude of flexibility toward the *ciz* as a whole.
Traditionally, songs have not been conceived as written items. Those which are notated are
frozen skeletal versions, and the existence of differing notated versions of a song does not
violate the idea that they are all the same song. In Ex. 2–4 below, the *sthai* section of a song in
Rag Bageshri demonstrates this point. 'Kauna gat bhaī' is notated in two important collections: *Krāmik Pustak Mālikā*, compiled by V. N. Bhatkhande, and *Rāg Vijñān*, compiled by
V. N. Patwardhan. The printed notations are reproduced in Exx. 2–4a and 4b respectively (in
their different notation systems), with transnotations in Western staff notation, and the text
in Text 15.

Example 2–4a

Example 2–4b

Irene Roy Chowdhury "Kaun gat bhaī" Sthai Example 2-5a
Rag Bageshri, Vilambit Ektal

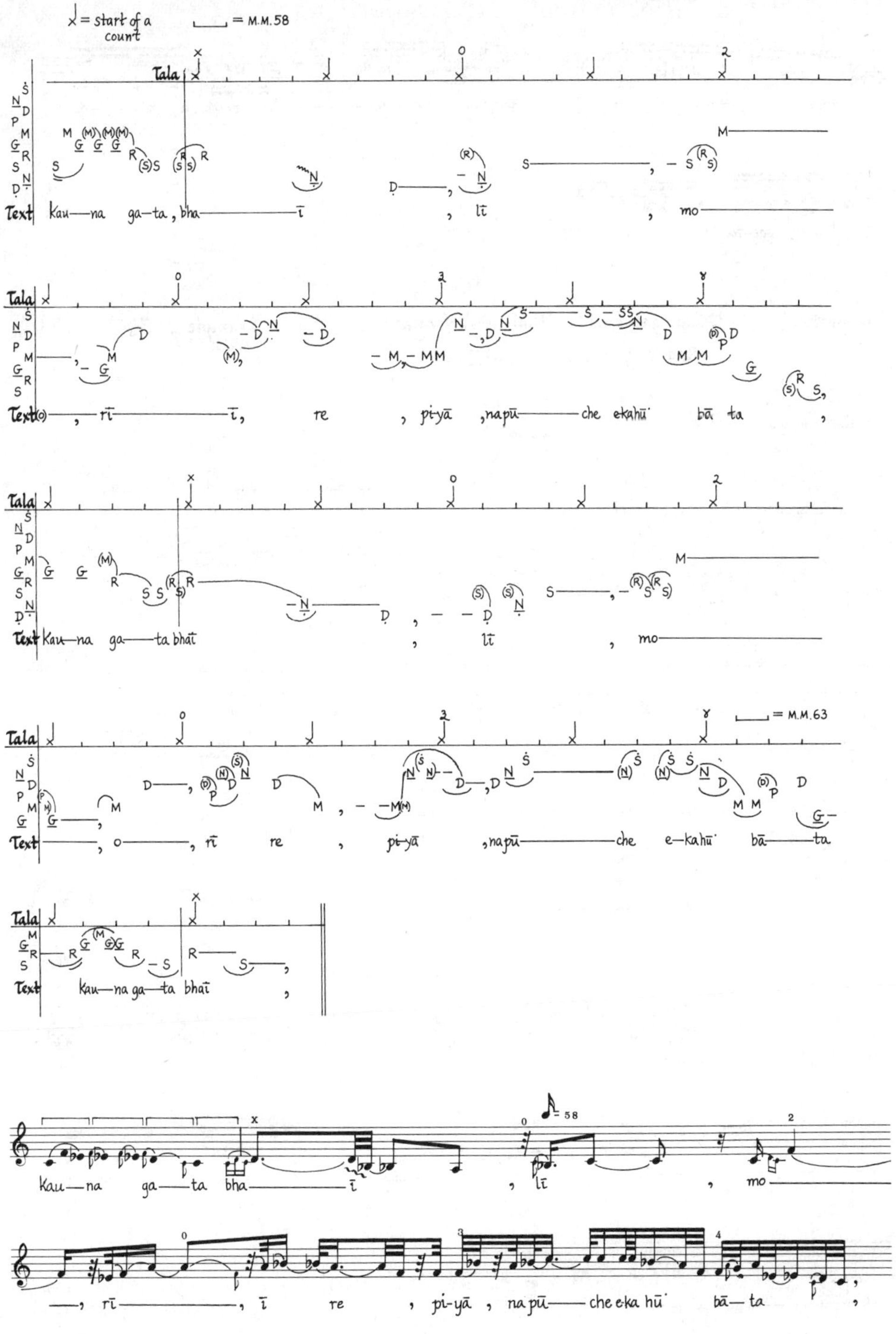

x = start of a count ⌐____⌐ = M.M.58

Text kau—na ga-ta , bha————ī , lī , mo—————

Text (o) , rī————ī , re , pi-yā ,na pū——che ekahū bā ta ,

Text kau—na ga——ta bhāī , lī , mo—————

⌐____⌐ = M.M.63

Text , o——, rī re , pi-yā ,na pū————che e—kahū bā——ta

Text kau—na ga——ta bhāī ,

♩ = 58

Kau—na ga——ta bha————ī , lī , mo——

——, rī————, ī re , pi-yā , na pū——che eka hū bā—ta ,

kau—na ga—ta bhaī   ,   lī   ,   mo——

————— , o———rī   re   ,   pi-yā   ,   na pū———che e-ka hū bā——ta

kau—na ga-ta bhaī   ,

Pran Nath   "Kaun gat bhaī" Sthai as Performed   Example 2-5b
Rag Bageshri , Vilambit Ektal

✗ = start of a count

TEXT 15

Sthai: What has happened that my husband never asks about me?
Antara: I have searched for him in one jungle, in all jungles, and in every corner. (Translated by B. D. Yadav.)

KAUNA GAT BHAĪ

कौन गत भई [ली] मोरी पिया न पूछे एक बात ।

Nor have *ciz* traditionally been intended to be performed in precise form. They have been transmitted orally without the intention of exact reproduction in the context of the *khyal* performance.[1] To demonstrate this, two performances of the *sthai* section of 'Kauna gat bhaī' are transcribed in Ex. 2–5; they are Selections 2A and 2B on the cassette.

Types of improvisation

Six types of improvisation are usually associated with *khyal*. (1) *Alap* is a manifestation of the *raga* of the performance by showing its characteristics in gradual but systematic fashion. In *khyal*, it is not *ragalap*, but rather *rūpakālāpti*, since the *alap* is done in the context of a *rūpaka* (Sanskrit, 'composition'), and is therefore metrical (rather than in free rhythm) and sung to a text (rather than to vocables, if a musician so chooses). (2) *Tans* are fast melodic figures of a virtuosic nature, sung to a vowel – usually 'ā' (i.e., called *akār*). (3) *Boltans* are *tans* sung to syllables of the *ciz* text (*bols*). (4) *Bolbant* is the use of the *ciz* text (*bols*) for purposes of rhythmic play. (5) *Sargam* passages are those enunciating the syllables for the pitches (Sa Ri Ga Ma Pa Dha Ni) as they are sung. (6) *Nom-tom* features rhythmic pulsations, achieved by pitch repetition, particular ornamentation, and enunciation of text syllables, vocables, or vowels.

1 Alap

The ways in which *alap* is carried out by different *khyaliyas* are numerous. A major distinction between artists lies in whether they sing *alap* on vowels (usually 'a'), or on vocables (such as 'de', 'na'), or to the *ciz* text (termed *bolālap*). The degrees to which they let their text be a rhythmic factor in *alap* also varies. Another major distinction is whether artists choose to present the *raga* in segments of pitch register (*merkhand*, focusing on combinations of three or four pitches in a cluster) or in a pitch-by-pitch manner (*badhat*). The pacing of *alap* can vary, as some artists dwell longer in one pitch register than in others. Another distinction is made as some mark off sections in their *alap* while others do not; those who do sectionalize it do so in a way of their own choice – for instance, by singing a passage of *bolalap* in an *alap* sung otherwise to a vowel, or by ceasing to sing for a brief rest (having accompanists provide continuity).

Selection 3 on the cassette is a segment (five cycles of the *tala*) of an *alap* in Rag Darbari Kanhra performed by Abdul Wahid Khan. It is an example of *bolalap* sung to the words 'gumānī jāga' (*avart*s 5–9 of the performance transcribed in Ex. 7–5 in Chapter 7). The

---

[1] I find that I must contradict G. N. Joshi (1976: 50) who wrote: 'A *Bandish* is supposed to be sung in its entirety with clear and perfect diction without causing any change in the originally conceived musical design'.

syllable 'ma' is particularly useful, and the singer treats it as he might a vocable. Rhythmic use of 'nī jāga' occurs at the end of the selection, serving to mark off that section of improvisation. In *merkhand* fashion, Abdul Wahid focuses in this section of *alap* on pitches Ma Pa Dha Ni Sa, extending improvisation down to Ga at moments and up to Re with 'jāga'. Producing subtle variation in the use of a limited amount of material is a challenge to the artist. This selection demonstrates as well the purposeful manipulation of vibrato, slurs, and, to a small extent, dynamics.

2 Tans

*Tan*s vary in shape, range, presence or absence of ornamentation, speed, and numerous other factors, since 'a fast melodic figure' can be almost anything. The matter of *tan*s is very confusing, and descriptions are unclear for the terms used. Some singers become known for singing *tan*s, perhaps *tan*s of a certain shape ('roller-coaster', for instance), while others dislike them and sing only a few in a performance because it is basic to *khyal* improvisation to do so. *Tan*s can be sung clearly 'like a string of pearls', or ornamented so heavily that the pitches are indistinguishable from one another.

In Selection 4 on the cassette, Bade Ghulam Ali Khan sings clear examples of *tan*s in Rag Malkauns (see Ex. 8–4 in Chapter 8 for a transcription). Those in the fifteenth cycle of the performance are sung to 'ā', rippling for the most part in straight ascent and descent. In the sixteenth cycle he begins them in a more focused style, then returns to sweeps, showing his ability to sing up to Dha in the high octave. His controlled use of vibrato as ornamentation in melodic descent, contrasting with slurs in melodic ascent, make these *tan*s interesting.

Another *tan* configuration is what I call 'plateau' *tan*s, in which each pitch in a series is sustained by a fast vibrato, creating an illusion of speed by ornamentation rather than by melodic motion. In Selection 5 on the cassette (see Ex. 7–1 in Chapter 7), improvisation in the eighteenth cycle of a performance in Rag Asavari by Gangubai Hangal begins with an ascending 'plateau' *tan* sung to the vowel 'ā'. She follows that by a fairly curvaceous, descending *tan* which leads into the texted cadential phrase 'Āye mātā bhavānī'. This entire selection shows the contrast of singing on a vowel (*akar*) using the song's text.

'Roller-coaster' *tan*s, those in which one 'phrase' encompasses several successive ascents and descents (or vice versa), are demonstrated in Selections 6 and 7 on the cassette: Kishore Amonkar singing *tan*s in Rag Jaunpuri and in Rag Bageshri respectively. These two selections demonstrate as well what I term 'loose vibrato' (in the former) and 'tight vibrato' (in the latter; see Exx. 6–3 and 6–4 in Chapter 6 for transcriptions).

In a remarkable performance of Rag Desi, Krishnarao Pandit offers a stunning series of *tan*s. In Selection 8 on the cassette, the *tan* in cycle 46 features the rhythm 5/4, while the *tan* in cycle 47 is in triplets, the first ornamented by oscillation, the second sung with a guttural sound, without vibrato. The melody tends to fall into repeating systematic patterns (as in *alaṅkārik tan*), but is actually tantalizingly irregular (see Ex. 3–4 in Chapter 3 for the transcription.)

3 Boltan

Boltan adds text to the description of *tan*s above. Theoretically, in *boltan* the *bol*s should be spaced in a sprinkling of *tan*s in such a way that the sense of the text is maintained. In Selection 9 on the cassette, sung in Rag Abhogi by Nisar Hussein Khan, the text 'jhana āyo' is rendered in melismatic *tan* fashion in cycles 53–6, contrasting with a long (*akar*) *tan*, in cycles 57 and 58 (see Ex. 5–3 in Chapter 5 for the transcription). The cadence to that section of improvisation is created by a rhythmic enunciation of the beginning of the song (*mukhḍā*), 'Jhana āyo re jha' in cycle 59.

A *khyal* singer can create *boltan*s that use the placements of the *bol*s for rhythmic interest, or *boltan*s that are indistinguishable musically from *akar tan*s. In Selection 10 on the cassette, both types are produced by Bade Ghulam Ali Khan (in Rag Malkauns, transcribed in Ex. 8–1 in Chapter 8). The end of the selection demonstrates text placement for rhythmic interest, where 'erī kaba ā' is repeated three times in a cadential figure called a *tihāī*. The fast sextuplets are sub-divided

$$4 + 2, 2 + 3 + 1$$
$$\text{e} - \text{rī ka} - \text{ba} \quad \text{ā}$$

the first two times, with the pattern shifted in the third text repetition to put the 'ā' on count 1 of the next *tala* cycle. Earlier in cycle 14 the *tan*s on 'ā' could alternatively be considered *akar tan*s on 'ā' of 'kaba ā', extending the 'ā'; in any case, there is no rhythmic text placement. At the end of cycle 12 the *tan*s on 'erī' and on 'kaba' are a nice compromise between the two types of *boltan*.

4 Bolbant

Bolbant is cultivated by musicians who excel in control of *tala*. Some artists create passages of *bolbant* with rhythmic placement of the straight lines of *ciz* text, as given, while others recombine the text words and phrases for variety. Many artists offer relatively simple syncopation patterns such as ♫♪ ♫♪ ♫♪ with one syllable per pitch, while others attempt such daring rhythmic play (*layakārī*) as ♫♫♫ ♫♫ ♫♫♫ ♫ ♫♫♫ ♫ ♩ with one syllable per pitch. The rhythmic variety that is possible is unlimited. In Selection 11 on the cassette, Vinayak Rao Patwardhan enjoys improvising with the text of a *ciz* in Rag Hamir, making particular use of off-beat placement of the syllables (see transcription in Ex. 3–10, *avart* 19). In Selection 12, from the same performance (see Ex. 3–11), the contrast between *bolbant* and *boltan* can be heard: melismatic *boltan*s on 'hā' of 'avagāhā (ā)' in *avart* 11 and on 'gā' at the end of the selection are very different from the rhythmically enunciated, straightforward *bolbant* in the rest of the example.

5 Sargam

These passages are used in different contexts by different *khyaliya*s. Most artists use them for speed, in the manner of *tan*s, but with clearer manifestation of mathematically proportioned rhythmic densities relative to the speed of the *tala* counts (double speed, quadruple speed, etc.) than a 'flowing' *tan* is likely to give. Another option is to use *sargam* in *bolbant*-like improvisation, and a few artists bring the text syllables into play. Selection 13 on the cassette is a short example of *sargam* in a medium-speed performance by Bade Ghulam Ali Khan; with *sargam* he contrasts primarily double-speed rhythm with increasing amounts of quadruple-speed *sargam* in cycles 107, 108, and 109 (transcription is in Ex. 8–2b in Chapter 8). In Selection 14 on the cassette, Amir Khan is singing in slow speed, but *sargam* improvisation increases the rhythmic density considerably (transcription is in Ex. 9–3 in Chapter 9).

Those two selections contrast with the lyrical *sargam* improvisation in Selection 15 sung by Nisar Hussein Khan (transcription is in Ex. 5–1 in Chapter 5).

6 *Nom-tom*

A limited number of *khyaliyas* perform *nom-tom*; it is a type of improvisation more usually associated with the majestic vocal genre *dhrupad* (in *nom-tom-alap*) than with *khyal*. In *dhrupad*, it always occurs as a part of the unmetered *ragalap* which is sung before the composition is presented, and it is sung to vocables. In *khyal*, it is sung before or after the composition is presented, to either vocables or text syllables. *Nom-tom* complements rippling *tans* and lyrical *alap*, eschewing in its pulsating drive the rhythmic complexity of *bolbant*. Marcato or some other ornamentation on each successive pitch and repetition of pitches creates more rhythmic 'punch' than, for example, an ordinary *sargam* passage would do. When performed by someone such as Kishore Amonkar, this type of improvisation is perhaps more appropriately described as singing 'with *jor*', or 'forcefully'. Selection 16 on the cassette, sung by Kishore Amonkar in Rag Pat Bihag (transcribed in Ex. 6–5 in Chapter 6), demonstrates a rather tuneful pulsating passage that is especially appropriate for *khyal*. In cycle 20, it is a marcato 'punch' on the vowel 'ā', contrasting with the *boltan* that follows; in cycle 23, the 'forceful' style initiates a passage of *bolbant*.

Structuring a *khyal* performance

While placement of the song at the outset of the performance is an important given element of the *khyal* form in particular, the other principle of placement to which a *khyaliya* adheres belongs to the sphere of Hindustani classical music in general: one pays attention first to melody, then to rhythm, then to speed. By strict adherence to these two placement principles, the following order of events would occur in *khyal* improvisation if the entire selection of possibilities were exploited: *ciz*, *alap*, *nom-tom* or *bolbant*, *boltan*, *tan*. *Sargam* could be brought into play wherever an artist wished, depending on the use to which he or she puts it.

There are two types of *khyal* performances. Those in which artists are expected to cover the range of possibilities, ideally giving attention to all musical elements – melody, rhythm, and speed – are called *baṛā khyal* ('large' or 'great' *khyal*). Those *khyal* performances in which attention to the melody is satisfied mostly by singing the *ciz*, thereby leaving improvisation to emphasize the musical elements of rhythm and, especially, speed, are called *choṭā khyal* ('small' *khyal*). In order to fulfill the ideal of giving attention to the three musical elements – melody, rhythm, and speed – *chota khyals* are rarely performed as independent pieces.

The matter of speed in *khyal* includes three different facets. As an element of music, 'speed', as referred to above, means virtuosity in singing at two, three, or four times the speed of the *tala* counts, as in *tan* and *sargam*. This is a matter of rhythmic density relative to the *tala* count. The other facets concern the rate at which the *tala* counts fall. The second facet is the level of speed at which the performance begins: *bara khyals* begin at a slow speed (*vilambit laya*) or medium speed (*madhya laya*), while *chota khyals* begin at a fast speed (*drut laya*). The third facet is the principle of acceleration through a performance, by which the rate of the *tala* counts gradually (or by sudden jumps) increases, for example, from $\flat = 84$ to $\flat = 104$ from the beginning to the end of a *bara khyal* performance, or, for example, from $\circ = 52$ to $\circ = 96$ from the beginning to the end of a *chota khyal* performance.

Whether it is a matter of *gharana* style or of individual choice, the artists who sing *khyal* have some leeway in the matter of speed. Their *vilambit laya* can either be very slow or rather slow, their medium-speed performances may begin at different speeds within that range, their fast speed may be not so fast or very fast. Acceleration patterns within a performance vary greatly, too. This range of acceptable possibilities contributes to making *khyal* such a flexible genre.

Singers seem to choose for *chota khyal* performances those *ciz* which have the most syllabic text settings. Whether all these songs were purposefully composed for performance at a fast speed is unclear. Since syllabic setting at a rapid pace is rhythmic in nature, the rhythmic aspect of *chota khyal* is enhanced by the nature of the *ciz* itself, which is likely to be repeated many times. Slow *bara khyals* are usually followed in performance by a *chota khyal*; in such instances the principle of acceleration through a performance is maintained across two items as if they were one.

The two *ciz* which an artist decides to link in a *khyal* performance should, theoretically, have complementary text content. If there are two *ciz* being performed, a *bara khyal* and a *chota khyal*, they are most likely to be in the same *raga* but in different *talas*, although it is not unusual for them to be in the same *tala*. It does happen that an artist will sing two such *khyals* in different but complementary *ragas*, but this is unusual. A number of artists enjoy pairing a *bara khyal* with a fast genre called *tarana* rather than with a *chota khyal*. Since the *tarana* is oriented to rhythm and speed like the *chota khyal*, the structural balance of the performance is not changed.

A few performers will link three items in performance, showing the three levels of speed from *vilambit* through *madhya* to *drut laya*. This will frequently include a change of *raga*, using, for example, one *raga* for the *vilambit khyal*, and a second *raga* for the other two. In this type of performance, a real distinction can be made for the sake of variety between *raga*-oriented *alap* at a slow speed and melodic improvisation closer to the image of the *ciz* at a medium speed.

Three other aspects of structuring a *khyal* performance remain to be discussed: (1) what happens before the *ciz* is sung; (2) details of the *ciz* as sung; and (3) the relationship of the *khyaliya* with his or her accompanist(s).

Most *khyal* singers anticipate their presentation of the *bara khyal* with a few moments of melody in the chosen *raga*; this is rarely named (though there is one instance in G. N. Joshi 1976: 48, who calls this *alap* and considers it the first section of *khyal*), and I have referred to it here as pre-*ciz alap*. Some artists sing this to vocables such as 'de', 'ne', or 'na'; others sing it to vowels (mostly 'a'); while still others sing it to the *ciz* text. For some, this melodic improvisation seems to be a vocal warm-up, taking only a few seconds. Others seem to intend to set the mood, singing for a minute or two, with the effect of beginning a *ragalap*, or of singing a 'mini-*ragalap*', or possibly of foreshadowing the tuneful *ciz sthai* to come. Other artists make this a major structural portion of their *bara khyal*, and surround their presentation of the *ciz sthai* with *ragalap* before and *rupakalapti* after, thereby using the song as sectionalizing material in *alap*. Selection 17 on the cassette is a pre-*ciz alap* in Rag Miyan ki Todi improvised by Latafat Husain Khan, sung to vocables until the initial phrases of the song 'Daiyā baṭh dūbhar bhaī' begins the *ciz* (see the transcription in Ex. 4–8 in Chapter 4). In the form of *ragalap*, he presents the *raga* in the area around pitch Sa (D̲, N S R̲ G), then in the second minute focuses in the lower register, and returns to the S R̲ G area in preparation for the song.

The *tala* begins with the song, as well, so the *tabla* player joins the ensemble at that point.

Flexible placement and use of the components of the *ciz* are among the options for structuring a *khyal* performance. The *sthai* and *antara* sections can be placed at different moments, and separate components of the *ciz* – the *mukhda*, the *sthai* text, and *antara*-type melody – can be utilized according to *gharana* style and/or individual style. This is discussed in the chapters that follow.

The composition is most likely to be sung with its sections (*sthai* and *antara*) separated in some way. In *bara khyal*, particularly at a slow speed, artists are likely to sing only the *sthai* at the beginning of the performance; then they will improvise new melody to the *sthai* text or to vocables or vowels. The *antara* will be sung at the point in the *alap* when the high pitch register is reached, but here there is an element of choice, as well, as to whether to introduce the important pitch Sắ by presenting the composition *antara* or by including it in improvisation before singing the song *antara*. A number of artists decide not to sing the second section of the song, thereby reducing the textual material of the performance to the *sthai* text only. Most of them, however, will begin their performance with the song compressed to *sthai* + *antara*-type melody in one unit, sung to *sthai* text. If artists wish to sing both sections of the song at the outset of the performance (as most do in medium-speed *bara khyal* and almost all in fast *chota khyal*), they are still likely to separate the two sections slightly by some improvisation on the *sthai* text, in the image of the *sthai* melody, before singing the *antara*. Or they might sing the first phrase of *sthai*, repeat it, sing the rest of the *sthai*, and then proceed to the *antara* without separating the two.

Use of the song as an element for repetition in the course of a *khyal* performance depends to some extent on speed. In slow *khyal* there is relatively little repetition of either the entire composition or even of whole sections; somewhat more repetition might occur in medium-speed *bara khyal*; and it is highly likely that the *ciz* will recur amid improvisation in *chota khyal*.

The first phrase (*mukhda*) of the *sthai* – text and melody – is the most important component of the *ciz*, for it provides material for most of the cadences in the performance. If the artist wishes to present the *ciz antara* gradually (for example, by repeating the first phrase or improvising on the text of the first phrase before singing the remainder of the section), and if he or she wishes to create a cadence or two in the process, the first phrase of the *ciz antara* (*antara mukhda*) will provide material for the cadence. Selection 18 on the cassette, sung by Bhimsen Joshi in Rag Lalit, demonstrates an *antara mukhda* – the phrase 'sovata sovata rī', which is used for cadences leading up to and including count 1 of cycles 16 and 17 of the performance. His return to the *sthai mukhda* 'Rain kā sapanā' marks the end of his improvisation in *antara* (see Ex. 7–2 in Chapter 7 for the transcription).

The *mukhda*, being texted, can be an element of rhythm if an artist so wishes. In slow *bara khyal*, however, many artists play down the rhythmic implications of the *mukhda* to such an extent that it blends in smoothly with the floating, *alap*-oriented context. The *mukhda* melody is likely to be changed somewhat during improvisation, even changed so much that its relationship to the composed *ciz mukhda* is reduced to text and the single important pitch on *sam* (count 1 of the *tala* cycle).

The text of the *ciz sthai* is utilized independently of its melodic setting in the texted types of improvisation (i.e. *bolalap*, *bolbant*, and *boltan*). It is the component of *khyal* which is most exploited for repetition in any performance of the genre.

The melody of the *ciz antara* is utilized independently of its text. The *antara* melody without its *ciz* text – being a stylized melodic contour and therefore referred to in this study as '*antara*-type melody' – is likely to be sung and resung toward the end of *bara khyal* and in *chota khyal*. While this distinctive melodic phrase (particularly the ascent to Sà) might be sung to vowels or vocables, it is most likely to be sung to the *sthai* text.

Ensembles

The basic performing ensemble for *khyal* consists of the featured soloist(s), an accompanist (or two) on a melody-producing instrument, a drummer, and one or two accompanists on the *tamburā*, the drone-producing instrument (see Plate 3, p. 55).

In the early history of *khyal*, the singers were exclusively male, but the number of female artists has been increasing through the decades. *Khyal* is usually sung as a solo, but there have also been numerous cases of male duo singers, usually family members who learned music together. Even when two soloists perform together (termed *jugalbandī*), they divide the improvisation between them so that there is still only one vocal part. They might sing together only the *ciz* and the *mukhda*. Their music-making is cooperative, not competitive, and it takes considerable skill and intimacy to create a performance to which each contributes equally.

A possible addition to this basic ensemble is a supporting singer (or two). This is a traditional part of performance training for aspiring young artists – a son (or daughter) or advanced disciple. This singer will improvise relatively quietly if the soloist wishes to rest, or the soloist will sing a passage and indicate to the supporting singer that he or she would like to have it repeated (for example, a *tan* repeated in *sargam*). Usually this supporting singer will also play the *tambura* during the performance. Even when the *tambura* player is not singing a supporting role, he or she will be musically close to the soloist.

The melody-producing instrument in a *khyal* ensemble is either a bowed lute (*sarangi*), or a portable organ (harmonium; see Plate 13, p. 265), or both. The role of the players on these instruments is to complement the vocal line of the soloist, by playing in heterophony a split second behind as the soloist improvises, by repeating ends of phrases for continuity during short breaks, or by repeating earlier phrases during longer breaks, should the soloist so desire. A few *khyal* singers set up a relationship that is close to a partnership with the *sarangi* player, giving him (always a male) opportunities to improvise rather than repeat during vocal breaks, or throwing him the challenge of repeating a phrase such as a *tan*. Repetition of a vocal phrase by the *sarangi* player can be heard in Selection 11 on the cassette (cycle 18 in Ex. 3–10 in Chapter 3). In Selection 19, sung by D. V. Paluskar, the *sarangi* is fairly prominent in the first half of the example (transcription in Ex. 3–13; the *sarangi* part is boxed).

Both the *sarangi* and the harmonium have been criticized as accompanying instruments for *khyal*. The *sarangi* was associated in the nineteenth century with light music and particularly with music for dancing girls; its tonal quality blends very beautifully with that of a female voice. Because of its musical and social associations and its tonal quality, it was not readily adopted into the ensemble by some of the leading male *khyaliyas*. Dilip Chandra Vedi recalled (Interview: 1978) that the *sarangi* was used for *thumri* and by female singers 'in the early days', and that around 1925 it became acceptable for *khyal*. Sumati Mutatkar of Delhi University also recalled (Interview: 1978) hearing that in the early decades of this century the *sarangi* was used to accompany only women singers of *khyal* and *thumri*, and that widespread

Plate 2   Ensemble (standing) of singers, *sarangi* players, and percussionists, accompanying a dancer, Delhi, c. 1820 (London, India Office Collection, No. Add. Or. 1)

sarangi accompaniment started in the 1930s or so. On the same day, Yunus Husain Khan, of the Agra *gharana*, commented that some of the singers in his family would not use the *sarangi* 'in the beginning' because of its association with dancers (Interview: 1978); his father, Vilayat Hussain Khan, did, however.

Complaints have also been made about the players of *sarangi*; they come from singers and have a slight tinge of competition about them. Vilayat Hussain Khan related the following story regarding the relationship between vocalist and *sarangi* player:

I still remember an anecdote regarding a Jalsa [musical gathering] that no sarangi player was allowed to sing with tampura; it was tabu . . . It was customary not to allow any instrumentalist singing with tampura until the person had abandoned those instruments and had spent the rest of his life in singing. Once it happened that a sarangi player who could sing fast started demonstrating his method; the convenor of the jalsa stopped him from singing and told him he could only sing when he had stopped playing sarangi for good. On hearing this from the convenor the man abandoned sarangi for good and began singing. After this decision he began singing with grace and was applauded by other vocalists. What I mean by stating this is that music was considered to be sacred and one of the finest branches of knowledge. To respect art and to keep up the standards of values were important traditions of society (1959: 6).

Sarangi players do not take formal instruction (*talīm*), it is said, and therefore they must learn what they know of *raga* and repertoire from the vocalists. Also, it is said, it is difficult to find a player with good intonation, or one who does not try to lead the singer and show off in his own right when that is not his role. On the other hand, vocalists agree that a good *sarangi* player greatly enhances a *khyal* performance. It will be increasingly difficult in the coming decades to find enough *sarangi* players to complement *khyal* ensembles, for few young musicians are studying the instrument.

The greatest difficulties with the harmonium are its Western-tempered tuning – a *sruti* harmonium was developed and was used by Abdul Karim Khan, but it was never widely adopted – and the impossibility of producing on it the *gamak*s (embellishments) so vital to Hindustani music. It has been associated also with lighter forms of music. For these reasons, All-India Radio (AIR), at the instigation of Rabindranath Tagore, disallowed its use in *khyal* ensemble in broadcasts from their stations. A number of respected musicians performed elsewhere with the harmonium, however, and it has become acceptable to almost everyone. In 1971, a symposium sponsored by the Sangeet Natak Akademi for All-India Radio presented the arguments for and against its use in Hindustani classical music; as a result of the papers presented and ensuing discussion, AIR decided to revise its policies in some respects.

One other possible substitution for *sarangi* or harmonium is the violin, the standard Western instrument played Hindustani-style. The only other stringed instrument used in *khyal* performance is the *svarmandal*. It is discussed in the chapter on Patiala (Chapter 8), since it is favored by Patiala singers.

The drum used in the *khyal* ensemble is the *tabla*; Vilayat Hussain Khan attributes its use to Sadarang (Nyamat Khan) in the eighteenth century (1959: 55). The *tabla* player is the timekeeper, drumming only the pattern of strokes associated with the particular *tala* (the *theka*), a role which may be relatively recent in *khyal*, for competition between the vocalist and *tabla* player in showing mastery over rhythm was practiced at the turn of the twentieth century (Deodhar 1973: 39). It also occurs in the performances of a few present-day *khyaliyas*.

Khyal, then, is an improvisational genre with a few distinguishing characteristics and a great deal of internal variety. *Khyal* as created by any one singer can be very different from that of another, and yet it can also be similar. A *khyal* singer develops his or her style as a result of both group tradition (*gharana*) and through his or her own creative individuality.

3   *Gwalior*

The context

In a vista dominated by the gorgeous, blue-tiled walls of an old palace, the city of Gwalior in the present-day state of Madhya Pradesh sits on a wide plain beneath the stately reminder of a long royal presence and a tradition of patronage that prevails even today. The palace was home to the fifteenth-century Rajput Tomar king Raja Man Singh and his favorite queen, the Gujari Mrignaina (the 'fawn-eyed'), for whom Man Singh organized a school of music. In the vicinity, some of South Asia's greatest singers were active, developing musical styles that spread and established Gwalior as a traditional center for vocal music. Twenty-eight miles from the palace is the birthplace of the great vocalist Tansen, whose musical genius sparkled at the court of the Mughal emperor Akbar.

The Tomar kings fought a losing battle against the advancing Mughals, and in 1526 Raja Man Singh fell to the forces of Akbar's grandfather, Babur. The Tomar Rajputs came to terms with the Mughals and, while the beautiful palace became a prison for political prisoners of the Mughals, the Tomar court remained important, providing political as well as musical talent. (Of the thirty-six vocalists and instrumentalists listed in the *Ā'īn-i-Akbarī*, the chronicle of the court of Akbar, fifteen are listed as Gwalior musicians, including the famous Tansen.)

Gwalior again became a focal point in the history of Hindustani vocal music when in 1726 the territory came under the rule of the Rajput house of Scindia. In that year Ranoji Scindia, with Malhar Rao Holkar, founder of the house of Indore, was authorized by Muhammad Shah in Delhi to collect revenues in the Malwa district. Ranoji's illegitimate son, Mahadji, established power in Malwa in 1769; thereafter, with the help of the Frenchman Benoit de Boigne – involved in the French–British intrigues – he established supremacy among other rulers in Hindustan. In 1785 he was responsible for helping to reinstate the blinded Mughal emperor Shah Alam to his throne.

Mahadji died suddenly in 1794 and was succeeded by Daulat Rao, a grandson of Mahadji's brother Tukaji. Daulat Rao, who ruled for more than three decades, moved his establishment from the old capital of Lashkar to an adjacent area where he founded the region's modern capital city of Gwalior. When he died without an heir in 1827, a series of power struggles ensued which eventually aided the British takeover in that area. Daulat Rao's widow Baiza Bai succeeded in placing an eleven-year-old distant relative on the throne – Jankoji Rao Scindia. When he died in 1843, without heir, his widow Tara Bai asserted herself and adopted a boy who ruled as Jayaji Rao Scindia.

By mid-century the British had become powerful in the region and Dalhousie had deprived the *rani* of the neighboring district of Jhansi of her title. This was the crucial period that culminated in the 1857 'rebellion' of native rulers against the British. The Rani of Jhansi joined forces against the British, but Jayaji Rao sided with the British. In response, the Rani of Jhansi attacked Gwalior, and in 1858 drove the young Maharaja Jayaji Rao from Gwalior fort. Jayaji Rao was eventually reinstated to his throne and in 1877 was rewarded for his loyalty to the British, with the right to a personal salute of guns and the title of Counsellor of the Empress (Queen Victoria).

Jayaji Rao (d. 1886) and his son and successor, Madhava Rao Scindia, were both generous patrons of the arts and were important in the history of *khyal*. Though these rulers of Gwalior were not Muslim, and though the Muslim population in Gwalior was far outnumbered by the Hindu, the singers whom the Scindias fostered and who established the oldest of the *khyal gharana*s, were Muslim – a heritage of the then defunct Mughal Empire.

Musicians of the Gwalior gharana

The history of the famed Gwalior *khyal* tradition actually starts in Lucknow, where in the first half of the nineteenth century there were two Muslim families who competed at singing *khyal*. The head of one was Makkan Khan, the patriarch of the other was Shakkar Khan. It is possible that they were brothers, related to musicians (Miyan Ghulam Rasul and his son Miyan Ghulam Nabi) who were associated with two other styles of vocal music – *qawwali*, a type of Muslim religious music, and *tappa*, a style with elaborate vocal ornamentation, developed from a Punjabi folk-song style (Mattoo 1960: 63).

Makkan Khan's family lived in Lucknow and included his son Nathan Pir Baksh, his grandson-in-law Kadir Baksh,[1] and his two great-grandsons, Hassu and Haddu Khan (see Charts 3–1 and 3–2). Of this group, Nathan Pir Baksh was considered a particularly fine *khyal* singer. Shakkar Khan's son Bade Muhammad Khan, the 'great' Muhammad Khan who is sometimes noted as being of the tradition of 'qawwal bacche', gained a reputation as an even greater musician than his father and served as a leading *khyal* singer in Gwalior. Bade Muhammad Khan was noted for singing *tan*s that few singers of his time could imitate.

In Lucknow, the competition between the two families increased, until it developed into total hostility. Tragedy struck the family of Makkan Khan when Kadir Baksh, still a young

---

[1] Vilayat Hussain Khan (1959: 146) traces the origin of the Gwalior *gharana* from the family of Kadir [Khadir] Baksh rather than from the side of Kadir Baksh's wife. According to this account as well, it was Kadir Baksh's family who was already in Gwalior, but there are discrepancies in several details in the genealogies presented by Vilayat Hussain (given here) and by Garg (given in Chart 3–2).

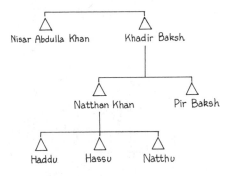

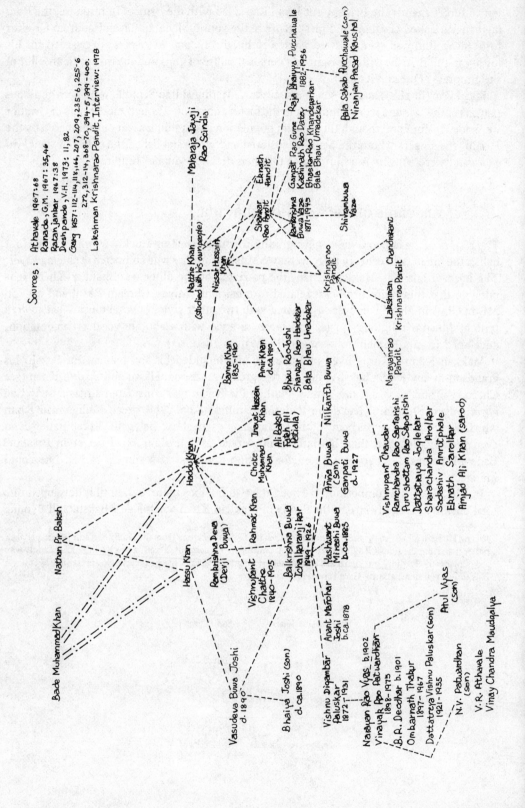

Chart 3-1: Gwalior Gharana Teaching Lines

Sources: Athavale 1967:68
Ranade, G.M. 1467: 35,46
Ratanjankar 1967:38
Deshpande, V.H. 1973: 11, 82
Garg 1957: 112-114, 164, 207, 209, 235-6, 255-6
272, 312-14, 368-70, 394-5, 399-400.
Lakshman Krishnarao Pandit, Interview: 1978

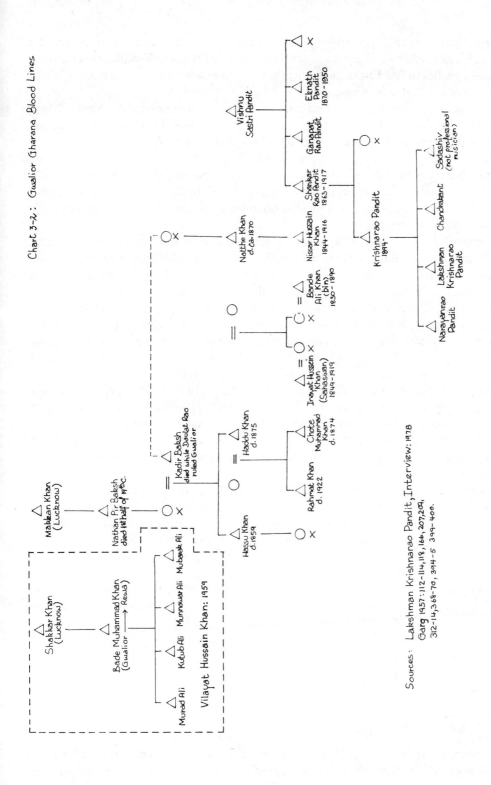

Chart 3-2: Gwalior Gharana Blood Lines

Sources: Lakshman Krishnarao Pandit, Interview: 1978
Garg 1957: 112-114, 118, 166, 207, 209,
312-14, 368-70, 394-5 399-400.

man and father of young boys, suffered an untimely death. The rumor circulated that the family of Shakkar Khan had been responsible for planning his death. Whether or not this was so, Nathan Pir Baksh fled Lucknow, taking the two young sons of his daughter and of Kadir Baksh – Hassu and Haddu Khan.

Their choice of Gwalior as a destination can be conjectured: a relative, Natthe Khan, served at the Gwalior court. In fact, he later became the *guru* of Maharaja Jayaji Rao and was so respected by the sovereign that it is said that 'the Maharaja *gandha bandh* even did [was formally initiated]' (Garg 1957: 199). It is possible that Natthe Khan was the brother of the late Kadir Baksh, as he is described as 'cousin brother' of Hassu and Haddu Khan (literally *cacere bhaī*, or 'descendant of paternal uncle-brother'). If Natthe Khan was already at the court under Daulat Rao, then it was probably with his intercession that Nathan Pir Baksh and his grandsons were 'sheltered' there.

The competition between Natthe Khan and Bade Muhammad Khan was probably keen. Trouble again developed between the two families. It has been said that the two boys, Hassu and Haddu, secretly stole opportunities to listen to Bade Muhammad Khan when he practiced, an activity that must have been difficult, because Bade Muhammad Khan tried to keep his *gāyakī* (singing style) concealed from others (Garg 1957: 231). 'Behind drapes' and 'beneath the throne' have been suggested as the boys' hiding-places, but a different picture is derived from the assertion that the musicians in Gwalior at that time even built special underground practice chambers to keep in the sound (Lakshman Krishnarao Pandit, Interview: 1978). In any case, after they had mastered even Bade Muhammad Khan's style of *tan*, they fulfilled a request by the *maharaja* to sing in court (*darbar*) – in the presence of their competitor – by singing not only with their own family's *gayaki*, but also that of Bade Muhammad Khan. The result was the departure of the great Muhammad Khan from the court of Gwalior to that of Rewa. He acquired fame, received generous support, lived a long life, and died in Rewa (Garg 1957: 400). Tradition still associates him primarily with Gwalior, however.

Of Hassu and Haddu, it is said that they 'gave new life to the Gwalior tradition' (V. H. Deshpande 1973: 50). With the genius of Hassu Khan, Haddu Khan, and Natthe Khan flourishing in Gwalior, the legendary fame of vocal music in that center became assured. All three had been trained musically within the family: Hassu and Haddu by their grandfather Nathan Pir Baksh and Natthe Khan 'by his own people' (Garg 1957: 199; see Chart 3–1).

Hassu Khan had an unusually good voice and was an extremely popular musician, so his death in 1859 (approximately eleven years before Natthe Khan and sixteen years before his brother Haddu) was considered a significant loss to the music world. It is said that his death was caused from singing an extremely arduous type of *tan* called a *kadak bijli tan*, which strong musicians knew at that time. The unlikely story is recounted in Garg that this occurred at a gathering, on a challenge from Bade Muhammad Khan, who asked him to repeat the *tan* (1957: 400).

The teaching line of Hassu Khan

Though historians frequently cite Hassu and Haddu Khan as the teachers of many musicians, the students of Hassu Khan were few because of his early death. Two of his outstanding students were Vasudeva Buwa Joshi (d. 1890)[2] and Ramkrishna Deva, otherwise known as Devji Buwa. Since both were teachers of Balkrishna Buwa, they played especially important roles in the transmission of the Gwalior tradition.

Vasudeva Buwa Joshi

Vasudeva Buwa Joshi, of a Chittapavan (Joshi) Brahmin family of Nagaon, in the Bombay area, journeyed as a teenager to Gwalior, because of its reputation for vocal music (Garg 1957: 255–6). He was able to make his way into the circle of students of the great *ustad*, who was very receptive to good Hindu students. After Hassu Khan's death, Vasudeva remained in Gwalior and attracted there many students from Maharashtra (G. M. Ranade 1967: 35). His most famous student was Balkrishna Buwa[3] (Vasudeva's son Bhaiya Joshi died an untimely death in about 1890, the same year in which Vasudeva himself died).

Ramkrishna Deva

Ramkrishna Deva, originally from the Poona area, studied first with *dhrupadiyā* Chintamani Misra and went to Gwalior after Misra died. Garg (1957: 322–3) stresses Ramkrishna's practicing of *tappa* and *dhamar* (rather than *khyal*) with Hassu Khan, and refers to some kind of deceit. Ramkrishna obtained a position with Maharaja Yashwant Rao Pavar of the Maharashtrian state of Dhar, where Balkrishna Buwa studied with him.

Balkrishna Buwa

Balkrishna, like so many musically inclined Hindu boys who were not born into families of professional musicians, had to seek out his own teachers. He was born in 1849 in the Kolhapur area (Chandur village; Garg 1957: 245). While his father was a good singer and approved of his son's liking for music, his mother firmly disapproved. He spent two years away, returned home for a year, at the end of which his father died, and then departed again to try to study with Ali Datta Khan, a situation that did not work out well. At about the age of fifteen he first went to Kolhapur to study with Bhau Buwa Kagwadekar, then to Sangli, Pandharpur, and Sholapur, and finally to the home of Ramkrishna Deva in Dhar. The relationship of Ramkrishna and Balkrishna was the traditional one: the devoted disciple serving the *guru* almost as a servant in a spirit of humility, the *guru* providing food, shelter, and clothing, along with musical instruction. During four years Balkrishna obtained about 400 *ciz* from Ramkrishna (Garg 1957: 322), until they fell out and Balkrishna was forced to leave his *guru*'s home. He next sought instruction from Vasudeva Buwa Joshi, with whom he trained (mostly in Gwalior) for several years. He may also have studied with Chote Muhammad Khan, son of Haddu Khan (V. H. Deshpande 1973: 82).

After completing his training, Balkrishna intended to settle in Bombay. He founded a *gāyan samāj* (singing society) and began a monthly paper called *Saṅgīt Darpan*. The Bombay climate was not good for him, however, and he developed asthma (Athavale 1967: 5). He was employed as state musician in Aundh, where he had a number of students (at least according to Garg 1957: 248), and was also state musician in Miraj, at least from 1887 to 1896 (Athavale

---

[2] Garg (1957: 255) gives Haddu Khan as his teacher, but V. H. Deshpande (1973: 82) and G. M. Ranade (1967: 35) cite Hassu Khan.

[3] Other students were Lakshman Rao and Krishna Sastri Shukla (Garg 1957: 256); the latter lived in Ujjain (Garg 1957: 135). Ganpati Buwa, a student of Balkrishna Buwa, also studied with Vasudeva for one year in Gwalior (Garg 1957: 135).

1967: 5). His final position was in Ichalkaranji, where he was a court musician, and he was subsequently known as Balkrishna Buwa Ichalkaranjikar.

Although it had been necessary for him to move around frequently for his musical training, Balkrishna had succeeded in obtaining many years of instruction in the Gwalior tradition. From an anecdote related by Deshpande, it appears that he took the study and transmission of a tradition very seriously. The anecdote concerns 'Baba' Sindhi Khan, the son of the Gwalior *khyaliya* Amir Khan who was a friend of Balkrishna. In 1917 in Bombay, Sindhi Khan paid his respects to the sixty-eight-year-old Balkrishna:

Balkrishnabuwa had eye-trouble and was resting with his eyes closed. Sinde Khan greeted him and telling that he was Amir Khan's son, sat near him. Without opening his eyes Balkrishnabuwa said, 'Shakal dikhav' (i.e., 'Convince me that you are Amir Khan's son'). Sinde Khan replied, 'Sir, if you open your eyes you will immediately see that my face resembles that of my father.' Without even stirring from his bed, Balkrishnabuwa said, 'I do not want to see the physical likeness. What I would like to see is how your music resembles that of your father.' Sinde Khan then began to sing. After a couple of *cheej*s Balkrishnabuwa got up, and fixing his eyes on Sinde Khan said, 'Your music has already convinced me that you are Amir Khan's son; now I can very well see that your features are also remarkably like your father's!' (V. H. Deshpande 1973: x).[4]

One of the prime deeds for which Balkrishna is remembered is his transmission of his tradition in the traditional manner. The names of several of his disciples are distinguished: Anant Manohar Joshi,[5] who won the President's Award for Hindustani Vocal Music in 1955;[6] Yashwant Mirashi Buwa who won the President's Award for Hindustani Vocal Music in 1961;[7] and Vishnu Digambar Paluskar.[8]

Among the early students of Balkrishna were also men from educated society in Maharashtra who, in keeping with the awakening of national pride, wanted to make music part of basic education. For this purpose they founded such societies as the Literary and Scientific Society and various *gayan samaj*. Their regular activities included concerts by famous musicians, discussion of musical topics, and publication of old and rare works on music. The Poona Gayan Samaj, founded in 1874, was one such society; it conducted music classes for its members and supplied music teachers to local schools. Another impetus to the popularity of classical music in Maharashtra at this time was the upsurge in interest in Marathi theater, in which well-trained male musicians, rather than actors with little musical training, played leading parts. Several *sangīt nātak mandali*s (music drama companies) were

---

[4] Sindhi Khan's older brother Pyar Khan had angered their father Amir Khan by studying the *gayaki* of Ali Baksh as well. In the Garg article on Sindhi Khan (1957: 390) it is remarked that even Sindhi Khan sang with a mixture of Gwalior *gayaki* and that of Ali Baksh.

[5] Born around 1878 in Aundh, Anant Manohar Joshi also studied with Rahmat Khan, son of Haddu Khan, according to Garg (1957: 83). He was known as 'Antu Buwa' (Ratanjankar 1967: 21).

[6] Through the Sangeet Natak Akademi, the President of India accords national recognition each year to a group of distinguished artists. Beginning in 1951 with the field of music, the honor has been extended to include the fields of dance, drama, playwriting and production. The award is sometimes referred to as the President's Award, sometimes as the Sangeet Natak Akademi Award.

[7] Born around 1883, Yashwant grew up in Ichalkaranji. He spent the years 1911–32 working with a drama company in the flourishing days of Marathi music theater. Then he taught in Poona (Garg 1957: 290–2) at the Gandharva Mahavidyalaya begun by Vinayak Rao Patwardhan, disciple of his *guru bhai* Vishnu Digambar Paluskar (Garg 1957: 172).

[8] Another good student was Ganpati Buwa Bhilavdikar (d. 1927), who was most noted for singing *tappa* and *tarana* (Garg 1957: 134–6).

started during the last quarter of the nineteenth century, and the theater flourished through-out the 1930s.

Perhaps it was just a sign of the changing times, or a feature of the particular situation in Maharashtra, or perhaps it was something in the attitude or personality of Balkrishna, but the paths followed by his students were not the same as the traditional path that he himself had followed. Yashwant Mirashi Buwa's involvement in the Marathi drama movement, and Vishnu Digambar Paluskar's involvement in public institutional teaching were remarkable.

Vishnu Digambar Paluskar

Much has been written and said about Vishnu Digambar Paluskar (1872–1931). He was born into a good family; his father was a *kirtankār* (a performer of religious discourses) from the princely state of Kurundwad, about 150 miles south of Poona (Athavale 1967: 1), and the family was of sufficient standing for Paluskar to go to English medium school with the Kurundwad ruler's son. He could have entered government service (or followed his father's profession), but an accident with exploding firecrackers damaged his eyesight to such a degree that he could no longer contemplate any profession that required a great deal of reading. He was sent for medical care to the neighboring state of Miraj, and was called to the personal attention of the ruler there. In Miraj the decision was made that Paluskar should leave formal schooling and begin musical training with Balkrishna Buwa, which he did when he was fifteen years old, in 1887. His nine-year period of training in the Gwalior style took the traditional form: 'He would daily devote two to three hours to memorizing the compositions and doing "riaz" or practice; two to three hours to cultivating his voice, and for about two to three hours he would take actual training in music from his Guru. Besides this, some of his time was spent in doing the household duties at his Guruji's house' (Athavale 1967: 7).

During the period of training, Paluskar became acutely aware of the difference between his own social standing and that of his *guru*. While he, as a disciple, would spend hours doing the requisite tasks for a man he was to respect above all others, at about the same time he would be an invited guest at state functions to which neither his *guru* nor his fellow disciples would be invited because of the low social status accorded to musicians. Being of a higher social status than his *guru* must also have caused Paluskar to question the necessity of putting himself in such a menial position. He began developing a plan for 'trying to remove the miseries of the musicians as well as of the students' (Athavale 1967: 8).

In 1896 he left Miraj to perform, following the route from Aundh to Satara and Baroda. He proceeded in a non-conformist manner: in Baroda, for example, where he knew no one, he decided to stay in a temple, avoiding 'the usual pattern of introducing himself to the outstanding musicians of the city or to the royal family or to other patrons of music' (Athavale 1967: 11). He did his *riāz* (practice) in the quiet early morning at the temple, and naturally was heard; ultimately he was invited by the *maharani* to perform and did so with success, 'rewarded with Rs. 700 in cash, over and above the shawl, which is traditionally given as a token of appreciation' (Athavale 1967: 13).

From Baroda Paluskar proceeded to Kathiawar (now Saurashtra), an area in which there were numerous royal states which patronized musicians. In Rajkot in 1897 he initiated a practice which he continued all his life and which was most significant for Indian music: since only a small and selected audience would be admitted to hear a concert at a royal court or in the home of a rich person, he decided to give his musical performances in public, charging admission fees. By this means he wished not only to make music accessible to the common man but to provide a means for musicians to earn a livelihood independently of rich patrons. Most traditional musicians (including his *guru*) opposed him, of course, saying that the art of music would be cheapened and commercialized (an argument that rages still!).

From Saurashtra, Paluskar travelled to Gwalior. This must have been important to him because, although he had been trained in the Gwalior tradition, he had never actually been there. 'That a musician coming from south could sing in the style of Gwalior School of Music with such purity and mastery, was a new experience for the Gwaliorians' (Athavale 1967: 18). Apparently he was successful, and was even praised by such artists as Shankar Pandit and Amir Khan. There he seems to have sung for the wealthy and royal, and to have taken introductions from the *maharaja* to leading personalities in other places.

By the turn of the century, and by a circuitous route, Paluskar reached Lahore in the Punjab. Lahore was a glorious center of culture, and there in 1901 he founded his famous Gandharva Mahavidyalaya, the first music institution to be supported by public rather than royal patronage. To staff his school he found it necessary to train his own teachers, whom he considered 'missionaries of music'. Athavale suggests that he got this idea from the world-wide network of Christian Missions (1967: 26). A group of some fifty or sixty carefully selected students would be trained for a nine-year period, supported by the institution (i.e., by Paluskar himself). Some would remain with him to teach, some would perform widely as artists, and some would be assigned the duties of starting and directing new branches of the Gandharva Mahavidyalaya in various places in India. The students resided in a hostel, were strictly (sometimes harshly) disciplined, and shared the everyday tasks of life. Paluskar saw this as different from the traditional system, though it seems to have resembled it in several respects.

To support his plan Paluskar made many performing and speaking tours. To improve the general image of the musician, he wore costly attire and travelled first-class in the train. To perform he would not sit in a position lower than that of his patron, as might happen when the musicians sat on the floor in the traditional fashion while the patrons sat in chairs in the modern fashion (Athavale 1967: 46); rather, he would insist that they be either all at floor-level or all elevated.

To be successful financially, Paluskar realized that to some extent he had to tailor his performances to the musical tastes of his audiences. Thus he included patriotic songs when the nationalist movement was in process, folk songs, devotional compositions, and other types of music in his presentations to royal audiences as well as to popular ones. For this he was roundly criticized by the traditionalists. He also introduced *tabla tarang*, in which a set of *tabla* tuned to a series of pitches is played in the manner of a *jaltarang* (Athavale 1967: 45).

By 1908 the Gandharva Mahavidyalaya had become an established institution, and its main location had shifted to Bombay, with Lahore as a branch. A regular syllabus was evolved, text-books were printed (on their own press), examinations were administered, and students began to come (which they had not for the first several months). To teach ladies Paluskar trained his wife and two nieces; otherwise, his 'missionaries' seem to have been non-Muslim and male.

Additional income for the school was provided in other ways which broke with tradition:

In those days, on the occasion of weddings and other similar ceremonies, people generally arranged music concerts of old professional musicians, and especially of lady artistes from the class of singing girls. Pandit Vishnu Digambar tried to break this tradition. He trained a special group of his students to give performances on such occasions. The intention was two-fold: firstly, to introduce artists of social standing for such functions and secondly, to collect funds for his institution (Athavale 1967: 36–7).

(Those 'old professional musicians' and 'lady artistes' were often the great Hindustani musicians of the time.) He even made the daring experiment of having the lady artistes from middle- and upper-class families who had become students sing in public when the school presented programs on its own behalf (Athavale 1967: 45):

Among Maharashtrian Hindus as in Hindu society in general, music was not considered as an art fit to be taught to the ladies of respectable class, in spite of the fact that they generally possess a charming musical voice in comparison to men. In social and religious functions of the ladies, they used to sing simple songs as handed down by tradition . . . Again ladies never attended any concerts of classical music, which were meant exclusively for the male sex. Girls of the older generation used to learn songs from their mothers or elderly ladies of the household, songs handed down from generation to generation. After schools for girls were started, some songs used to be taught but these were forgotten soon after they left the school. There was, however, no idea of teaching classical music and the utmost limit was to teach them to play a few songs on the harmonium or the Sitar. Music as a career was altogether unthought of till the beginning of the broadcast era (G. M. Ranade 1967: 56–7).

In 1911 Paluskar received the consent of the Governor of Bombay to confer degrees in music. After four years a student would receive the 'Sangit Praveshika' degree, and after five additional years a student would be referred to as 'Sangit Pravin' (Athavale 1967: 37). At a conference in 1916 Paluskar was asked critically: 'How many Tansens has your institution produced so far?' What he could say in response was important for the continuity of the art-music tradition, though it may have been difficult to realize at the time: 'Even the great Tansen himself could not produce another Tansen, but I have done what even Tansen could not do. I have produced thousands of Tansen's good appreciative listeners with musical ears, through my institution, and through my extensive tours' (Athavale 1967: 46–7). Indeed, the twenty-five branches of the school have to date produced thousands of musically knowledge-able students.

Toward the end of his life Paluskar turned inward and focused a good part of his attention on the worship of Lord Rama. When he died in 1931 he left one ten-year old son, Dattatreya Vishnu Paluskar, the only surviving child of twelve offspring. His legacy was also carried by a roster of disciples, among them Narayan Rao Vyas, Vinayak Rao Patwardhan, B. R. Deodhar and Omkarnath Thakur.

Dattatreya Vishnu Paluskar

Dattatreya Vishnu Paluskar (1921–55) was born when his father was quite old, and he regretted never having heard his father sing when he was at his best. Much of his training came from Narayan Rao Vyas, Vinayak Rao Patwardhan, and Paluskar's cousin-brother Chintamani Rao Paluskar (Saxena 1955: 17). D. V. Paluskar was recognized as one of the leading young artists of his time, with a resilient voice that was compared favorably to those of Bade Ghulam Ali Khan and Omkarnath Thakur. Like many singers of his generation, he felt that once he had mastered his *gharana*'s *gayaki*, he could feel free to take from other *gharana*s what he liked (Garg 1957: 174). Like his father, D. V. Paluskar was religious and took part in *kirtan*s and *bhajan* singing. It was a shock to the musical world when he died suddenly in his mid-thirties.

Vinayak Rao Patwardhan

Vinayak Rao Patwardhan was born in Miraj in 1898 (Garg 1957: 352) or 1899 (disc notes, GCI EALP 1314). One account states that he lost his parents as a child, and it was an uncle who tended to his musical education, taking him to study with Vishnu Digambar Paluskar in Lahore in 1907 when Patwardhan was nine years old. By 1919 he had achieved the Sangit Pravin, the highest degree in the Gandharva Mahavidyalaya (disc notes, GCI EALP 1314), and he assisted his *guru* by teaching in the Bombay, Lahore, and Nagpur branches of the Gandharva Mahavidyalaya (Garg 1957: 352). Much to Paluskar's disapproval, Patwardhan was lured in 1922 to the Maharashtrian stage, to join the Gandharva Natak Company of Bal Gandharva where he remained for nine years and established a good reputation.[9] When Paluskar died in 1931, Patwardhan gave up his stage career for teaching. The next year he founded the Poona branch of the Gandharva Mahavidyalaya, to which he devoted the remainder of his long life. For teaching purposes he published the seven-volume collection of compositions called *Rāg Vijñān* (1960). He continued to perform, both alone and with Narayan Rao Vyas, and toured Russia and Eastern Europe. In 1972 Patwardhan was honored by the Government of India with the Padma Bhushan for his life-long service to Indian music.[10] He died on August 23, 1975.

Among Patwardhan's excellent students is the inimitable, energetic, and enthusiastic Vinay Chandra Maudgalya (b. 1918), who has built the New Delhi Gandharva Mahavidyalaya into one of the capital's major teaching and performing institutions.

Narayan Rao Vyas

Narayan Rao Vyas (b. 1902) was also involved with Marathi theater music and is a versatile musician who plays *tabla*, harmonium, and *jaltarang* (Program, Sangeet Natak Akademi Awards 1976). His forte, of course, is *khyal* and, like his *guru* V. D. Paluskar, he renders *bhajan*s beautifully. In 1976 he received the President's Award for Hindustani Vocal Music from the Sangeet Natak Akademi.

B. R. Deodhar

B. R. Deodhar was born in Miraj in about 1901 and studied with Nilkanth Buwa Alurmath (Vishnu Digambar Paluskar's *guru bhai*). He wanted very much to study with Paluskar himself, but his family would not permit him to go to Bombay, however, until Paluskar visited Miraj and took Deodhar to Bombay with him. He studied music until 1921, when he left to follow Mahatma Gandhi's non-cooperation movement. Just at that time Deodhar met an Italian scientist-musician, Dr G. Scrinzi, who had settled in Bombay. Dr Scrinzi thought it a good idea to train an Indian musician and scholar in Western music, so he hired a piano and gave lessons to Deodhar, who within a year passed three examinations in the theory of Western music at London's Trinity College of Music, before returning to Indian music.

Deodhar's career has been varied. He held a music position with the Krishna Film

---

[9] In his chapter 'V. N. Patwardhan', Chaubey gives 'about seven years' for the length of his stage career and gives 1912 as the year when Patwardhan became a student of Paluskar (1958: 72).

[10] Each year in January the President of India honors outstanding citizens to mark the anniversary of the Republic. The three categories of award are Padma Vibhushan (the highest award), Padma Bhushan, and Padma Shri. Among the recipients of these awards are distinguished performing artists, as well as scientists, industrialists, and the like.

Company, experimenting with instrumental ensemble music (*vadya vrinda*) for films, and then turned to musical research. He edited, from 1948, a monthly publication, *Saṅgīt Kāla Vihār*, featuring histories of *gharana*s and articles on music,[11] and also wrote the multi-volume work *Rāg Bodh* (1947). In the mid-1960s he was appointed Principal of the College of Music and Fine Arts of Benares Hindu University, a college begun and developed by his *guru bhai*, Omkarnath Thakur.[12]

From Hassu Khan (d. 1859), then, the *khyal* style of Gwalior was passed through generations primarily of Maharashtrians: Vasudeva Buwa Joshi (d. 1890), who remained in Gwalior to teach; Ramkrishna Deva, who was court musician of Dhar; and in the next student generation Balkrishna Buwa, who was court musician of Miraj and Ichalkaranji (d. 1926). With Balkrishna's students it can be seen that times had changed: royal courts had been replaced by the government of the Republic of India, and awards were given to Anant Manohar Joshi and Yashwant Mirashi Buwa not by royalty but in the name of the President by the Sangeet Natak Akademi, independent India's national academy of music and drama. With Vishnu Digambar Paluskar (d. 1931), widespread public education in Indian art music both reflected and created socio-cultural change that has been sustained by a further generation of disciples – including Vinayak Rao Patwardhan (d. 1975), Narayan Rao Vyas (b. 1902), B. R. Deodhar, D. V. Paluskar (d. 1955), and Omkarnath Thakur (d. 1967), and by their students and their students' students, down to the seventh generation from Hassu Khan. With Haddu Khan, who lived sixteen years beyond his brother, the line of transmission retained a somewhat more traditional character.

The teaching line of Haddu Khan

Banne Khan and Amir Khan
Among the many good disciples of Haddu Khan was Banne Khan (1835–1910), a singer of *dhrupad* and *dhamar*, originally from Amritsar (Garg 1957: 235–6) but living in Lucknow (Garg 1957: 387). In Lucknow he heard the *khyal* singing of Hassu and Haddu Khan and went to Gwalior to study. It is said that he was treated like a member of Haddu Khan's family (indeed, he must have been one of the few Muslim disciples), and that Haddu, who had long waited for the birth of a son, was about to adopt Banne Khan when finally a son was born to him (Garg 1957: 235–6). Banne Khan played an active part in Gwalior musical life, until he received a position in Hyderabad, where he spent the remainder of his life.

With Banne Khan in Hyderabad was Amir Khan, his cousin-brother and disciple (Garg 1957: 288). Amir Khan (d. c. 1910) became one of the great musicians in Gwalior, and was an admirer of the singing of the young Vishnu Digambar Paluskar around 1899 (Athavale 1967: 18). He had four sons, among them Sindhi Khan (see p. 42 above). Besides the family of Banne Khan, the only Muslim musicians of note in the line of Haddu Khan were those of his own family.

---

[11] Vamanrao [Vaman Hari] Deshpande drew heavily from this publication for his Marathi-language book *Gharāndāj Gāyakī* on *gharana* (1961), now published in English translation as *Indian Musical Traditions: An Aesthetic Study of the Gharanas in Hindustani Music* (1973).

[12] Because Omkarnath Thakur developed a musical style of his own, distinct from the style of Paluskar, discussion of him and his student Balwant Raj Bhatt appears in Chapter 9, among the 'independent' musicians.

Muhammad Khan and Rahmat Khan

Haddu Khan is said to have married twice; his first wife gave him two sons and his second two daughters, both of whom were married to great musicians (see Chart 3–2). The elder son, Muhammad Khan (called Chote, 'small'), and the younger, Rahmat Khan, were both trained in music by their father. The elder son was guided as well by the famed *pakhāvaj* player Nana Saheb Panse in Indore (Garg 1957: 166). Chote Muhammad Khan performed at court in Baroda and was establishing a reputation as a good *khyal* singer in Bombay when he developed a drinking problem and died, in 1874.

Rahmat Khan also left Gwalior to establish himself as a performer. He travelled to Benares (where he stayed for some time), sang in the grand music festival held in 1900 by the Nepali ruler (to which so many great musicians were invited), and then lived in Bombay for several years, associating with his *guru bhai* Vishnupant Chattre until the latter's death in 1905 and then with Vishnupant's brother Kashinath Pant. Rahmat Khan later served in Kurandavar, where he died in 1922. Although he was known as a fine singer with *khāndānī gayaki* (of his family's style), with a good voice and interesting *tans*, he is not among the best remembered musicians of his time, which reflects the difficulty of being the son of a great musician, namely Haddu Khan.

Nissar Hussain Khan

Natthe Khan's son Nissar Hussain (1844–1916), a musician remembered with near-reverence, received formal music training from his father from the age of twelve and later studied with Haddu Khan. Upon his father's death around 1870, Nissar Hussain succeeded to his father's position as court musician under Maharaja Jayaji Rao, who had long been an admirer of his singing. The support he received was lavish, as support for the best *darbar* musicians usually was. In addition to a salary he was given food, clothing, and a house. When Jayaji Rao died in 1886 it was undoubtedly disruptive for Nissar Hussain, for the new prince, Madhava Rao, was too young to rule and all patronage was suspended. Nissar Hussain, a bachelor, had no family to worry about, but neither did he have sons to train in the family tradition.

It is at this point in the Haddu line (and, indeed, in the Gwalior *gharana* narrative) that accounts of the Muslim line of musicians end and the story takes two directions: the first concerns the family with whom Nissar Hussain took up residence when his court service was terminated; the second concerns a number of individuals who studied with Hassu (already discussed), Haddu, or Nissar Hussain Khan and with whom the Gwalior tradition became widely diffused. With the exception of Amjad Ali Khan, the noted *sarod* player, no further outstanding Muslim musicians have been associated with the tradition.

The Pandit family, with whom Nissar Hussain went to live around 1886, was Hindu; that was significant, but it must be remembered that there were relatively few (upper-class) Muslims in Gwalior, and Muslim musicians generally associated with Hindus – Brahmin Hindus, in fact, for Hindu singers were usually from Brahmin families. (For a Muslim to associate with Hindus was an ordinary matter, but for them to share a dwelling was extraordinary.) The Pandit family was Kattar Brahmin (Garg 1957: 369) or Dakshini Brahmin (Garg 1957: 118), originally Maharashtrian (Garg 1957: 368). The head of the family, Vishnu Pandit, was a *kirtan* singer, but not of a family trained in classical music (*śāstriyā sangīt*). He was a friend and contemporary of Hassu and Haddu Khan and Natthe Khan, all court musicians, and he often visited their home. Thus a long-term relationship existed between the two families, and it is not altogether remarkable that Nissar Hussain should have lived with the Pandit family. Vishnu Pandit had four sons, two of whom, Shankar and Eknath, became disciples of Nissar Hussain and studied with him for four, five, or six years, serving him as true disciples, even though they were Brahmin and he Muslim.[13]

Nissar Hussain, a very well-versed musician, as the best musicians of his time tended to be, possessed a large repertoire of old compositions and sang *dhrupad*, *dhamar*, *khyal*, *thumri*, *tappa*, *bhajan*, and even the light-music form *dādra* (in *dadra tala*) (according to Garg 1957: 210). Among his best students were the Pandit brothers, Bhau Rao Joshi, and Ramkrishna Buwa Vaze. Nissar Hussain died in Gwalior in 1916.

Shankar Rao Pandit and Eknath Pandit

Shankar Rao Pandit, the third son of Vishnu Pandit, born in Gwalior in 1863 (Garg 1957: 368), may have studied with Balkrishna Buwa or only with Nissar Hussain, but in either case his training was in the tradition of Haddu Khan. In addition to singing *khyal*, he was noted for *tappa*, having learned from one Devji Buwa of Gwalior, and he also sang *tarana*. He was most famous for rendering Rag Yaman, although he sang many other *ragas*. Shankar performed in numerous places such as Lucknow, Calcutta, Poona, Bombay, Alwar, Jaipur, Jullundur, and Baroda. According to Garg, he was sought by the rulers of Satara (near Poona), of Kishangarh, and of Alwar to be a court musician, but he chose not to leave Gwalior. Shankar's younger brother Eknath Pandit (b. 1870) is reported (in Garg) to have studied with several musicians not referred to in the article on Shankar: *tabla* with Jorab Singh, *sitār* with Babu Khan Saheb, and *bīn* with Miyan Mujaffar Khan.

Teaching was important in the careers of both the Pandit brothers. Some time after 1917 Eknath taught for seven or eight years in the Poona Gayan Samaj (a private institution founded in 1874), and it seems he continued teaching throughout his life, for he was appointed to teach at a school that the Gwalior Maharaja had instituted, from around 1930 to 1936. With his son Krishnarao Pandit, Shankar Pandit founded a teaching institution, the Gandharva Vidyalaya, situated across the railroad lines from Gwalior in Lashkar; while it was

---

[13] Garg (1957: 112) gives their ages at the time of beginning instruction as about twenty-one and about eighteen respectively, but if Shankar were born in 1863 (p. 368) and Eknath were born in 1870 (p. 112) then the instruction would have begun in two different years – 1884 and 1888, both of which are later than the date of Haddu's death, cited as 1875 (p. 395). The birthdates cited in Garg and other biographical sources must often be assumed to be close rather than exact (even when the cautious 'approximately' is omitted), because such records were not always kept carefully; dates of death are probably more consistently reliable.

There is further confusion in the Garg accounts regarding the musical training of Shankar and Eknath. According to the Garg article on Shankar (1957: 368–70), it was he (not Vishnu) who lived during the era when Haddu, Hassu, and Natthe Khan were court musicians and he often went to their home to hear them sing. In order to ready himself for musical instruction, Shankar first studied with Balkrishna Buwa, and later took Nissar Hussain as his *guru*.

According to the Garg article on Eknath Pandit (1957: 112–14), Vishnu Pandit frequented the house of the *ustad*s Hassu and Haddu Khan, and requested them to instruct his sons Shankar and Eknath, which they did along with Haddu's son Rahmat Khan. After eight to ten months, Shankar and Eknath also studied with Natthe Khan. Later they studied with Nissar Hussain Khan. There is consensus of opinion, at least, that Shankar and Eknath both studied with Nissar Hussain in their own home, and this is confirmed by Shankar's grandson Lakshman Krishnarao Pandit (Interview: 1978).

supported by the Gwalior government, it was not a royal institution.[14] The Vidyalaya offered instruction in vocal and instrumental music. The Gwalior Maharaja, Jayaji Rao, honored Shankar in 1945 with the title 'Sangit Ratnalankar' and awarded him a supervisor's stipend in his school, the Madhav Sangit Mahavidyalaya, in 1947 (Garg 1957: 120). Among Shankar's students were Ramkrishna Buwa Vaze (who had also studied with Nissar Hussain Khan), Raja Bhaiyya Pucchawale, Ganpat Rao Gune, Kashinath Rao Datey, and Bhau Umadekar Itaydi. When Shankar died in 1917 (just six months after Nissar Hussain Khan), his family renamed their music school after him: Shankar Gandharva Vidyalaya.

It is crucial for the history of the Gwalior *gharana* that Eknath Pandit attracted the attention of V. N. Bhatkhande, who was collecting songs from traditionally trained musicians (see p. 135). From Eknath in c. 1914–15 Bhatkhande managed to obtain about 250 songs, which he prepared for publication. In about 1917, Maharaja Madhava Rao Scindia of Gwalior met Bhatkhande in Bombay and became interested in his work. The *maharaja* (incognito) visited the music classes which Bhatkhande was teaching in Bombay and saw him notating music. Impressed, he invited Bhatkhande to develop a scheme for a music school (as Bhatkhande had already done for the *maharaja* in Baroda) with full details of courses of study, mode of training, examinations, and the like. For qualified teachers, 'the Maharaja called all musicians, employees of the State as well as others, and made them sing before Pandit Bhatkhande so that he could select those whom he found suitable to be appointed to the posts of teachers in the proposed Music School' (Ratanjankar 1967: 37).

Among the musicians selected to teach in the *maharaja*'s school (Madhav Sangit Mahavidyalaya) were students of Shankar Pandit: Raja Bhaiyya Pucchawale, Krishna Rao Datey, Bhaskar Rao Khandeparkar, and a Shri Gokhale. They were sent to live in the Gwalior palace in Bombay while training under Bhatkhande in his new systematic type of music instruction:

In drawing up the course of studies Bhatkhande asked them to write their Dhrupads, Horis and Khayals in notations and sing them to him to enable him to make a section out of these for teaching. They hesitated because they had learnt the compositions from their Guru, Shankar Rao Pandit, the famous Khayal singer of Gwalior, with great efforts and this was then considered a treasure to be guarded and not given. But Bhatkhande placed before them a whole file of Khayals from their Guru's tradition which he had collected some years before, from Eknath Pandit (known also as Maoo Pandit), the younger brother of Shankar Rao Pandit. He also sang some of the Khayals, as he had learned them from Maoo Pandit. It was a revelation to these musicians to hear him sing compositions belonging to their Gharana. This vanquished them. They wrote their Khayals and sang them without hesitation. There were of course slight differences, here and there, in the versions of the Khayals, which was but natural as they had learnt them, without the aid of notation, vocally. Among them, Bhatkhande considered the versions sung by Sri Poochhwale to be very little altered in and nearer the original as taught by Shankar Rao Pandit (Ratanjankar 1967: 38).

Raja Bhaiyya Pucchawale

Raja Bhaiyya Pucchawale (1882–1956) was of a Maharashtrian family, originally from Satara state but associated with Pucch, the *jāgīrdār* village in Bundelkand in which his great-great-grandfather, great-grandfather, and grandfather had worked. The 'mutiny' of

[14] Similar institutions were being founded in various places, but usually under the auspices of royalty; the most important exception was the Gandharva Mahavidyalaya founded by Vishnu Digambar Paluskar in 1901 in Lahore (see p. 44).

1857 uprooted them, and they moved to Gwalior. Raja Bhaiyya's father Anand Rao was a *sitar* player, so Raja Bhaiyya absorbed music at home and then received instruction in vocal music from a succession of teachers, among them Baldevji, for three years, and *dhrupadiya* Vaman Buwa Deshpande, for ten years (according to V. H. Deshpande 1973: 83). As a young man, Raja Bhaiyya apparently played harmonium well enough to accompany good musicians.

According to an anecdote related in Garg (1957: 319–20) Raja Bhaiyya first heard the singing (a *thumri*) of Shankar Rao Pandit on a phonograph record and determined to study with him. Shankar did not quickly agree to teach him because he had not taught anyone as a formal disciple for a while, but finally instruction began in 1907 when Raja Bhaiyya had reached the relatively advanced age of twenty-five. As Raja Bhaiyya gained skill, Shankar would have him practice holding his *tambura* with one hand and playing the *tal theka* on a *tabla bāyan* with the other.

After Shankar's death Raja Bhaiyya became involved with Bhatkhande and the *maharaja*'s new music teaching institution, the Madhav Sangit Mahavidyalaya. After serving as instructor there for twenty-four years he was appointed principal (1941) and retired in 1949. He published instruction books during his teaching career and became known throughout North India, as the books were adopted as text-books in various institutions. The texts were the four-part *Tān Mālikā*, *Sangītopāsana*, *Thumrī Tarangiṇī*, and *Dhrupad-Dhamār Gāyan*. In 1956 he was given the President's Award for Hindustani Vocal Music by the Sangeet Natak Akademi, an award which came days before his death.

Thus, in Gwalior the contemporary reputation for vocal music relates to teaching as well as to performing. It is striking, for example, to read the biographical article in *Hamāre Sangīt Ratna* (Garg 1957: 299–301) on Mushtaq Hussein Khan (Sahaswan/Rampur), whose life spanned the same period (c. 1880–1964) as that of Raja Bhaiyya Pucchawale (1882–1956), and learn of the individual musical achievements of the former in contrast with the essentially didactic achievements (in print as well as orally) of the latter. Both artists earned the President's Award for Hindustani Vocal Music. Had the Rampur Nawab, Hamid Ali, who arranged to have some of his musicians give compositions to Bhatkhande, also been interested in starting a music teaching institution, the circumstances might have been different, but the 'old tradition' of exclusivity was maintained at Rampur until the court disbanded (see Chapter 5). The tradition of Gwalior was considerably diffused at a comparatively early stage with the publication of many of the traditional compositions by Bhatkhande, and was consistently diffused thereafter with public teaching institutions initiated and staffed by Gwalior *gharana* musicians.

Krishnarao Pandit and his sons

Shankar Rao Pandit's son Krishnarao Pandit (b. 1894), a traditionally trained *gharānedar*, helped found his family's teaching institution, the Gandharva Vidyalaya, but then became a court musician. He first worked in Satara (near Poona), and then served as a court musician in Gwalior (c. 1914–19). Unlike most court performers, he also wrote books on music – on harmonium playing, and on *sitar*, *jaltarang* and *tabla* playing, notably *Sangīt Sargam Sār*, *Sangīt Ālāp Sanchārī*, and *Sangīt Pravesh*.

After Independence, in 1948, when Gwalior state was merged with Madhya Pradesh, the *maharaja* ceased his patronage of music. It was not that he no longer had the money, but that he no longer had the same status to maintain – and patronage of musicians had been an important part of maintaining status. Gone was the era when the best musicians were paid handsomely (e.g., Rs. 1,000 had been paid monthly to Bade Muhammad Khan, in comparison with Rs. 50–60 to a soldier). In Gwalior musicians had enjoyed such financial status that some shopkeepers would loan mortgages, with *raga*s for collateral, even though they themselves could not sing (Lakshman Krishnarao Pandit, Interview: 1978).

Three of Krishnarao Pandit's sons became musicians (see Chart 3–2). Narayanrao taught at the Madhav Sangit Mahavidyalaya which became the Madhya Pradesh Government Music School in Gwalior. Chandrakant is principal of the family's Shankar Gandharva Vidyalaya in Lashkar. Lakshman Krishnarao Pandit (known as L. K. Pandit) taught in his family's school in Lashkar, then was a music producer for All-India Radio, and since 1976 has taught in the Faculty of Music and Fine Arts of Delhi University.

Lakshman Krishnarao Pandit

Lakshman Krishnarao Pandit (b. 1934) began his training with his father at an early age. His first performance was at the famed Hardvallabh festival, where so many young musicians have made their debuts. A ninety-year-old musician who heard him sing but had not heard the announcement thought it was his father singing. It is important to Lakshman that his vocal tradition is a family one, and he points out that members of his family have studied only with other members of the family. Like his father and grandfather he sings *khyal*, *tappa*, and *tarana* (they also sang *dhrupad*), as well as slow-speed *tarana*, medium-speed and fast *tap-khyal* (*khyal* based on *tappa*), and *tap-tarana* (*tarana* based on *tappa*). They used to sing *chaturaṅg* – a composition with multiple *antara*, including *khyal*, *sargam*, *tarana*, and *pakhavaj bol*s (sung like *chota khyal*, with more emphasis on rhythm). They also sang *trivat*, a type of composition including *khyal*, *tarana*, and *pakhavaj bol*s, also at a fast speed and with emphasis on rhythm.

For Lakshman, a total *gharana* is, in musical terms, not a matter of family but of a style tradition which continues for many years. Nor is a *gharana* 'a still pool; rather, it's a flowing river'. Things will continually change, 'because an artist is not a carbon copy – if he were, the art would diminish as multiple carbon copies get dimmer and dimmer' (Interview: 1978).

Musical styles of Gwalior *gharana* musicians

Any discussion of the style characteristics of the Gwalior *khyal gharana* must be undertaken at a high level of generalization and with the expectation of discovering offshoot styles. This is because of the age of the *gharana* and also because of the Maharashtrian personalities in the *gharana* who believed so strongly in public music education, which resulted in diffuse transmission.

To some extent, this diffuse transmission has two aspects that can (and must) be viewed separately. One is the widespread diffusion of compositions of the *gharana*, through notations published both by relative outsiders such as Bhatkhande and by the *gharana* musicians themselves, in such collections as Vinayak Rao Patwardhan's *Rāg Vijñān* and others mentioned above. With such publications, the possession of compositions (which had been a measure of personal access to the tradition) gave way to a pride in knowing compositions. In addition, relatively private knowledge of the histories of compositions (generations of receivership), including knowing who composed them, was to a large extent lost when the same musicians who permitted notation of their repertoires refused permission for acknowledgement of themselves as sources of the repertoire, much less providing histories of the songs. Thus large numbers of compositions about which specific information must formerly have been transmitted as part of the material itself have now come to be called merely 'traditional compositions' – a tremendous historical generalization. The Gwalior repertoire was more widely diffused earlier than other traditional repertoires for two reasons: it was the oldest and most respected *gharana*, and so those who searched for authentic compositions were naturally drawn to it; and the Maharaja of Gwalior encouraged (or demanded) that the musicians cooperate with those who searched.[15]

The second aspect of the diverse transmission in the Gwalior tradition – the one discussed here – concerns the actual manner of performing the songs and of improvising *khyal*. It is particularly with respect to this that the possibility of offshoot styles arises. V. H. Deshpande reminds us that Ghagghe Khuda Baksh, who 'founded' the Agra *khyal gharana*, initially received his training in Gwalior (1973: 50), and that 'knowledgeable musicians of the older generation used to say that they could see marked differences between disciples of Haddu and Hassu Khan' (1973: 86). For more recent times, Deshpande attributes the origin of the Alladiya Khan style to the Gwalior *gharana* (1973: 49). The example of the individualistic *gharana* musician Omkarnath Thakur has already been cited, and Deshpande adds another individual to this roster: 'Vazebuwa called himself a follower of the Gwalior *gharana*; however, his style was distinctive and could better be described as the "Vazebuwa style"' (1973: 11). Deshpande sees so much variation in the styles of Gwalior *gharana* musicians that he even seeks an explanation for the existence of the Gwalior *gharana*: 'It is quite possible that because the number of disciples of different musicians was limited in the early period, all of them were bracketed in one gharana' (1973: 86).

The discussion below of Gwalior *gharana* musical activity and style takes into consideration the reality of the situation as suggested by Deshpande. First, the sketchy musical information available about musicians in the early period is presented; then attention is given to the line from Natthe Khan and Haddu Khan through Nissar Hussain Khan to the Pandit family; and finally the discussion concentrates on the line of descent from Hassu Khan, focusing on performances by disciples and other successors of Vishnu Digambar Paluskar.

Gwalior *khyal* style in historical perspective

Bade Muhammad Khan and Hassu and Haddu Khan

V. H. Deshpande (1973: 50) credits the founding of the Gwalior *khyal* style to Bade Muhammad Khan and, from the tales in the lore recounted above, rightly so. Bade Muhammad Khan was known for his *tans* – clear and mellifluous ones (Garg 1957: 231). Details of the musical style of Nathan Pir Baksh, the doyen of the family of *khyal* singers who competed with Muhammad Khan, have been neglected in articles, with greater attention given to his part in moving his family to Gwalior, most notably his grandsons Hassu and Haddu Khan. Of their kinsman Natthe Khan, who was already residing in Gwalior, we are told that he took part in *kirtan* and *bhajan*, along with the Hindus in Gwalior (Garg 1957: 199).

[15] Naomi Owens (Rajshahi University, Bangladesh) has conducted research on the origins of the songs in the *Krāmik Pustak Mālikā* and has produced a paper (unpublished) about the role of the Gwalior establishment.

Hassu Khan apparently had a wonderful voice (Garg 1957: 399), a better natural voice than that of his brother Haddu Khan. The two boys mastered the singing style (*gayaki*), including the *tan*s, of Bade Muhammad Khan. Haddu Khan spent all his life with his brother until Hassu's death (1859), and the two of them sang in various places, including Jaipur when the Gwalior Maharaja took them there, but it is not explicitly stated whether Hassu and Haddu sang *jugalbandi* (as partners), or if the elder, Hassu, sang with Haddu supporting him, or if the two sang separately.

After Hassu's death, Haddu continued a brilliant career on his own. According to the article on him in Garg (1957: 395) he liked particular *raga*s: Miyan Malhar, Yaman, Malkosh, Todi, Bihag, and Darbari Kanhra. He would begin his *khyal*s in a very restful, slow tempo. After singing both sections of the song in that way as well, he would sing *boltan*s and *tan*s, and then slow *khyal* would be followed by a fast *chota khyal*. He sang lyrical and clear *tan*s, taking in the high register (Garg 1957: 395; this description sounds more like contemporary *khyal* than other descriptions of the *khyal* of this early period would confirm).

Musicians in the line of Haddu Khan

The information available on the styles of these musicians is sketchy. It falls into three categories: (1) the structuring of the performance – slow beginning, singing both *sthai* and *antara* with two types of improvisation ensuing, and following on with a fast *khyal*; (2) the types of improvisation included – *boltan* and *tan*; and (3) details about one element in the performance – the *tan* style.

Sons of Haddu Khan

Of Haddu Khan's sons Chote Muhammad Khan and Rahmat Khan, assurances are made in the Garg article that they received from their father all the attributes of Gwalior *gayaki*. Rahmat is praised particularly for his strong and mellifluous voice and for his prepared *tan*s (Garg 1957: 312, 314).

Nissar Hussain Khan

Nissar Hussain Khan (d. 1916), son of Natthe Khan and *guru bhai* of Haddu's sons, mastered every aspect of *gayaki* and had a large collection of old compositions. His was a deep voice, strong and dignified, and he could sing *tan*s of two-octave range.

Krishnarao Shankar Pandit

Of the Pandit brothers who studied with Nissar Hussain Khan, Eknath and Shankar both apparently acquired a vast repertoire of *khyal*s (Garg 1957: 114, 369). A list of musical practices in the *gayaki* of Shankar's son Krishnarao Shankar Pandit is given in Garg (1957: 120). A particular characteristic of his *gayaki* is establishing the *laya* from the outset, doing *alap* with *sthai*. This was reiterated by G. N. Joshi (1976: 47): 'Pandit Krishnarao Pandit, the octogenarian doyen of the Gwalior School, starts his exposition straight away with a Bandish and Rhythm, doing away completely with the preliminary *ALAP* movement' (here Joshi is showing the contrast with the Agra practice; see Chapter 4 below on the Agra *gharana*, particularly pp. 107ff., on Faiyaz Khan). Krishnarao's performances confirm the fact that he does indeed launch straight into the *bandish*, avoiding even the very short pre-*ciz alap* which most artists present even before medium-speed *khyal*s.

Plate 3 Krishnarao Shankar Pandit (center) of the Gwalior *gharana*, with accompanying ensemble, Delhi, 1955 (photo by permission of the Sangeet Natak Akademi, New Delhi)

The article in Garg also enumerates a varied selection of embellishments as achievements of Krishnarao, and also *alankārik tan*, which is declared to be a speciality both of him and of the *gharana* (1957: 120). A performance broadcast on AIR in 1968 of the *khyal* 'Mhāre dere āo' in Rag Desi provides excellent examples of both these characteristics of Krishnarao's *khyal* style; that performance was in a rapid medium-speed. The text and translation of 'Mhāre dere āo', given below, is pertinent to Exx. 3–1 to 3–4, transcribed from the same performance.

TEXT 16

Sthai: म्हारे देरे आओ [आवो जी] महाराजा बज के बीन के ।
Antara: बजावो जी राज ॥

Sthai: Oh Lord come to our home. I have been praying for your coming.
Antara: Don't talk about past things. Please play sweetly on the *bin*.

Early in this Desi performance Krishnarao offered two particular types of embellishment. In the eleventh *avart* (*tala* cycle) (see Ex. 3–1a) the sustained pitch Ga was treated with a subtle fluctuation within the pitch.[16] Then, in *avart*s 12 and 13, after the quick ornamental

[16] V. H. Deshpande (1973: 10) refers to this fluctuation as *kan*, as is discussed in Chapter 7 on the Kirana *gharana*. I hesitate to name these embellishments without learning from each musician what he or she calls them, because terminology is one of the most individualistic (or possibly *gharana*-related) matters in Hindustani music. A systematic consideration of terminology in current usage, by whom, and with what connotations, is a task which needs to be undertaken.

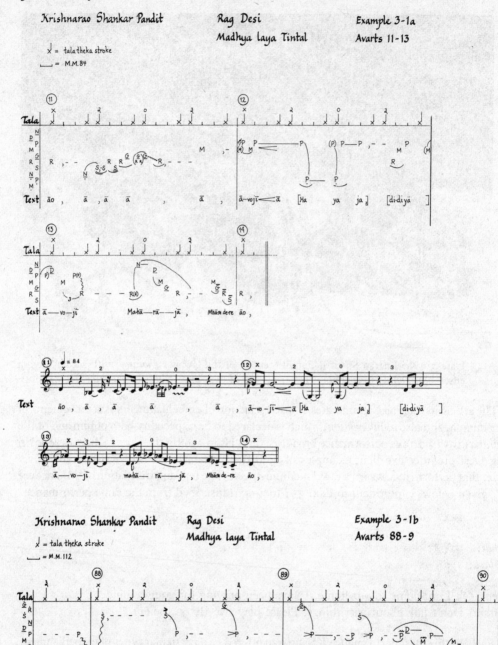

Krishnarao Shankar Pandit   Rag Desi   Example 3-1a
                              Madhya laya Tintal   Avarts 11-13

Krishnarao Shankar Pandit   Rag Desi   Example 3-1b
                              Madhya laya Tintal   Avarts 88-9

leaps from Pa down to Pạ and back, the move from Re up to <u>Ni</u> was accomplished without apparently touching the pitches in between. Another breathtaking instance of a leap without connecting the pitches in between occurred in *avart* 88–9 (Ex. 3–1b, on 'mahā'); relatively few *khyal* singers attempt this type of figure.

Musical contrast through varying embellishments was brought into full play in this performance, as shown in Ex. 3–1a, where quick leaps contrast with quick embellishments (*khatka* or *murki*) on Pa at the beginning of *avart* 12, with a fast, vibrato, descending connection between Pa and Re in count 3 of *avart* 13, and with the legato line from <u>Ni</u> back down to Re in the *tala* subdivision marked by 'o' (counts 9–12 of the sixteen-count *tintal* cycle).

In *avart* 41 (Ex. 3–1c) a strong attacking ornament that gives the effect of repeating the pitch is featured on 'mhāre dere', but that is contrasted quickly with the legato descent on 'āo'. Krishnarao seemed to enjoy variation between descending lines and ascending ones following in quick succession (or vice versa), as in Ex. 3–1d (*avart* 52), where each pitch in descent is approached by a 'grace note' from below, and then each pitch in ascent is approached from above. In *avart* 59 a fast vibrato on the prolonged pitch Ma is contrasted

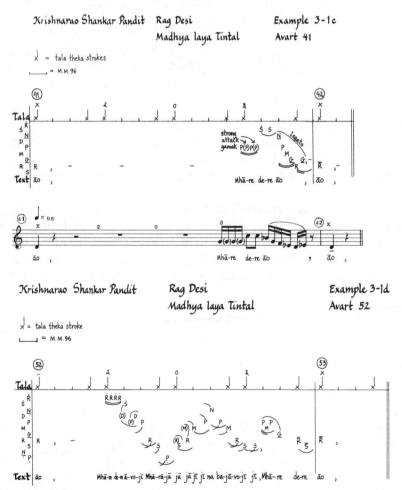

Krishnarao Shankar Pandit   Rag Desi   Example 3-1e
                            Madhya laya Tintal   Avarts 78-9

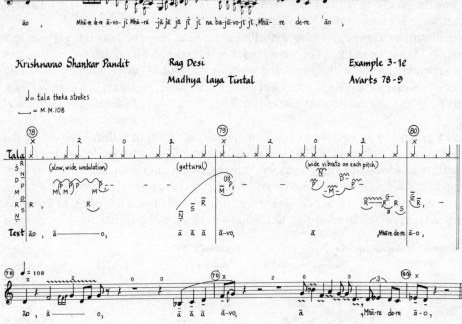

with a staccato delivery of the *mukhda* 'Mhāre dere āo'. In *avart* 78 (Ex. 3–1e) two phrases
with slow, wide, undulating vibrato surround a marcato motive produced with a guttural
voice that Krishnarao produced elsewhere in the performance. The melodic content of the
three phrases is beautifully conceived: a unit showing pitch Pa in context, terminated by the
mukhda 'Mhāre dere āo'.

Rag Desi, with its distinctive *vakra* ('crooked', 'curving') motion, provides a wonderful
opportunity for display of the *alankarik* passages (showing the shape of the *raga*, as in practice
exercises) mentioned in the Garg article (1957: 120). Some such passages are straightforward,
as is *avart* 22 in Ex. 3–2a (follow the pattern beyond N̲ S R N̲). The end of *avart* 26 in Ex. 3–2b
(the descent from the pitch Dha) is another characteristic phrase in Rag Desi. A phrase

Krishnarao Shankar Pandit   Rag Desi   Example 3-2a
                            Madhya laya Tintal   Avart 22

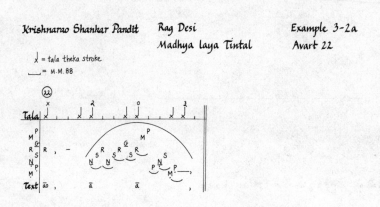

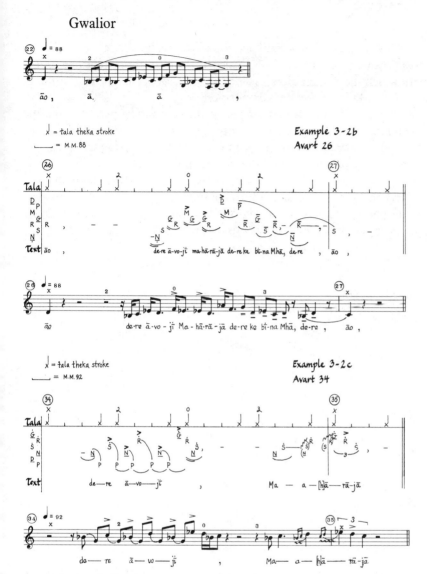

Example 3-2b
Avart 26

Example 3-2c
Avart 34

particularly *alankarik* in nature, showing the pitch Pa in relationship to other pitches in the *raga*, is transcribed in Ex. 3–2c (first half of *avart* 34).

Krishnarao made most passages – even *alankarik* ones – more complex by rhythmic play (*layakari*), which is a characteristic of his style. In Ex. 3–2b (*avart* 26) the words (*bols*) of the text are brought into rhythmic play (*layakari*) in the type of improvisation called *bolbant*; some stressed syllables ('re' and 'ja' most notably) shift the expected speech accents, and the marcato style of stress toward the end of the phrase shifts attention away from the melody of that characteristic Desi phrase toward the rhythm. Likewise, the *alankarik* phrase in Ex. 3–2c is made interesting rhythmically, as the rhythmic groupings are shifted off the beat by the text placement but also by vocal stress and slurs. Other examples of Krishnarao's exceptional skill in controlling rhythm are shown in Ex. 3–3. In Ex. 3–3a the rhythmic play in the descending passage in *avart* 42 contrasts markedly with that in the ascending passage in *avart* 44. Using the same text in *avart* 65 (Ex. 3–3b), he made a succession of short units (see breath marks in the notation) rather than a conjunct, long *bolbant* unit. Variety is marked in Ex. 3–3c (*avarts* 76–7), by use of ornamentation and also by the *tihai* (thrice-repeated phrase 'Mhāre dere āo') with which the passage ends. As is usual in vocal music, the *tihai* is not as exact rhythmically as it would be in a drum composition.

Another consistent feature of this Desi performance is that the *sarangi* player shared the performance, for Krishnarao gave him time for masterly repetitions. The relationship comes across as a cooperative, not a competitive one. In the full *avarts* of vocal rest (43 and 45) in Ex. 3–3a, for example, the *sarangi* player repeated the passage just sung.

The characteristics enumerated for the medium-speed *khyal* style of Krishnarao Shankar Pandit – use of *alankarik* melodic passages, *layakari*, contrasting types of vocal production and embellishments, the pairing of phrases with contrasting melodic direction – are all shown in Ex. 3–4, *avarts* 46 and 47, two successive passages from this exemplary Desi performance.

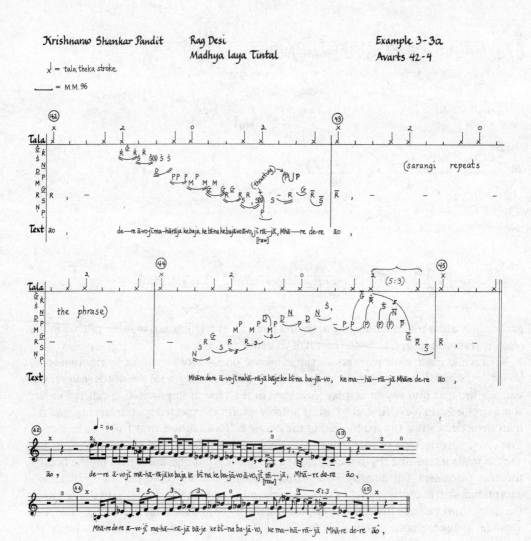

Krishnarao Shankar Pandit   Rag Desi   Example 3–3a
Madhya laya Tintal   Avarts 42–4

Krishnarao Shankar Pandit   Rag Desi   Example 3-3b
                              Madhya laya Tintal   Avart 65

𝄎 = tala theka stroke
⎯⎯⎯ = M.M. 104

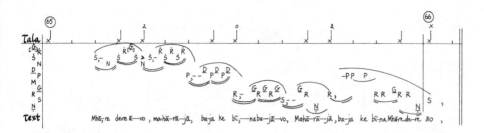

Krishnarao Shankar Pandit   Rag Desi   Example 3-3c
       𝄎 = tala theka stroke Madhya laya Tintal   Avart 76-7
       ⎯⎯⎯ = M.M. 108

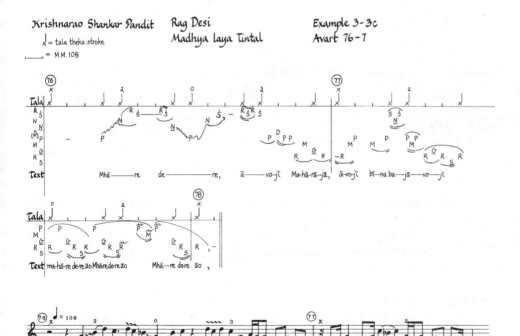

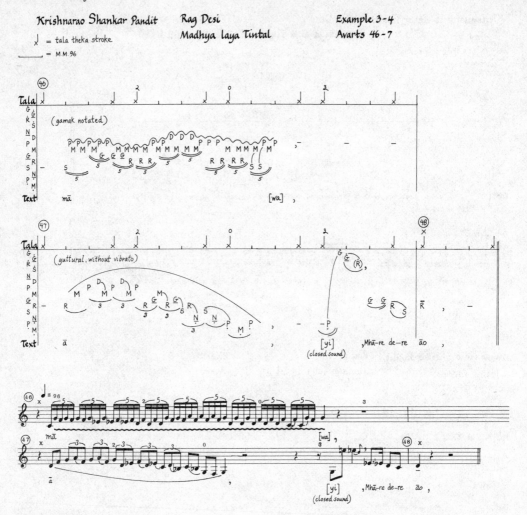

Krishnarao Shankar Pandit   Rag Desi   Example 3-4
Madhya laya Tintal   Avarts 46-7

♪ = tala theka stroke
___ = M.M. 96

With so much attention to rhythm in this *madhya laya* performance, the feeling for the *raga* might easily have been submerged. But that is part of what makes Krishnarao's improvisation so artistic. Even while an intricate combination of vocal and musical elements were at play simultaneously, his shaping of melodic units was cohesive and beautifully designed to lead logically from one to the other. The man is clearly a master.

Chandrakant Krishnarao Pandit

A performance by Chandrakant Krishnarao Pandit, a son of Krishnarao Shankar Pandit, can be distinguished immediately from one by his father from the brief pre-*ciz alap* that precedes the song. In structuring the performance further, Chandrakant first presents the *sthai* of the composition, then, singing in a reposeful, even legato style, he offers a correct view of a *raga* in *bara khyal* improvisation, relying on *sthai* text; the Garg article on his father (1957: 120) had led us to expect this. He is likely to present the *antara* of the composition after improvising into *antara* range on the *sthai* text. This structure of his slow *khyal* contrasts with his rendering of fast *chota khyal*, in which he is likely to present both sections of the composition at the outset.

Unlike his father, who relished rhythmic play, Chandrakant uses *layakari* infrequently. One example is shown in Ex. 3–5; after prolonging pitch Ni (before offering Sá in *alap*) in a *tintal* performance of 'Koyala bole māī' in Rag Bhairav, he introduced a shapely *tihai*.

Instead of *bolbant*, Chandrakant emphasizes *boltan* after his *alap*. He also sings many *sapat* (straight, linear) *tan*s, rendered in a clear fashion; these may be reminiscent of his predecessor Haddu Khan's *boltan* and also his clear *tan*. Chandrakant sings both *boltan* and *tan* in *chota khyal* as well as in *bara khyal*.

During the improvisation in the *chota khyal* 'Piyā milana kī bārī' that followed 'Koyala bole māī' Chandrakant presented a phrase such as his father might sing, an *alankarik* extension from pitch Ga on 'piyā milana', resolved on 'kī bārī'. The passage ends with a *tihai*, as shown in Ex. 3–6.

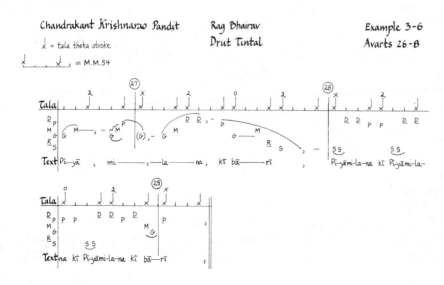

Lakshman Krishnarao Pandit

Reviews of Lakshman Krishnarao Pandit are likely to invoke reminders of his musical heritage, as in: 'He has inherited all the wealth of his father's deep knowledge. This worthy son of Pandit Krishan Rao has fully grasped the essential features of Gwalior "Gayaki"' (*Times of India*, 1968f). Likewise, 'Lakshman Pandit, the son of the illustrious Pandit Krishan Rao Shankar of Gwalior, in his vocal rendering of the difficult Raga Marwa underlined the value of "authentic" and systematic training' (*Times of India*, 1970g). Lakshman seems to feel musically close to his father, too, for in an interview (1978) he mentioned his father three times, citing similarities in their musical practices.

References to Lakshman's training carry reaffirmation of traditional musical values, for this artist was raised in a traditional musical family but he is also a graduate of Agra University. Lakshman stresses his opinion that *gharana* is a style, not a family tradition. While members of his family have studied only with family, they are all involved in teaching non-family members.

Lakshman is credited as well with 'erudition', 'aesthetic sensibility', 'inspiring music', and 'sincerity' (from a selection of reviews). As to his feeling for *raga*: 'It was as though the artiste had brought himself into complete communion with the Raga, and was conveying its innermost meanings, its deepest lyrical secrets' (*Statesman*, 1970). Further, it has been remarked that 'there is dignity and appeal in his cultivated voice' (*Times of India*, 1968j); it is 'broad and open' (*Times of India*, 1971). Lakshman described his own vocal production as open, without falsetto, indicating that in vocal training Gwalior *gharana* musicians develop their range from *mandra* to *tar saptak*. He produces a resonant, pulling legato in his slow *alap*, and his judiciously employed *mīnd*s (slurs) are effective.

Three reviewers of a *bara khyal* performance of Rag Eman [Yaman] by Lakshman in October 1968 (at Sapru House in the Rag Rang Festival) described what was apparently an artistic exposition, while praising different aspects of it. The *Indian Express* reviewer (1968) said: 'his slow exposition has expanse'. The critic for the *Times of India* (1968f) heralded 'his faithful presentation of the "gayaki". He sang in full voice, attacking each note at its core. In the upper octave, his sa-ri-ga assumed a tremendous impact and power . . . Crisp and tiny embellishments thrown in between the soft and tranquil strains heightened their effect'. For the *Hindustan Times* (1968) the critic wrote: 'Eman had an excellent balancing, the way he delineated it, as though bar by bar. Laxman employed brilliant devices of springing occasional flashes across'.

Another superb performance by Lakshman, on AIR in 1969, featured Rag Komal Re Asavari, which he sang for 28 minutes and 18 seconds (28:18) – just under 23 minutes of *bara khyal* and the remaining 5½ minutes of *chota khyal*. The structuring was indeed expansive, more so than some of his *bara khyal* presentations, perhaps because he chose to sing in *tilwada tal*, the slow sixteen-count *tala* in which few artists now sing. (By contrast, his slow *ektal* performances are likely to be somewhat faster.) This adherence to speed distinction between *talas* is one way in which Lakshman has indeed maintained tradition.

A description of the structural proportions of this exemplary *bara khyal* performance in Re Asavari is presented here to demonstrate what the reviewers described as 'expanse' and 'balancing' in Lakshman's creative style. In that performance (as usual in his *bara khyal*, but not in his father's) Lakshman introduced the *raga* with a relatively lengthy pre-*ciz alap* (2:15), sung to indistinct syllables. Its shape was as inclusive a *sthai* melody as a *ciz sthai* might be (D to D), rather than seeming to be the initial portion of a pitch-by-pitch *raga* exposition. After the *ciz sthai* was presented, emphasis was placed for three full minutes on *mandra saptak* phrases, focusing particularly on the cluster M, P, and D; then for the next minute and a half the middle register to D was explored. Thus, this was not a pitch-by-pitch, *badhat*-type *alap*. His entire *alap* was *bol alap*, on *sthai* text.

As he approached the eighth minute of this Komal Re Asavari *khyal* (at 7:53), Lakshman took an entire *avart* break during which the *sarangi* player improvised in the vein of what had been sung. Such breaks seem to be characteristic of Lakshman's *bara khyal* performances. His introduction of pitches Ni and Sȧ took from 9:52 to 14:28, so he took even more time in *antara* range than in *sthai* range. He sang the *antara* after introducing Sȧ; and he utilized the *antara mukhda* until he had sung it all. This one can also expect Lakshman to do in other *bara khyal* performances. Rather than complete his *alap* improvisation in *antara* range on *ciz antara* text, however, Lakshman returned to the *sthai* text and *mukhda*, and ascended further, to Rė. In this slow exposition, he sang clearly and forcefully up to Ma in *antara* range, and ended the *avart* with a *tihai* – the first purposeful rhythmic element in the presentation. In structuring this *bara khyal* then, Lakshman took well over half his allotted time to present the composition and especially the *raga*. Such proportioning manifests the ideal which distinguishes a slow *khyal* performance from even a medium-speed *bara khyal* performance (like the Desi *khyal* sung by Lakshman's father and described above): relatively more emphasis on the *raga*, and relatively less emphasis on rhythm, meter, and speed.

One trait of the *alap* sung by Lakshman seems characteristic of his *bara khyal* performances: in presenting the *raga* he keeps the pitch territory that he has already covered fresh in the mind, by referring back to it in rather wide-ranging phrases (like his father's) – as in improvisation emphasizing *madhya* Dha:

In the tenth minute of the Komal Re Asavari improvisation, after he introduced Ni, he dipped back down to

(The ⌇ here indicates a slow undulation as he connects the pitches.) His retreat from pitch Ni also prolonged the suspense leading to the introduction of Sȧ.

The *tihai* with which Lakshman marked the end of his *alap* seems to be a type to which he is partial: the initial words of the *mukhda* are repeated, leaving the final word (or *sam*-syllable)

till the end; in this case it was 'Raba mera/raba mera/raba mera vohī'. In the *chota khyal* of this performance it was 'tuto/tuto/ japare rām'. In another performance it was 'bana/bana/bana tan' (Rag Kedar). Lakshman's brother Chandrakant also sang this type of *tihai*; an instance was shown in Ex. 3–6 above.

Several types of improvisation occur in performances by Lakshman. Ex. 3–7 (from a fast *khyal* in Rag Kedar) shows a *boltan* on 'pā' of 'pāyala' ('anklets'), which makes no rhythmic use of the text. Like many of Lakshman's *tan*s, this *boltan* has the shape of successions of ascending or descending lines broken with intermittent melodic leaps – an octave, a seventh, a fifth, a fourth (like his father he is skilled in melodic leaps). Lakshman's *tan*s seem to be long, for the most part, as contrasted with many of his father's *tan*s, which are brief motives repeated immediately by the *sarangi* player. In Lakshman's slow *tilwada tal* performance described above even the *tan*s were relatively slow, featuring a loose-sounding, slow *gamak* intermeshed with legato motives and sustained pitches. Reviews have noted the force with which he can sing *tan*s. In keeping with the ideal of a balanced structure, Lakshman also puts some *bolbant* in his performance. No single type of improvisation is allowed to predominate.

Lakshman states that, like his father, he preserves the *sargam* type of improvisation for practice, and thus it is absent from his performances.

Lakshman's relationship with his accompanists borders on partnership. It is not quite that, however, for while the *sarangi* player is given an opportunity to repeat *tans*, Lakshman usually starts another before the *sarangi* repetition is completed; even when the overlap is minimal, the relationship between the two is clear. This can be rather abrupt, as was a moment near the end of *bara khyal* in the Komal Re Asavari performance when the *sarangi* player (Sabri Khan, a skilled artist) was in the process of reproducing not only the pitches in a passage, but a purposeful, slow, shaking *gamak* as well, and Lakshman cut it off, beginning another forceful *gamak tan*.

Lakshman's relationship with the *tabla* player seems to depend on the structuring of the performance. When he takes long *avart* breaks during his *alap*, the *tabla* player continues with calm *theka*, while the *sarangi* player improvises quietly, in order not to disturb the *alap* context. In *chota khyal*, on the other hand, the *tabla* player takes brief solos. In the Kedar *chota khyal* cited above, the *tabla* player even began 'solo' before Lakshman had finished melodic units. The two ended the *chota khyal* together, with Lakshman's *tihai* rhythm matched by the drummer.

In the styles of Gwalior *gharana* musicians in the teaching line of Haddu Khan, only a few traits seem to be consistently characteristic: both sections of the composition will be presented; there will be *boltan*; *tans* will be rendered in a clear fashion; and they will cover a wide range. Beyond these general characteristics, other traits will probably be manifested: the vocal quality will be strong and open; the *antara* of the composition in a *bara khyal* performed will be presented only after *sthai* improvisation; *alankarik* passages will be prominent in the melodic improvisation; and some *layakari* will be sung, if only *tihais*. The other traits noted in the above discussion relate to individual singers and provide a basis for comparison with other Gwalior singers, in a larger sampling of performances. Such traits are the great variety of embellishments and the principle of contrast used by Krishnarao Pandit, and the near-partnership relationship which Lakshman seems to enjoy with his accompanists.

Musicians in the line of Hassu Khan

In the line of Hassu Khan, through Vasudeva Buwa Joshi, Ramkrishna Deva, and Balkrishna Buwa, came musicians such as Vishnu Digambar Paluskar, who assumed the role of musical missionary to the public in North India. Most musicians in this line were attracted to music as an occupational choice (rather than a hereditary likelihood) – an old Brahmin ideal which fitted nicely into the socio-cultural changes in India in the first half of the twentieth century (however unconsciously, at first, the ideal was played out). By natural musical inclination, the common Gwalior tradition in which all were trained has been manifested in various ways.

In the following section performances by disciples of Vishnu Digambar Paluskar – Vinayak Rao Patwardhan and Narayan Rao Vyas – and by V. D. Paluskar's son D. V. Paluskar, who studied primarily with Vinayak Rao Patwardhan, are analyzed.

Vinayak Rao Patwardhan and Narayan Rao Vyas

For Patwardhan, a renowned musician of the Gwalior *gharana*, the word 'facile' seems particularly appropriate – facile in voice and facile in manipulation of musical materials (see Chaubey 1958 for a negative view of this). The discussion of performances by him emphasizes types of improvisation rather than large-scale structural aspects of style.

Probably because of his natural voice, Vinayak Rao Patwardhan spent an unusual amount of performance time improvising in the high register. One could expect him to sing phrases with Má several times in improvisation (see Exx. 3–8, 3–9, 3–10, and 3–11, where Ma is notated as F) and to offer Dhá as his ultimate high pitch (see Ex. 3–9). Also showing his vocal facility is a melodic figure which seems to have been almost a signature phrase for him, as shown in Ex. 3–8: a light leap up, followed by a legato descent – a very long, pulling *mind* phrase. Through counts 2 to 5 of the *ektal* cycle shown there, he ascended from Sa to Sá, then moved Rė–Sá with a *mind* descending to Ma. Counts 6 and 7 include an ascent from Pa to Má, followed by the *mind* down to Dha. In Ex. 3–9, from the same recording in Rag Anandi Kedar (GCI ECLP 2766), the tempo is faster, but the figure is still there in the *tihai* (on 'udho') which ends the *avart*.

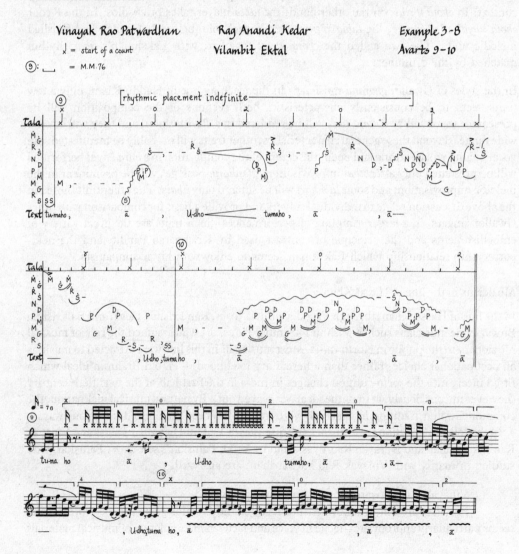

Vinayak Rao Patwardhan   Rag Anandi Kedar   Example 3-8

ↀ = start of a count   Vilambit Ektal   Avarts 9–10

⑨: ⌊ = M.M. 76

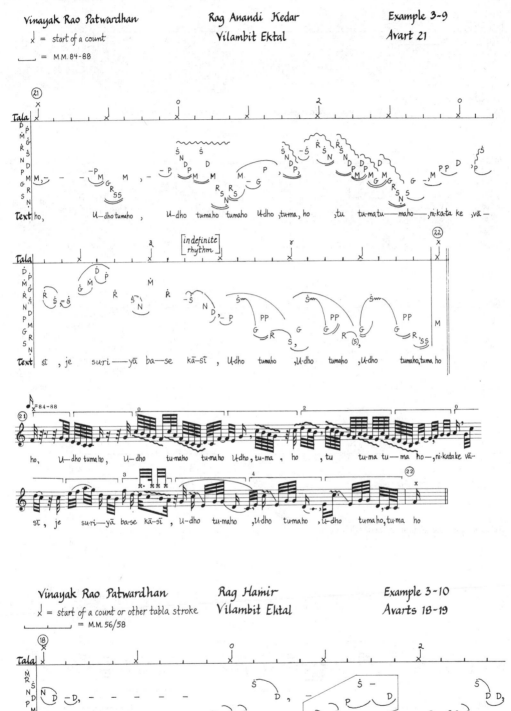

Vinayak Rao Patwardhan   Rag Anandi Kedar   Example 3-9
 𝄩 = start of a count   Vilambit Ektal   Avart 21
 └─┘ = M.M. 84-88

Text: ho, U—dho tumaho, U-dho tumaho tumaho U-dho ,tu-ma, ho ,tu tu-ma tu——maho—,ni-ka-ta ke ,va—

Text: st , je su-ri——ya ba-se ka-si , U-dho tumaho ,U-dho tumaho ,U-dho tumaho,tuma ho

Text: ho, U—dho tumaho, U—dho tu-maho tu-maho U-dho ,tu-ma , ho , tu tu-ma tu——ma ho—,ni-katake va—

Text: st , je su-ri——ya ba-se ka-si , U-dho tu-maho ,U-dho tumaho ,u-dho tumaho,tu-ma ho

Vinayak Rao Patwardhan   Rag Hamir   Example 3-10
 𝄩 = start of a count or other tabla stroke   Vilambit Ektal   Avarts 18-19
 └─┘ = M.M. 56/58

Text: pa—ti , ka-ra-na ca-hu , ka-ra-na ca—hu raghupa—ti,

sarangi

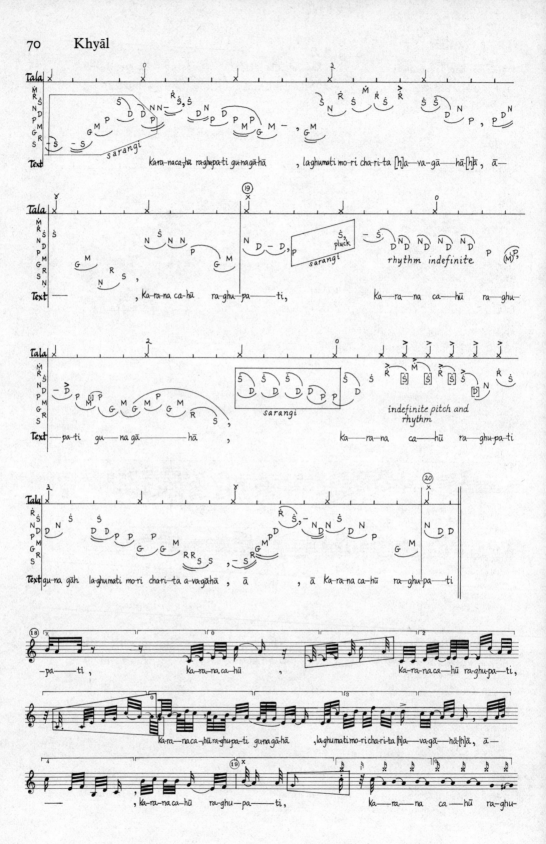

Vinayak Rao Patwardhan

𝗑 = start of a count

_____ = M.M.50

Rag Hamir

Vilambit Ektal

Example 3-11

Avarts 11-12

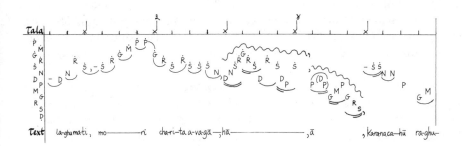

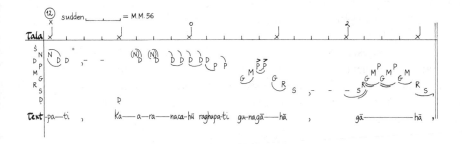

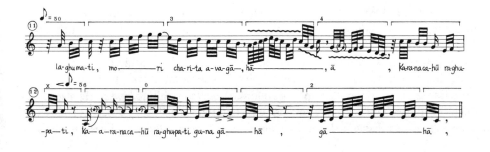

In another display of vocal facility, Patwardhan loved to repeat a brief melodic motive in two different *saptak*s in quick succession, as in Ġ Ṙ Ṡ G R S. With fine control, Patwardhan made judicious use of dynamic contrast, as can be seen in Ex. 3–8. In count 4 (*avart* 9) he made a swell on 'dho' that was complemented beautifully by the *tabla* player, who increased the tension in his part as well by increasing the rhythmic density of his strokes; the swell in both voice and drum ended abruptly on count 5, and Patwardhan began his descending *mind*. He used *mind*s in other contexts, as well, as in Ex. 3–10, in *avart* 19, counts 2 and 3, 7, and 8, where he created rhythmic play against the *tabla theka* with a series of *mind*s between two pitches, defying the definition of the counts by the drummer.

While Patwardhan, like other Gwalior singers, did not sing *sargam* in *bara khyal*, he sang passages with rhythmic enunciation that non-Gwalior singers might produce with the *sargam* syllables. An instance of this is shown in Ex. 3–8, *avart* 10; the contrast with the preceding *avart* is clear and effective. This type of rhythmic enunciation differs from that in Ex. 3–11, where for a moment (in *avart* 12 of a Rag Hamir performance) he produced rhythmic enunciation with ornamentation that is associated with the type of improvisation called *nom-tom* (at 'karana cahū').

Two other types of improvisation that Patwardhan cultivated were *boltan* and *bolbant*. Ex. 3–9, *avart* 21, of his Anandi Kedar recording features *boltan*s in counts 1 to 6. They are descending *tan*s, as a great number of Gwalior *tan*s are likely to be. He featured *bolbant* in his *bara khyal*, *chota khyal*, and also in the genre *tarana*, which he sometimes sang in lieu of *chota khyal*.

Patwardhan enjoyed interplay with his accompanists. In the Hamir recording the violinist had the opportunity to play phrases between the vocal phrases (not exact repetition either melodically or rhythmically). But what highlighted the interplay particularly was the violinist's reproduction (at those moments of vocal silence) of the vocal techniques, as well as of pitch or pitch contour (see Ex. 3–10, especially count 6 of *avart* 19, as the violinist reiterated the *mind*s but not the rhythmic placement). Patwardhan also sometimes interacted with his *tabla* player; Chaubey (1958: 73) comments on his 'duels' with the *tabla* player in *tarana*.

For Narayan Rao Vyas, *guru bhai* and sometime singing partner of Patwardhan, three distinguishing traits are important: two concern his structuring of a *bara khyal*, and the third his *tan*s. Unlike singers in Haddu Khan's line, it seems that Vyas preferred to sing his *alap* to vowels (*akar*) rather than to the composition text (*bolalap*); he reverted to *bolalap* when he wished to demarcate a section of his improvisation. When in his *alap* improvisation he reached the *antara* range, he was likely to make abundant use of the *ciz antara*: for a number of *avart*s the *antara mukhda* provided melody for cadences. Ex. 3–12, from a recording of Rag Gaur Malhar, shows his approach to and presentation of the *antara* of the *khyal* 'Sāvana me jhuki'. In addition, he often repeated the *ciz antara* later in the performance.

The third characteristic concerns the shape of his *tan*s. Two melodic shapes which Vyas seems to have enjoyed are the 'ever-higher' and 'ever-lower' shapes, as well as a combination of the two, played out in a number of ways. One is a series of descending linear *tan*s, each begun higher than the previous one. Another involves 'roller-coaster' *tan*s, with each successive pinnacle rising higher or, in descending roller-coaster *tan*s, falling lower. He also sang *tan*s in which the highest pitch register remains constant while successive descents go lower. Vyas also seems to have relished a descending *tan tihai* – three *tan*s followed by the *mukhda*.

Narayan Rao Vyas   Rag Gaud Malhar   Example 3-12
                                  Madhya laya Tintal

𝄽 = start of a tala subdivision

⌐──┐ = M.M. 132

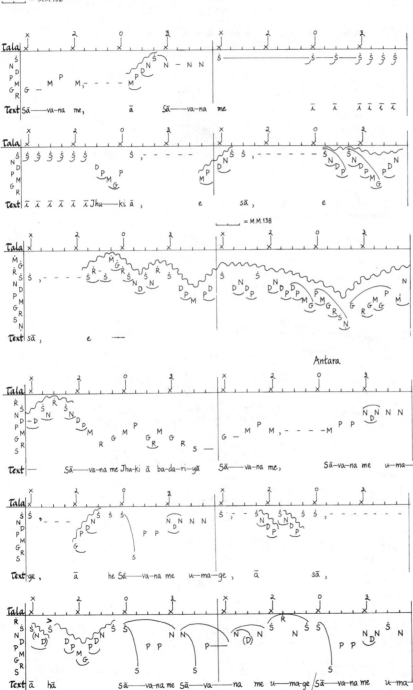

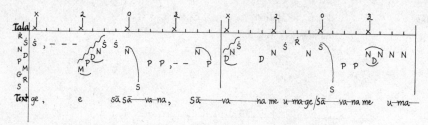

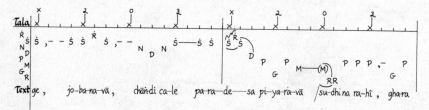

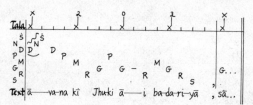

The recording on GCI EALP 1314 includes a *jugalbandi* performance of *khyal* – *madhya laya ektal* Rag Malgunji – performed by Vinayak Rao Patwardhan and Narayan Rao Vyas, followed by a *tarana*. The *tans* determine that the performance is unmistakeably *khyal*, but there are many resemblances to the way *dhrupad* is performed in an *alap-dhrupad* sequence and portions of the *alap*. In this *jugalbandi* performance Patwardhan shows off his propensity for high register in phrases reaching up to Má and Pá and for pulling, *mind*-like legato descent. The voice of Vyas can be distinguished in the duet by its natural vibrato.

Dattatreya Vishnu Paluskar
   In describing D. V. Paluskar's style, V. H. Deshpande stressed that the young artist was catholic in spirit when it came to *gharana* style characteristics. From Agra he took *boltans* (though it is not clear why, because Gwalior musicians revelled in *boltan*); from Kirana he took *surilapan* – singing *alap* with sweet expressiveness; and from Alladiya Khan he is said to have taken *vakra tans* (1973: 15). Whatever the origins of his style characteristics, D. V. Paluskar shared enough of the Gwalior style that no one considered him independent of it.
   Like Narayan Rao Vyas, D. V. Paluskar sang *alap* to vowels rather than to the *ciz* text, bringing text in for contrast (but without clear sectional demarcation). And, like Vinayak Rao Patwardhan, he sometimes treated his audiences to *nom-tom*-like *bolbant* after Sá had been introduced in *alap*.
   Like other Gwalior *gharana* singers, D. V. Paluskar enjoyed vocal leaps. Phrases such as

pivoting on one pitch and including leaps, featured in his Rag Kamod performance. Instances

D.V. Paluskar   Rag Kamod   Example 3-13
                                 Drut Tintal   End of the khyal

   ⅄ = start of a tala subdivision

   ⅄_____ = M.M. 72

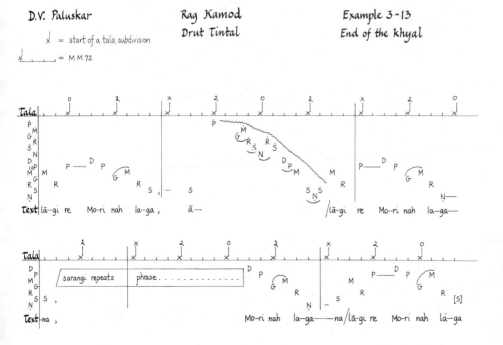

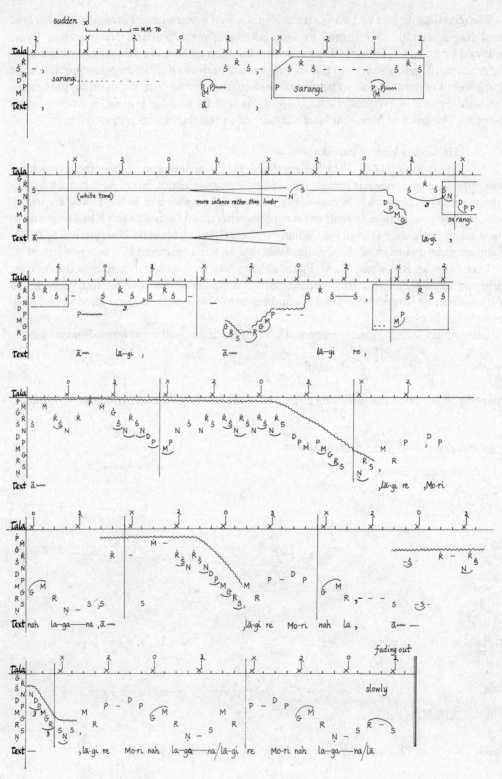

of very wide leaps are shown in Ex. 3–13, from a *chota khyal* in Kamod. In his Bageshri Kanhra [Kanada] *khyal*s, such leaps hardly ever occurred, so this must be seen as one he could exploit in *raga*s conducive to it but not as a characteristic of every performance.

Ex. 3–13 serves as well to demonstrate three other characteristics of D. V Paluskar's performances. First, his singing of *akar tan*s, which he featured to a far greater extent than his Gwalior predecessors. Secondly, dynamic expressiveness, as shown in the swell on 'ā' in the seventh full *avart* in Ex. 3–13. Thirdly, he liked to sing with *mind*s, but between two pitches rather than in longer units.

With respect to the shaping of *tan*s, D. V. Paluskar used variety. Many *tan*s were descending, as expected from a Gwalior musician. Particularly in Rag Kamod, he would dwell on the alternation of two pitches with fast *gamak*, then shift to two other pitches in the same way, and then gradually widen the range of the *tan*. In whatever *raga*, he liked *tan*s with leaps, followed by a fast *gamak* prolongation on the pitch at the end of the leap.

Generalizations about musical style characteristics

Singers in the line of Hassu Khan structure their *khyal* performances in similar ways. First, one can expect them to have cultivated a wide vocal range (from Ga or Ma to Pā or Dhā) and to display it in performance. One can also expect them to be so secure in intonation that the many melodic leaps (octave or more) they make will be in correct pitch. Improvisation before the *ciz* will not seem to be the beginning of an *alap*, or a truncated *alap*; instead, it will probably be in the image of the *ciz* – shapely, and possibly taking in most of the middle octave. This will either be sung on *ciz* text or on syllables such as 'de' and 'a'.

Distinctions seem to be made between *laya* (speed) in the structuring of performances. In slow *khyal*, the *ciz antara* is likely to be presented in the *antara* portion of the *alap*, or it might be omitted. In medium-speed *khyal*, both sections of the song will most likely be presented together at the beginning. In fast *khyal*, the *antara* will follow multiple statements of the *sthai* at the beginning. In slow *khyal*, *alap* will present the *raga* in pitch clusters, sung probably to vowels (*akar alap*), using text to provide contrast until the higher pitch register is approached (usually Dha or Ni). At that point, the text (*bols*) will become more prominent. This contrast of *akar* and *bols* makes it clear that *bols* connote rhythm to Gwalior musicians, for attention to rhythm begins as *tar saptak* is reached. Medium-speed *khyals* will probably not feature any systematic *alap*, although *mandra saptak* will be referred to in an early cycle of the *tala*. The text is prominent throughout such performances.

Boltans will be there, but in different amounts with different performers. *Bolbant* will be there – again, in different amounts and with different degrees of complexity. *Avarts* of *boltan* and *bolbant* will be intermixed; that is, the performances will not be divided into segments by each type of improvisation.

Tihai is a predictable element in this style. Some Gwalior artists in Hassu's line are likely to sing *tihai* in *chota khyal* more than in *bara khyal*, or in some *bara khyal* but not all, while others make abundant use of this rhythmic cadence.

An element which seems to play a greater part in the Gwalior *gharana* than in the styles of younger *gharanas* is *nom-tom*, the pulsating rhythmic play associated with *alap-dhrupad*. The musicians generally follow *bara khyal* with *tarana* rather than with *chota khyal*; one even utilizes elements of *tarana* in *chota khyal*. Those artists who cultivate *tarana* and *nom-tom* are likely to be the ones who enjoy interplay with their accompanists.

With the exception of D. V. Paluskar's performances, *akar tans* occur in nominal amounts, and at the very end of *bara khyal*. Nor are there necessarily very many *akar tans* in *chota khyal*. *Sargam* is also used relatively little, and mostly at faster speeds – in *madhya laya* selections or in the *chota khyal*; it is used in *tarana* by those artists who sing *tarana*.

Summary

Comparison of this selection of performances from two lines of Gwalior musicians reveals a number of *khyal* performance characteristics that are held in common, and a few distinct to each line. Several characteristics seem to be individual (relative to the group), and one generational. These conclusions, based on a selective number of performances, should serve as a springboard for further analysis of other performances.

Common characteristics

Gwalior artists (with one exception) precede the song with a pre-*ciz alap*, that is, more *ciz*-like than song-like, and this is sung either to *bols* or vocables. They distinguish between slow (*vilambit*) and medium-speed (*madhya*) *bara khyal* performances in three major ways: *vilambit laya* is for *alap*-type improvisation, while *madhya laya* only suggests *alap*-like improvisation by more reference to the low register at the outset than elsewhere; otherwise, rhythm is prominent throughout the improvisation. In *vilambit laya* performances, their *alap* is organized in pitch-register segments (rather than pitch-by-pitch development), and they present the *ciz antara* after improvising in *antara* range. In *madhya laya* performances, they improvise on text rather than on vowels.

They cultivate a wide range and continue to show it throughout a performance, whether in the process of *alap* or in *tan*s. They are skilled at melodic leaps and include a number of them in a variety of contexts throughout a performance. With the exceptions noted below, they sing more *boltan*s than (*akar*) *tan*s. A good percentage of their *tan*s are descent-oriented (confirming the statement in Bhatta 1968: 31); and many *tan*s are *alankarik* in structure, in the sense that they systematically develop a melodic idea.

Rhythmic play of some sort is cultivated by all these artists: some excel in *bolbant*, while others hardly cultivate it; they all seem to enjoy *tihai*. On the matter of embellishments, they all sing with *mind*s, but this seems to be a category of individual preference. As to ensemble, interplay with the melody-producing accompanist (*sarangi* or violin) is frequent, while interplay with the *tabla* player is more dependent on individual styles.

These generalizations accord with those made about the Gwalior *gharana* style by V. H. Deshpande in his *Indian Musical Traditions*: linear *tan* studded with *gamak*s, aimed at covering all three registers (1973: 51), and (simple) fusion of *svara* and *laya* (1973: 70), by which he means fusion of attention to *raga* and to rhythm. Deshpande's comment about the Gwalior *gharana* style being 'middle of the road with regard to exploitation of the principle of musical contrast' (1973: 37) seems to apply more aptly to individual singers than to all.

Distinctions between the Hassu and Haddu line

In the line of Haddu Khan (i.e., in the performances of the Pandit family), *alap* in slow *bara khyal* is sung to text, while in the line of Hassu Khan *alap* is sung to vowels until the *antara* range is reached, at which point *bol*s are brought into play primarily as an element of rhythm. The Pandit family singers do not use *sargam*, whereas those of the other line sing *sargam* sparingly in medium-speed *bara khyal* and *chota khyal*. Five other characteristics are tentatively suggested on the basis of this selection of recordings: (1) the Pandit family practices little or no cultivation of *nom-tom*, while it is strongly characteristic of the other line; (2) the Pandit family seems careful to present the *ciz antara* in every *khyal*, while it may be left out by singers in the other line; (3) in *madhya laya* performances, the Pandit singers present the *antara* late in the improvisation, while singers in the Hassu Khan line place the *antara* either with *sthai* at the beginning or late in the improvisation; (4) some of the Hassu-line singers seem to replace *chota khyal* with *tarana* more frequently than members of the Pandit family do; and (5) dynamic expression through vocal techniques, such as swell, seems to be cultivated by singers of the Hassu line more than by the Pandit family singers.

Characteristics of individual styles

Krishnarao Shankar Pandit sings to pre-*ciz alap*, and he encompasses an amazing variety of embellishments. Lakshman Krishnarao Pandit divides his *alap* with long breaks during which the *sarangi* provides continuity, and he gives a particularly prominent role to the *tabla* player. One of his favorite *tan* shapes is a large melodic leap followed by a descent (without *mind*), and these may come in series; Lakshman, along with D. V. Paluskar, features *tan*s of pitch plateaux created by *gamak*s, though Paluskar's include more leaps. Lakshman is noted for singing *tan*s with force. Lakshman Pandit and Narayan Rao Vyas both pay relatively prolonged attention to *antara* – to *antara* range in *alap*, using the *antara mukhda* for that stretch of time, and possibly repeating the *ciz antara* in the course of their improvisation. Vinayak Rao Patwardhan favored, especially, a *tan* shape of a large melodic leap followed by descent, but the descent is a long, pulling *mind*. D. V. Paluskar made nominal use of *boltan*s, preferring *akar tan*s instead.

One characteristic seems to be attributable more to different generations than to any other factor (though it could be attributed to individuality): there seems to be a reduction over the years in the cultivation of the principle of contrast. As pointed out in the analysis above, the two singers in this sample who cultivated contrast as a major musical factor were Krishnarao Shankar Pandit and Vinayak Rao Patwardhan. This single element made their performances strikingly different.

4   *Agra*

The context

Agra lies roughly 200 kilometers south-east of Delhi. Its early history is obscure, but it was possibly the home of Rajput peoples who fell to the invading Afghanis in the latter part of the twelfth century. About 300 years later, the greatest of the Afghani Lodi kings, Iskander (Sikander), made it his home (1489–1517). On the eastern side of the Yamuna River he constructed a fort and a seat of government which he called the city of Sikandra. His choice of Agra presaged a movement of various rulers of the Mughal dynasty to and from Delhi–Agra. The great Mughals left their mark on Agra with the construction on the western side of the Yamuna River of the great Agra Fort, palaces such as Akbar's Fatepur Sikri, where the great vocalist Tansen reigned as musical monarch, and the incomparable Taj Mahal, the tomb which Shah Jahan had constructed for his beloved wife Mumtaz.

Despite their enjoyment of Agra and their palaces on the banks of the Yamuna, the Mughals recognized Delhi as the capital of their far-flung empire. Indeed, Shah Jahan designed yet another city for Delhi (there have been seven across five millennia), and by 1666 Agra district had dwindled in importance. After Shah Jahan no Mughal ruler paid much attention to Agra. In 1761 the city was taken by the Jats of Bharatpur and in 1803 it came into the hands of the British. Thereafter it remained a sizeable military and administrative cantonment, and in 1863 it was constituted a major municipality.

There is no historical tie between the great courts of the Mughals and the traditions of the great Agra *gharana*. The Agra *gharana* of *khyal*, post-dating the Mughal presence in Agra, is named after the home place of the 'founding family', whose musical talents were fostered elsewhere.

Musicians of the Agra *gharana*

Early history

The history of the Agra *gharana* is a long one, dating far beyond the early nineteenth century when one member of the *dhrupad*-singing family learned *khyal* and changed the course of family music history. According to Yunus Husain Khan (Interview: 1978), at the time of Allauddin, one of the early Afghani Muslim *sultan*s of Delhi (1296–1316), this family of musicians was Hindu Rajput and resided in Rajasthan.

The family has been associated with Agra since the sixteenth century, when one Sujan Singh and his brother Bichitra settled there. They converted to Islam as well; Sujan, who made the pilgrimage to Mecca and is thus called 'Haji', is also referred to as Subhan Khan (cf.

Agarwala 1966: 20, 29). Subhan or Sujan Khan is said to have lived to be 125 years of age; the family possessed *dhrupad* and *dhamar* compositions of his. The brothers Subhan and Bichitra were contemporaries of the great singer Tansen and also court musicians to Akbar, which probably explains the move to Agra. Both musicians are listed in the *Āʾīn-i-Akbarī*, the chronicle of the court of Akbar, which lists musicians as it does learned men, poets, and grandees of the empire. Of the thirty-six imperial musicians listed, the first six are mentioned thus:

His Majesty pays much attention to music, and is the patron of all who practise this enchanting art. There are numerous musicians at court, Hindūs, Īrānīs, Tūrānīs, Kashmīrīs, both men and women. The court musicians are arranged in seven divisions, one for each day in the week. When his Majesty gives the order, they let the wine of harmony flow, and thus increase intoxication, in some, and sobriety in others.

A detailed description of this class of people would be too difficult; but I shall mention the principle musicians.

1 Miyān Tānsen, of Gwālyār. A singer like him has not been in India for the last thousand years.
2 Bābā Rāmdās, of Gwālyār, a singer.
3 Subhān Khān, of Gwālyār, a singer.
4 Srigyān Khān, of Gwālyār, a singer.
5 Miyān Chand, of Gwālyār, a singer.
6 Bichitr Khān, brother of Subhān Khān, a singer. (Abul Fazl-i-ʿAllami 1977: 680–1).

In the genealogical tracing of his early family history, Yunus Husain Khan makes no mention of Gwalior, but he does include a 'Surgyan Khan', specifying that he was also court musician to Akbar. That is likely to be the same person as the Srigyan Khan listed above, since he is also from Gwalior, although his family relationship is not included in the *Aʾīn-i-Akbarī* list as others' are. According to Yunus Husain, Surgyan Khan married a daughter of Tansen; an article by Garg (1957: 222) states that a 'Sujan Sahab' married a daughter of Tansen. Yunus Husain's reconstruction of his family genealogy is shown in Chart 4–1; the vertical lines indicate sons born 'in the line', rather than (necessarily) a father–son succession. Yunus Husain's account does not agree in every detail with his father Vilayat Hussain's published account (1959), but the general lines are clear.

Until Ghagghe Khuda Baksh, the family was one of singers of *dhrupad*, *sadra*, and *horī/dhamār* (springtime songs, usually about Lord Krishna). Their tradition of *dhrupad* singing is called the Nauhar *banji*.

Ghagghe Khuda Baksh

Ghagghe Khuda Baksh (1790–1880 or c. 1800–c. 1850–60) apparently changed his family's musical history for purely practical reasons: he had a *ghagghe* (raucous) voice, which was problematic for singing in his family's style. Although he learned music from his elders along with other members of his family, no one paid much attention to him or encouraged him because of his unsatisfactory voice quality. Consequently, he left Agra for Gwalior. There he was taught by Nathan Pir Baksh, who took him as a disciple because, it is said,

83

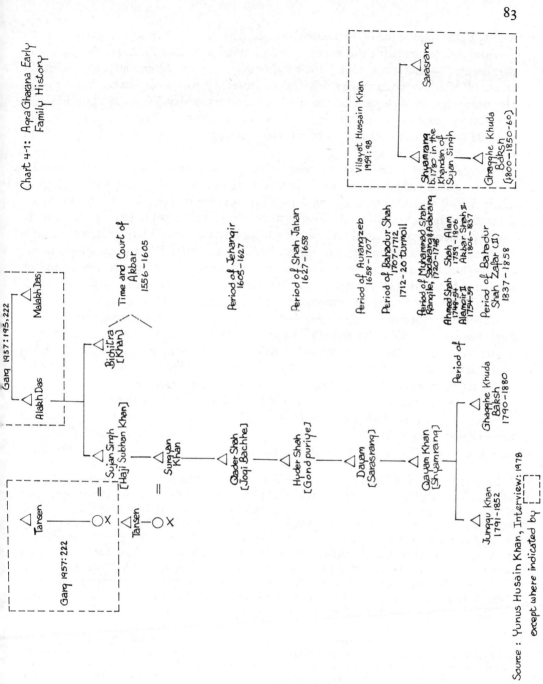

Chart 4-1: Agra Gharana Early Family History

Gang 1957:195, 222

Malakh Das

Alakh Das

Bichitra [Khan] — Time and Court of Akbar 1556-1605

Gang 1957:222

Tansen

Tansen

Sujan Singh [Haji Subhan Khan]

=

=

Sunayan Khan

Qader Shah [Joqi Bachhe] — Period of Jehangir 1605-1627

Hyder Shah [Gond puriye] — Period of Shah Jahan 1627-1658

Dayam [Sarasrang] — Period of Aurangzeb 1658-1707

Period of Bahadur Shah 1707-1712, 1712-20 turmoil

Period of Muhammad Shah Rangile, Sadarang & Adarang 1720-1748

Ahmed Shah 1748-54, Alamgir II 1754-59

Shah Alam 1759-1806, Akbar Shah II 1806-1837

Qayam Khan [Shyamrang] — Period of Bahadur Shah Zafar (II) 1837-1858

Period of

Junqqu Khan 1791-1852

Ghaqqhe Khuda Baksh 1790-1880

Vilayat Hussain Khan 1954:98

Sarasrang

Shyamrang b.1780 in the Khandan of Sujan Singh

Ghaqqhe Khuda Baksh (1800-1850-60)

Source: Yunus Husain Khan, Interview: 1978 except where indicated by [ ]

Khuda Baksh was the son of Nathan Pir's *ustad*.[1] According to Kapoor (though in terms of everyday Indian family life this seems scarcely credible), Nathan Pir Baksh taught Khuda Baksh secretly – unknown even to Nathan Pir's family – in the underground room in which he practiced. Hard work and much cultivation improved Khuda Baksh's voice. 'Years passed. He used to take lessons in the morning and practice the whole day. In his spare time he served the Ustad(s). Due to the good training of his guru(s) and the efforts of the student, God rewarded him with the anticipated result. Now his voice was clear [and accurate in pitch]' (Vilayat Hussain Khan 1959: 100).

When Ghagghe Khuda Baksh (no longer 'Ghagghe' but forever known as that) returned to Agra, his accomplishment astounded his family, and his achievement in the new style of music (*khyal*) was obviously accepted by them because it was taken up by successive generations and developed in distinctive ways. There was possibly some resentment by Gwalior musicians of Khuda Baksh's accomplishments, for tales of recriminations remain in the lore. Kapoor recites the story of Hassu, Haddu, and Natthe Khan challenging him and accusing him of merely copying the Gwalior style of their family.[2] They threatened him with death (by the sword) if he dared to take possession of what he had learned and call it the Agra style of music, but the timely intervention of the Gwalior Maharaja saved the situation.

Khuda Baksh became a well-known and respected singer. He won favor with Maharaja Shivadan Singh of Alwar (in Rajasthan) and was one of the great musicians employed in Jaipur in the reign of Maharaja Sawai Ram Singh, along with his intimate friend Bairam Khan (d. 1852) (cf. Kapoor 1957), the great Dagar family *dhrupadiya*, and Mubarak Ali Khan, famed for his *qawwali*-style *khyal* singing (Vilayat Hussain Khan 1959: 69).

As was the custom at the time, Khuda Baksh was invited to sing in several courts which seem to have constituted what we would now call a 'concert circuit'. On one such occasion he visited Rampur at the invitation of Nawab Kalve Ali Khan. Vilayat Hussain Khan's description of that visit is given here because it includes much detail about patronage of the time:

As a regular procedure [Kalve Ali Khan] wrote a letter to Maharaja Ram Singh, requesting that he send Ghagghe Khuda Baksh to Rampur so that he could hear him. The Maharaja was glad to send Khan Sahab to enrich his reputation and made arrangements for his journey. On his arrival at Rampur Nawab welcomed him with great eclat; he told Khan Sahab, 'Rest for a couple of days from your journey and then I shall ask you to take the trouble to sing'. After a couple of days he was called to the palace of Nawab Sahab for a demonstration. Khan Sahab and his accompanists appeared. He was asked to sit in a room where the instruments were tuned under supervision and there he waited. After some time the Nawab called for him. The time of the year was sultry and the Nawab resposed in a room around which *khas-khas* [fragrant grass] was hanging, and the mind remained cool due to the aroma of rose and *keora* [incense]. The wind created by the fan made the room cool. Khan Sahab on arrival, saluted the nawab

---

[1] According to Kapoor (1957) and Vilayat Hussain Khan (1959: 99), Shyamarang would have been Nathan Pir Baksh's *ustad*. No specific mention is made of this in the Garg article on Nathan Pir (1957: 198) or in any other source I have found. Vilayat Hussain's account is confusing because he speaks of two singers, Natthan Khan and Pir Baksh, both of whom 'had learned *hori* and *dhrupad* from Agra *gharana* . . . So they told Khuda Baksh, you belong to our Ustad's *khandan*; if you want to learn *asthai-khyal* we shall be only too pleased to teach you' (1959: 99). Vilayat Hussain continues in his chapter on the Gwalior *gharana* to speak of two different musicians and he recounts the lineage as shown in the insert in the Gwalior genealogical chart (Chart 3–2, p. 39). Compare that lineage with the more generally accepted one in Chapter 3.

[2] Kapoor (1957) refers to the 'Gwalior style of their father', but Nathan Pir Baksh was their grandfather. Kapoor's source may have been Tassaduq Hussain Khan's book *Calendar Musiqi*, unpublished according to Vilayat Hussain Khan (1959: 118), which Kapoor mentions in passing.

and started singing. The change of temperature caused Ghagghe's voice to be adversely affected. After a few minutes, try as he did, the voice gave no avenues for improvement, and many of the *kanas* [subtle melodic fluctuations] could not be produced at will. On hearing this, the Nawab turned to Bahadur Husain and asked him, 'You have been praising him so highly, but he appears to have nothing'. On hearing this Khuda Baksh was so ashamed that he began to perspire even in the cool of the room. Just at that moment he was trying to sing a *tan*, but he was unsuccessful because his voice responded improperly. Just at this opportune moment, the eldest son, Mian Ghulam Abbas Khan, who was singing along with him, broke into the *tan* attempted by his father and produced a new one out of his own imagination. Khan Sahab was all the more ashamed. He could not restrain himself and resolved to sing finally, regardless of what happened. As soon as he reached the top Sa, suddenly his voice cleared; it was just like the emergence of the moon from a clouded sky. Thereafter Khan Sahab sang with the fullest confidence. It made an instantaneous appeal on the mind of Nawab Sahab who began to praise him without restraint. During those days it was the rule in the state of Rampur that whenever the Nawab praised a musician a reward should also be forthcoming. So presently a *tali* – a bag containing Rs. 500 – was placed before Khan Sahab. Khuda Sahab built up such a musical atmosphere that he was lost in his music, as was Nawab Sahab. Each time the Nawab repeated the praise, a bag of money was given to the musician. The performance lasted for a couple of hours. At the end the Nawab had to admit that he had never before been so greatly influenced by music. After that Nawab Sahab kept him for two weeks and listened to him with great interest. On departure he was again amply rewarded.

At the time of his departure Khan Sahab requested the Nawab 'I have heard a great deal in praise of Your Majesty's music. If you are pleased to honor me with your singing I shall be happy'. The Nawab replied, 'Bhai, I would certainly sing before you and I shall do it this evening'. At five o'clock in the evening Nawab called for him. On his arrival the Nawab started to tune his *tamburas*; the *tambura* was correctly tuned as though there were a shower of musical tones. Then Nawab Sahab started singing and the listeners were agape with wonder. Khan Sahab Ghagghe too was swayed by the emotional appeal of Nawab's music and praised him spontaneously. On his return to Jaipur the Nawab wrote another letter to the Jaipur Naresh requesting him to convey his gratitude to Khan Sahab and to him as well for kindly acceding to his request for a chance to hear Khuda [Baksh] (Vilayat Hussain Khan 1959: 102–3).

Further Agra *gharana* family history can be traced through two lines. On Ghagghe Khuda Baksh's side the important names are Ghulam Haider Khan (called Kallan Khan), Ghulam Abbas Khan, Tassaduq Hussain Khan, and Faiyaz Husain Khan (see Chart 4–2), who were centered in Jaipur and Baroda. The other line, through Junggu Khan, Ghagghe Khuda Baksh's brother, includes the illustrious names of Natthan Khan, Vilayat Hussain Khan, Khadim Hussain Khan, Latafat Husain Khan, and Yunus Husain Khan, who were centered in Mysore and Bombay and then in Delhi. In musical terms, however, the two lines are as one, owing to the teaching patterns (see Chart 4–3). From Vilayat Hussain's account, for example, we deduce that Khuda Baksh taught (among others) his brother's son Sher Khan, and Sher Khan gave initial training to Khuda Baksh's son Ghulam Abbas (1959: 103), after which Khuda Baksh seems to have taken over his own son's training. Because of the shared teaching roles of the two branches of the family, it is appropriate to discuss the Agra musicians generation by generation across the lines, counting Ghagghe Khuda Baksh as the first generation.

The second generation

The second generation of Agra *khyal* singers consisted, in one line, of Ghagghe Khuda Baksh's sons Ghulam Haider Khan (d. 1925, called Kallan Khan) and Ghulam Abbas Khan (1809, 1818, or 1820–1932 or 1934) and, in the other line, of Junggu Khan's son Sher Khan

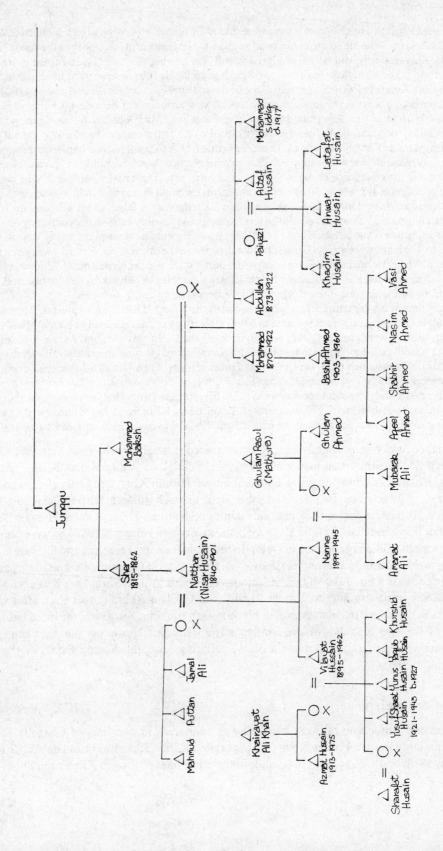

87

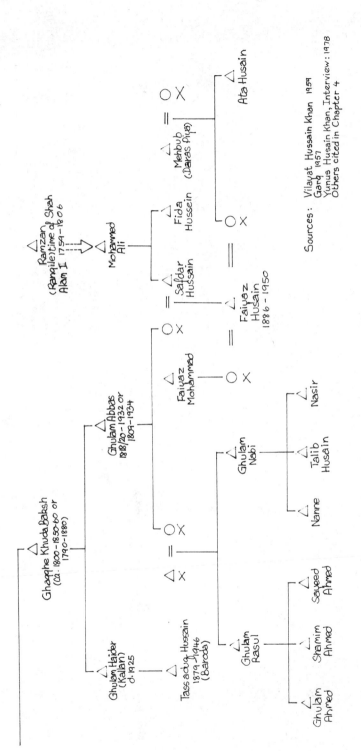

Chart 4-2: Agra Gharana Blood Lines

Sources: Vilayat Hussain Khan 1959
Garg 1957
Yunus Husain Khan, Interview: 1978
Others cited in Chapter 4

88

Chart 4.3 : Aqra Gharana Teaching Lines

Sources: Vilayat Hussain Khan 1959
Garg 1957
Yunus Husain Khan, Interview: 1978
Others cited in Chapter 4

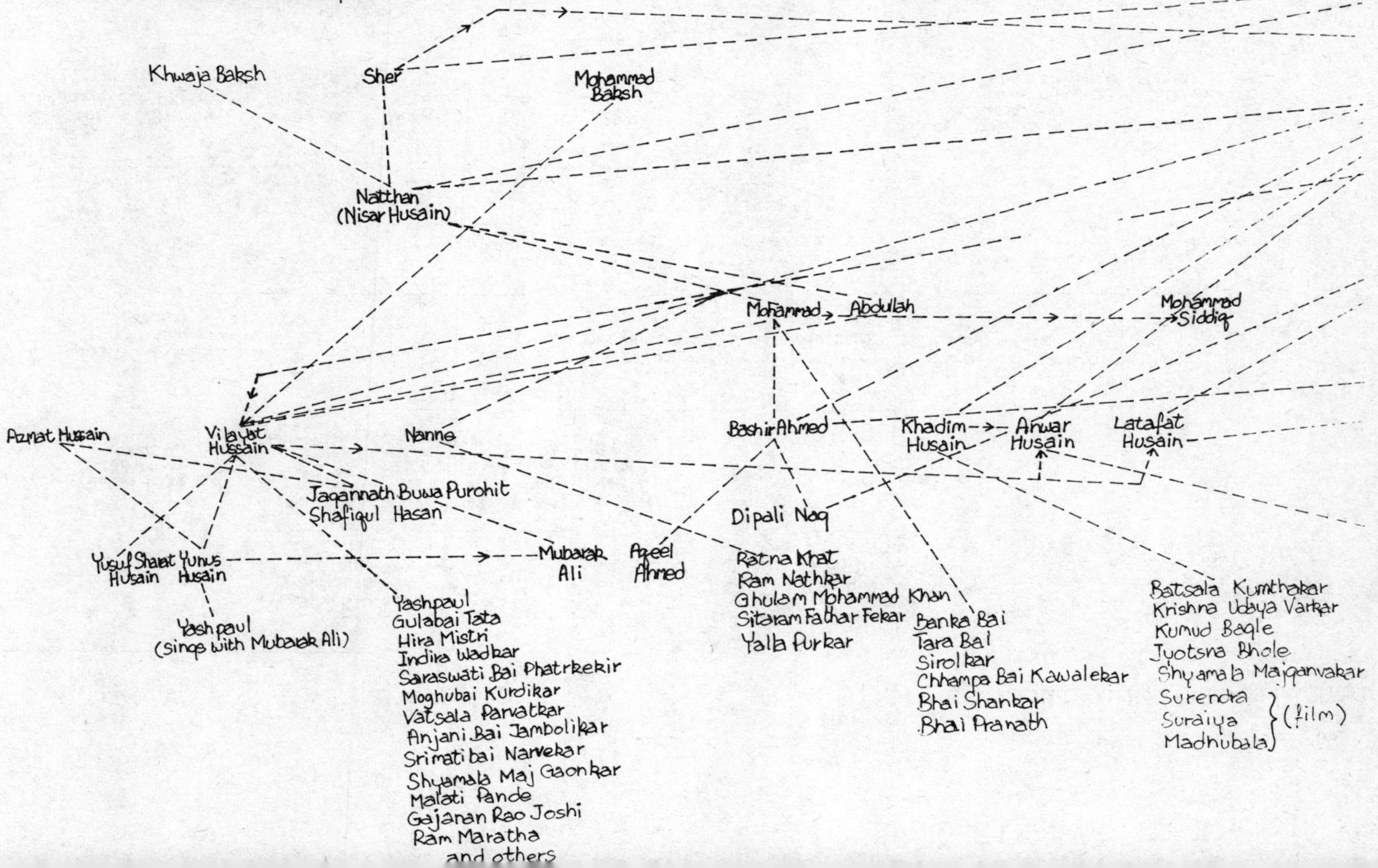

Khuaja Baksh

Mohammed Baksh

Sher

Natthan (Nisar Husain)

Mohammed → Abdullah

Mohammed Siddiq

Khadim → Anwar Husain

Latafat Husain

Bashir Ahmed

Dipali Nag

Aqeel Ahmed

Nanne

Jagannath Buwa Purohit
Shafiqul Hasan

Mubarak Ali

Vilayat Hussain

Yusuf Shaat Yunus Husain

Yashpaul (Sings with Mubarak Ali)

Pariat Husain

Batsala Kumthekar
Krishna Udaya Varkar
Kumud Bagde
Tuotsna Bhole
Shyamala Majpanwabar
Surendra
Suraiya } (film)
Madhubala

Ghulem Mohammad Khan
Sitaram Fabhar Fekar
Banka Bai
Tara Bai
Sirol kar
Chhampa Bai Kawalekar
Bhai Shankar
Bhai Pranath

Ratna Khat
Ram Nathkar
Yalla Purkar

Yashpaul
Gulabai Tata
Hira Mistri
Indira Wadkar
Saraswati Bai Phatrbekir
Moghubai Kurdikar
Vatsala Panvatkar
Anjani Bai Jambolikar
Srimati bai Narvekar
Shyamab Maj Gaonkar
Malati Pande
Gajanan Rao Joshi
Ram Maratha
and others

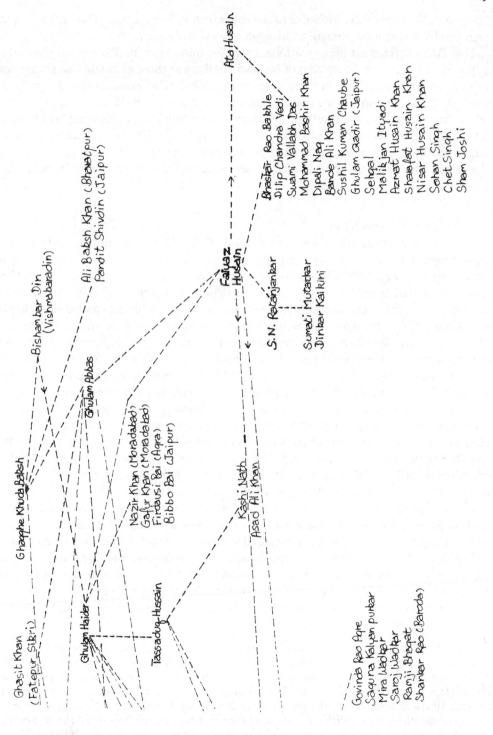

(1815–62). Sher's brother, Mohammad Baksh, known as Sonji, a court musician in Jaipur, seems to have remained primarily a *dhrupad* and *dhamar* singer.

Sher Khan devoted his life to teaching, living for thirty years in Bombay (cf. Garg 1957: 195). 'He never forgot the upkeep of his own family; somehow or another he always sent money home' (Vilayat Hussain Khan 1959: 103). According to Yunus Husain Khan (Interview: 1978), Sher Khan was the first member of the family to go to Mysore. Vilayat Hussain tells of Sher being honored as well by his contemporary, the Gwalior musician Haddu Khan (d. 1875), and by Maharaja Jayaji Rao Scindia (1959: 104). This is significant, given the family history of competition with Gwalior musicians. During the last five years of his life Sher Khan retired to Agra where he died in 1862, at the age of 46 or 47 (Vilayat Hussain Khan 1959: 104).

Ghulam Abbas Khan

Ghulam Abbas Khan was born in 1809 (Yunus Husain Khan's chart) or 1818 or 1820 (Vilayat Hussain Khan 1959: 104) in Agra, and according to Vilayat Hussain he began musical training with Sher Khan (possibly because he was growing up in Agra where Sher was, while his father was away – in Jaipur or travelling on the concert circuit). Agra *gharana* accounts record that Ghulam Abbas learned *khyal* with Sher, while he studied *hori–dhamar* with Ghasit Khan, his maternal cousin (Vilayat Hussain Khan 1959: 105, and Rampala Mehra 1969: 38). We know of his ultimate training with his father, Khuda Baksh, through the anecdote about their performance in Rampur for Nawab Kalve Ali Khan, cited above.

According to Vilayat Hussain, although Ghulam Abbas never accepted a position as court musician, he was a highly respected singer, much in demand by the rulers of Alwar, Jaipur, Tonk (all in Rajasthan), Mysore, and other places (1959: 105). In 1907, the Maharaja of Mysore invited him to perform at the time of the Dussehra festival (the important ten-day Hindu festival celebrating the victory of the deity Rama over the demon Ravana, as told in the epic *Ramayana*), and he was presented with a purse of gold, among other rewards. Muslim musicians as well as Hindu travelled at Dussehra, one of the busiest times of the year, to perform in musical festivities throughout the subcontinent.

Just as Khuda Baksh had been invited by Nawab Kalve Ali Khan to sing in Rampur, Ghulam Abbas sang there for Kalve Ali's successor, Nawab Hamid Ali Khan. An anecdote told by Vilayat Hussain (1959: 33–4) included some details of cultural interest. According to Vilayat Hussain, Nawab Hamid Ali had ceased to invite outside musicians to perform in Rampur because his own group of court musicians satisfied his connoisseur's appetite for music. Once Ghulam Abbas was visiting nearby Moradabad and decided to visit Rampur and pay his respects to the *nawab*. He stayed with Muljik a member of the court, and requested him to arrange an audience with the *nawab*.

The Nawab ordered him [Mulji] to bring Ghulam Abbas with him the next day. The next day Khan Sahab reached the palace and the Nawab acceded to the request to let him in to pay salaam. On entering Khan Sahab made a kingly bow and sat after receiving permission. The Nawab asked about his welfare and talked with him courteously. Ustad Wazir Khan [scion of the Seniya tradition of *bin* playing] was present. All of a sudden the Nawab said, 'Mian Ghulam Abbas, I have stopped listening to music'.

The rejoinder from Khan Sahab was that the act was very wise, since the Nawab had already heard all the musicians of India, and secondly, he was equal to none in his knowledge of music. Why then should he become disturbed while listening to others? Whatever Huzzar had done was wisest. Then, keeping the train of thought lively, Khan Sahab said, 'I have stopped singing also, now that I am old and have sung enough in my life I want to visit Qa'aba and do Haj; may God fulfill my desires'.

The Nawab listened to all of this silently and after some time said, 'Mian Ghulam Abbas, I've heard all the musicians of India, but have found only two men who are expert in laya'.

Khan Sahab: 'And, pray, who are they?'

Nawab: 'Firstly, Bindadin of Lucknow, and secondly, Ustad Wazir Khan Sahab'.

Khan Sahab said at once, 'Sir, you forget one man'.

The Nawab was perplexed and said: 'That is absolutely incorrect if there is any third, name him'.

At once Khan Sahab said, 'Sir, you are the third man. Almighty God has bestowed you with laya and sur both'.

Nawab Sahab was very pleased to hear this and said, 'It is your affection for me that makes you say so'. After some time the Nawab inquired: 'Ghulam Abbas, tell me what sort of player Musharraf Khan of Jaipur is'.

Khan Sahab: 'How can one speak of the greatness of Musharraf Khan! He is one of the best *bin* players of India'.

Nawab next inquired: 'What sort of *bin* player is Ustad Wazir Khan?'

Khan Sahab, pointing towards Wazir Khan, said, 'It doesn't belong to any class'.

Nawab Sahab was astonished to hear this, and somewhat angrily asked: 'Did you say "it" for my Ustad?'

Khan Sahad: 'Sir, there are three types of *bin*'.

Nawab: 'How?'

Khan Sahab: 'Real, Imitation, and seasonal'.

Nawab Sahab again asked, 'Please explain'.

Khan Sahab: 'Real *bin* is that which is being played from fourteen generations past; genuine methods, teaching or process are also involved. Imitation *bin* is that which is a mere carbon copy of some music heard. The third type is seasonal which means that the musician is a *bīnkār* or a *sitariyā* according to his whim, or somebody else's whim. He's serving the opportunity and acting accordingly. Now, on looking at these *bins* more attentively it is evident that a genuine style is really a genuine style, and a counterfeit one is really counterfeit. Now Khan Sahab Wazir Khan is a real *bin* player; the *binkars* of India learn from him and imitate him. Khan Sahab doesn't belong to anybody but all others emanate from him'.

Ghulam Abbas had hardly uttered the whole sentence than the Nawab got up, jumping with delight and praised him copiously for his ability. He was so pleased with him that he rewarded him with Rs. 1000.

Vilayat Hussain described Ghulam Abbas as a good conversationalist in Hindi and Persian who could charm his audiences with a sprinkling of poetry in those languages (1959: 106), but one could also describe him as a good politician.

We gain a second impression of Ghulam Abbas from Vilayat Hussain, who knew him and as a youth heard him sing. Ghulam Abbas took good physical care of himself in order to be a good singer. 'He would often say that he practiced celibacy until he was 30 and concentrated on *sur*' (1959: 105). 'And, eating well but only at mealtimes, Ghulam Abbas would say "A vocalist cannot sing if he does not take enough food"' (*ibid.*).

He used to walk very slowly . . . The reason was that he never wanted to exert his lungs unnecessarily. I never heard him complain of cough or cold, so he had perfect breath control. In the mornings he used to do 21 push-ups; he prepared a syrup out of 21 almonds, along with five black pepper seeds mixed with some sugar. At night before retiring he used to take half a seer of milk. This is why his physical capabilities remained the same until his death (1959: 105–6).

Ghulam Abbas Khan died in 1932 (Vilayat Hussain Khan 1959: 106) or in 1934 (Yunus Husain Khan: chart), or in 1935 (Yodh 1978: 20). He had passed on his musical tradition to his brother Kallan Khan (Ghulam Haider Khan), in the next generation to his cousin Natthan Khan and to Natthan's son Vilayat Hussain Khan, as well as to his own grandson Faiyaz Khan.

Kallan Khan

Kallan Khan (Ghulam Haider Khan) was the younger brother of Ghulam Abbas and the youngest son of Khuda Baksh. He does not seem to have studied with his father; Vilayat Hussain recounts that he studied for ten or twelve years with his brother Ghulam Abbas and with Bishambar Din, a disciple of his father. By that circuitous means Kallan 'fully followed the style of his father . . . There is no doubt that Khan Saheb was a representative singer of his *gharana*' (Vilayat Hussain Khan 1959: 106, 107).

During the time of the Jaipur Maharaja Madho Singh, Kallan Khan was appointed court musician and was one of the musicians there who hosted dinners and musical gatherings for visiting musicians. Such occasions highlighted musical life in the courts, though they were not court functions *per se*. Vocalists and instrumentalists gathered in the home of a leading musician to enjoy music with the most rarefied and demanding audience imaginable. Such gatherings kept musicians from the whole of India in touch with each other and undoubtedly contributed greatly to the transmission of materials and ideas and the making or breaking of musical reputations.

One curious piece of information about a Kallan Khan in Jaipur could be important in terms of the patronage system, if it could be confirmed. Kapoor (1957) reported that during the time of Akbar (1556–1605) this family of musicians acquired a *jāgīr* in Gaundpur, in Alwar (Rajasthan), i.e., a piece of land, the income from which was assigned in lieu of salary. A Garg article (1957: 196) mentions a music-loving Jaipur *jagirdar* Nawab Kallan Khan in whose 'context' one could hear a great deal of music. If these two pieces of information were related, and Kallan Khan of the Agra *gharana* were Nawab Kallan Khan, it would mean that Kallan Khan was of a landowning family – an unusual status for a family of professional musicians. The family was apparently relieved of that status, however, by the British, for helping the freedom fighters in the 'mutiny' of 1857.

Kallan Khan accepted as disciples non-family members as well as *gharanedar* pupils (see Chart 4–3). Among his *gharanedar* pupils were his son, Tassaduq Hussain, Vilayat Hussain, and Vilayat Hussain's younger brother Nanne; then, in the second generation after Kallan, Bashir Ahmed, Khadim Husain, and Anwar Husain (Vilayat Hussain Khan 1959: 106–7); of all those family members, only his own son and Faiyaz Khan were on his side of the family).

Kallan Khan preferred not to travel to the many conferences that were so popular in the early decades of the century, though 'once on persuasion of Bhatkhande he went to Lucknow for a demonstration in the All-India conference' (Vilayat Hussain Khan 1959: 107). He died in 1925 in Jaipur, before his long-lived older brother Ghulam Abbas.

The third generation

In the third generation after Khuda Baksh, the only *khyal* performer was Natthan Khan, Sher Khan's only son. In the other line, Ghulam Abbas had daughters, and Kallan Khan's son Tassaduq Hussain was born thirty-nine years after Natthan Khan.

Natthan Khan

Sher Khan's son, Nisar Husain, who became known by the name Natthan, was born in 1840 (Yunus Husain Khan: chart). When he was two his father moved to Bombay (presumably from Agra), and Natthan was taken there later (Garg 1957: 195, 354). When his father returned to Agra after teaching in Bombay, the young boy was presumably taken back to Agra as well.

Natthan's father died in 1862, when he was twenty-two, and accounts of his life report that his training was taken over by Ghulam Abbas (Garg 1957: 195). Ghulam Abbas was not a court musician and he seems to have been living in Agra; this is certainly suggested by the article in Garg, which reports that when any musician came to Agra there was a feast at the home of Ghulam Abbas, and a musical sitting: 'Natthan Khan thus listened with intense concentration to the songs of singers and he tried to reproduce the specialities of various singers. He also obtained some compositons from the *dhrupadiya* Ghasit Khan of Fatepur Sikri' (Garg 1957: 195–6; see also Vilayat Hussain Khan 1959: 107).

After completing his formal instruction (*talim*) in Agra, Natthan Khan went to Jaipur, where he presumably stayed with his 'uncle' Kallan Khan. He may have studied there with Mubarak Ali Khan, vocalist in the *qawwal-bacchu* (or *qawwali*) style (Wadhera 1954a, citing Vilayat Hussain Khan). In Jaipur he heard numerous musicians and began to establish a reputation for himself. His stay there seems to have been a long one – ten or twelve years (Garb 1957: 196) – after which he began to perform in numerous places on the concert circuit, including Delhi. Among other places, he visited Baroda, but not at the invitation of the royal family. There he stayed with Faiyaz Mohammad Khan, where many students assembled every day, among them Bhaskar Rao Bakhle who became Natthan's disciple and a famous musician. Vilayat Hussain states that the *maharaja* and *maharani* heard Natthan at that time and 'were greatly affected by his music and used to respect him very highly' (1959: 108).

Once he had left Jaipur and begun to travel, Natthan Khan apparently made Bombay his base (c. 1878 or 1880–90; Garg 1957: 196 and Vilayat Hussain Khan 1959: 108). This seems likely, since his father had stayed in that city to teach, and it was the major urban center in the Rajasthan and Baroda sphere. Vilayat Hussain explains Natthan's settling in Bombay in terms of a fairly unusual circumstance – patronage by a female professional singer:

At Bombay Bawali Bai of Goa became his disciple. She compelled Khan Sahab to stay in Bombay 10–12 years; she learned a lot from Khan Sahab and served him faithfully. She defrayed all of Khan Sahab's expenses and never allowed him to accept a job. The result was that she was unequalled in talent in the whole country. The rulers of Rampur, Mysore and Kolhapur [Maharashtra–Mysore border] invited her often and used to listen to her with pleasure and presented her with diamonds and precious metals. There is no doubt that Natthan Khan taught his disciples in the same way as he taught his own children (1959: 109).

The British-built cities in those days were becoming increasingly important centers of cultural activities. Wealthy Indian businessmen became patrons, and the rulers of the independent princely states kept residences in those cities. It was in Bombay in 1890 that the Maharaja of Mysore, Chamaraj Wadiyar, heard Natthan Khan perform and, according to Yunus Husain, was so impressed that he took Natthan Khan to Mysore as court musician (Vilayat Hussain Khan 1959: 109). Natthan Khan was fifty years of age at that time, and he remained in Mysore until his death at sixty or sixty-one, in 1900 (Garg 1957: 197) or in 1901

(Vilayat Hussain Khan 1959: 112). After he died, all his *khandan* (family) went to Dharwar and then to Bombay (Garg 1957: 197).

Both Vilayat Hussain and the Garg article relate an anecdote about Natthan Khan and the Maharaja of Mysore, which Vilayat Hussain says 'illustrates the interest the rulers and nobles took in music in the past and how they respected the musicians and tried to please them' (1959: 110). The anecdote concerns a gold bracelet (Garg 1957: 196), studded with diamonds and some pearls and engraved with the emblem of the state (Vilayat Hussain Khan 1959: 109) that the *maharaja* had awarded Natthan Khan when he was particularly pleased with his singing. The *maharaja* ordered him to wear it whenever he appeared at court. Some time later, on the occasion of Dussehra, the *maharaja* noticed Natthan Khan without the bracelet and questioned him; Natthan Khan replied that he had transformed it into food for his children.

The Maharaja Sahab burst into laughter on hearing this and gave him a new bracelet from his own hand. With his own hands he put it on the musician's wrist and told him, 'This bracelet belongs to the *darbar*. Leave it for wearing in the court. If you have any necessity in the future please tell me'. Similarly, once while listening in the *darbar* Khan Sahab was presented with a diamond ring as reward (1959: 109–10).

The disciple most frequently associated with Natthan Khan is Bhaskar Rao Bakhle (see Chapter 9). Vilayat Hussain, Natthan Khan's most famous son, was only about six years old when his father died and Nanne Khan was only one or two. While the Garg article assured us that through Vilayat Hussain his father's *gayaki* survived (1957: 197), Wadhera (1954d) cited Vilayat Hussain as saying that he listened to his father's music with the indifference of a child and remembered nothing of his style. As discussed below, Vilayat Hussain received his training from other members of his family. Natthan Khan's older sons Mohammad Khan and Abdullah Khan were trained by their father, however (Vilayat Hussain Khan 1959: 113).

The fourth generation

The fourth generation of prominent Agra *gharana khyal* singers includes Natthan Khan's older sons Mohammad Khan, Abdullah Khan, and Mohammad Siddiq Khan. Natthan Khan's daughter, Faiyazi, is also remembered by name because she married a prominent musician from Atrauli, Altaf Husain Khan, and their sons carried on the Agra tradition. In the other Agra line is Kallan Khan's son, Tassaduq Hussain Khan. Seven years after Tassaduq Hussain, Faiyaz Husain Khan was born in the same line, and sixteen years later Vilayat Hussain Khan in the other line.

Mohammad Khan (1870–1922), Natthan Khan's eldest son, was born in Agra. He started his musical training with his father, but learned many compositions of *hori, dhrupad, tarana,* and *khyal* 'from all the elderly people who were still living' (Vilayat Hussain Khan 1959: 112). He had just moved from Agra to Bombay in 1901 (at the age of thirty-one) when his father died. After attending to the affairs of the family in Agra, he settled in Bombay, where many people outside his family wanted to study with him. Mohammad was a generous and attentive teacher and carried on the style of his renowned father. He taught his younger brothers and later his own son, Bashir Ahmed Khan. Vilayat Hussain tells of Mohammad that he had a great liking for Urdu poetry and sang *sher* (a verse in the song from *ghazal*) well and with understanding (1959: 113). Natthan Khan's second son, started his formal instruction (*talim*) with his father and accompanied him to Mysore. The Maharaja of Mysore assigned separate pay for him even before he completed his training with his father (Vilayat Hussain Khan 1959: 113). On his father's death in 1901, when he himself was twenty-eight, Abdullah left Mysore and was never again a court musician. He settled in Bombay (Yunus Husain Khan, Interview: 1978), and also travelled to perform in many places, including Hubli, Dharwar, Kolhapur, Poona, Bagalkot, Bijapur, Sholapur, Delhi, Jullundur, and Kashmir. Abdullah apparently was a talented composer, as is shown by his 'Erī ali piyā bin' in Rag Yaman (Chaudhuri 1966: 2). He died in his home town of Agra at the age of forty-six (Vilayat Hussain Khan 1959: 113–14).

Mohammad Siddiq Khan, the third son of Natthan Khan, learned from his older brother Mohammad. He was becoming an accomplished musician when, in 1917, according to Vilayat Hussain, his heart stopped as he sang in a Holi concert in Indore and he died (1959: 114).

Nane Khan (1899–1945), Natthan's youngest son, was born a year or two before Natthan died, in Mysore. His training was with Kallan Khan rather than with his older brother, but after *talim* he too went to live in Bombay. He also possessed the family flair for poetry; writing under the *mudra* ('pen name') 'Shakir', he composed poems in Hindi and Urdu and also wrote musical compositions (Vilayat Hussain Khan 1959: 114). The members of this *gharana* are proud of their literary and musical creativity. Like other members of his family he taught many students, being generous with his musical knowledge. He died in Agra at the age of forty-six.

In the other line, Kallan Khan's son and disciple Tassaduq Hussain Khan (1879–1946) was also born in Agra, and was employed in Baroda for twenty-two years, at the Sangit High School (Vilayat Hussain Khan 1959: 118). He wrote in Hindi under the *mudra* 'Vinod', and also knew Persian and Urdu.

Faiyaz Husain Khan

Faiyaz Husain Khan (1886–1950) was born in Agra (or in Sikandra, near Agra, according to Chaubey 1958: 2) at the home of his maternal uncle under sad circumstances, for his father, Safdar (Sabdar) Husain Khan of the Rangile *gharana*, had died some three to four months earlier. Rather than remain with her husband's family, Faiyaz Khan's mother returned to her father's home, and the boy was raised by Ghulam Abbas Khan, his maternal grandfather, in Agra (Chaubey 1958: 29; cf. Yodh 1978: 19).

Between the ages of five and twenty-five Faiyaz was given *talim* by his grandfather (Garg 1957: 222), who made the boy memorize a vast number of melodies. Ghulam Abbas' brother Kallan Khan taught him as well (Daniélou 1951: 57), as did Fida Husain Kotavala, his paternal uncle (Garg 1957: 222). Ghulam Abbas had Faiyaz listen to all the important contemporary musicians whom he hosted in Agra, and he would explain to him the technique of each one (Daniélou 1951: 57). Faiyaz also heard the best musicians when he toured with his grandfather for a good part of each year; their annual tours took them to Natthan Khan in Mysore (Deodhar 1981: 29). Faiyaz had been trained in *dhrupad* and *dhamar* as part of his *gharana*'s mode of instruction, and during his tours he listened to the best *dhrupad* singers as well. However widely he travelled throughout his life, Faiyaz kept close ties with Agra, returning there for the days of the Muslim festival Muharram (Garg 1957: 223).

In 1906 (Garg 1957: 223; Deodhar 1981: 29) or 1907 (Daniélou 1951: 57), when he was twenty or twenty-one, Faiyaz sang in Mysore on the occasion of the Dussehra festival and was awarded his first gold medal. He eventually accumulated a number of medals; 'he took a childish delight in [them] and used to wear them all at the time of important performances' (Daniélou 1951: 57). Further, Faiyaz 'had never learnt to save [money] but he did keep all his medals and when he visited (for the first time) a town for a recital, he was fond of pinning them on his sherwani, walking down the bazar with his silver-handled stick, and getting a feel of the place' (Deodhar 1981: 32).

In 1911 Faiyaz was again shown appreciation by the Mysore ruler who dubbed him 'Aftāb-ki-Musiqi', ('the Sun of Music') (Garg 1957: 223), a title by which he was known for the rest of his life. Wadhera (1953a) gives the date as 1919, and Vilayat Hussain (1959: 116) gives 1925 and suggests that Faiyaz was offered a post as a court musician in Mysore but refused. In Baroda in 1911 (Garg 1957: 223) or 1912 (Daniélou 1951: 57), when Sayaji Rao came of age and became *maharaja* of that princely state, he invited Faiyaz to be a court musician on a generous salary. Vilayat Hussain dates this event in 1915, with the following account:

During those days [1915], Baroda State had few good musicians. Faiyaz Mohammad Khan [Father of Faiyaz Husain's first wife] was urged by the Maharaja to tour the country in search of young talent. When Khan Sahab reached Agra, he was delighted to hear Faiyaz Husain Khan. Hence he was invited for a *jalsa* during the Holi Festival. The Maharaja then decided to retain Faiyaz Husain Khan as a state-employee, at a salary of Rs. 100 per month. His emoluments increased progressively after every successive audition by the Maharaja. After a couple of years, the salary per month was Rs. 350 and he was seated with nobles in the *darbar* (1959: 115–16).

In 1918–20 (Vilayat Hussain Khan 1959: 116) or 1921, Faiyaz was invited to sing in Indore at a fabulous musical competition: 'Faiyaz Khan was acclaimed as the best musician of India in 1921 when the Maharaja of Indore invited as many as 500 musicians from far and near and the court of Indore kept ringing with melodies for a whole month. The Ustad was awarded a prize of Rs. 22,000' (Wadhera 1953a). Another account of a concert in Indore, possibly the same concert, relates that 'Maharaja Tukoji was so pleased with his performance that he removed his precious bejewelled necklace and presented it to the musician, a gift of over 12,000 rupees' (Daniélou 1951: 57).

Faiyaz performed widely, and participated in music conferences arranged by Bhatkhande. Vilayat Hussain mentions that at the Lucknow Conference in 1925 the title 'Sangit Chudamani' was conferred on him, and in Allahabad he earned the titles 'Sangit Bhaskar' (Sun) and 'Sangit Saroj' (Lotus). The same year he won acclaim in Calcutta, Jaipur, Jodhpur, Alwar, Palanpur, Idar, Champanagar, Banaili, Mahisadal, and other places (1959: 117). He sang from the major radio stations and made commercial recordings, as did most musicians of his generation. His fame spread throughout the country.

There is no doubt that Faiyaz was an exceptionally fine musician and charismatic performer, for source after source mentions the sway he had over audiences and the role he played in popularizing classical music among the masses of India. One such commentary relates how he would become engrossed in the atmosphere of the *raga*, in the theme of the song, and in the rhythm of the composition, to the point where he almost forgot himself. His bodily movements and facial expressions would reflect all that, and he communicated his 'bubbling joy of life': 'Unless a person was deaf or was intentionally controlling himself, it was next to impossible not to be influenced by the delightful, picturesque and technically perfect recital' (Thakur 1966: 30).

Faiyaz, six feet tall, attractive in appearance, fond of perfumes, and romantic in nature (Thakur 1966: 31), apparently exuded emotion. He was spoken of as sincere, but by nature capricious, impatient, and outspoken. 'He would speak out whatever he wished even during his [AIR] broadcast. Thousands of listeners once heard him snubbing an accompanist on the mike . . . At a certain conference held at Bombay, his indignation over a musician singing the same raga at a number of musical gatherings was publicly noticeable' (Wadhera 1953a).

Although Faiyaz never liked to teach (Daniélou 1951: 57), many people learned from him, both his family and outsiders (see Chart 4-3). He married twice, but had no son, and thus was frequently accompanied by Ata Hussain Khan, the brother of his second wife (the son of Mehbub Khan, 'Daras Piya') (Daniélou 1951: 57). As this eulogy by Daniélou suggests, Faiyaz's life seems to have been a happy one:

Unlike most artists whose existence is a long story of hardships and difficulties, Faiyaz Khan never knew what the problems of life are. His way was strewn with flowers. Born in a well-to-do family of accomplished musicians he was from childhood surrounded by music and grew up in the midst of songs. Music was never for him something outside life. It was music which appeared as the main everyday preoccupation. The problems of maintaining a family were mere insignificant details for which the gods provided without anyone bothering about it (1951: 56).

Because of a lung problem, Faiyaz was not able to sing in his last years, and he died of tuberculosis on November 5, 1950, at the age of sixty-four. The entire country mourned his passing, for in addition to the loss of the man as a musician, his death marked the near-end of the period of traditional musicians who had been maintained by wealthy princes – the passing of a long era and great tradition in Indian music history.

Vilayat Hussain Khan

Faiyaz Khan's cousin Vilayat Hussain Khan was born (according to his own account) in Agra in 1895 (at Agra Fort, according to Yodh 1978: 18). There are conflicting accounts of his birthdate (e.g., Garg 1957: 354; V. H. Deshpande 1973; Yunus Husain's chart). Young Vilayat Hussain joined his father Natthan Khan in Mysore, and was there until Natthan died in 1901 (or 1900, according to V. H. Deshpande 1973). Vilayat Hussain, then five or six years old, went to Jaipur, first to Kallan Khan, and then to live with his great-uncle Mohammad Baksh, known as Sonji (Vilayat Hussain Khan 1959: 128), who treated him like a son and initiated his musical training (Garg 1957: 354). Vasudev (1961: 51) gives a mysterious account of this: 'His father's uncle spirited him away from Mysore to Jaipur'. Wadhera (1954d), says he went to live in Jaipur with his 'grandfather', a loose honorary designation for any relative of that generation, for his father's father, Sher, had died in 1862.

In his book *Saṅgītajñoṅ ke Samsmaran* (1959), Vilayat Hussain was specific about his musical instruction, giving in detail what genres, techniques, even particular *raga*s he learned from each of his forty-two 'teachers'. His account begins with Karamat Khan of the family of *darbar* singers of Delhi, who was employed in Jaipur and who taught him *svara* and *tal*, *alap*, and *dhrupad*. From Mohammad Baksh he learned *alap*, *dhrupad*, and *hori*; from Kallan Khan, *asthai-khyal* (*badhat*, *layakari*, *sargam*, *upaj*), that is, how to sing. Ghulam Abbas Khan taught him compositions in particular *raga*s, as did his elder brothers Mohammad Khan and

Abdullah Khan, each of his maternal uncles, and numerous others, both family and non-family. As the list continues, it is clear from whom he acquired a large repertoire of compositions (and therefore *raga*s) in the various genres. His training in how to sing and create a good performance he had received from older musicians in his early years of intensive work.

Vilayat Hussain mentions another manner of gaining experience: 'sitting' with Faiyaz Khan, Tassaduq Hussain Khan, and Abdullah Khan (1959: 130). The Garg article states that for a time after his Jaipur training, Faiyaz took responsibility for him. When Faiyaz sang a *mehfil* (private concert), he would first have the boy Vilayat Hussain sing for a little while, and then, when Faiyaz took his place to sing and would in time produce *tan*s, Vilayat Hussain would repeat the *tan*s in *sargam* (Garg 1957: 354–5).

In 1914, when he was nineteen, Vilayat Hussain went to live in Bombay with his older brother Mohammad Khan (Garg 1957: 355). He studied with Mohammad for about six years, but also began to appear in numerous musical programs and to establish a reputation for himself. When Mohammad died, Vilayat Hussain assumed the responsibility of the upkeep of his family. In the 1920s he was assisted by a 'generous gentleman', Ganpat Rao Manerikar, who arranged numerous programs in his residence in Bombay (Yodh 1978: 21). Vilayat Hussain began to acquire a number of students (see Chart 4–3) and appeared in conferences, such as that in Allahabad in 1932 (Chaudhuri 1966: 3).

In his article on Vilayat Hussain, Sadhuram Yodh stresses the role of Vilayat Hussain in radio broadcasting, from as early as 1928, when Bombay Broadcasting Company started public broadcasts. While many artists were unwilling, Vilayat Hussain agreed to and did perform on the air:

Vilayat Hussain and his pupils sang on radio Shivmat Bhairav, Hussaini Todi, Dhanashri, Ramgauri, Nayaki and Shahana Kanada as well as many such 'aprachlit' *Ragas* and popularized their '*Chijas*'. This created a commotion in the musicians' world and Vilayat Hussain got rebuts from some noted singers who just could not expect such a thing from one of their own. He took pains to convince them that the times were changing fast and the musicians should come forward to present their real art through the Radio. He contended that the support of the masses was more beneficial to the artists than to the masses (Yodh 1978: 22).

Two years later (1930), when the broadcasting system was taken over by the Government of India, Vilayat Hussain was appointed a member of the Local Advisory Committee.

The Station Director of A.I.R. Bombay had the insurmountable task of persuading reputed vocalists and instrumentalists of famous Gharanas to figure on radio . . . Vilayat Hussain together with some of the members of the Advisory Committee had to comb the city of Bombay and had to advise for touring the adjoining states, including Rajputana and Central India where many famous artists lived. They would employ every means in their power to induce these masters to give radio programmes (Yodh 1978: 21).

From 1935 to 1940 (Garg 1957: 355) Vilayat Hussain was a court musician for Maharaj Raj Wadiyer (Yunus Husain Khan, Interview: 1978) in Mysore where his father had been a court musician some thirty years earlier and where he had spent his early childhood. For some time after that he gave music instruction to the royal children in Kashmir (Garg 1957: 355) or to the Maharaja Karan Singh himself (Yodh 1978: 23). Vilayat Hussain would have liked to return to Agra to live, and did so for about six months some time around 1951, but he returned to Bombay when it became apparent there was no way to support himself in Agra (Garg 1957: 355).

Another move in 1955 took him to Delhi's Bharatiya Kala Kendra, a teaching institution established by the Government of India as a means of supporting musicians and training young prospective artists in the traditional arts. All-India Radio attracted him away, however, and he served as music director from 1956, first in Bombay, then soon afterwards back in Delhi. Another government institution, the Sangeet Natak Akademi (National Academy of Music and Drama), commissioned and published his valuable book *Saṅgītajñoṅ ke Samsmaran* ('Reminiscences of Musicians') in 1959. Thus, Vilayat Hussain was a recipient of the new patronage system of the government, established when India became an independent nation.

Saṅgītajñoṅ ke Samsmaran, cited frequently in this study, was written in Urdu, but published in Hindi translation.[3] In it are reminiscences about music and musicians which Vilayat Hussain had heard from Ghulam Abbas Khan, and anecdotes and information that he had collected from musicians and kept in a diary. The published version 'was, however, not approved by Khan Saheb and he was much critical of it and stated that the matter was not put before the public in the way he desired it to be, as the contents were some what rather distorted and expurgated' (Yodh 1978: 28). He had composed about 200 Urdu verses to portray the basic qualities of the style of famous musicians and these were deleted from the book. Vilayat Hussain studied with the Urdu poet Simab Akbarabadi (Yodh 1978: 18); his pen name in Urdu writings was 'Shafak'.

Vilayat Hussain's musical performances apparently emanated a certain sternness – a style in opposition to the romantic style.

In his person, Vilayat Hussain betrays the same stern quality that one finds in his music. His features are sharp and well defined, his jet-black hair is oiled and neatly plastered down either side of his temples, his lips are thin. The black or white *sherwani*, which he normally wears, with wide-bottomed white pyjamas, gives him an inviolable buttoned-up look from which, one feels, no unnecessary romanticism would ever be allowed to break loose. One eye is unserviceable, but the disadvantage is ruled with such confidence that one seldom notices it. The only concession to weakness, it seems, is in the evidence of the *pan*-stained teeth. Even as one feels, however, that the passion and dedication which must have informed most of his life have unluckily not found an external stamp, he utters some ringing verses in Urdu and rolls his tongue over the warm cadences in Braj Bhasha. To have a taste for poetry is one thing: when the compositions are his very own, you cannot accuse a man of lacking passion in his make-up (Vasudev 1961: 51).

In his Braj Bhasha poetic composition he used the pen name 'Pran Piya'. On May 12, 1962, six days before he died, Vilayat Hussain sang a National Program on All-India Radio. He died with a reputation for having been one of the most authentic exponents of Agra *gharana* (*Times of India*, 1962).

The fifth and sixth generations

In the fifth generation (see Chart 4–2) are Bashir Ahmed Khan (son of Mohammad Khan), the three sons of Faiyazi, and six sons in the other line. Born a 'half-generation' later was Vilayat Hussain's son Yunus Husain Khan, among others. Mention must also be made of Vilayat Hussain's son-in-law, Sharafat Husain Khan. The sixth generation includes Bashir Ahmed's sons, most notably Aqeel Ahmed Khan.

[3] Some of the English translations given here are reproduced by courtesy of Sara Stalder.

Bashir Ahmed Khan (1903–60) was born in Agra and educated within the *gharana*, particularly by Kallan Khan, who taught many family members (Vilayat Hussain Khan 1959: 118 and Yunus Husain Khan, Interview: 1978). Bashir Ahmed transmitted his tradition to his son Aqeel Ahmed and also to one particularly outstanding non-family member, Dipali Nag, who is discussed below. Both are active in the concert sphere.

Natthan Khan's daughter, Faiyazi, was married to a leading musician from Atrauli, Altaf Husain Khan, a court musician in Jaipur. They had three sons who became good musicians. Khadim Husain Khan, the eldest, studied with his father and also with Kallan Khan, in Jaipur. Likewise, Anwar Husain Khan studied with Kallan Khan, but after Kallan died in 1925 he studied with Khadim Husain, who had settled in Bombay; he also studied with Vilayat Hussain Khan (1959: 119). Both Khadim Husain and Anwar Husain were heavily involved in teaching, primarily of people outside the family (see Chart 4–3). Their younger brother, Latafat Husain Khan, studied with Tassaduq Hussain Khan and then with his elder brother Khadim Husain, with Faiyaz (whose style he is said to have imbibed) and with Vilayat Hussain (Vilayat Hussain Khan 1959: 120). Latafat Husain has made solo commercial recordings, and has also performed *jugalbandi* with his brother Khadim Husain.

Yunus Husain Khan

Yunus Husain Khan is the leading Agra *gharanedar* of his generation. Born in Agra, on November 15, 1927, he is proud to be the eleventh direct descendant in his line. Yunus Husain began studying at seven or eight years with his father, Vilayat Hussain, and he sang in *darbar* in Mysore when he was very young (between 1935 and 1940 when his father was court musician there). He also learned from Faiyaz Khan and from Azmat Husain Khan, his maternal uncle. He began singing on All-India Radio in his brother Yusuf Husain's place when Yusuf Husain died in 1945.

Yunus Husain has performed internationally – in 1954 in Afghanistan, and in 1973 in Europe and the United States. Such opportunities for Indian musicians multiplied between the 1950s and 1980s, not only because there is an enthusiastic demand for them in the West, but because India, as an independent government, has organized many cultural tours. From 1962 to 1964 Yunus Husain was a composer for AIR; he composes under the name 'Darpan'.

A 'Husaini singer', Yunus Husain composes and performs *khyal*s based on Sufism. He is a disciple in the Chisti sect of Sufism (both the Nizami and Sabiri branches) and is known for singing Muslim religious songs (he also sings traditional *khyal* and *thumri*, of course). Among the *raga*s he has composed, for example, is Husaini Bhairav (Banerji: 1972).

Yunus Husain was formerly on the Faculty of Music and Fine Arts at Delhi University. In addition to teaching vocal music there, he was director and conductor of the Sargam Choir. According to the Sargam Choir program notes, the group was begun in 1972

to provide a forum for the students to participate in musical activity in a general way and also to experiment in the field of choral singing under the guidance of experienced teachers. The choir sings classical and light classical modes, folk and regional varieties, devotional and patriotic themes suitably adapted for choral rendering . . . Ustad Yunus Husain Khan with his creative talent and rare vision has already given a new direction and opened fresh avenues for musical expression.

Yunus Husain is now a professor of music at Visva-Bharati University in Santineketan.

In terms of transmission of the tradition, the Agra *gharana* can be contrasted with the Gwalior *gharana* discussed in the previous chapter. Whereas the role of family heredity has diminished greatly in the Gwalior *gharana*, the number of *gharanedar* in the Agra group has increased with each generation. Whereas the Gwalior tradition was diffused widely beyond a family at a fairly early period, transmission of the Agra tradition has been controlled for the most part within the family. With such controlled transmission, it is not surprising that the number of non-family bearers of the Agra musical tradition are few, relative to those in the Gwalior tradition. Among the most noteworthy non-family Agra *gharana* musicians have been Jagannath Buwa Purohit and S. N. Ratanjankar, the noted musicologist, Dinkar Kaikini, Sumati Mutatkar (Dean of Music and Fine Arts at Delhi University), Dipali Nag, M. R. Gautam (who has been Head of the Department of Performing Arts at Benares Hindu University and is Vice-Chancellor of Indira Kala Sangit Vishwa Vidyalaya, University of Music and Fine Arts in Khairagarh, Madhya Pradesh), the Kichlu brothers (one of whom heads the ITC Sangit Akademi in Calcutta), and Jyotsna Bhole. (Bhaskar Rao Bakhle and Dilip Chandra Vedi, who studied with other *gharana*s as well, are discussed as independent musicians in Chapter 9.)

Dipali Nag

Among the non-family Agra *gharana* musicians, Dipali Nag is an unusual figure in that she is both a prominent vocalist in her own right and an established patroness of other vocalists. She is the daughter of J. C. Taluqdar, a well-known historian of India's Mughal period. Though her family is Bengali, she was raised and educated in Agra, receiving an MA in English there. Taluqdar decided that his daughter would study with Faiyaz Khan, and, because of the family friendship, Dipali was permitted to learn with the children of the *gharana* in her home town of Agra. In addition to studying with Faiyaz Khan, she studied with Tassaduq Hussain Khan and Bashir Ahmed Khan, both Agra *gharanedar*. According to Dipali, the *ustads* did not object to teaching non-family women, but they did not teach their own daughters.

Dipali started broadcasting in 1939, when Faiyaz took her to AIR and told them to let her perform without audition; such was the advantage of being a pupil of such a respected *ustad*. Also in 1939 she made a commercial recording which was particularly successful because it included a composition by Faiyaz Khan (Rag Jaijaiwanti: 'Jhana, jhana, jhana more pāyal'), which the producers had put into Bengali. Dipali was dubbed the young girl with the Muslim-style singing. She says: 'My father protected me from the praise I received and [aside] from the earnings!' In 1944, when Dipali was just married and living in Calcutta, Faiyaz Khan summoned her to come and sing with him; she said it was a remarkable experience, due partly to the difference in their voices.

Dipali Nag has been active in the music sphere in numerous ways. She has broadcast from many AIR stations (including a Sangist Sammelan Series in 1972), has performed widely (including the Tansen Festival in Gwalior in 1970), has been televised in Delhi, Paris, and London, has made appearances in Hawaii and on the West Coast of the United States, has published criticism (*The Statesman*), articles, and books, has lectured widely, has served as examiner of music for educational institutions, and has been a teacher, an AIR producer, and conductor of a choir (Sapta Sur) in Delhi and Calcutta. She has been part of government-sponsored cultural delegations to Czechoslovakia, the USSR, and Iran. And, as a doyenne in Delhi, she has hosted numerous *mehfils* in her home, which has served as a gathering-place for musicians and connoisseurs (*samajdārlok*) of music.

Musical styles of Agra *gharana* musicians

Generalisations about the *gharana* style

A profile of the Agra *gharana* musical style is perhaps easier to draw than other *gharana*s, because the basic distinguishing characteristic has been consistently maintained for a relatively long time. That basic characteristic – to which most other Agra characteristics can be related – is enunciated by all sources: the *khyal* style has been kept close to *dhrupad*. This has been achieved, as Vamanrao Deshpande (1973) emphasizes in his volume on Hindustani music, primarily by a 'heavy bias in favor of *laya* (rhythm), which is one of the major characteristics of *dhrupad*'. Other specific characteristics of the Agra *gharana* musical style which are generally cited are: full presentation of the *sthai* and the *antara*; clear enunciation of those texts; and cultivation of *boltan*s and *bolbant* (rather than *akar*). Still further characteristics that keep Agra *gharana khyal* style close to that of *dhrupad* are concerned less with treatment of the text than with *gayaki*: the robust or powerful voice, with a certain aggressiveness, and with the notes attacked rather than invoked. Dipali Nag described the style as masculine and strong (Interview: 1978). Such remarks are customarily made about *dhrupad* singing style. Other comments made about Agra vocal quality (that it is 'gruff', for example) neither relate to *dhrupad* style nor seem to be characteristic of the *gharana* style in general.

Some remarks on Agra style concern the tempo of performances: 'Gwalior and Agra have a relatively faster tempo [than other *gharana*s] although it is slow as compared to film (or lavni) music' (V. H. Deshpande 1973: 77); and 'their inspiration is best in madhya laya' (Vasudev 1961: 51). Dipali Nag confirmed that Agra singing was likely to be in *bara bara laya* (medium speed). Conversely, in my sampling of *bara khyal* performances, I find that the Gwalior *gharana* musicians pace themselves faster than Agra *gharana* musicians, and that Agra musicians do not sing consistently faster (or slower) than musicians in *gharana*s other than Gwalior.

Two other characteristics mentioned with respect to Agra – beautifully proportioned form and correctness of *raga* – lie more in the general realm of good Hindustani musicianship and are likely to be attributed as well to other *gharana* styles. One fairly recent characteristic which seems to be perceived as being 'close to *dhrupad*' relates to form and *raga* – a relatively extensive *alap* preceding the *ciz*.

Each of these characteristics will be elucidated through analysis of performances of a selection of Agra *gharana* musicians. In addition, comments on the music of early Agra musicians for whom no recorded music is available are necessary to lend historical perspective to the present situation. It must be remembered that for the early musicians we have only generalized lore from a few, diverse sources.

Early Agra *gharana* musicians

The Agra *gharana khyal* style was developed by a group of musicians whose family tradition was *dhrupad*. Scattered comments about repertoire and performances remind us that members of the family did not stop singing *dhrupad* when they began singing *khyal*. Furthermore, the fact that it has remained customary up to the present generation for Agra *gharanedar* to sing both *khyal* and *dhrupad* was probably a primary factor in the development of a *khyal* style that was 'close to *dhrupad*'.

For the 'founder' of the Agra *khyal* style, Ghagghe Khuda Baksh, sources mention only his raucous voice (discussed earlier) and two other items of information. Like so many of his successors, Khuda Baksh composed songs; his 'Kaise sukh sohe' in Rag Bihag has been singled out for plaudits (Wadhera 1954d). For Khuda Baksh (and for most of the other members of his family), Vilayat Hussain refers to '*asthayi khyal* singing style'. The contexts in which he used the term *asthayi* (अस्थायी) were, for example: अस्थायी-ख्याल की गायकी पर इनको पूरा-पूरा अधिकार था   ('He had full command of *asthayi khyal* singing style', 1959: 103); रिश्तेदारों से भी सैकड़ों चीज़ें याद की' जिनमें होरी धुपद सरगमें तराने अस्थाइयां ख्याल सभी कुछ शमिल था । ('From his relatives he learned numerous things, among them *hori*, *dhrupad*, *sargam*, *tarana*, *asthai*', p. 112); मैंने लाचारी-तोड़ी की अस्थायी याद की और बहार भीमपलास मारवा पूरबी आदि रागों के तराने याद किये ।   ('I remembered [learned] *asthayi* of Rag Lachari-Todi and *tarana*s of Rags Bahar, Bhimpalas, Marwa, Purba and others', p. 132).

Of Sher Khan (1815–62) we learn from Vilayat Hussain (1959: 103) that 'he had full command over *asthayi* singing and had a very effective way of singing. He had a powerful way of singing *tans* and phirat'. By *phirut* Vilayat Hussain seems to mean 'with flexibility', in that a musician can sing slowly while emphasizing the *raga* (as in *alap*), but he can also sing in medium and fast speeds while using the ornamentation style and *tans* of *khyal* (p. 110). Thus, it would appear that powerful *tans*, as well as expressive *alap*, were features of even the earliest Agra *gharana khyal* style.

Ghulam Abbas Khan

Of Ghulam Abbas (1818 or 1820–1932, or 1809–1934) we learn from Vilayat Hussain that he was a high-class (or high-ranking) *asthayi-khyal* singer. 'He had good breath control and the listener was charmed when Ghulam Abbas held one note . . . Whenever he dwelled on one pitch and gradually treated it with creative gestures, it made a deep impression' (1959: 104). According to Vilayat Hussain's account, Ghulam Abbas conscientiously worked at perfecting this singing of *sur* (pitch). Chart 4–3 shows that he took great interest in teaching; thus his emphasis on *sur* and his voice culture must have been transmitted to successive generations in his family.

Kallan Khan

Of Kallan Khan (Ghulam Haider Khan, d. 1925) Vilayat Hussain relates that he was very expressive with a very clear and good voice and that he was considered one of the best singers of his time (1959: 106). Thus, we consistently learn that Vilayat Hussain considered vocal quality and good control and expressiveness of voice important characteristics of his ancestors' musical style.

Later Agra gharana musicians

Natthan Khan

With accounts of Natthan Khan (1840–1901) we read that he sang with great expression and vigor (Vilayat Hussain Khan 1959: 111). But with Natthan Khan we begin to get more detailed and varied comments on singing style and performance characteristics. To the statement that he sang with great expression and vigor can be added the words 'majesty' or 'dignity', pertaining to the tempo at which he sang (Garg 1957: 159). In the following anecdote related by Vilayat Hussain Khan, the impression gained is that the slow speed of Natthan Khan's singing seems to have been peculiar to him, not a general characteristic of his *gharana*

Once Natthan Khan Sahab went to Delhi and received an invitation by the renowned singer Bahadur Husain Khan. All the musicians of the city gathered there. After dinner, the music started. When Natthan Khan began his music, he was accompanied by Muzaffar Khan, the famed *khandani tabla* player of Delhi. Natthan Khan began asthayi in *tilwada tal* [slow, sixteen-count *tala*], but the laya was not accompanied to his taste. He asked Muzaffar Khan to play a bit more slowly. So Muzaffar Khan, who was playing simple, pure theka, played so slowly that it was difficult for listeners to respond to the sam. This laya was nothing uncommon for Natthan Khan Sahab and he began singing with great expression and vigor [the force of a lion] (1959: 110–11).

Natthan Khan, as the anecdote continues, respected Muzaffar Khan's playing and later asked the *tabla* player to play something for him – presumably a solo. But Muzaffar Khan was exhausted from the effort of playing *theka* so slowly, for he is said to have replied 'Khan Sahab, I am having difficulty playing theka in this laya; you are the one who can perform in this laya without fatigue'. The picture one gets is of *khyal* being sung at a relatively lively pace (medium speed) at Natthan Khan's time (1840–1901), and of Natthan Khan singing more slowly than was usual.

Several sources suggest that in the 'early days' of *khyal* it was not sung particularly slowly either. Two such assertions are cited here. Yunus Husain Khan stated in 1969 that in the 'older days' the tempo of many great singers was slow but lively (i.e. medium speed), but that singing had become slower in the last twenty-five to thirty years. He cited from the 'older days' not only his father, Vilayat Hussain Khan, but Bade Ghulam Ali Khan (1903–68) of Patiala, Krishnarao Pandit (b. 1894) of Gwalior, and Mushtaq Hussein Khan (1874, 1878 or 1880–1964) of Sahaswan. Sumati Mutatkar, a musicologist at Delhi University and a respected singer of the Agra *gharana*, commented in 1969 that medium speed was formerly related to the pulse rate, but that now a *khyal* is often begun slower than that, and the speed is gradually increased to medium speed and then to fast speed. There seems to have been a gradually increasing differentiation of the three levels of speed in *khyal* performance.

Other comments about Natthan Khan relate to his relish of rhythmic play (*layakari*): Saxena (1956a) notes his 'imbedding of pattern weaving with laya variations' (called *laya phirat* and *boltans*), while Rampalal Mehta (1969: 38) notes his enunciation of the *bols* (text), emphasis on *bolbant*, and *layakari* with a variety of rhythmic relationships, including *dugun* (2:1), *caugun* (3:1), *aithgun* (8:1), and *adi* (uneven subdivision).

In *alap-dhrupad*, emphasis on rhythm comes in two places: first it is found in the unmetered *nom-tom-alap* section of the performance sequence which follows the grand *ragalap*. *Nom-tom-alap* is sung on vocables such as 'na' and 'ne'; thus, the presence or absence of a text is not a determining factor for creating an emphasis on rhythm. Emphasis on rhythm in *alap-dhrupad* also comes in the *dhrupad* section, when a composition is sung, and text and *tala* are introduced into the performance. Rhythmic play here used the text (*bolbant*) and involves rhythm relative to meter. In this metered context, the rhythmic play can either be 'with' the meter (as in subdivision of counts in such relationships as 2:1, 4:1, 5:1) or it can be 'against' it (as in cross-rhythms).

In *khyal*, the same set of rhythmic possibilities is present as in *dhrupad*. The difference lies in the fact that in *alap-dhrupad* these characteristics are not opinions: there must be *ragalap* (slow, unmetered, in 'free' rhythm); there must be *nom-tom-alap* (emphasis on rhythm in an unmetered context); and there must be *dhrupad* with *bolbant* improvisation (emphasis on rhythm in a metered context). In *khyal*, the slow, unmetered, 'free' rhythm would lie in the pre-*ciz alap*, as would the emphasis on rhythm in an unmetered context, albeit in a truncated section. Because the composition is sung close to the outset of the *khyal*, however, the unmetered factor is minimized. Slow, 'free' rhythm (i.e., de-emphasis of rhythm) must be an illusion created within the meter. If emphasis on rhythm of a *nom-tom* sort is desired, the particular sort of ornamentation, melodic pattern, and vocable pattern must be brought into play within the meter. Emphasis on rhythm in a metered context is clearly the most obvious option in *khyal*.

In *khyal*, emphasis on rhythm is an option, and the musical means by which one emphasizes rhythm are also optional. The Agra *gharana* – more than any other – has opted to emphasize rhythm, and to do it in ways similar to those used in *dhrupad*. For Natthan Khan, those ways involved enunciation of the *bols* and *layakari* in *bolbant*.

Natthan Khan's skill with *tala* must have been formidable. An episode related by Vilayat Hussain tells of one occasion when this was proved. Natthan Khan was in Dhawar, at the home of Bhaskar Rao Bakhle. He was practicing one morning, accompanied by Kamta Prasad, a reputed *tabla* player who was visiting him. They were engrossed in very slow *jhumra tala*, when Natthan Khan suddenly remembered an important engagement. When he stopped singing to explain that to Bakhle, Kamta Prasad began to play a *tabla* composition, a *gat*, perhaps to regain Natthan Khan's attention for, as Vilayat Hussain related it:

The listeners and even Kamta Prasad were certain that Natthan, who was talking, would not be able to catch the sam. However, when only one-fourth of the gat remained, Khan Sahab began singing a tan with many arabesques and ended at the sam with complete grace. Kamta Prasad was amazed and left the tabla to address Natthan: 'You are the king of laya, and laya is your slave. When you started talking I thought you would miss the sam, but I was wrong; you came at the sam as though nothing had happened' (1959: 111–12).[4]

Natthan Khan was noted for his skill in creating *tan*s as well. Vilayat Hussain remarked that his father (Natthan) gave a new turn to the Agra style with *tan*s of crisp and 'knotty' movements (influenced by the famous Mubarak Ali Khan whom he would have heard in Jaipur; Wadhera 1954b). He is also reported to have sung *boltan*s, *tan*s merging within the syllables of the *ciz* text (Garg 1957; 196). Rampalal Mehta adds that he would close a *boltan* passage with *tihai* (1969: 38), thereby creating striking rhythmic contrast.

Another characteristic of Natthan Khan's *khyal* performance was his choice of *ciz* in which the text fell in *atit* or *anagat* relationship to the *tala* (Rampalal Mehta 1969: 38) – just before or just after *sam*. This was another instance of his love of rhythmic play.

Only those particularly pertinent elements of Natthan Khan's sons' musical style will be mentioned here (except for Vilayat Hussain). Mohammad Khan (1870–1922) enjoyed rare

---

[4] This has all the ingredients of many similar anecdotes: a place, a cast of highly respected musicians, a situation of musical participation, a contest with a 'winner', and the 'loser' addressing the 'winner' with acknowledgement of his mastery. 'King' is a frequent expression of adulation.

*raga*s and popularized them among his students (Vilayat Hussain 1959: 113). Abdullah Khan (c. 1873–1922), who was with Natthan for a considerable time, was noted, like his father, for rephrasing the words of the song and for *layakari*. His breath control must have been excellent, for he sang long *tan*s in one breath and came well to *sam*. His *tan*s were clear (Vilayat Hussain 1959: 113). For Mohammad Siddiq, Vilayat Hussain's comments sound like those for his predecessors – powerful voice and vigor and also exciting *tan*s (1959: 114).

Plate 4   Faiyaz Khan of the Agra *gharana*

Plate 5   Dipali Nag of the Agra *gharana* at her home in New Delhi, with the author, 1978

Faiyaz Husain Khan

The greatest Agra *gharana* singer of the generation after Natthan Khan was Faiyaz Husain Khan. Faiyaz benefitted from musical traditions and training not only from his maternal side of the Agra family under discussion here, but also from his paternal side, the outstanding musicians of the 'Rangile' *gharana* from Ramzan Khan and Mohammad Ali Khan to Fida Hussein Khan and Faiyaz's father Safdar Hussain Khan (see Chart 4–3; cf. V. H. Deshpande 1973: 42, 82). In addition, Faiyaz's own talent and creative genius contributed to the shaping of his musical style. It is not my intention to analyze all the derivations – if, indeed, such a clear analysis were possible – but some of his style characteristics were clearly held in common with other singers of the Agra tradition.

For singers who performed within living memory, we can derive details on such attributes as vocal range (well over two and a half octaves for Faiyaz) and natural pitch register. Faiyaz had an unusually low-pitched voice which contributed to the effect of his singing; and he had the vocal *power* that was cultivated by his *gharana* predecessors (Daniélou 1951: 57). Descriptions of his vocal quality range from 'clear and sweet' (Vilayat Hussain Khan 1959: 115) to 'broad, full husky' (V. H. Desphande 1973: 13). Vasant Thakur dubbed it 'broad, masculine' (1966: 31); and Dipali Nag reiterated 'masculine'.

Because of the exceedingly low pitch-register of Faiyaz's natural voice, it was difficult for his disciples to sing with him in performance or in practice, as the traditional manner of learning calls for. Dipali Nag (who also has a naturally low-pitch voice and sang with Faiyaz) commented that those of his disciples who tried to conform to that low pitch risked ruining their voices (Interview: 1978). It is possible that the desire to emulate Faiyaz's low voice produced the 'gruff', 'grating', 'husky' vocal quality noted by V. H. Deshpande (1973: 16) and Amar Nath (Interview: 1978) as characteristic of Agra *gharana* vocal production. In any case, comments about other Agra *gharana* singers contradict this generalization: 'the beautiful voice like a lion of Sharafat Husain' (Dipali Nag, Interview: 1978); 'the deep, rich voice of Latafat Husain' (*Times of India*, 1970d); the 'full-throated' (*Indian Express*, 1972c), 'broad, rugged' (*ibid*, 1971), 'powerful' (*Times of India*, 1966) voice of Yunus Husain Khan.

Vamanrao Deshpande, for whom tempo was an important criterion for generalizations about *gharanas*' styles, commented indirectly on the tempo one could expect from Faiyaz: 'A broad, full husky but inelastic voice will shine best in very slow tempo and although it might be exploited to produce quick tans its most effective exploitation will always be found in slow tans (Faiyaz Khan)' (1973: 13). Shinglu, the music critic for the *Statesman* of Delhi, commented (in 1978) that Faiyaz sang less slowly than Amir Khan (see Chapter 9 below, on independent musicians), but not briskly.

With tempo, as with other elements of performance, however, it is necessary to stress Faiyaz's remarkable flexibility. Vasant Thakur commented that in fast *khyal* as well Faiyaz was in his element (1966: 31). Indeed, any artist who was proclaimed to be equally at home singing *alap-dhrupad*, *dhamar*, and *hori*, *khyal* and *thumri*, and even the light genres *dadra* and *ghazal* would have had to be facile in every tempo.

The variety of forms which Faiyaz performed appears to be rather unusual for an Agra *gharana* musician. The article on him in Garg explains his espousal of the light forms as follows: 'At the insistence of his audience he might even sing ghazal. Hearing him sing ghazal, listeners were astonished that this artist who was a living manifestation of the *śāstriya saṅgīt* tradition could also sing ghazal so well' (1957: 223). More usual, perhaps, was his flair for *thumri*. 'In his "Thumri", which is unmatched for its romantic hilarity and lyricism, Faiyaz Khan evinced a preference for the "Poorab Ang" [of Benares]' (Wadhera 1953a). 'When asked once from whom he had learned *Thumri* . . . he said that he never studied it but merely picked it up by hearing' (Daniélou 1951: 56). Such eclecticism should not be surprising when it is recalled that in the period of Faiyaz's early musical training with Ghulam Abbas he had learned by memorizing a vast number of melodies and by listening critically to the singing of many musicians (Daniélou 1951: 57).

Faiyaz's repertoire was apparently enormous and was enhanced as well by his own songs. His genius was manifested not only in performances but in compositions which bear his *mudra*, Prem Piya. One published description of his composition style seems particularly apt: 'Each letter and syllable in the composition is given a quality of precise power, a meaningfulness both musical and literary' (*Times of India*, 1970a). Among his most popular *khyal* compositions are 'More mandir ablo nahīṅ āye' in Rag Jaijaiwanti, and 'E meṅ chodo' in Rag Sughrai (Garg 1957: 224). Another of his *khyal* compositions, 'Bāram bār vārī re mā', in Rag Gara Kanhra *ektal*, is discussed below as performed by Sharafat Husain Khan, whose style is said to resemble Faiyaz's. In addition to many *khyal* compositions, he wrote *dhamar* (e.g. 'Ālī thap bājan lāge' in Rag Jaijaiwanti), *thumri* (e.g. 'Mose karat barjorī' in Rag Gara), *sadra* (e.g. 'Khwājā Mohiuddin' in Rag Shri), and *tarana* (e.g. 'Ode tānā dira tānā' in Rag Bahar). These are among the selection of Agra *gharana* compositions published in Rampalal Mehta (1969).

The art of *layakari*, which one comes to expect from Agra *gharana* musicians, was practiced by Faiyaz. 'Gifted with a voice that was richer than that of any other musician, his inimitable style of "Rag Barhat" (elaboration), bejewelled with a most lively "layakari" made him the idol of audiences everywhere' (Wadhera 1953a). Vasant Thakur credited him with a perfect sense of rhythm (1966: 30). Dilip Chandra Vedi, who studied with Faiyaz, pronounced him (Interviews: 1978) one of the best *bolbant* singers. Dipali Nag considered him expert at coming to the *sam* (Interview: 1978). These statements indicate that Faiyaz was likely to make rhythm a musical factor where it was expected – in *bolbant* and at *sam*, but also in *rag barhat* (*badhat*).

Faiyaz introduced into *khyal* performance the singing of *alap* before the *bandish* (Yunus Husain Khan, Interview: 1978). That *alap* (the *rag badhat*) included the 'lively layakari which made him the idol of audiences everywhere'; he developed 'his own style of "alapchari", with "Nom, Tom" giving it an entity quite different from the "Alap", in "Dhrupad" and the prevalent form of "Khayal"' (Wadhera 1953a). As stated by Dipali Nag (Interview: 1978), this 'Nom, Tom' is 'singing with *jor*'. In Exx. 4–1, 4–2, and 4–3, this long pre-*ciz alap* with *nom-tom* is demonstrated with passages from a performance of one of Faiyaz's favorite *ragas* – Jaijaiwanti – which was broadcast on Radio Pakistan. The pre-*ciz alap* was long indeed for a *khyal*, 15:40. Precise time in the performance is given below, to demonstrate proportions in the structuring of the selection.

While there was no feeling of pulse at the outset of this *alap* there was apparently no intention to exhaust all the melodic possibilities for a very few pitches (such as one would expect in *alap* before *dhrupad*). In the first two and a half minutes Faiyaz introduced the pitches Ma, Pa, Dha, Ni, and Ni *komal* of the lower octave in one improvisational unit, and the pitches Re and Sa in the middle octave in a second unit on the vocables 'ni', 're', and 'na'. At 3:28 came the first feeling of pulsation – too early for an *alap-dhrupad* performance. That first hint of *non-tom* is shown in Ex. 4–1; it was the first 'ni re re na' shown in the transcription which introduced the pulse; thereafter the feeling of pulsation was affected by pitch repetition with the characteristic *nom-tom* embellishment (the approach from above), rather than by vocable repetition. Interim sustained pitches make this a 'hint' at *nom-tom* rather than consistent pulsation.

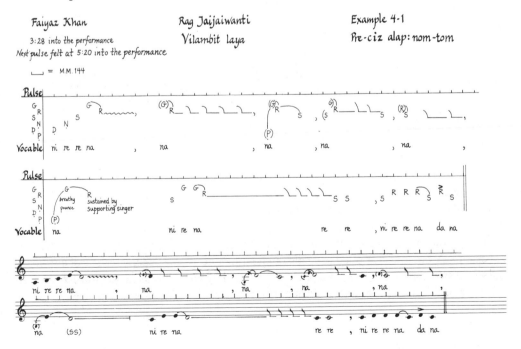

Faiyaz Khan   Rag Jaijaiwanti   Example 4·1

3:28 into the performance   Vilambit laya   Pre-*ciz* alap: nom-tom
Next pulse felt at 5:20 into the performance

After the short passage shown in Ex. 4–1 the hint at pulsation was dropped, not to recur until 5:20 into the performance. Pitch Ga was the focus of the next unit of improvisation; then both Ma and Pa in the following unit, and Dha and Ni *komal* in the next, as the *raga* was shown in lovely, floating melodic improvisation. The first sustained occurrence of *nom-tom* came at 12:10 into the performance; in it pitch Sá was introduced for the first time in a most dramatic manner (this is shown in Ex. 4–2). The pulse rate is the same as in Ex. 4–1, but the pitches come at twice the rhythmic density. The *nom-tom* is characterized by quick successions of vocables on quick successions of pitches. Vocable 'di' sets off most melodic–rhythmic groupings; vocable 'ne' comes within phrases, and 'na' is used for prolonged pitches. Groupings were created within longer phrases (see the phrase marks in Ex. 4–2): after the *sarangi* repetition (boxed) of the initial phrase, for example, Faiyaz sang a grouping of three ('ne ne ne'), then of four ('di ne ne ne'), then of two ('di ne'), and then a longer grouping to achieve the shifting rhythmic combinations characteristic of *nom-tom*.

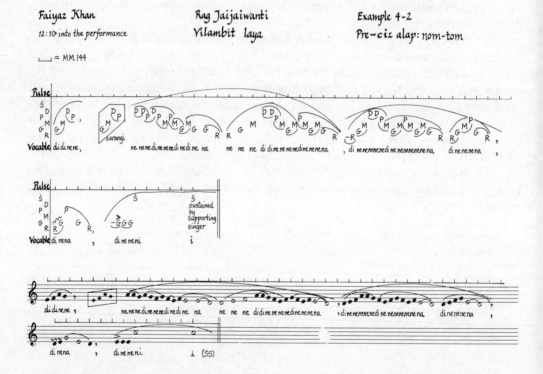

Faiyaz Khan

12:10 *into the performance*

⌞⌟ = M.M. 144

Rag Jaijaiwanti
Vilambit laya

Example 4-2
Pre-ciz alap: nom-tom

In the fourteenth minute of the performance came a much lengthier unit of *nom-tom*, the last major unit of the *alap*. Here (see Ex. 4–3) the pulse is faster, and the functional placement of the syllables 'di', 'ne', and 'na' is less consistent. Also introduced is a *gamak* (embellishment) sounding like a loose-jawed dip, which I have transcribed as ⌣; this *gamak* is instinctively associated with *nom-tom*. It creates what sounds like pitch repetition (see line 3 of the example), but is also applied to single pitches (see line 4). Also characteristic of *nom-tom* is the successive iteration of the same pitch, enunciated by vocables, as in line 5 of Ex. 4–3. By this type of improvisation, *alap* is brought to a climax of rhythm and speed.

Faiyaz Khan

In 14th minute of the performance

Rag Jaijaiwanti

Vilambit laya

Example 4-3

Pre–ciz alap: nom-tom

⌐⌐ = M.M. 176

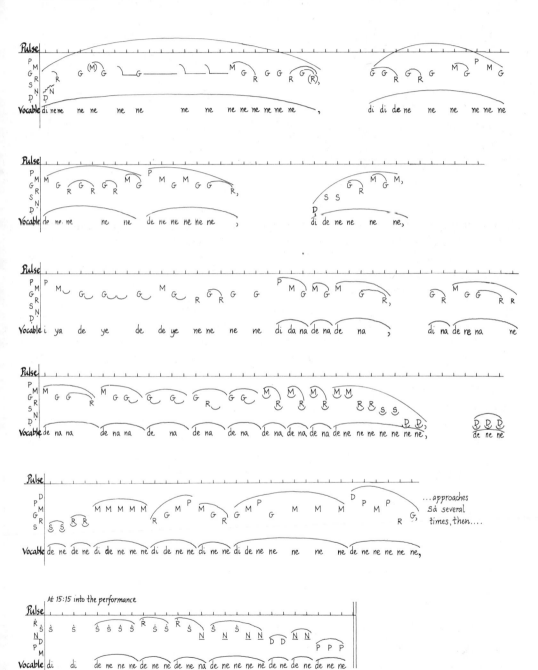

...approaches
Sā several
times, then....

At 15:15 into the performance

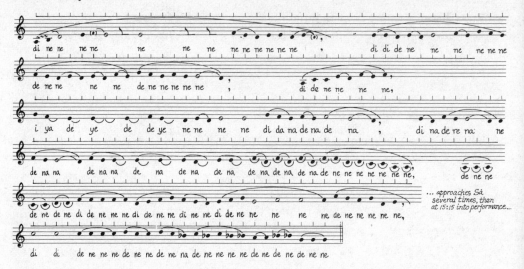

The lengthy pre-*ciz alap* and Faiyaz's cultivation of *nom-tom* were individual innovations in *khyal* performance style, but they were so widely adopted after him that they have now become associated with the Agra *gharana* tradition in general. Furthermore, these two innovations are commonly perceived as ways in which the Agra style has been kept 'close to *dhrupad*'. Why Faiyaz chose to perform *khyal* in this way is not clear, but I would like to suggest that he may have wanted to merge *dhrupad* into *khyal* at a time when audiences no longer wished to hear the extended *alap-dhrupad* selections that constituted a good portion of the performances of Agra *gharana* musicians. In order to maintain valued *dhrupad* heritage, it seems that *khyal* performance was increasingly 'dhrupadized', although we do not know exactly when Faiyaz began doing this and exactly what he changed.

In this performance of Jaijaiwanti, Faiyaz proceeded to a medium-speed *ektal bara khyal* and a fast *tintal chota khyal*. In Ex. 4–4 his first *tans* are shown. Rather than assert that his *tans* were any slower or faster than other artists' (they do not seem sufficiently consistent in this respect to assert that), I think it is more significant to point out two other aspects of Faiyaz's *tans*. First, he varied the speed of his *gamak* (in this instance, vibrato), thereby creating the effect of greater and lesser speed; in this example the melodic pace is slowed when the *gamak* is slower (see counts 6 and 7), but the vibrato speed is likely to change even within consistent

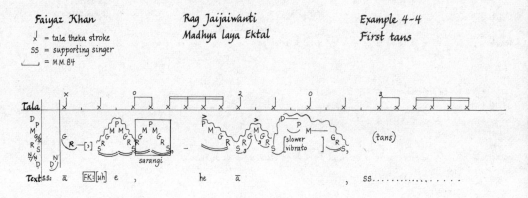

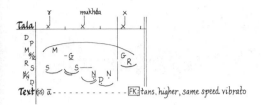

rhythmic density. Secondly the element of *layakari* appears even in *akar tans* (see counts 4–5 where *layakari* makes an intricate passage of essentially straight down–up–down melodic notion); the *tans* are 'clear' in that their pitches, even at a fast speed and sung with *gamak*, can usually be ascertained easily.

Faiyaz was also a master of *boltans*, especially those in which the *bols* contributed a definite rhythmic factor. This is demonstrated by Ex. 4–5, from the medium-speed *khyal* in Jaijaiwanti, particularly in the second *tala* cycle.

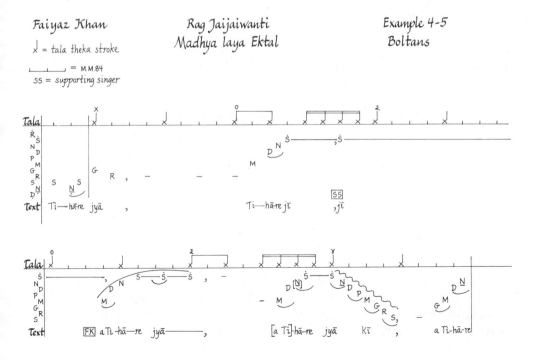

Faiyaz was also known for *bolbant*. Ex. 4–6 is a *bolbant* passage from the *chota khyal* of the same Jaijaiwanti performance. In it he combined clever *bol* placement with melodic twists and turns within a small range (the first two *tala* cycles). Then the phrase 'sagarī raina meṅ jā' is presented, first complete and then in parts – 'raina meṅ jā' (twice) and 'sagarī rain'. 'Jā' on count 1 of the third cycle starts a fresh idea: shifting rhythm, as in emphasis on each syllable 'ga-rī rai-na meṅ jā-ge' (twice), changing to different emphasis patterns for the last two repetitions of 'sagarī raina meṅ' in the example. Flashing by at a rapid speed, this is a stunning passage, vividly portraying the text, 'awake through the whole night of rain'.

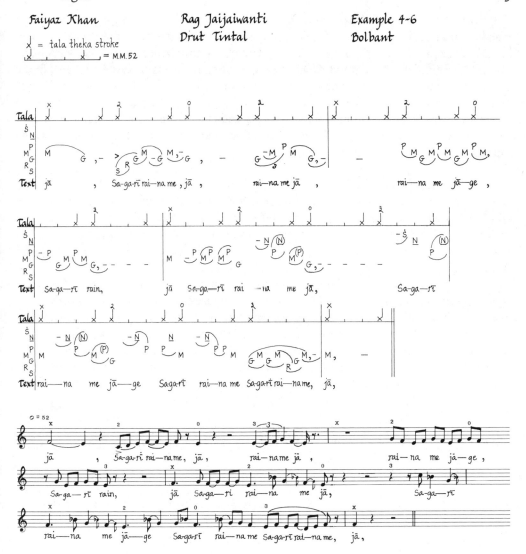

Faiyaz Khan   Rag Jaijaiwanti   Example 4-6
           Drut Tintal   Bolbant

Indeed, Faiyaz was lauded for his care for the meaning of the texts. And, significantly, he was likely to dwell on phrases of the *ciz* other than just the first *sthai* phrase. Both of these elements of his performance style were described by B. R. Deodhar, from a delightful performance of the Basant composition 'Piyā saṅg khelo rī' in *drut tintal*:

The gist of the song is: a young, rather impetuous girl reminds her friends of the approach of spring, of the joyous atmosphere around them. She asks them to wear colourful garments, weave garlands for the Beloved and rush to play with him. She is impatient to start. Occasionally she pleads with them; sometimes she rushes around, urging them to hurry. Khan Sahib expressed every shade in her mood through the stress on words, the play with notes, and the expressions on his face. Sometimes, instead of the first line of the *cheeza*, he picked on a line in the *astai* and *antara* and dwelt on it. His play with the line *Daru ho garao* (the last line of the *astai* in the *cheeza*) was so elaborate that for the time being one felt that it formed the opening line of the composition (Deodhar 1981: 31).

Faiyaz Khan was a very influential singer. A brief list of the leading Agra *gharana* musicians who have been said to sing with his style includes Bashir Ahmed Khan (grandson of Natthan Khan), Sharafat Husain Khan (grandson-in-law of Natthan Khan, son-in-law of Vilayat Hussain), and Latafat Husain and Khadim Husain (also grandsons of Natthan Khan). In the next generation are Aqeel Ahmed (son of Bashir Ahmed) and Dipali Nag, whom Vilayat Hussain claimed was Bashir Ahmed's best student (1959: 118). From a selection of recorded performances of Sharafat Husain, Latafat Husain, and Dipali Nag, the style characteristics of the Agra *gharana* and of Faiyaz Khan are examined more closely in the discussion which follows.

Sharafat Husain Khan

In February 1969 Sharafat Husain sang a National Programme on All-India Radio which featured a thirty-minute *vilambit-drut khyal* in Rag Gara Kanhra, followed by a ten-and-a-half-minute *drut khyal* in Rag Pancham Sohini. All three compositions were by Faiyaz Khan 'Prem Piya': Bāram bār vārī re mā,' 'Tan, man, dhan sab vārun ali', and 'Hamāre ding āojī'. The slow-speed *ektal* performance of the first of these compositions, 'Bāram bār vārī re mā', in Rag Gara Kanhra, serves as a 'textbook' manifestation of Faiyaz's style through both composition and performance, because of the potentialities he envisaged in it. Sharafat Husain began his performance with a brief pre-*ciz alap*, which was shorter than one he would probably have sung in a context less constrained in time, but it was longer (1:16) than most pre-*ciz alaps* that are heard not only in AIR broadcasts but at all. That is to be expected from an Agra *gharana* musician after Faiyaz Khan. Sharafat Husain's voice was powerful with controlled, resonant, sustained tones of *dhrupad-alap* style. The 1:16 pre-*ciz alap* gave us the pitches around Sa (N̩S, S (S)Ȓ , S̃R̩N̩). Then just before the *ciz mukhda* we glimpsed P̩N̩ S—R N̩S , heralding the *mukhda* of the *ciz* and the approach

to it – P̩N̩S—N̩SR G̲ R S – which recurred through the ensuing metered development of the *raga*.

It was just over two minutes of slow, powerful, sustained singing before that *mukhda* was heard again to mark off a portion of the *alap*. The musical phrases which it marked off had included S N̩ D̩P̩ , M̩P̩N̩—, P̩S , M̩P̩D̩N̩ S—Ñ̩D̩ N̩D̩ N̩S , thus taking us down to Ma, and showing us both forms of Ni in context, in pitch-segment fashion rather than pitch-by-pitch.

Again, there was just over two minutes of slow, powerful, sustained singing before the *mukhda* recurred. In those two minutes the region Pa to Sa was still heard, but the pitches just above Sa were emphasized more, including S G̲—R S G̲R, R M G̲R, G̲ SR N̩, S (N̩ S) . Ma was just touched, not stressed.

Beyond this point (5:42 into the performance) there was no further real exploration of the lower octave. The gradual rise to Så was pursued, with *mukhda*s occurring after units just over a minute long. One ensuing unit introduced the contrast between Ga and Ga, the next rose to Ma several times, but it was clear that Ma is not a pitch to be 'stood upon' in this *raga*. As long as he was focusing on Ga and Ma-Ga, Sharafat Husain kept referring back down into the lower octave to Pạ-Sa.

In the ninth minute of the performance, he took us up to Pa, then in the next unit stressed Pa, and Dha, and even Ni-Dha. That unit lasted only 1:27 (from *mukhda* to *mukhda*), and the effect was a contraction in the amount of time he was going to take to get up to Så. Having glimpsed Ni, however, he backed off and for one *tala* cycle dwelled in lower *sthai* territory:

$$\underset{\text{M̥}}{P} N S , S R^{\underline{G}} S^{R} \quad N . . . . .$$ Most tantalizingly in the next cycle, just into the

thirteenth minute of the performance, he touched – just touched – Så in the process of reviewing now-familiar *raga* materials in ever-fresh ways.

Up to this moment the performance did not differ from many other *bara khyal* performances – apart from the relatively long pre-*ciz alap*. The text to which this was sung should be noted. The first phrase of the *ciz sthai*, 'bāram bār vārī re mā', was used throughout with the *mukhda* on 'bārama Bā'. It is a cleverly conceived text, because two of the three initial consonants – 'b' and 'v' – are pronounced almost indistinguishably. The consonant 'm' can be sung as a nasal. The remaining syllables – 'ra' (bārama), 'rī' (vari), and 're' – are the same syllables that constitute the vocables to which *dhrupad alap* is sung. In this *khyal* performance, they can either impart a linguistic meaning or not, as the singer or hearer wishes.

Into the fourteenth minute of Sharafat Husain's performance, that text was put to the second potential use that was probably conceived by Faiyaz Khan – *nom-tom*-like pulsation. This lasted for a period of just over two minutes (broken up by *mukhda*); a portion of it is transcribed in Ex. 4–7. In the third and fourth complete cycles of the *tala* notated in Ex. 4–7 (after the long break), the reiteration of contiguous pitches Ma–Ga Ma–Ga, Re–Ga Ga–Re, with change of syllable on each, created *nom-tom*-like pulsation. The shifting rhythmic groupings in the fifth cycle continued the effect. Having included emphasis on rhythm in this performance through *nom-tom*, Sharafat Husain utilized *tans* for the bulk of the music improvised after the *alap*. Through his improvisation he revealed an acceptably wide vocal range, descending to Mạ and ascending to Må.

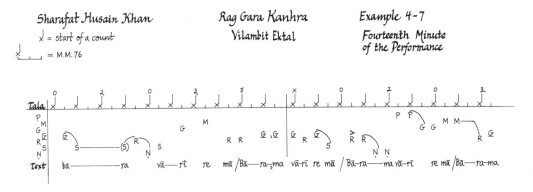

Sharafat Husain Khan
𝄎 = start of a count
𝄎⌐⌐ = M.M. 76

Rag Gara Kanhra
Vilambit Ektal

Example 4–7
Fourteenth Minute
of the Performance

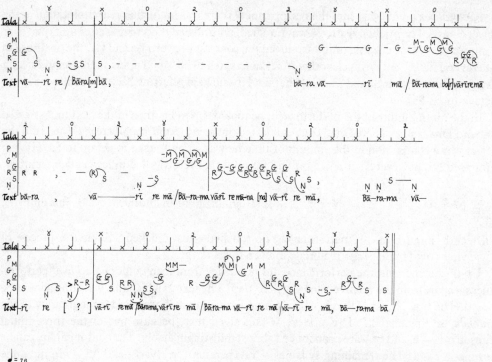

In the *drut khyal*, he again played with sustained melody contrasted with *tans*, but a great deal of the interest lies in the composition itself. He played with the text, repeating two words, then three, and more parts of the *ciz* than the opening line. It is not intricate rhythmic play, however.

Some of Sharafat Husain's *tans* were of a type which become familiar when one listens to a number of Agra performances. The pitches are treated as plateaux, each prolonged with fast vibrato, and thus the succession of pitches is relatively slow, while the vibrato is fast:

. The result is a slow, clear *tan*. Singers of other *gharana*s produce this type of *tan*; it is not characteristically Agra.

Two other characteristics of Sharafat Husain's chota *khyal* performances are pertinent. It cannot be predicted from performance to performance whether he will present *sthai* and *antara* together at the beginning of the *drut* speed, but he will eventually present the whole *ciz*. Also, he gives the *tabla* player a fast solo at the beginning, and at least one brief solo during the *drut*.

Latafat Husain Khan

With a performance of 'Daiyā batha dūbhar bhaī' in Rag Miyan ki Todi, Latafat Husain (see Plate 6, p. 128) provides excellent illustration of the manner in which an individual artist draws on the tradition and distinguishes himself within it. In this *khyal* performance there are clear traits which he may have learned with Natthan Khan, and also traits of Faiyaz Khan's style that are now considered characteristic of Agra in general.

The pre-*ciz alap* was as long as 4:33. The *alap* after the *ciz* effectively ended by 12:40, but the 'two *alaps*' consumed half the total time of this *bara khyal* performance. In the pre-*ciz alap* (see Ex. 4–8) Latafat Husain explored the lower octave and showed off his excellent range, reaching down to Sa. (Note that in the transcription the durations are spaced as if against a pulse; no pulse was felt during this section, however.) This pre-*ciz alap* was subdivided by a *samalap* phrase which is derived from the *ciz mukhda*. It was sung to the syllables 'ri', 're', 'ne', and possibly 'le',

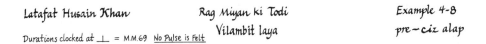

Latafat Husain Khan   Rag Miyan ki Todi   Example 4-8
                                              Vilambit laya   pre-ciz alap
Durations clocked at ⌐ = M.M.69   No Pulse is Felt

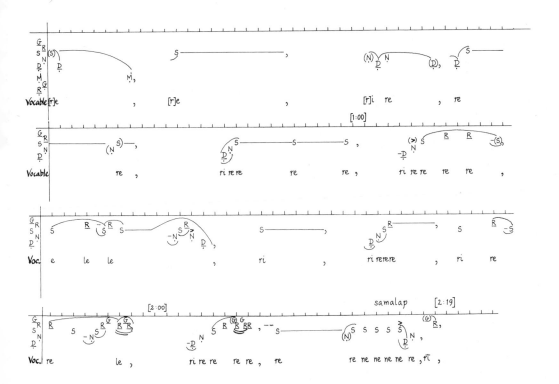

The manner in which Latafat Husain rendered the *ciz sthai* in the first two cycles of the *tala* of this performance serves as an example of how a singer of *khyal* can create the illusion of 'free' rhythm within the meter: in slow speed, the text and melody of the composition were rendered so indistinctly that it was difficult to distinguish the song from what preceded it. The text syllables are difficult to hear even when you know what they must be; in fact, the vocables of the pre-*ciz alap* were more clearly enunciated!

In terms of range, the melody in the first seven cycles of the *tala* was taken up only to Pa, so a good portion of the performance was devoted to *sthai* improvisation. *Antara* range was entered on *sthai* text. In cycle 9, the introduction of Dha and also Rè-Ni, indicates a contraction of the time taken to introduce new, higher pitches, as in Sharafat Husain's performances. Cycles 10–12 of *antara*-range improvisation are shown in Ex. 4–9. In cycles 13–14 Latafat Husain introduced the *antara* of the composition, then returned for the cadence to the *sthai mukhda*.

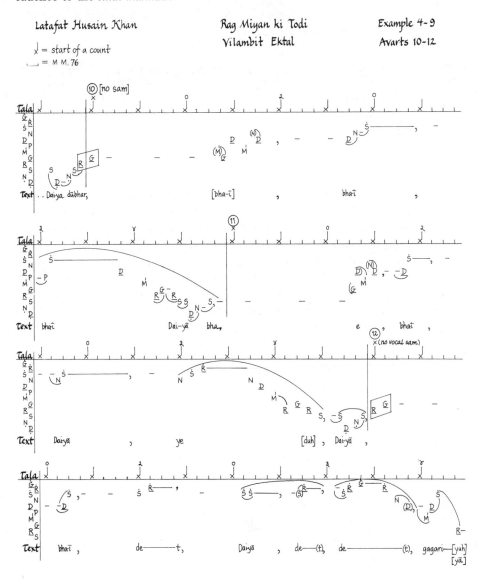

Latafat Husain Khan   Rag Miyan ki Todi   Example 4-9
                                       Vilambit Ektal   Avarts 10-12

𝄒 = start of a count
⌣ = M.M. 76

The words 'no *sam*' in the transcription in Ex. 4–9 indicate a characteristic of Latafat Husain's performance that distinguishes it decisively from Sharafat Husain's but relates it to Natthan Khan's: a preference for making texts fall *atit-anagat* to *sam* (Rampalal Mehta 1969: 38). In a total of thirty-five cycles in this Miyan ki Todi performance, Latafat Husain stopped his *mukhda* before *sam* (*atit*) nineteen times; twice he broke just at *sam* and sang the pitch just after *sam* (*anagat*); nine times he hit right on *sam*, but for two of those he took a quick breath just before, that caused one to think he would not hit *sam*; the first counts of the remaining five cycles he sang through without creating a cadence. An *atit* cadence is shown in Ex. 4–10a below and an *anagat* cadence in Ex. 4–10b.

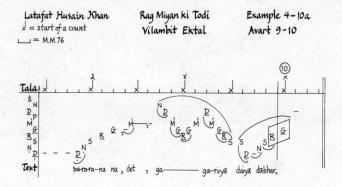

ba-ra-ra-na na, det ,   ga——————— ga—ri-yā dai-yā dūbhar,

Latafat Husain Khan   Rag Miyan ki Todi   Example 4-10b
ꭓ = start of a count   Vilambit Ektal   Avart 7-8
⌐⌐ = M.M.76

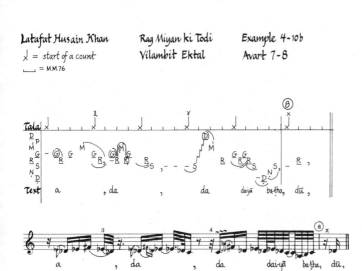

a   , da   ,   da   daiyā   ba-tha, dū ,

a   , da   ,   da   dai-yā   ba-tha, dū,

Latafat Husain's *nom-tom* came in cycles 16 and 17 and was created not by enunciation of the *ciz* text but by enunciation of the pitch syllables – by *sargam*. Since Latafat Husain placed rhythmically pulsating *sargam* at this strategic point in the *khyal* performance – when the *alap* is finished and rhythm becomes more prominent – and since this was the only occurrence of *sargam* in this performance, it would appear that he was using it as a type of *nom-tom*. Numerous non-Agra musicians sing *sargam* at this point in the performance structure. It is striking that the *sargam* syllables are similar to *nom-tom* vocables in that they are not linguistically meaningful.

The remainder of Latafat Husain's performance (cycles 18–35) can be characterized as follows: (1) contrast of sustained high-pitched melody with a rhythmic *bolbant* ending (two cycles' duration); (2) contrast of *gamak boltans*, to a rhythmic *bolbant* ending (see Ex. 4–11 below); (3) full cycles of *bolbant*; (4) *gamak* (jerky, heavy) *boltans* ending with the *mukhda*; and (5) fast vibrato *akar tans*, ending with the *mukhda*.

In an interview in 1978, Dipali Nag noted a 'jerky style' of the Agra *gharana*, referring possibly to a type of vocal production called *jhatka* that is described as 'jerky' or 'jagged'. Under (4) above it is noted that Latafat Husain rendered *boltans* with a *gamak*, or in a style that was heavy or jerky. In the *drut khyal* which followed the *khyal* described above, he produced *tans* with the same effect; this effect does not seem prominent in all Agra *gharana* singers' styles, however.

Ending a passage of *boltan* with a rhythmic *tihai* has been cited as a characteristic of Natthan Khan's style (Rampalal Mehta 1969: 38). In Ex. 4–11 such a passage is transcribed from this Rag Miyan ki Todi *khyal* by Latafat Husain. The *boltans* are of the type which have no rhythmic intricacy introduced by the *bols*; they might as well be *akar tans*.

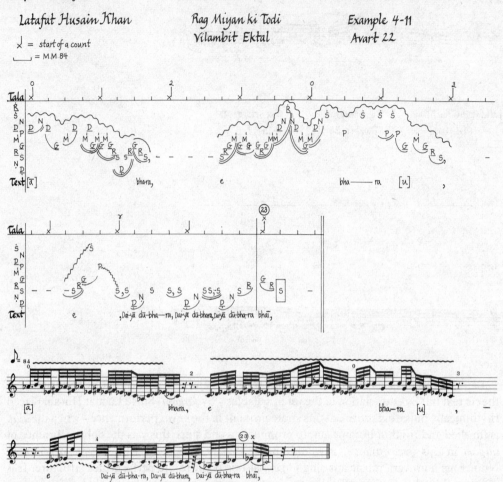

Latafat Husain Khan   Rag Miyan ki Todi   Example 4-11
                               Vilambit Ektal   Avart 22

Dipali Nag

From her musical performances it is clear that Dipali Nag takes very seriously the privilege she had of studying music along with the children of Agra *gharanedar*, for her *khyal* style manifests adherence to tradition. Her clarity of text, for example, and her utilization of the *ciz* text are exemplary.

While most *khyal* singers employ mostly the first phrase of the *ciz sthai* as text for melodic improvisation, Agra *gharana* singers are likely to improvise a great deal on the remainder of the *sthai* text as well. This was mentioned earlier for Faiyaz Khan and Sharafat Husain, and it is also demonstrated here in Table 4–1 where the text of an entire *khyal* performance is transcribed: 'Bhore hī āye' in Rag Lalit, as sung by Dipali Nag in an All-India Radio broadcast in 1968. The *mukhda* phrase 'Bhore hī ā [ye]' ('came early in the morning') is complemented by 'tuma alakha jagāye' ('you uttered a blessing'). While one published notation of this song has a *jogi* (ascetic) come early in the morning and utter the blessing (*Krāmik Pustak Mālikā*, iv, p. 508), Dipali Nag has made 'you' come to give the blessing, thereby making the song more personal.

TEXT 17

Sthai: भोरे ही आयें मोरे दुवारे तुम आके अलख जगायें ॥

Antara: सोहनी सूरत मोहनी मूरत नैना रसीले अलसाने ॥

Bhore hī āye

Sthai: You came early in the morning and awakened us by saying 'alakh' as soon as you arrived at the gate.

Antara: You are beautiful in appearance and attractive in body. Your eyes are beautiful and charming.

Table 4-1   Dipali Nag, parse of text 'Bhore ī āye' in Rag Lalit

Improvisation after the *ciz*	*Mukhda*	×
1 Bho'—re hī' ā' āye' āye' / bhore' bhore' bhore' ā' ————————→	bho' re hī'	ā
2 Bhore hī' / bhore hī / bho'—re hī āye / bhore hī' / bhore hī āye' āye' ā āye' bhore hī' /→	bhore hī'	ā
3 Bho'—ra hī ā' / bhore' bhore' bhore bho' re hī ā' / bhore hī ā' / bho'—re' hī ā—ye tum āy alakha' jagāye' jagāye' jāga————————→	bhore hī'	ā
4 Bhore' bhore' bhore' hī' ā' ye' / bhore hī' / ra hī' āye' tum āy alakha' / bhore' tum āy ala'—kha jagāye bhore' hī / ————————→	bhore hī'	ā
5 Bhore' hī' hī' / bhore hī' / bhore hī' / bho'—re hī' ā' ā' ȳe' tuma' alakha jagāye' / ala'—kha' jagāye————————→	bhore hī'	ā
6 Bhore hī' / bho'—re' hī ā'—ye' tuma' alakha' alakha' ja'—gā' gāye jagāye' alakha jagāye / ————————→	bho' re hī'	ā
7 Bhore' hī' / bho'—re' hī' tuma' alakha' jagāye' / alakha jagāye' / alakha jagāye' / alakha jagāye' / alakha jagāye tuma jagāye ————————→	bho' re hī'	ā
8 Bho'—re hī' jagāye' jagāye' jagāye' jagā' jā—gā' āye jagāye tuma alakha jagāye'————→	bhore hī'	ā
9 Jagāye' jagāye' jagā'—āye' jagā' ja—gāye tuma' tuma' alakha' jagāye' tum āy alakha jagāye' alakha jagāye ————————→	bho' re hī'	āye
10 Bhore' hī' ā' ā' ā' ā' āye' tuma' alakha jagāye' tum āy alakha jagāye ——→	bho' re hī'	ā tuma' āye'
11 Jagā' jagā' ja'—gā' jagā' jagā' jagāye / bhore hī ā' ————————→	bho' re hī'	āe
12 Jagā' jagā' jagā' ja' gā' ja' gā' jagāye' bhore' hī āye / jaga' ————————→	bho' re hī'	ā
13 Jagāye' jagā jagā' gāye' gāye' jagāye / bhore hī ā'—ye' / bho'—re' hī ā āye / bhore hī āye tum āy alakha jagāye / bhore hī' āye' tuma' ala'—kha jagāye / ANTARA: Sohanī sūrata' mū' mūrata' a' a mai' ke' sūrata laga'—āye' e' e'————————→	bho' re hī'	ā
14 Bhore hī ā' ā' ā' āye / bhore hī ā'—ye tu'—māy alakha jagāye' bhore hī āye tum āy alakha' / bhore hī āye tum āy alakha jagāye / bhore hī āye' ————————→	bhore hī'	ā
15 Bhore hī āye tum āy alakha jagāye' / bhore hī ā' / bhore hī āye tum āy alakha jagāye' / bhore hī āye tum ay alakha jagā' / bhore hī āye tum āy alakha' jagāye / bhore hī' āye' tuma' alakha' bhore hī āye / bhore hī āye' ————————→	bhore hī	ā
16 A' a' a' a' a' bhore hī āye tum āy alakha jagāye bhore hī' āye' āye' ————————→	bhore hī	ā//

Note: ' indicates breath; / indicates end of text phrase; → indicates *mukhda* follows.

The text was clear even in *alap* (*bolalap*), though it was not enunciated rhythmically before she wished it to be, and then most frequently at the end of a cycle, as the approach to *mukhda* drew near (as in Latafat Husain's performances). In Ex. 4–12 below, the transcription of the third textual unit shown in Table 4–1 demonstrates how she brought text, melodic motion toward the *mukhda*, and rhythm together by means of a textual *tihai* on 'jagā [ye]', the last word of the *ciz sthai*, even in the context of *bolalap*. The slow speed and her legato singing, and the focus on a few pitches (Nị Re Ga, resolving to Sa) in this *alap* context, combined with subtle use of the elements of test, rhythm, and meter, provide a beautiful example of how *bara khyal* is a genre distinct from *Dhrupad*, though sharing elements with it.

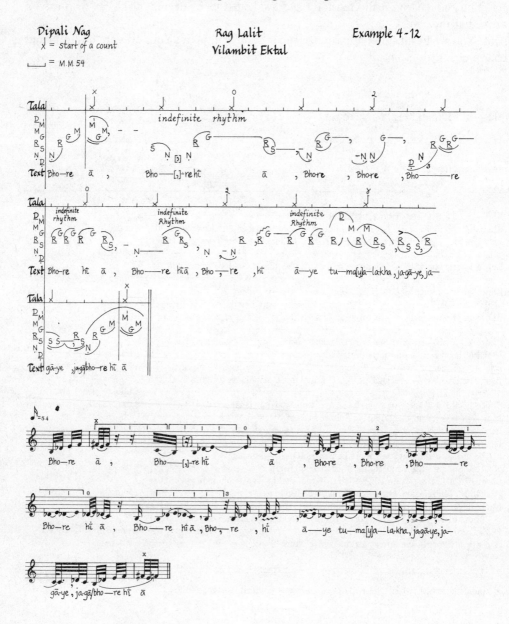

Use of the 'alakh jagāye' phrase increased in this *alap* as Dipali entered *antara* range, stressing pitch Dha in textual unit 6; she used this last portion of *sthai* text almost exclusively, until she sang the *ciz antara* in text unit 13. It appeared that she was preparing the way for the *ciz antara* by using the text phrases which immediately precede it. The textually dense unit 14 in Table 4–1 is the setting for *bolbant* which clearly demarcated the end of the *alap* portion of this *bara khyal* performance.

Dipali also uses the song text for *bolbant* and *tihai* in her *khyals*. She seems to prefer *akar tans* to *boltans*, thereby providing contrast to her use of the text, but there are no long stretches of dizzying *akar tans*. Nor is there cultivation of *sargam*. Clearly, the use of the *ciz* text is an important element in her style.

In accordance with the purest classical music ideals in Hindustani vocal music, Dipali Nag sings almost all of her *alap* with little ornamentation, offering reposeful, sustained tones graced only by a few pointed moments of vibrato. In the proper place – toward the end of the *alap* (as she ascended to Ni in the Rag Lalit performance, textual unit 7 in Table 4–1) – she begins to use her voice differently, giving 'color' with slow undulations within a pitch, at first purposefully narrow $\sim\!\!\wedge\!\!\wedge$ then wider $\sim\!\!\wedge\!\!\vee$ on pitch plateaux, a slow version of the *tan* style noted above for Sharafat Husain. She also sings *minds* connecting several pitches, which is startling, because *minds* are not a cultivated element of Agra style. Apart from *minds*, it would not be possible to mistake Dipali Nag's *khyal* performances for those of any other *gharana*; hers is the Agra tradition in the line of Natthan Khan, Faiyaz Khan, and Bashir Ahmed Khan.

Vilayat Hussain Khan

It is recounted in Garg (1957: 354) that when Vilayat Hussain was ten years old he sang in performance under the wing of his more musically established cousin Faiyaz Khan: he sang *dhrupad* and *hori* and *nom-tom* in a low and strong voice. Listeners were astonished, we are told, and uttered the exclamation of praise 'vah-vah'. Chaudhuri, similarly tells how a program would open with Vilayat Hussain singing *dhrupad* and *dhamar*, and then Faiyaz would take the platform. It is pertinent that Vilayat Hussain was firmly grounded in *dhrupad* singing because his son Yunus Husain, commenting (Interview: 1978) that his father sang *alap* in *khyal* before singing the *ciz*, explained that this was due to his experience in singing *dhrupad* (thus implying that it was not due to the influence of Faiyaz Khan).

Vilayat Hussain's performance of *khyal* was credited with such qualities as 'neatness', 'beautifully-proportioned form' and 'dramatic contrasts'. More particular to the Agra *gharana* he was lauded for his *boltan* and rhythmic play (V. H. Deshpande 1973: 42); Desphande upbraided him, however, for 'neglect of *svara*' (1973: 43).

Vilayat Hussain was noted for an unrivalled repertoire: 'The stock of classical songs of varied form and styles, in an almost unbelievable number of Ragas – both rare and better-known – he had at his disposal, was in itself an achievement which could bring distinction and all-around recognition to any musician of Hindustan' (Pant 1966: 1). Among those *ragas* were rare ones, which he was noted for popularizing. Included in his repertoire were many of his own compositions, written under his *mudra* 'Pran Piya'. Among the most famous are 'Man moha lino Shyām Sundar Ne' in Rag Raisa-Kanhra, 'Ajhu na Āye Shyām' in Rag Anandi, and 'Main vārī vārī Jāūngī' in Rag Yaman (see Chaudhuri 1966: 3 and Rampalal Mehta 1969).

Plate 6   Vilayat Hussain Khan of the Agra *gharana* (right), author of *Saṅgītajñoṅ ke Samsma-ran*, in a practice session, with Latafat Husain Khan (left front) (photo by permission of the Sangeet Natak Akademi, New Delhi)

Yunus Husain Khan

It is striking that commentaries on the singing of Vilayat Hussain's son Yunus Husain rarely relate his style to his father's or to Faiyaz Khan's, or, for that matter, to any other specific Agra *gharana* predecessors (see *Times of India*, December 19, 1970, for one exception). He is very much like his father, however, in his love and talent for composition. Under the *mudra* 'Darpan' he composes songs in *raga*s he created, as well as new compositions in traditional *raga*s. Some of his *raga*s are Nauhar Todi, Sujani Malhar, Dev Yani, Jogwanti, Lalita Sohini, and Hussaini Bhairav. He clearly enjoys performing his own compositions.

In some respects, Yunus Husain has asserted his own musical preferences. Two are striking, given his Agra tradition. First, his rejection of Faiyaz Khan's relatively lengthy pre-*ciz alap*: 'It is propaganda that Agra sings *alap* before the *bandish*'. Perhaps with these words he was trying to declare his independence from Faiyaz, since he stated unequivocally (Interview: 1978) that it was Faiyaz who initiated that Agra custom.

According to his own statement (Interview: 1978), Yunus Husain prefers not to sing very slowly: 'If you sing very slowly, you can't enjoy the *tala* and percussion'. His enjoyment of percussion constitutes the second respect in which Yunus Husain expresses his own musical preference: in some of his performances the *tabla* player is a partner rather than a time-keeper. In a performance of Rag Lalita Gauri in 1969, for example, the *tabla* player initiated the *chota khyal* in the active manner of an instrumental performance. Then in that same performance Yunus Husain challenged the *tabla* player, Sardar Khan, in *dhrupad*-like simultaneous rhythmic improvisation as he sang *sargam-layakari*. He made a similar challenge to the *tabla* player Ghulam Ahmed Khan in the *chota khyal* portion of a performance of Rag Shudh Sarang, broadcast on All-India Radio (December 8, 1969). While this is extraordinary in *khyal*, where the *tabla* player is usually a keeper of the *tala*, it is significant to note that Yunus Husain, like his Agra predecessors, was keeping his *khyal* 'close to *dhrupad*'.

Yunus Husain's performances of *khyal* differ greatly from each other. In most performances one hears a great deal of *sargam*, in some none at all (e.g. in his Sujani Malhar recording). In most performances one hears *bolbant* (but not particularly intricate rhythmically); in some no *bolbant* (again, the Sujani Malhar recording exemplifies this). In some performances his *tans* are both *boltans* and *akar tans*; in others only *akar tans*. In the Sujani Malhar performance, there is a more conscientious *alap* than is usual for Yunus Husain; more usually his *raga* improvisation retains the image of the composition relatively clearly. Yunus Husain could perhaps be dubbed a creative musician who emphasizes individuality within tradition.

Summary

A characteristic frequently cited for Agra *gharana* performances – the lengthy *pre-ciz alap* – dates from Faiyaz Khan and seems to be considered an option rather than a necessity by musicians of the present generation.

In presenting the *ciz* in *bara khyal*, Agra artists seem to act as predicted: they present the entire composition. Particularly in slow-speed performances, they place the *ciz antara* within *antara ke alap*, or as closure for it, thus avoiding serious interruption of the *alap*-style development of the *raga* at the outset (this they share with Gwalior artists). In *chota khyal*, the *sthai* and *antara* are either presented together at the beginning, or the *ciz antara* is sung after quite considerable improvisation on the *sthai*.

Keeping *khyal* performances 'close to *dhrupad*' is the characteristic cited most often for the Agra *gharana* style. Emphasis on *laya* is a prime factor in this, and it is maintained in the following ways: (1) *boltan*; (2) *bolbant*; (3) use of a large proportion of the text provided by the *ciz*; 4) and a variety of ways of skilfully approaching *sam*, including (a) *tihai* and (b) *atit-anagat* approaches; 5) *nom-tom* and *nom-tom*-like rhythmic emphasis; and 6) a lively relationship between singer and *tabla* player. Different Agra artists use a different selection of these, and to different extents.

The first three features are text-related; since improvisation on a *dhrupad* is text-oriented, they could indeed be seen as characteristic 'close to *dhrupad*'. *Boltan* is a synthesis of elements from the two sets of musical associations – *dhrupad*/text and *khyal*/tan. *Boltans* have been mentioned in Natthan Khan's 'repertoire', and they seem to have been a consistent feature in the singing of generations of Agra singers.

Also relating to text treatment is the general statement about Agra style that texts are clearly enunciated. This statement usually intends a comparison of this *gharana*'s regard for text to that of other *gharanas*, in which texts are unintelligible, relatively speaking, this generalization seems accurate. Analysis of performances suggests a refinement, however: enunciation of the text is willfully employed for musical ends as, for example, in performances by Latafat Husain Khan.

Bolbant has been cited for Natthan Khan, Abdullah Khan, Faiyaz Khan, and Vilayat Hussain Khan in the 'older' generations of Agra singers. In a consideration of a limited selection of performances by Sharafat Husain Khan and Yunus Husain Khan, however, *bolbant* does not appear to be a predominant element; what *bolbant* there is is not markedly intricate.

Enjoyment of rhythmic play and *tala* has been observed for Natthan Khan, Abdullah Khan, and Faiyaz Khan, in terms of 'coming well to *sam*'. Natthan Khan, by his choice of *ciz*, and, two generations later, Latafat Husain Khan, by his performance practice, favor coming to *sam atit* or *anagat*; also characteristic of Natthan Khan, and heard in performance by Latafat Husain, is the sequence of *boltan* leading to *tihai* (as far as I know, however, Latafat Husain did not study with Natthan, who died in 1900 or 1901). The extent to which rhythmic play is likely to be carried on in *chota khyal* (i.e., in fast speed) in the performances of Agra *gharana* musicians is also evidence that they were wholly at ease with *tala* and *laya*.

With respect to other elements in Agra *gharana khyal* improvisation, only a few generalizations are possible at this point. The above selection of performances showed *sargam* used by only two artists – Yunus Husain Khan and Latafat Husain Khan; it does not seem to be a consistent or important element in the form. With respect to style, the shape of *tans* does not appear to be particularly distinctive, either as cited in commentaries or heard in performances. Several performers sang *tans* featuring plateaux, which are created by pitches prolonged with a *gamak*; this does not seem to be distinctive of the Agra style. Dipali Nag's comment (Interview: 1978) that fast *tan* singing is not cultivated in Agra style is pertinent; no Agra artists seem to emphasize virtuoso display through speedy *tans*, although they certainly can and do produce fast *tans*. Rather, a relatively slow speed of *tans* seems to be their characteristic. While V. H. Desphande (1973) spoke of the slow *tans* of Faiyaz Khan, comments about the *tans* of his predecessors tend to mention clarity and flexibility rather than speed; this appears to be pertinent for the styles of Faiyaz Khan and of recent Agra artists.

The cultivation of a powerful voice and aggressive singing style (the lack of *minds*, for example) seem to have been important in Agra *gharana* training. The gruff vocal quality of Faiyaz Khan, cited often as 'the Agra vocal quality', does not seem to be characteristic.

The interest in composition of a number of Agra *gharana* musicians is distinctive, and particularly so when the relative age of the *gharana* is considered, for they could have been content with a body of traditional compositions. The varied repertoire of types of music they have preferred is also a vigorous element in their tradition.

Performance characteristics and preferences of individual Agra *gharana* artists have, of course, been important. Major individual contributions such as those of Ghagghe Khuda Baksh, Ghulam Abbas Khan, Natthan Khan, and Faiyaz Khan seem to have been absorbed into the tradition, but a few comments about more individualistic traits have also been noted above. Rare *ragas* were enjoyed by Ghagghe Khuda Baksh, and many years afterwards by Vilayat Hussain, and the creation of new ones by Yunus Husain. For Abdullah Khan, long *tans* in one breath have been noted. For Faiyaz Khan and Vilayat Hussain Khan, the large and varied nature of their repertoire is impressive. Dipali Nag sings relatively more examples of *mind*, while Latafat Husain Khan is likely to exploit the 'jerky *gamak*' that is also produced by a group of Gwalior *gharana* artists. Latafat Husain and Yunus Husain sing *sargam*, while Sharafat Husain and Yunus Husain enjoy interplay with the *tabla* player in the ensemble.

From commentaries on Agra *gharana* artists' styles, and from analysis of performances, one perceives a cohesive tradition. This consists of a propensity for composition, strong vocal production, and a balanced sense of proportion in structuring performances, with cultivation of rhythmic elements and utilization of the *ciz* text as two particularly distinguishing characteristics. Most of these are ways in which Agra *khyal* performances have been kept 'close to *dhrupad*'.

5 Sahaswan/Rampur

The context

The Sahaswan of Rampur *khyal gharana* was developed by musicians from Sahaswan (primarily) who received patronage at Rampur. Both places are in the east of the modern state of Uttar Pradesh: Sahaswan is a large village in the Badayun district which bounds Rampur on the south. From Sahaswan/Badayun many distinguished musicians from a group of interrelated families have come, among them those who were responsible for the development of a *gharana* at Rampur. Their familial and professional network has included the cities and regions of Lucknow, Atrauli (Aligarh district), Gwalior, Nepal, Baroda, and, most decisively, Rampur.

The princely state of Rampur had its origins in the tangled political history of the seventeenth and eighteenth centuries. Two Afghani brothers, Shah Alam and Husain Khan, arrived in the subcontinent in the latter part of the seventeenth century to seek service under the Mughal emperor. Shah Alam's son, Daud Khan, was very successful in this, and in 1719 Daud's adopted son, Ali Mohammad, received the title of *nawab* and a grant of the greater part of Rohilkhand, which encompassed Rampur.

In 1745 Ali Mohammad incurred the wrath of Safdarjung, the powerful *subahdar* of the neighbouring kingdom of Oudh who was a powerful ally of the Mughal ruler (called Protector). Ali Mohammad was forced to relinquish his lands. However, as a result of the power struggles in Delhi upon the death of the Mughal Muhammad Shah in 1748, Ali Mohammad's lands were returned to him. On his own death, his estates were divided among his sons, and the *jagir* (land grant) of Rampur went to a younger son, Faiz-ullah Khan. In 1793 Faiz-ullah died and there was dissent within the family, which resulted in the murder of Faiz-ullah's eldest son. The British and the powerful ruler of Oudh intervened and installed Ahmad Ali Khan, Faiz-ullah's grandson and the son of his murdered eldest son.

In 1857, the politically decisive year when several rulers of princely states attempted revolt against the British, the Nawab of Rampur, Muhammad Yusuf Ali Khan, allied with the British. For his loyalty he was awarded more land and an increased gun salute. He was succeeded by his son, Muhammad Kalve Ali Khan, who was followed briefly by his son, Mushtaq Ali (1887–9), who was in turn succeeded by his son, Hamid Ali Khan, then a minor. As *nawab*, Hamid Ali Khan Bahadur became one of the great patrons of the arts; it was under his patronage that the Sahaswan/Rampur *khyal gharana* developed.

Rampur is situated slightly to the north and east of Delhi, a drive of four to five hours through the towns of Ghaziabad, Moradabad, and Bareilly (Bareli) on the road to Lucknow (once the capital of Oudh). It is like a small city, trim at the perimeter as if it had once been surrounded by walls, and graced with entrance gates in Mughal style. From the road that almost encircles it, the aspect of Rampur is dominated by the domes and spires of the palace in the 'fort', which once was the residence of the *nawabs* but now houses the renowned Raza

132

Library. The 'fort', the central focus of the town, was obviously built less for purposes of defense than for providing a central princely residence and government complex. The fort walls are neither particularly high nor particularly formidable, and the buildings inside manifest no suggestions of martial preparedness. Their yellow and white façades, almost rococo in design, lie in a spacious, well-planned complex that could have been a university instead of a government administrative center. Around the walls of the fort is a bustling and incredibly crowded bazaar, where pedestrians, bicyclists, and rickshaw-walas make it perfectly clear to the occasional automobile driver that his presence is inappropriate and unappreciated. Buses are parked alongside the fort wall, but, even though one can see them, it is hard to believe that they are really there and could move among the crowds.

During the period 1911–31, when the British shifted their headquarters in India from Calcutta back to Delhi and began constructing a new capital, New Delhi, one of their intentions was to establish a firmer and more centrally located presence in India. Indian nationalist movements were springing up throughout the country, and the British Raj was determined to avoid a repeat of the 'mutinous' events of 1857. Throughout the Indian countryside one can see the architectural results of the concerted early twentieth-century efforts of the British to remove key *rajas* and *sultans* and *nawabs* from their residences in the centers of each city and state – new palaces in outlying 'suburbs', hidden from view by spacious grounds, edifices in which the classic Indian concepts of space and aesthetics were replaced (sometimes successfully) by combinations of Western and Indian spatial and aesthetic characteristics.

During the decentralization process in the 1920s the Raza family, the rulers of Rampur, moved to a new palace on the outskirts of Rampur. The change of aesthetic in the new palace bears eloquent testimony to the change of life brought about by an endorsement of the British presence, for the extremely large, long building resembles the red sandstone governmental structures of New Delhi. One entry into the palace is made through a high-ceilinged room of marble dominated by a staircase: architecturally one has left India for Europe. Hallways lined with mirrors alternate with hallways wainscoted in dark wood; an enormous dining-room is decorated with French paintings of the nineteenth and early twentieth centuries; a large 'living-room' is filled with overstuffed sofas and chairs and decorated with portraits of King George V and Queen Mary; a reception room is lined with portraits of the Rampur *nawab*s.

The largest entry portico of the palace leads to the throne room. From the throne (crystal, on a slightly raised Indian-style platform of carved white marble) at the far end, one looks out at a large rectangular room with pillars down either side creating aisles and at the *zenana* above, an enclosed balcony from which the women could watch any proceedings in privacy. In front of each pillar is a seating arrangement of three chairs around a small table; nowadays a rolled-up carpet is laid over a few chairs. One had the impression in 1978 that the carpet could be unrolled, the lights switched on, and normal court life resumed.

Completely Western in conception is one room in this palace designed specifically for performances of various sorts. The chair for the *nawab* in the rear, under a wall-decoration of a violin (or guitar?), faces a wooden floor (for roller-skating, I was told) of parquet design and a raised theatrical stage with a multi-colored lighting system, curtain, etc. Here it was that music, dancing, and theatrical productions took place.

Both palaces of the *nawab*s of Rampur once hosted glorious performances of music and dance patronized by rulers who were themselves well-trained musicians. When in 1857 the renowned artistic patronage of Wajid Ali Shah of Lucknow (Oudh) ended, the Rampur Nawab Kalve Ali, advised by his younger brother Haider Ali, was determined to establish at Rampur a musical *darbar* equal to that which had existed at Lucknow. This the brothers did under the leadership of their *ustad*, the great *sursringar* player Bahadur Hussein Khan, and his nearest relative by marriage, Amir Khan, *dhrupad/dhamar* singer and *bin* player. Musicians they employed included Mohammad Hussein Khan (*bin* player), Boniyat Hussain Khan (*sarangi* player), who left Gwalior to assume the position in Rampur, singers of *khyal*, *thumri*, and *tappa*, and also *sarod* players and others (Roy Choudhary 1973: 6).

Kalve Ali Khan ruled for about twenty years (1860–80?). In the following period the state was for some years under direct rule of the government; during the interregnum Bahadur Hussein Khan, Amir Khan, and some of their disciples were taken under the wing of Haider Ali at his *zamindārī* (estate) in Cilsi, to the south of Rampur. When the next *nawab*, Hamid Ali, was installed in Rampur in 1889, he was only fourteen; his uncle Haider Ali assisted him in re-establishing a coterie of performing artists at court and Hamid Ali gained full power in 1896. The chief disciple of Bahadur Hussein and Amir Khan, Wazir Khan, a direct descendant of Tansen and a fine *bin* player (Ratanjanker 1967: 40), went to Rampur around 1900 to be chief court musician. Haider Ali's son, Sadat Ali (called Chhamman Saheb), who had also become an accomplished musician, went to Rampur to be Home Secretary of State, and in music had almost the same position as Wazir Khan (Roy Choudhary 1973: 7).

Under Nawab Hamid Ali Khan some of India's greatest musicians practiced their art; Wazir Khan, *bin* player and *dhrupadiya*, and his students Allauddin Khan and Hafiz Ali Khan; *bin* players Mohammad Hussein Khan and Nabi Baksh; *sarod* player Fida Hussein Khan; *rebab* player Mohammad Ali Khan; *sarangi* player Bundu Khan; *sitar* players Hafiz Khan and Karim Khan; the great *tabla* player Ahmed Jan Thirakwa; and Kathak dancers such as Acchan Maharaj and Kalka Prasad (N. R. Singh 1964: 10). Bhaiyya Ganpat Rao, famous for his harmonium playing, also resided at the Rampur court for a time. The leading singers were Kale Nazir Khan, Haider Khan, Inayat Hussein Khan, and Mushtaq Hussein Khan. 'All-night performances were a nightly routine at Rampur and on special occasions, musicians of repute from other parts of the country would be invited to participate in the jashans [festivities]' (N. R. Singh 1964: 10–11).

After the death of Hamid Ali, his son Raza Ali Khan became *nawab*; he continued the Rampur court's patronage of musicians, and musical festivities. The advent of the rainy season (*sawan*) was one such traditional time of celebration, for the rain-clouds offered relief from the searing heat and choking dust-storms of summer. Mushtaq Hussein Khan, the *khyal* singer, reflected on the *sawan* season in Rampur (N. R. Singh 1964: 22):

'It is beyond me to describe the joy and the grandeur of the *Sawan* festivities of Rampur of those days. Famous musicians gathered in the gardens and parks of the Nawab's palace, and there were veritable feasts of *Malhars* and *Kajris* [songs]'.

On one such occasion, when it had not rained for a good many days, Nawab Raza Ali Khan remarked, 'In spite of so much of *Malhar* [rag], the weather remains unaffected'. He smiled and said, 'Let us see if Mushtaq Hussain's *Malhar* can persuade the weather to melt in mercy'. Mushtaq Hussain Khan complied promptly, after uttering a silent prayer to his *Pir* and began singing a *Malhar*. He became so deeply engrossed in the music that he did not even notice that there was a bustle in the gathering. It actually started to rain! Very modestly, Khan Sahib says 'It was only a coincidence, of course, but even so, it was an unforgettable experience of my life!'

It is important to note the exceptional degree of personal involvement of the *nawab*s and members of their family in music in Rampur (similar to that of Wajid Ali Shah in Lucknow, in Oudh). One reads, for instance, how Nawab Kalve Ali Khan may have influenced the performance style of the traditional musicians in his employ when he 'asked Bahadur Hussain and Amir Khan to display in *sursringar*, *veena*, and *dhrupad* with the same charm as was achieved by the best female vocalists in India . . . Bahadur Hussain achieved this in his *sursringar* display and Amir Khan in his *dhamar* songs' (*sic*: not in *vīṇā* music and *dhrupad*) (Roy Choudhary 1973: 6).

The ruling family of Rampur seems to have been involved not only in musical patronage but also in performance. Nawab Hamid Ali's musical expertise appears to have been systematic and theoretical. Atiya Begum reports a visit to Rampur in 1924 when His Highness Hamid Ali Khan 'expounded the 13 Todis, 18 varieties of Kanhra, 4 of Bhiraon, and 14 of Kalian, rendered the extinct tals (time) of Brahma, Rudra, Shiva, and also the four classical styles of Natch (dancing)' (1942: Foreword). Facing a patron of such knowledge, 'even top-ranking musicians shuddered at the thought of having to perform before him. His practised ears would detect the slightest deviation. Nor would he hesitate or lose time to take the defaulting artiste to task' (N. R. Singh 1964: 10).

Active involvement in musical activities, interest in the systematic approach to music, and patronization by Rampur royalty of the finest traditional musicians all coincided at one 'moment' in the modern musical history of North India in the 1910s – when V. N. Bhatkhande was present in Rampur. Like the eloquently different styles of palace architecture, this 'moment' typified the meeting of tradition and change in the sphere of music (the situation is described in Ratanjankar 1967: 35–43).

Bhatkhande was a Brahmin Hindu musicologist whose musical interests lay in systematizing and theorizing about modern Hindustani (rather than primarily ancient Indian) music on the basis of what was being practiced. To accomplish this he procured from traditional musicians songs that had been transmitted orally and harbored in their families from generation to generation. Many musicians regarded these as personal property, to be treasured and taught only to those disciples of their choosing, even within the family. Bhatkhande also treasured the songs, as a means of learning about *raga*s, but he saw them as part of the musical heritage of the culture at large, songs which should be shared by all (lest they be lost) through the means of musical notation. He procured the songs in diverse ways: sometimes they were taught to him willingly by musicians who endorsed his efforts; sometimes musicians were required by patrons to 'give' them to him. The latter was the case in Rampur.

The ruler of Rampur, Hamid Ali, became acquainted with Bhatkhande's work in music through two sources – through a respected vocalist in his employ, Kale Nazir Khan, and also through the *taluqdar* (landlord) of a neighboring region in Uttar Pradesh, one Raja Nawab Ali, who had earlier been responsible for Kale Nazir Khan's knowledge of Bhatkhande's work. Nawab Hamid Ali invited the Hindu *pandit* to Rampur, and many discussions of theory ensued. 'Naturally there was some resistance . . . as Rampur was one of the purest strongholds of conservative and uninterrupted classical tradition' (Ratanjankar 1967: 41, 40). But gradually Bhatkhande converted the *nawab* to his point of view, with the results related below, in the words of Ratanjankar, whose loyalty is clearly to Bhatkhande rather than to the traditional musicians who must have found nothing humorous or comic in them (contrary to Ratanjankar's suggestion) and to whom 'new ideas' were a threat to their art and way of life.

There is an interesting and true anecdote about Bhatkhande's stay and work in Rampur. It illustrates not only his devotion to music but his practical sense which was fully aware of the prevailing atmosphere of prejudice and suspicion against new ideas. He was a shrewd man of the world and knew how to get round difficulties smoothly, sometimes comic and sometimes humorous, which came in the way. Ustad Wazir Khan was the Guru of the Nawab and he had a large collection of original Dhrupads and Horis of great value as they had been transmitted from the time of Tansen. Naturally Wazir Khan did not like to give these compositions to Bhatkhande as he considered them to be a precious treasure of his family. However, though Wazir Khan was the Guru of the Nawab, he was also the Durbar musician and therefore the Nawab's employee.

Pandit Bhatkhande thought carefully over the situation and ultimately decided that the best way to secure his object was to get the cooperation and help of the Nawab Sahib. The Nawab was himself a very good musician. He decided to become the pupil and disciple of the Nawab, which the Nawab naturally considered a great honour, because in those days to become or accept a disciple was an important formal occasion and it conferred great honour on the Guru when he had as disciple a personality like Bhatkhande. Panditji began to take lessons from the Nawab and after some days requested him that he was very keen that the treasures of the Rampur tradition should be recorded by notation in the music books so that they will be permanently available to music-lovers. The Nawab enthusiastically agreed with the idea and ordered Wazir Khan to give Pandit Bhatkhande whatever he wanted. Wazir Khan had no option when his employer ordered him to do this and Bhatkhande thus got the priceless collection of Dhrupads and Horis of the Senia Gharana. It is a humorous illustration of what stratagems he had to resort to in order to achieve his laudable and noble objective. Needless to say he had great regard for the Nawab Sahib, his guru (Ratanjankar 1967: 41–2).

To artists who pleased him, Nawab Hamid Ali was extremely generous in distributing rewards. The great Wazir Khan 'lived like a prince in a palace with sentries at the gate' (Shankar 1973: 11). Mushtaq Hussein Khan recalled those days at Rampur with nostalgia. Tears would come to his eyes as he remembered the wonderful music of the great masters, and 'with utter humility he confesse[d], "I am but what Rampur made of me – a pale shadow of the galaxy of masters who adorned the Court of Nawab Hamid Ali Khan"' (N. R. Singh 1964: 11).

Musicians of the Sahaswan/Rampur *gharana*

The chief *khyal* singers at the Rampur court were Mahbub Khan, his son Inayat Hussein Khan (1849–1919), Inayat's brother-in-law Haider Khan (1857–1927), and Mushtaq Hussein Khan (d. 1964), who was son-in-law successively to both Haider Khan and Inayat Hussein Khan. All these singers were related both by blood or marriage and by musical training (see Charts 5–1 and 5–2); they were of the Sahaswan *gharana*, named for their ancestral home Sahaswan.[1]

The members of the Sahaswan families of musicians have consistently received training from each other, as shown in Chart 5–1. The only outsiders listed among the teachers in the biographical sources were the *bin* (and *sursringar* and *rebab*) players and *dhrupad* singers Bahadur Hussein Khan and later his grand-nephew Wazir Khan (1860–1927), both of whom

---

[1] Dates and relationships shown in Charts 5–1 and 5–2 are derived from the following sources: Garg 1957: 107–8, 211–12, 220–1, 299–301, 403–4; Agarwala 1966: 27; N. R. Singh 1964: 1, 4, 5, 20, and family tree chart; Wadhera 1978: 14; Vasudev 1964; and Misra 1952: 20. The only discrepancies among these sources are the dates of Mushtaq Hussein's birth and the relationship of Inayat Hussein Khan to Haider Khan. Vasudev (1964) cites Mushtaq Hussein as saying that Haider was Inayat Hussein's nephew, but Garg (1957: 403) says that Inayat Hussein married Haider to his sister.

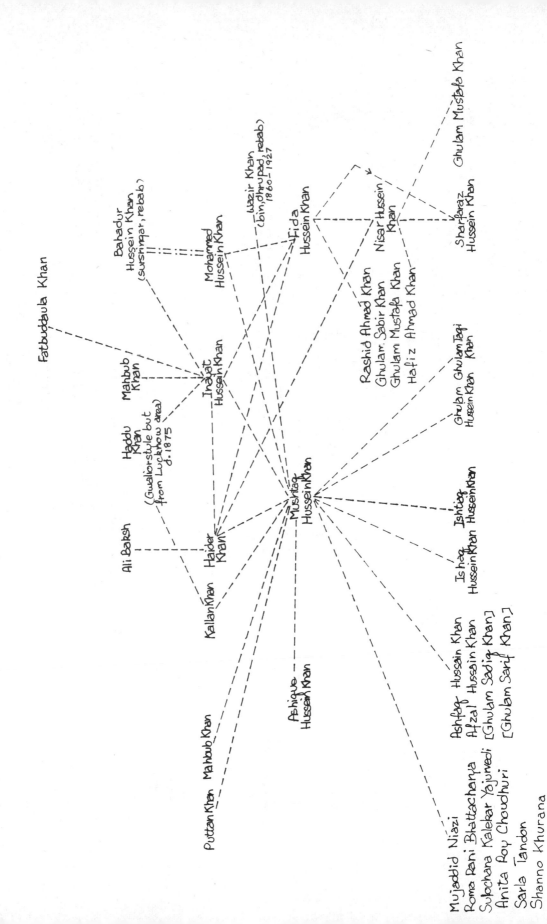

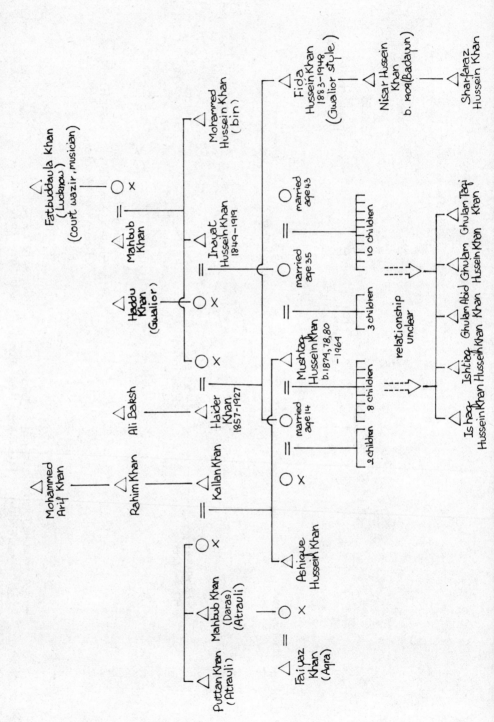

Chart 5-2: Sahaswan Gharana Blood Lines

served under Rampur *nawab*s, and Haddu Khan (d. 1875), of the Gwalior *gharana*. Haddu taught both Kallan Khan and Inayat Hussein Khan.

Inayat Hussein Khan

While it has been established that Inayat Hussein Khan studied with Haddu Khan of the Gwalior *gharana*, it is important to establish whether or not his basic intensive training was in the Gwalior style. It seems that it was not. Naina Singh asserts that 'Enayat Hussain Khan started his career as the son-in-law of the famous Ustad Haddu Khan of Gwalior. But his real master was Ustad Bahadur Hussain Khan, a direct descendant of Mian Tansen' (1964: 5). What she means by 'real master' is intimated by an anecdote both she and the Garg article (1957: 107) relate: as a disciple of Bahadur Hussein, Inayat Hussein concentrated for four years just on rendering pitches correctly and for two-and-a-half (or five) years after that on only Rag Gaur Sarang. Garg (1957: 108) suggests – by a paragraph change – that Inayat Hussein studied with Haddu Khan after he had finished his period of prolonged training, i.e., when he was travelling. In Gwalior he went to the home of Hassu and Haddu Khan and they, being pleased with Inayat Hussein's *gayaki*, married him to a daughter. After this event he began to receive training but *only for a short while*; no details of that training are given. Inayat Hussein entered service first in Rampur and then in several other courts (probably because of the death of Nawab Kalve Ali Khan), settling finally in Hyderabad.

Because Inayat Hussein received instruction from Haddu Khan (however brief), Sahaswan vocalists tend to be listed among Gwalior *gharana* musicians (see, for example, Agarwala 1966: 27). Little is made of the 'fact' that another singer of the same generation as Inayat Hussein also studied with Haddu Khan – Kallan Khan, father of the great Mushtaq Hussein Khan. There does not seem to have been reinforcement of Gwalior *gayaki* by Gwalior musicians instructing successive generations of Sahaswan singers.

Inayat Hussein Khan, with his Gwalior style and his training (from Tansen) in the Seni tradition, was the most important teacher among the Sahaswan musicians of his generation. Relatives from two lines went to him – Mushtaq Hussein Khan from one line and Haider Khan, and then Haider's son Fida Hussein Khan, from the other line. While Mushtaq Hussein and Haider remained tied to the Rampur court, Fida Hussein (and later his son) made a career as a court musician in Baroda and is thus referred to as being 'of Baroda'.

Haider Khan

Haider Khan (1857–1927), of the same Sahaswan generation as Kallan Khan and only eight years younger than Inayat Hussein, for some reason did not study with Haddu Khan. He trained with his father, Ali Baksh, and then with Inayat Hussein. Haider began his career as a court singer in Rampur. While the life of musicians at a generous court is usually described in idyllic terms, the death of their patron could create difficult circumstances. On the death of Nawab Kalve Ali Khan, Haiden Khan, Inayat Hussein, and several other Rampur musicians joined the service of Maharaja Shamsher Janga Bahadur in Nepal. Some of the Rampur musicians, among them Haider Khan, returned to Rampur when court patronage resumed under Hamid Ali Khan. Toward the end of Haider Khan's life, he lived and taught in Bombay.

Fida Hussein Khan

Fida Hussein Khan (1883–1948) was initiated into musical training by his father Haider Khan and then received training from Inayat Hussein Khan and from Inayat Hussein's brother Mohammad Hussein Khan, a *bin* player of the Seni tradition. At first Fida Hussein's voice was considered poor and *ustad*s did not want to work with him, but with diligent practice of only *svar* and exercises through every night for ten years, he gradually developed musical competence. He became a court musician in Baroda, where he served for twenty years; there he was the equal of Faiyaz Khan of the Agra *gharana*. In 1940–1 he was in Rampur for a short stint of service, after which he became a radio artist, and retired finally to his ancestral home in Badayun.

The students of Fida Hussein Khan manifest both a dissolution and a continuity of tradition. Ghulam Sabir Khan apparently became a *sarangi* player, while Ghulam Mustafa Khan, a respected singer, is said to have been influenced greatly by Amir Khan (*Times of India*, 1968g). Hafiz Ahmed Khan, who was also a student of Nisar Hussein Khan, an accomplished singer of *khyal* and *tarana*, is now one of the best-known musicians of this tradition.

Mushtaq Hussein Khan

The attribution of the Gwalior style to Sahaswan musicians continued with Mushtaq Hussein Khan (1874, 1878 or 1880–1964). Susheela Misra (1952: 20) cites three requisites of Gwalior-style *khyal* singing, and then says of Mushtaq Hussein: 'he is easily the best exponent

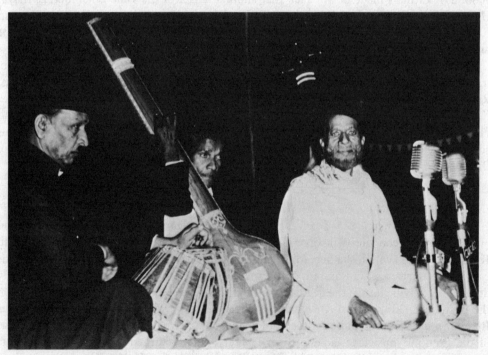

Plate 7   Mushtaq Hussein Khan of the Sahaswan *gharana* (right), with the *tabla* player Ahmed Jan Thirakwa (left) (photo by permission of the Sangeet Natak Akademi, New Delhi)

of Gwalior Gayaki today'. Uma Vasudev (1964) reported an interview with the *ustad*: 'In view of the several inspirations that went into his work I was anxious to have it confirmed from his own lips where, among the ramifications of *gharanas*, he would put his style. He was confident enough in his assessment of his contribution to this field to say that it should be termed after the place of his birth: "The Sahaswan *gharana*, of course." But he traced his ancestry to the time and house of Tansen'.

Mushtaq Hussein was initiated into musical training at the age of ten by his father, Kallan Khan, and was also taught by his older brother, Ashique Hussein Khan. Then followed a series of *ustads*: Haider Khan in Nepal, and his maternal uncles Mahbub Khan and Puttan Khan of Atrauli, who supervised his training until he was summoned to Rampur by Inayat Hussein Khan. He then accompanied Inayat Hussein to Hyderabad for a further ten or eleven years of study. Mushtaq Hussein also studied with Inayat Hussein's brother, Mohammad Hussein Khan, a *bin* player, and with Wazir Khan, a *bin* player and *dhrupadiya* in Rampur.

Mushtaq Hussein Khan became a court musician in Rampur when he was thirty-five or possibly forty years old, under Hamid Ali Khan. He was allowed to travel widely from Rampur and performed at numerous music conferences and on All-India Radio. Under Nawab Raza Ali Khan, Mushtaq Hussein became chief court musician. He was given the President's Award for Hindustani Vocal Music in 1951, the first to receive this award. Upon retirement from Rampur in 1956, when the court establishment was disbanded, he taught in New Delhi at Bharatiya Kala Kendra, one of the new urban institutions which were springing up to foster musical training for the general populace. In 1957 he was awarded the prestigious Padma Bhushan, awarded by the Government of India to individuals in a number of fields for outstanding contributions to the nation.

In the next Sahaswan generation of singers are Mushtaq Hussein's five sons. He married Haider Khan's daughter when he was fourteen, then Inayat Hussein Khan's daughter when he was thirty-five (N. R. Singh 1964: 3; cf. Garg 1957: 300); of the twenty-three children from these two unions, seven survived. Two of Mushtaq Hussein's sons, Ghulam Hussein Khan and Ghulam Taqi Khan, perform together in *jugalbandi* (*Hindustan Times*, 1968) as well as solo (*Indian Express*, 1971e). The most prominent of Mushtaq Hussein's sons is Ishtiaq Hussein Khan. The other line of Sahaswan singers of the next two generations includes Fida Hussein Khan's son, Nisar Hussein Khan, and Nisar Hussein's son, Sharfaraz Hussein Khan.

When Mushtaq Hussein was teaching at Bharatiya Kala Kendra in New Delhi, his students of the Sahaswan/Rampur tradition included, for the first time, people outside the family. They were, for the most part, non-Muslim, and they included women. One of those women, who is developing into an accomplished musician, is Sulochana Yajurvedi, née Kalekar. She received her early musical training from Mushtaq Hussein Khan and from Bhola Nath Bhatt of Allahabad. Though she holds the Sangeet Alankar from Gandharva Mahavidyalaya in Poona (Vishnu Digambar Paluskar's institution), she has been referred to as 'the only lady representative of the great Rampur tradition of vocal music at present' (*Program of the Shankar Lal Festival of Music*, 1978a).

Ishtiaq Hussein Khan

Ishtiaq Hussein is the most prominent among Mushtaq Hussein's five sons. His career has been determined by a feature of the *gharana* system; while the father is living, the son usually remains his disciple (*shagird*), singing with the father (*ustad*) in a supporting performing role. Mushtaq Hussein Khan lived until 1964, when Ishtiaq Hussein was in his fifties (or possibly his sixties). While he is acknowledged to carry the family tradition – indeed, he filled his father's position at Bharatiya Kala Kendra in New Delhi – it is regrettable that he did not have the opportunity in his maturing years to develop his own distinctive style. Ishtiaq Hussein is now resident at the International Tobacco Corporation's Sangeet Research Academy, an institution devoted to the preservation of *khyal gharana* traditions.

Nisar Hussein Khan

Nisar Hussein (b. 1909), on the other hand, had the opportunity to become a court musician in his own right at Baroda when his father Fida Hussein Khan passed away in 1948. Nisar Hussein had been initiated into musical instruction from the age of five by his paternal grandfather Haider Khan, and at the age of eleven made a trip with him to Delhi. There a European heard the young boy sing and recommended him to Maharaja Sivaji Rao of Baroda. Nisar Hussein journeyed to Baroda to join his father and began to study with him there (Garg 1957: 211). He remained in the service of the Maharaja of Baroda most of his life, but performed widely in concert, on the radio, and for recordings. As most musicians seem to have done, he then retired to his birthplace, Badayun.

The marriage of Inayat Hussein Khan to Haddu Khan's daughter, which introduced the Gwalior *gharana* style, serves as a prime example of the direct relationship between social system (marriage patterns) and musical style. The extent to which Sahaswan singers of *khyal* – usually referred to as the Rampur *gharana* (though one line served in Baroda) – are carriers of the Gwalior *khyal* style and the extent to which their style is musically distinct will be considered after the musical analysis that follows.

Musical styles of Sahaswan/Rampur *gharana* musicians

Inayat Hussein Khan

Commentary about Inayat Hussein does not refer directly to his training in Gwalior *gayaki*. Rather, we learn that he sang *dhrupad*, *dhamar*, *khyal*, and *tappa*, which was said to have been his speciality. He is said to have sung *tarana*s as some Gwalior musicians did, but these were composed by Bahadur Hussein, a Rampur musician (Roy Choudhary 1973: 6), and is said to have been 'king of laya' (Garg 1957: 108). We are told in Garg that his *tan*s were animated and lyrical, and that his tone, voice, and placement of pitch were all very beautiful. He composed excellent songs under the names 'Inayat Piya', and 'Inayat Miyan'. He seems to have been a well-rounded musician and very highly respected.

Haider Khan

For Haider Khan, a comment has been made which is resonant with the Gwalior *gayaki* ideal of a wide vocal range: he was famous for being able to sing all the pitches in *ati tar saptak* (the octave above *tar saptak*). In his *tan*s every detail could be heard clearly. His special characteristic was the proper rendering of pitches.

Fida Hussein Khan

Fida Hussein, too, developed his vocal range; he could reach up to *ati tar* Sa and, furthermore, could go from *mandra* Sa to *ati tar* Sa in one breath, singing every pitch in between. While his voice is described as deep and resonant, he is said to have sung continually in a very high pitch but with the chest voice (rather than falsetto) that is the accustomed manner in Hindustani vocal music. Expressed in terms of another Hindustani vocal ideal, it was said that Fida Hussein could match the tone of his voice to that of a *tambura*. Finally, the article in Garg proclaims that his style of voice was that of Hassu and Haddu Khan of Gwalior (1957: 221).

Nisar Hussein Khan

The article in Garg refers to Nisar Hussein not as a Gwalior *gharana* musician but as a musician in the Seni tradition (1957: 211). Nisar Hussein is particularly noted for singing *tarana*, which, in *khyal* performances, he often substitutes for the fast *khyal* composition. His *khyal* performances manifest his control over all aspects of his music – melodic and rhythmic. The principles of variety and contrast are highly cultivated by Nisar Hussein; these are especially evident in his presentation of the *ciz* (composition) and of particular melodic material, in the different types of vocal production and embellishment that he uses, in his successions of rhythmic figurations, and in his placement of the various types of improvisation.

While many *khyal* singers settle into a pattern for presenting the *ciz* (the *sthai* and *antara* together at the beginning, or separated by improvisation), Nisar Hussein's method differs from performance to performance. In his recording of *vilambit* Gobardhan Todi (GCI ECLP 2260) he presented both *sthai* (with repeats) and *antara* initially, before any *alap*. In his *vilambit* Jaijaiwanti radio broadcast (a longer performance) he sang the *ciz sthai* and followed it by improvisation that included *sargam* and *tans* before the *antara* was sung, just three *tala* cycles before the end of the performance, which lasted approximately twenty-one minutes.

In choosing a *khyal* in Rag Jaijaiwanti, Nisar Hussein chose a *raga* which calls for melodic contrast, namely in the interplay of two forms of the pitches Ni and Ga. Ex. 5–1 presents part of a slow-speed Jaijaiwanti performance which demonstrates this. In *avart* 7 he used Ga as far as the pulling *mind* through G̲a in count 10; in *avart* 8 the play with both forms of Ni was tantalizing until he settled into Ni *shuddh* (transcribed ♮) toward the end of the cycle.

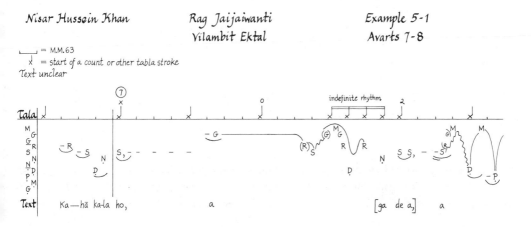

Nisar Hussein Khan   Rag Jaijaiwanti   Example 5-1
                            Vilambit Ektal   Avarts 7-8

⌐⌐ = M.M. 63
✗ = start of a count or other tabla stroke
Text unclear

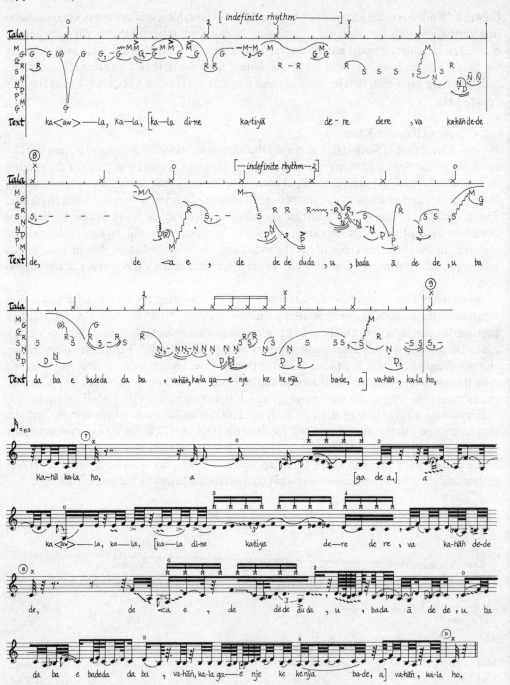

One type of contrast in vocal production which is peculiar to Nisar Hussein is coupled with the occurrence (and recurrence) of *antara*-type melodic improvisation in his *bara khyal*. To provide a contrast, for instance, with a tight vibrato and *tan* context, or with a soft, gentle *alap*

style, he will throw his voice on ascending pitches in *antara*-shaped melody relatively loudly, connecting the pitches in a legato way that sounds uncontrolled, off-pitch, and meandering, though it is none of these. This is probably what Chaubey was describing when he wrote:

There is no need for a musician to travel over the third octave just to enjoy a free return journey to his pitch. What is his object in exhibiting the range of his voice? Does it sustain his theme? Does it enhance the artistic grace of his style? Is it to exhibit his vocal agility? In doing all this, the voice changes its character and assumes a feminine shrillness that does not agree with his masculine assumptions (1958: 96).

And this is probably the same effect that was described in a performance by Hafiz Ahmed Khan (who studied with Nisar Hussein's father and with Nisar Hussein): 'Alongside this natural breath and brilliance of his voice, conspicuous and persistent crooning and curbing in the higher reaches of the pitch sounds incongruous. Moreover, the habit tends to throw his sense of tune into a false focus' (*Times of India*, 1968d). Nisar's Hussein's son, Sharfaraz Hussein, does this too.

Nisar Hussein exploits ornamentation effectively, frequently as a means of contrast. *Minds* are important in his vocal style, as are different widths of vibrato and the contrast of vibrato with pure tones. These are demonstrated in Ex. 5–2, *avarts* 52–9 of a medium-speed Abhogi performance in *jhaptal*. *Avart* 52 is the *sthai mukhda* with which he finished the previous structural unit. *Avarts* 53–8 comprise the new material in the next unit, which is brought to an end by repetition of the *sthai* in *avart* 59. Within this unit Nisar Hussein used a series of effects: (a) sustained pitch (Ma); (b) vibrato on several pitches, with the final pitch resolving into pure tone with a change of syllable to 'yo'; then (c) the same sequence as in (b), embellished by the pure tone starting on a relatively closed 'a', and proceeding to an open 'ā' before changing to 'yo'; (d) a succession of vibrato–*mind*–pure tone–vibrato–*mind*–vibrato.

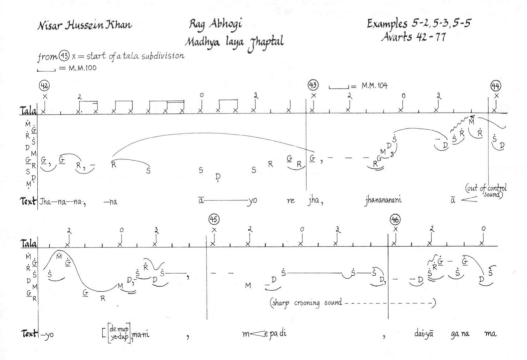

Nisar Hussein Khan

Rag Abhogi
Madhya laya Jhaptal

Examples 5-2, 5-3, 5-5
Avarts 42 - 77

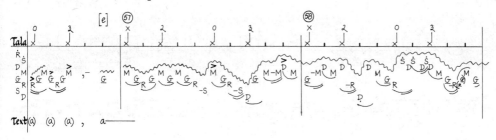

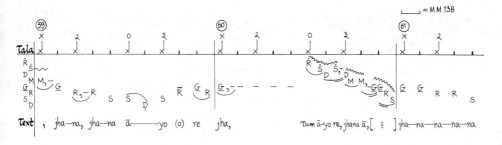

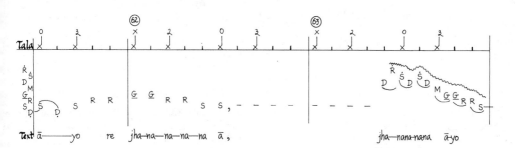

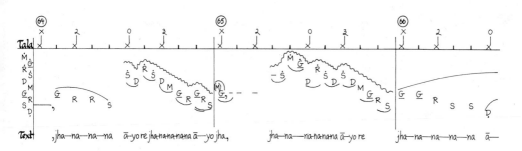

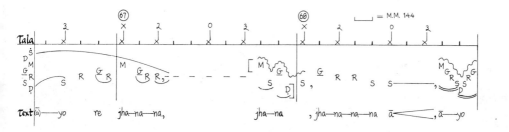

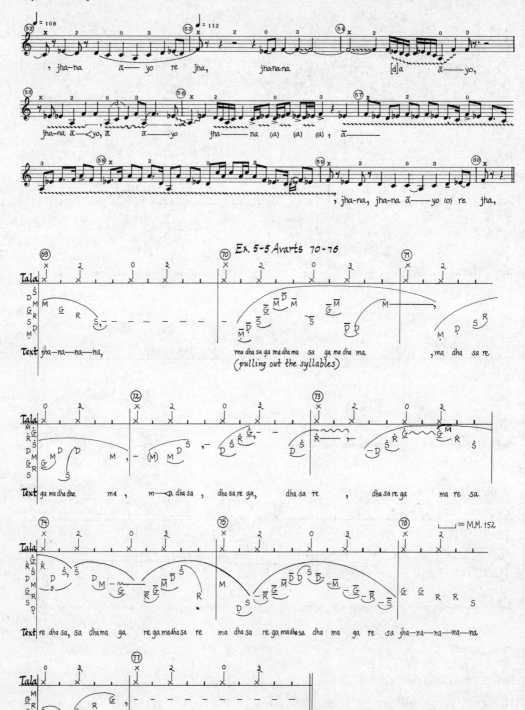

madha sa ga madha ma sa ga ma dha ma sa gama dhama
(pulling out the syllables)
, ma dha sa re ga madhadhadha ma , m—sa dha sa ,

dha sa re ga , dha sa re , dha sa re ga ma re sa re dha sa , sa dha ma ga re ga ma dha

sa re ma dha sa re ga madha sa dha ma ga re sa jha—na—na—na—na ā————yo rī ,

In Ex. 5–3 consecutive phrases in a multiple-cycle unit feature a succession of contrasting rhythms: (a) syncopation in *avart* 49 is followed by (b) irregular rhythm in *avart* 50, which is followed by (c) more patterned rhythm. The melody here is *tan*-like, but the speed is relatively so slow that rhythm rather than speed is perceived as the significant element of the unit.

Nisar Hussein also cultivates rhythmic contrast within a single *avart*, as for example with *sargam*. He begins a phrase with regular double- or quadruple-speed pitches/syllables, then gradually shifts into interesting and intricate rhythmic play, with starts and stops, syncopation, and varying rhythmic densities.

Contrast achieved by juxtaposition of different types of improvisation is shown in Ex. 5–4 from the same Rag Abhogi performance. Here the types of improvisation are *boltan* and *bolbant*; *boltan* in particular is featured in Nisar Hussein's performances. The *boltan* in *avart* 78 is the type which makes no internal use of the text and might just as well be *akar*; it is unusual, however, to hear *tan* on the vowel 'ī', as here in 'erī'. In *avart* 79, on the other hand, the syllables (however indistinctly rendered) are placed for rhythmic purposes. When the *bolbant* in *avart* 80 is heard, we realize that the three successive *avarts* contain progressively more emphasis on rhythm.

Nisar Hussein Khan   Rag Abhogi   Example 5-4
✗ = start of a tala subdivision   Madhya laya Jhaptal   Avarts 78 - 80
⌐———⌐ = M.M. 152

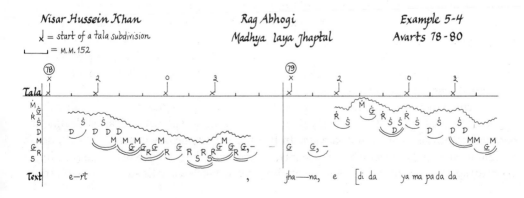

To Nisar Hussein Khan clarity of text, whether *bandish bol*s or *sargam* syllables, usually means emphasis on rhythm. When rhythmic play is not a concern, the *bol*s will not be enunciated clearly. For example, when he presents the text of the *ciz* at the outset of a slow-speed *bara khyal*, it is likely to be unclear (*madhya laya* text will be clearer); but the text in *chota khyal* will be clear.

A number of Nisar Hussein's *tan*s are reminiscent of *tan*s of the Gwalior *gharana*. Displaying his secure sense of pitch in many *tan*s, he leaps gracefully between widely spaced pitches, as a Gwalior musician would. He also repeats a motive an octave higher, at very fast speed. He can cover a wide range in one *tan*, encompassing one and a half octaves or more. For the most part, Nisar Hussein adheres to the prescription of the *raga* in *tan*s, unlike his cousin Mushtaq Hussein in his *sapat tan*s. And the pitches in Nisar Hussein's *tan*s are clear; this is partly due to his use of a tight, narrow vibrato rather than a heavier, wider *gamak* that tends to hide the pitches.

Unlike musicians of the Gwalior *gharana*, Nisar Hussein exploited *sargam*, for different effects. In his *vilambit* Jaijaiwanti performance, he sang *bolalap* style, but occasionally substituted *sargam* syllables and pulled them out vocally, connecting the pitches with *mind*. Shortly after that he used *sargam* for the sake of speed through a passage of increased density in a stable of *tala* counts, and then used it in *bolbant* style, for rhythmic effect. He also sang *sargam* with vibrato and *gamak*s, so that a phrase would sound more like *akar tan* than *sargam*. He did not rely on heavy use of *sargam*, however. There was no *sargam* at all in his *vilambit* Gobardhan Todi performance. Ex. 5–5 shows an exceptionally tuneful *sargam* passage from the medium-speed Abhogi performance; the melody, which traverses two octaves, is occasionally highlighted by *mind*s and ornamental vibrato.

In listening to performances by Nisar Hussein Khan, one is struck by the smooth manner in which he leads up to the *mukhda*; there is no feeling of sudden arrival or disjunction between improvised phrase and *mukhda*. In Ex. 5–2 the *tan* melody in *avart* 58 is a series of descents (from pitches to which he has leapt), and he made the last pitch of the *tan* (on *sam*, of *avart* 59) appear to be the crest of the descending *mukhda* melody on 'jhana, jhana āyo'. In the remainder of the examples the improvisation leads to Sa before the *mukhda*, but with ample time to feel that the phrase is finished before the *mukhda* arrives.

The description of Nisar Hussein's style in Garg serves as a useful summary:

In his singing is a great variety of *gamak*, *boltan*, and *sargam*; in his singing style, fruition of *sthai* and *antara* comes together with improvisation of very beautiful *swar*. A clean kind of *akar* in his voice, clarity of *tans* from *mandra* Sa to *ati tar saptak* Sa, *sargam*, novelty [freshness?], uncommon *boltans*, *tans* of a set of difficult pitches, and 'granular' *tans* are achieved in his artistry in a special, attractive way (1957: 211).

Sharfaraz Hussein Khan

Sharfaraz Hussein is still in the process of developing his own distinctive style, but he shows clear signs of Sahaswan family training and tradition. Like his father Nisar Hussein, Sharfaraz cultivates *mind*, and this is one of the best aspects of his *gayaki*. He also cultivates contrast through ornamentation and through different methods of vocal production. In Ex. 5–6, from a performance of Rag Chhayanat, the wilful use of vibrato is highlighted, especially in *avart*s 16 and 18; dynamic swells are featured in *avart* 16, count 9, and in *avart* 17, counts 5 to 6. Sharfaraz Hussein, like Nisar Hussein, gives out that 'crooning and curbed'-sounding *antara*-type melody, ascending and descending with pitches seeming to slur across beats (but not actually doing so); that occurred just before the *mukhda* in *avart*s 16 and 17, and within *avart* 18. His vocal quality is lighter than Nisar Hussein's, however, and the effect is not so powerful.

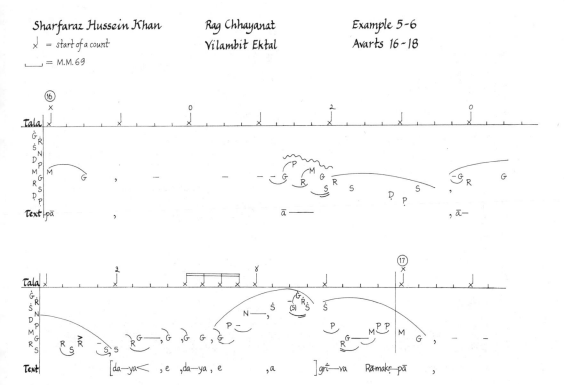

Sharfaraz Hussein Khan   Rag Chhayanat   Example 5-6
ᴊ = start of a count   Vilambit Ektal   Avarts 16-18
⌐⌐ = M.M. 69

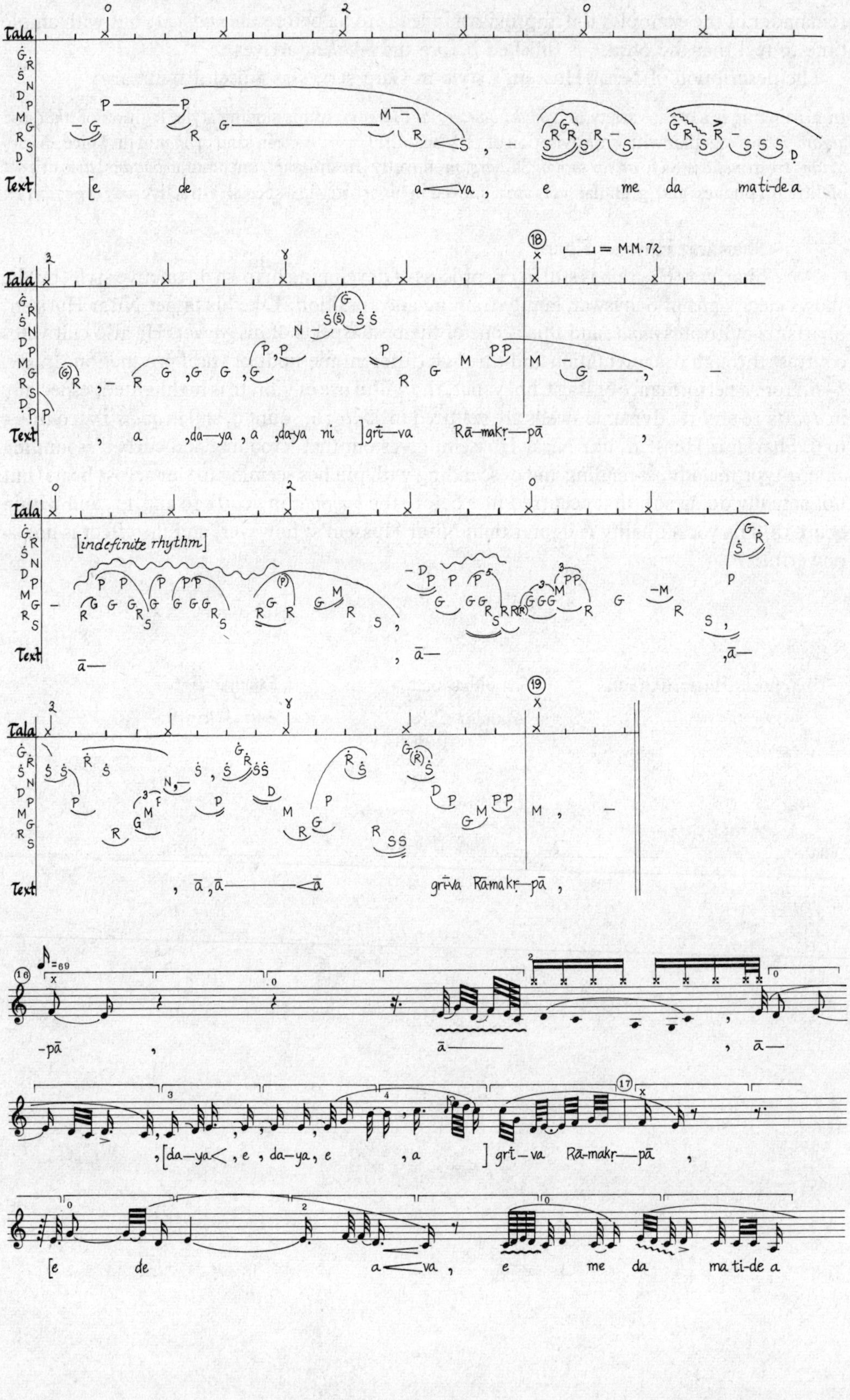
Tala
Text
[e de a va , e me da mati-de a
, a ,da—ya , a ,da-ya ni]grī-va Rā-makṛ—pā ,
18 = M.M. 72
[indefinite rhythm]
ā— , ā— ,ā—
, ā ,ā— ā grī-va Rā-makṛ—pā ,
19
16 = 69
-pā , ā— , ā—
,[da—ya , e , da—ya , e , a] grī—va Rā-makṛ—pā ,
17
[e de a va , e me da ma ti-de a

Also like his father, Sharfaraz Hussein sings *tans* with leaps and contrasting widths of vibrato (Ex. 5–7). He also vacillates between clarity and non-clarity of text. He is not so particular about singing the *ciz antara* as his father, however, and is likely to omit it even in *chota khyal*.

Sharfaraz Hussein Khan   *Rag Chhayanat*   Example 5-7

x = *start of a count*   *Vilambit Ektal*   *Avart 26*

⌐___⌐ = M.M.72

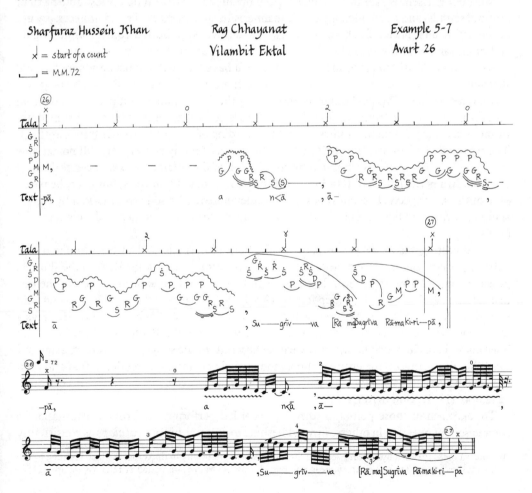

Mushtaq Hussein Khan

Mushtaq Hussein is known for having been a well-rounded musician. In addition to singing *khyal*, he sang *dhrupad*, *dhamar* and *hori*, *thumri*, *tappa* (N. R. Singh 1964: 14), and *tarana* (Srinivasan and Niranjan 1959). He also sang *sadra*, which were compositions in a *tala* of ten counts, performed in a style somewhat different from *khyal*. (*Sadra* have now been incorporated into *khyal* style, as compositions in *jhaptal*.)

Mushtaq Hussein is particularly associated with a form called *rag sagar*, which is similar to the Karnatak *rāgamālikā* and features a succession of *ragas*. Mushtaq Hussein is said to have received the inspiration for composing *rag sagars* from Basat Khan (brother of Bahadur Hussein Khan, *bin* player), who composed one using fourteen *ragas* (Vasudev 1964).[2] Mushtaq Hussein composed six *rag sagars*, one of them using eighteen *ragas*; another twenty. As a *raga* is sung, its name is woven into the song-text, often with play on the double meaning of the name (for instance 'hamir', meaning 'rich', or 'kalyan', meaning 'good' or 'welfare'). Mushtaq Hussein's *rag sagars* must have been a particular source of delight to his knowledgeable and system-oriented patrons, the *nawab*s of Rampur, though the connection is not made in written sources.

Mushtaq Hussein is said to have had superb breath control, with no undesirable nasal or guttural sounds, and he avoided unseemly mannerisms such as excessive and unnecessary use of the jaw in *tan*s (N. R. Singh 1964: 13, 18). He cultivated poise and control while singing and often sang with his eyes closed in intense concentration (Vasudev 1964).

As to tempo, Mushtaq Hussein felt that every *tala* has a tempo that must be adhered to, and that singing in a very slow tempo mars the innate character of a *tala* (N. R. Singh 1964: 18). Indeed, recordings of his performances released by the Gramophone Company of India from the All-India Radio Archives confirm this. His *khyal*s in *tintal* move at a pace which is medium by modern standards (though indicated on the recording of Bihag on GCI ECLP 2608 as slow). The *rupak tal Gunkari selection* (GCI ECLP 2573) is considerably slower, but still not so slow that the *tala theka* must be elaborated by subdivision of the counts, as slow-speed *theka* now must be. In a performance of Rag Barwa rebroadcast (probably) in 1968, however, he paced *ektal* at the slow speed of recent times. As Vasudev noted, 'His style was marked by a great stamina in the slow tempo and an otherwise "golden mean between fast and slow tempo"' (1964).

In structuring his *khyal* performances, Mushtaq Hussein is said to have adhered to a definite pattern. Before the *ciz*, he 'creates the proper atmosphere of the Raga in the shortest possible time' (Misra 1952: 20). The *alap* is not sung as a free exposition before the *ciz*; instead, the development of the *alap* follows closely the structure of the piece being sung, and is incorporated within the rhythmic structure of the *ciz* (N. R. Singh 1964: 13). He sings a 'neat rendering of the Asthai and Antara . . . Then follow the Badhat (elaborations), the bolalaps and tans in which he skilfully weaves the words of the songs into beautiful alaps and tans' (Misra 1952: 20); 'the entire composition, asthai and antara, is rendered first and then the melodic variations in *akar* (ā vowel), *bols* (words), and *sargam* (sol-fa) in the three degrees of tempo' (N. R. Singh 1964: 14).

To take each of those points in turn, his recorded performances provide affirmation in some cases but question in others. I would hesitate to describe his pre-*ciz alap*s as consistently

---

[2] Chaubey (1958: 17) attributes the *rag sagar* to the *soz* (composed in twenty to thirty *ragas*) which are sung by the Shia Muslim community of Lucknow, near Rampur, during the Muharram period of religious mourning.

'taking the shortest possible time'. The *rupak tal* selection in Gunkari was very long by *khyal* standards, perhaps because he was singing with someone else (possibly Ishtiaq Hussein), in the alternation style of *jugalbandi*. In the slow-speed Barwa *khyal* his solo pre-*ciz alap* was relatively long as well. It could be that this element of his performances differed according to the speed he chose for the particular *tala* – a longer pre-*ciz* before slower-speed *khyals*.

The observation that Mushtaq Hussein adheres closely to the structure of the *ciz* in his *alap* is consistently borne out in the recordings. This is true for melodic improvisation in pre-*ciz alap* and for improvisation after the *ciz* has been presented. His is a 'tuneful' style of *bolalap*, rather than one devoted to purposeful exposition of the *raga*.

The entire composition – *sthai* and *antara* – is indeed rendered first in the published recordings. In the Barwa radio performance, on the other hand, he presented the *ciz sthai*, repeated it, and then began lengthy improvisation, which took a long time to reach *antara* range. No distinct *ciz antara* was heard. It is possible that the slow speed of that selection determined a different structuring in terms of presentation of the *ciz*. Of the types of improvisation Mushtaq Hussein is said to have enjoyed, *boltan*s can be heard in the recordings, many of them of the type where syllable placement is purposefully rhythmic. *Sargam* is also there, but it is by no means an important element. Not mentioned in descriptions is *bolbant*; he sings it, however, at the end of his Gandhari *khyal* (GCI ECLP 2538), and it is complemented by an off-beat exchange with the *tabla* player.

Mushtaq Hussein sang *sapat tan*s

in which all the notes come gushing up and then down 'like a jet of water from a fountain'. He is a stickler for the rules of the raga, but when he comes to these tans, he sets these rules aside for a while, and takes all the seven notes up and down in regular successions. In these taans, he often covers all the three octaves (Misra 1952: 20).

Garg cited Mushtaq Hussein himself:

He said that when doing alap one should maintain the separate shape of each raga, but in tans it is difficult to keep intact the form of the raga. In his opinion when doing sapat or three-octave tans, it is not inappropriate to include all the pitches. Singers of old did this in sapat tans in [the performance of] ragas (1957: 300).

Numerous *sapat tan*s are sung in his recorded performances.

Another type of *tan*, in which he climbed to the high octave and then abruptly back down, he called ' "Jahez ki tan", or *tan* received in dowry from the illustrious Haddu–Hassu family of Gwalior' (Chaubey 1958: 18). Whether they are 'Jahez ki tan' or not, Mushtaq Hussein does sing a number of *tans* that resemble Gwalior *tans* – those with leaps between pitches, reaching ever higher, and then tumbling down:

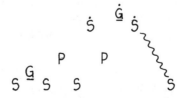

Chaubey, who compared Mushtaq Hussein's *tans* to skating – as an erratic glide – commented: 'Every time he does that, I watch him panic-stricken like a spectator who watches a dangerous circus trapeze. How relieved I feel when I see him returning to the terra firma of his voice!' (1958: 18). This comment was really concerned with Mushtaq's desire to show off a Gwalior-style high-register vocal range which he did not actually have. In his recorded performances Mushtaq Hussein's *tans* extended even up to *ati tar* Sa, but the 'erratic glide' is missing. Since he dipped down to *mandra* Ma as well, it is clear that he did achieve a wide vocal range, and kept it until he made the recordings in his late eighties or early nineties. According to N. R. Singh (1964: 13, 17) every *tan* was to end on pitch Sa (though this is arguable), and Mushtaq Hussein trained his students for intricate *tan* elaborations as a preliminary to the approach of the final *sam*.

One distinctive musical feature of Mushtaq Hussein's improvisation involves dynamics, a melodic phrase, and a particular vowel: he would loudly sustain *tar* Sa on 'i' (for example, 'pi' of 'piyā'), then dip down to Pa, and then return to *tar saptak* for a very soft phrase. In Rag Mirabai ki Malhar (GCI ECLP 2538), for example, he sang (a), as shown below; in Rag Bihag (GCI ECLP 2608) he sang (b); in Rag Gandhari (GCI ECLP 2538) he produced (c).

(In Gunkari, GCI ECLP 2573, his loud, sustained Så occurred on the vowel 'ā'.) It cannot be asserted that this unusual emphasis on 'i' is due to the natural flow and placement of text syllables, because in the word 'piyā' it is the 'ā' that should be lengthened.

Mushtaq Hussein used ornamentation sparingly in this selection of recorded performances. In his Barwa radio broadcast he exploited a *gamak* called *murki*, a fast, short 'trill'. He placed it, for example, on the initial pitch of a melodic unit, and then expanded the tight, concise vibrato characteristic of *murki* into a wide vibrato within a few pitches of the start of the phrase. *Murki* also occur in the Barwa *khyal* on initial pitches of numerous *mukhda*, as if to announce the arrival of the end of the melodic and metric unit. In Ex. 5–8 the *mukhda* of the first five *avarts* of that performance are transcribed, to show Mushtaq Hussein's use of ornamentation and also to demonstrate the variability of a 'composed' *mukhda*. (The text is absent from the example because it was unclear in the recording; clarity of text is not an attribute of Mushtaq Hussein's *khyal* style.)

Two further details of Mushtaq Hussein's recorded performances concern the role of his accompanists. In one exceptional instance in the Gunkari performance, the *sarangi* player led the improvisation: about three-fourths of the way through he played a rhythmically enunciated passage, which was imitated by Mushtaq Hussein and then by the second singer (Ishtiaq Hussein?) in turn. A rhythmic exchange with the *tabla* player in the Gandhari performance was noted earlier. In the Gandhari recording the *tabla* player had a brief solo, during which Mushtaq Hussein rested before his units of improvisation. Since that happened in the Barwa *chota khyal* as well, it seems as if Mushtaq Hussein permitted his accompanists to make individual contributions to the performance.

Lastly, whenever Mushtaq Hussein rested between units, he consistently resumed singing with the *mukhda*. This contrasts with the practice of most singers, who begin again mid-cycle with newly improvised music. See, for example, the transcription in *sargam* notation which includes Exx. 5–2, 5–3, and 5–5; Nisar Hussein Khan began new improvisational units in *avarts* 43, 49, 53, 60, and 63, in each case with new material. In *avarts* 67–9 he repeated the *mukhda* in embellished fashion, as a demarcation before *boltan*-type improvisation and *sargam*.

Sulochana Yajurvedi

In keeping with the Rampur tradition, Sulochana 'has done commendable work in applied research in music and has composed and produced hundreds of new musical compositions. She is in possession of a large number of rare compositions of music. She surpasses anyone in her repertoire of *ragas* and she has the honour of not repeating *ragas* at stage concerts' (*Program of the Shankar Lal Festival*, 1978a). Like her teacher, Mushtaq Hussein Khan, and his teacher before him, she sings *tappa* and *jhaptal* compositions.

Sulochana Yajurvedi has a good, contralto-like voice, which has been described as 'broad' and 'powerful with melodic fullness' in reviews in Indian newspapers (*Times of India*, 1968a and 1978). Her structuring of *bara khyal* performances follows Sahaswan tradition: *ciz* leading to *alap* through *antara* range, with a small degree of acceleration. In her radio broadcast of Rag Bilaskhani Todi in 1978, she followed a *vilambit khyal* with a *madhya laya jhaptal* composition, in which she achieved a fast pace by using quadruple-speed passages. In a Shankar Lal Festival performance she treated her audience to a succession of three *khyals* – slow, medium, and fast.

In contrast to Nisar Hussein Khan, who made improvisation lead smoothly into the *mukhda*, Sulochana works the *mukhda* smoothly into the ensuing *tala* cycle. In *bolalap* context particularly she continues the style of the improvisation with the *mukhda*. The *sam* is felt, but then she goes beyond it to carry on the *sthai* phrase. She uses a great deal of ornamentation, even near the beginning of the *bara khyal*. Ornamentation and dynamic swells contribute an element of contrast to her style, as with other musicians of the *gharana*. She might lean into a sustained pitch with a gradual increase of volume, or she might let a slight vibrato creep into an initially pure tone. *Mind*s are especially important in her vocal vocabulary. Her particular way of rendering them for special effect is pleasing: in a descending interval (Sa to Pa, or Sa to Ma, or Sa to Ga, for instance), she will begin quite softly and lean into the descent, increasing the volume carefully. Occasionally she will do this in an ascent as well. When she sings one of these *mind*s and then waits for the *sarangi* player to imitate it, the effect is quite dramatic. Another instance of eloquent usage of *mind* is when she makes a fast, highly ornamented ascent to a pitch and then descends in *mind*, with dramatic contrast.

Sargam plays a part in both her *bara* and *chota khyal*. Her pronunciation of 'dha' and 'sa' is distinctively 'dho' and 'so'. One of her styles of using *sargam* is for rhythm in *nom-tom* style, as she emphatically pronounces the syllables in duple or triple succession. She might sing each of these with a *gamak*, creating further rhythmic interest:

$$\overline{\underline{R}\,\underline{R}}\,\overset{\frown}{\underline{G}\underline{G}}\,\overline{\underline{R}\,\underline{R}}\,\overset{MM}{\frown}\,\overline{\underline{R}\,\underline{R}}\,\overset{\frown}{\underline{G}\underline{G}}\qquad or\qquad \overset{\overline{RRR}}{}\,\underline{NNN}\,\underline{DDD}\,\overset{SSS}{\frown}\,\underline{NNN}\,\overset{SSS}{\frown}$$

Since she also sings many *tan*s with melodic leaps, some as great as an octave, her *tan*s, like those of other Sahaswan/Rampur singers, resemble Gwalior *gharana tan*s.

Sulochana likes to combine several types of improvisation in one *avart* of the *tala*. She is likely to sing *sargam* for only part of an *avart*, then switch smoothly to using *bol*s in a similar vein (double-speed, for instance). Or she might build *boltan*s of the pitch-plateau type and then proceed to some other type of double-speed improvisation. She might even combine, within one *avart*, *sargam*, then *tan*s with *gamak*, and finally *bol*s in a pulling kind of legato singing that is distinctively her own.

Sulochana Yajurvedi's relationship with her accompanists resembles that of Mushtaq Hussein with his. She sings with a *sarangi*, which beautifully complements her vocal quality, and gives the *sarangi* player a meaningful part in the performance by providing opportunities for him to repeat a motive that she has just sung. In her Shankar Lal Festival performance she gave the *tabla* player three chances for solos lasting two *avart*s; this is fairly unusual in *bara khyal*.

Summary

Several performance characteristics shared by Sahaswan *gharanedar* and their students are also features of Gwalior *gharana* style. One is the cultivation of a wide vocal range: Inayat Hussein Khan and Fida Hussein Khan are remembered for reaching as high as *ati tar saptak*. A second concerns the shapes of *tan*s. *Sapat tan*s are sprinkled throughout performances by Sahaswan/Rampur musicians; Mushtaq Hussein Khan regarded *sapat tan*s as melodic moments when one could step outside the *raga*. *Tan*s with melodic leaps are also characteristic of Gwalior-style *tan*s. The third characteristic shared with Gwalior style is the cultivation of the principle of contrast. In structural terms this means, for example, including in a single cycle of the *tala*, *sargam*, *tan*, and *bolbant*. In stylistic terms it means varying vocal expressiveness by changing gradually from a non-*gamak* context to one with *gamak*, as in moving from a pure tone to vibrato, or vice versa, and using dynamic contrasts.

Performance characteristics shared by Sahaswan *gharanedar* and their students which distinguish their style from that of the Gwalior *gharana* include melodic expressiveness. While Sahaswan musicians pay attention to rhythm in the form of *bolbant* (e.g. Nisar Hussein Khan) or occasional *tihai* or *nom-tom* (Sulochana Yajurvedi), rhythm is definitely secondary to melody. Furthermore, speed is not a special concern of these artists, and acceleration of the rate of the *tala* counts, particularly in *bara khyal*, is minimal.

Sargam is utilized, albeit sparingly, by these musicians. Nisar Hussein sang *sargam* relatively early in the slow improvisation, as well as later in a rhythmic context. While *boltan*s occur, they are not among the principal types of improvisation cultivated by Sahaswan/Rampur singers.

In structuring their *khyal* performances, these musicians are likely to sing the entire *ciz* at the very outset. Inayat Hussein, Mushtaq Hussein, and Sulochana Yajurvedi were noted for performing and composing large repertoires of compositions. Of interest in an ancillary way is the inclusion of *tappa* and *tarana* as traditional parts of Sahaswan singers' repertoires.

Use of the *ciz* text varies from artist to artist. Nisar Hussein and his son Sharfaraz Hussein regarded text as an element of rhythm and made it clear or unclear as they wished. For the most part, Mushtaq Hussein made the texts unclear. Sulochana Yajurvedi, on the other hand, expends considerable effort in expressing the meaning of the text.

A few characteristics appear to be important for distinguishing individual styles within the group. For Nisar Hussein and his son Sharfaraz Hussein, the 'crooning' into *antara* range is unique. Mushtaq Hussein's tuneful *alap* is significant relative to his group tradition, while his sustaining of Sȧ on the vowel 'i' in the particular context described above is unique. His clear distinguishing of levels of speed according to the *tala* he is using may have been fairly common practice in performing *khyal* in the first three decades of the twentieth century, but it is striking in terms of modern performance practice in the 1970s. For Sulochana Yajurvedi the meaningful rendering of the text and *nom-tom*-style *sargam* stand out as unusual for a Rampur musician. Peculiar to her (or at least very unusual) is the incorporation of the *mukhda* into the ensuing cycle of the *tala*.

6 *Alladiya Khan*

The context

The Alladiya Khan *gharana* is the only *gharana* named for a person rather than for a place. Perhaps because of the desire to refer to *gharanas* by place rather than by person – which in this case is problematic – it is often called the Jaipur *gharana*. Joan Erdman, in her article on the *maharaja*'s musicians in nineteenth-century Jaipur, identified musicians of the 'Jaipur *gharana*' as those who were integrated into the musical activities of the *maharaja*'s household and who identified themselves to those outside the patron's household by the rubric 'Jaipur *gharana*' (1978: 365). While Alladiya Khan grew up in the area around Jaipur, and at least one member of his family served there, the style of *khyal* he espoused was not specifically associated with musicians of the Jaipur household or with members of his family before him. Thus, this *gharana* is more aptly named after Alladiya Khan himself. In any case, Alladiya is the central figure. A sketch of his family history is in order; this falls into two periods, neither of which is entirely clear.

Alladiya Khan's family history (see Chart 6–2) names as the earliest known ancestor Baba Vishwambhara Das, an ancestor of Swami Haridas (who was *guru* to the great singer Tansen in the sixteenth century) (V. H. Deshpande 1972: 2; see also Garg 1957: 274). The family was Hindu–Gaud Brahmins from the north of India, and Shandilya *gotra* (Garg 1957: 274). Alladiya's ancestors may have been in the service of Nizam Chahi, and then for some time served the Mughal Badshah Aurangzeb (1618–1707). In Aurangzeb's time (Garg 1957: 274), or that of his son, Shah Alamgir (Garg 1957: 97), the family was forced to become Muslim. The story of the conversion was important to Alladiya:

'You know we were forced to a conversion by Aurangzeb – hardly 200 years ago. My eighth ancestor was a Hindu. My fifth ancestor and many of us wanted to come back to Hindu fold, but, Hindus did not accept us back!' He became red and full of emotion – and we left it at that.

Once he recounted to me how his ancestor who was with a Hindu King, sacrificed his religion in order to save his king, and ultimately, though his ancestor became a Muslim, the king was released only after he was forcibly converted! – 'well, well, well, these are things of the past – now I am a Muslim – and I pray Allah as a Muslim!' (Shukla 1971: 21).

More recently Alladiya's family has been associated with Atrauli, near Aligarh in Uttar Pradesh, where a number of families of musicians have lived. He was supposedly of the Mohalla Choudharian group of Atrauli musicians (Agarwala 1966: 33), and is sometimes referred to as 'of' the Atrauli *gharana*. The date of Alladiya's family's move from Atrauli to Rajasthan is not entirely clear. V. H. Deshpande's suggestion (1972: 2; probably based on Govindrao Tembe's biography of Alladiya) is that they migrated from Atrauli in Alladiya's grandfather's time (early nineteenth century; see Garg for a much earlier possible connection with Rajasthan).

160

Chart 6-1 : Alladiya Khan Gharana Teaching Lines

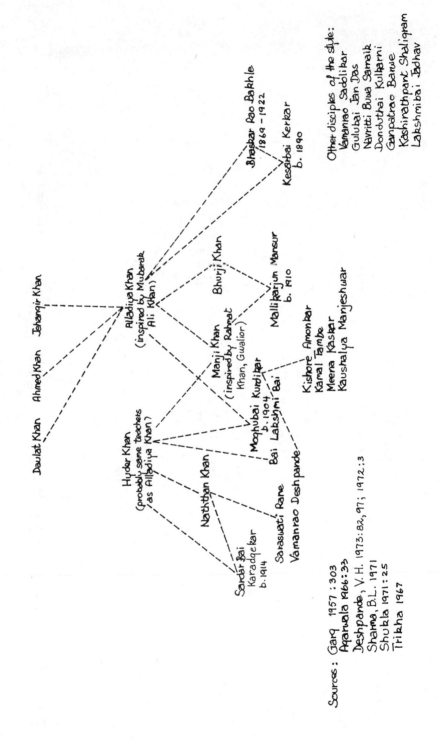

Daulat Khan

Ahmed Khan Jehangir Khan

Alladiya Khan
(inspired by Mubarak
Ali Khan)

Bhurji Khan

Manji Khan
(inspired by Rahmat
Khan, Gwalior)

Mallikarjun Mansur
b. 1910

Bhaskar Rao Bakhle
1869 - 1922

Kesarbai Kerkar
b. 1890

Kishore Amonkar
Kamal Tambe
Meena Kaskar
Kaushalya Manjeshwar

Hyder Khan
(probably same teachers
as Alladiya Khan?)

Naththan Khan

Moghubai Kurdikar
b. 1904
Bai Lakshmi Bai

Sarasuati Rane
Vamanrao Deshpande

Sardar Bai
Karadgekar
b. 1914

Other disciples of the style:
Vamanrao Sadolikar
Gulubai Jan Das
Navrriti Buwa Samaik
Donduthai Kulkarni
Ganpatrao Barve
Kashinathpant Shaligram
Lakshmibai Jadhav

Sources: Garg 1957: 303
Agarwala 1966: 33
Deshpande, V.H. 1973: 82, 97; 1972: 3
Sharma, B.L. 1971
Shukla 1971: 25
Tribha 1967

162

Chart 6-2: Alladiya Khan Gharana Blood Lines

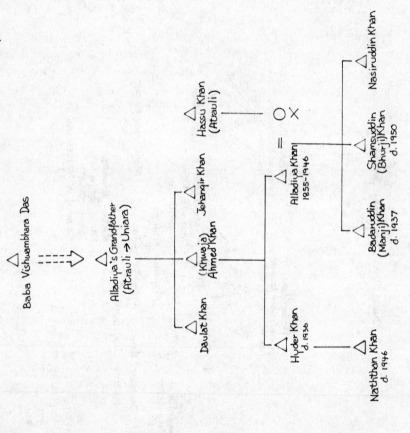

Sources: Agarwala 1966:3; Deshpande, V.H. 1972:2; 1973:50

Garg 1957:96, 274; Sharma, B.L. 1971:42

Shukla 1971:16.

The history of musical patronage in Rajasthan is a rich one, and numerous courts there at various times generously fostered the arts. Musicians dismissed by Aurangzeb had fled to Alwar, and even courts entangled in the constant struggle against the Mughals had sponsored musicians at court. At Alwar, Tonk, Udaipur (Mewar), Bikaner, Bharatpur, Jodhpur, Jaipur, and temple centers such as Nathdwara the classical arts flourished. In Rajasthan some of the greatest singers of India practiced their art, particularly those of the four great styles of *dhrupad*.

In the area around Jaipur there were several centers of musical patronage. In addition to the Jaipur court itself (ruled by Rajput *maharajas*) there was the state of Tonk (ruled by Muslim *nawabs*) and the principality of Uniara (Uniyara). The *jagirdars* of Uniara attracted many musicians from Atrauli (in Uttar Pradesh), who then settled in Rajasthan (B. L. Sharma 1971: 34). This may have been the cause of Alladiya Khan's family migration to Rajasthan, for it was in Uniara that they seem to have settled (V. H. Deshpande 1972: 2 and 1973: 47n; Ratanjankar 1966: 30).

The family musical tradition was apparently *dhrupad* singing, in the Dagar style (Shukla 1971: 17). Alladiya's father Khwaja Ahmed Khan served Nawab Ibadullah Khan of Tonk (B. L. Sharma 1971: 34; see Chart 6–2). His paternal uncle Daulat Khan served Maharaja Mansingh of Jodhpur; his paternal uncle Jehangir Khan lived in Jaipur, served in Uniara, then served the Nawab of Tonk, and later returned to Uniara where he settled for life (B. L. Sharma 1971: 35, 42). The members of the family seem to have received their musical training within the *gharana*, i.e., from each other (see Chart 6–1).

Musicians of the Alladiya Khan *gharana*

Alladiya Khan

Alladiya is said to have been born in Jodhpur around 1855 (Shukla 1971: 19). He received his initial musical training from his father, but his father died when he was young. Alladiya's main *talim* (formal instruction) was with his paternal uncle Daulat Khan (Garg 1957: 97) or with his other uncle Jehangir Khan (V. H. Deshpande 1972: 2; B. L. Sharma 1971: 41), who sang *dhrupad*, *dhamar*, and *khyal*, and was a great scholar of music. Thus, Alladiya lived in Jaipur, Tonk, Uniara, Jodhpur, and other places for a considerable time (B. L. Sharma 1971: 41; Shukla 1971: 19). Alladiya's brother Hyder Khan may have been with him much of the time, because he too is mentioned as having served at Uniara (B. L. Sharma 1971: 34).

The greatest influence on Alladiya as a singer of *khyal* was Mubarak Ali Khan, whom Alladiya presumably heard at the Jaipur court (perhaps in the 1860s or 1870s). Mubarak Ali was the son of Bade Muhammad Khan, who had been famous at the Gwalior court; their family were noted for their *khyal* singing, in the *qawwal baccha* style, not for *dhrupad*. Alladiya never took formal instruction from Mubarak Ali and is said always to have regretted it (V. H. Deshpande 1972: 3). The reasons why he did not, as related by Shukla, reveal several attitudes prevalent at the time and still lingering:

Music as an art was highly respected in those days and the Dhruvapada singers were, by and large, considered to have the sine qua-non of musical knowledge and were savants 'consilio et animis'. Mubarak Ali was indisputably a very great musician of his times. His art, however, lacked the majesty and maturity of the Dhruvapads. But in Khayal singing, however, he had no equal . . . Khan Saheb

Plate 8   Alladiya Khan, the only individual singer for whom a *khyal gharana* is named (photo by permission of the Sangeet Natak Akademi, New Delhi)

further added that, although he himself belonged to a Dhruvapad Gharana of Dagar style and though he descended from a Brahmin family of the Gaud sect and Shandilya Gotra, he very much wanted to be a disciple of Mubarak Ali Khan – in fact he was not only prevented from becoming a disciple of a mere Khayalia, but Mubarak Ali himself also said that he may learn from him but he (Mubarak Ali) will not 'sin' by converting a Dhruvapadia – and a Brahmin at that . . . [according to Alladiya], Mubarak Ali was the pioneer in introducing the intricate note patterns and complicated nuances and twists in the classical music of Khayal (Shukla 1971: 17).

Alladiya's career was not especially smooth. After completing his period of study he left Rajasthan for the Deccan, accompanied by his brother Hyder Khan. First he worked in Baroda state, not at the court but in the service of the Shrimant Gayan Vad; his arrival there in Rajput-style clothing must have created something of a sensation, because it is mentioned not only in his biographical sketch in *Hamāre Saṅgīt Ratna* but also in that of his son Manji Khan (Garg 1957: 94, 274). In Poona (at the Kirla Sakar Natak Mandali) he presented his first *mehfil* (private concert), and favorably impressed the best musicians in that city. He worked in various states in the Deccan, including Kagan (Ratanjankar 1966: 30) and also resided in Bombay periodically.

When Alladiya was about forty (c. 1895), serving at Ambetha, the prince required him to sing every morning, every afternoon, and every night successively for a number of days. His voice became gruff and hoarse; it took him two years to improve it again, but its original resonance and attractiveness were gone. At that point, according to V. H. Deshpande, Alladiya had to develop singing and performance styles that depended less on *alap* (1972: 3). He drew on his family training in *dhrupad* and the inspiration gained from Mubarak Ali's *khyal* singing, and so developed a distinctive style of *khyal*. He cultivated difficult aspects of the musical art: he was apparently proud of creating a difficult style and became widely renowned for it. His contemporaries nicknamed him 'Avghad Das' ('Devotee of the Difficult'; V. H. Deshpande 1973: 53).

Alladiya performed *dhrupad*, *dhamar* and *hori*, *tarana*, and *khyal*. In addition, he was famed for singing *sadra* (compositions in a *tala* of ten counts – *jhaptal*):

It is not perhaps widely known that the noted musicologists of 6 or 7 decades ago (particularly 1907–1917), who appreciated Khan Saheb's music, were mainly concerned with his 'Sadra'. No one is known to have sung 'Sadra' in Khayal style before Alladiya . . . Sadra is a distinct style and Alladiya Khan sung it, entwined with his immemorable intricate structure, preserving its pristine purity (the gravity of a sadra) and still in a novel form! (Shukla 1971: 22).

Unlike most *khyal* singers, Alladiya did not sing the light genre *thumri*. A likely explanation for this is that he was from a family of traditional *dhrupad* singers, who usually have nothing to do with *thumri*.

In about 1900 Alladiya took on a student whom he loved – Bhaskar Rao Bakhle, a great musician who studied with several outstanding teachers (see Chapter 9). Alladiya used to stay in Bakhle's house in Bombay and give him lessons at night (Garg 1957: 269). Bakhle occasionally assisted Alladiya in concerts – an honor accorded only the best disciples – and in 1922 when the young musician died Alladiya was clearly distressed. Shukla recalled the effect this had on his performance at a private concert held in Bombay in 1922; even with the distinguished presence of the rulers of Miraj, Kolhapur, and Dewas among the invitees who were celebrating the birthday of the patron, Sir Vitthaldas, Alladiya was not able to overcome his grief:

Alladiya Khan, assisted by his eldest son Nasiruddin . . . as well as Hyder Khan, began his recital with an alap in Nayaki followed by a Dhamar in the same Rag . . . The performance failed to produce the desired effect. When Sir Vitthaldas inquired after Khan Saheb's health, Khan Saheb broke into tears: 'My Bhaskar! I am feeling lonely without him!' – and wept like a child! – and the musical sitting abruptly closed with a feeling of sorrow (1971: 16).

Alladiya's longest term of service at a single court seems to have been in Kolhapur, where he went c. 1914–15 and remained until about 1929 (cf. Garg 1957: 197). According to Alladiya himself, he was also attached to a Shaiva temple at Kolhapur (Shukla 1971: 21); apparently *dhrupad* continued to be performed in temples, even by Muslim musicians. While in Kolhapur, Alladiya won a gold watch from the *maharaja* for his skill in wrestling (Shukla 1971: 24), an activity apparently enjoyed by numerous Indian musicians.

Upon leaving the Kolhapur court c. 1929, Alladiya moved to Bombay. His brother Hyder Khan may have still been with him, teaching the family *dhrupad* tradition until his death in 1936.

Manji Khan and Bhurji Khan

Alladiya married the daughter of Hassu Khan, a *dhamar* singer of Atrauli (Agarwala 1966: 33), and had three sons: Nasiruddin Khan, the eldest (Shukla 1971: 16); Badaruddin, called Manji Khan; and his *suputra* (the son of whom he was particularly proud) Shamsuddin, called Bhurji Khan (Garg 1957: 95; Agarwala 1966: 33). Alladiya's brother Hyder Khan also had a son, Naththan Khan, but among them all Manji Khan was the musical genius.

Manji Khan studied *dhrupad* with his uncle Hyder Khan and then took training with his father (for teaching lines see Chart 6–1). He seems to have been Alladiya's greatest joy, until he became fascinated with the singing style of Rahmat Khan of the Gwalior *gharana* and adopted it into this *gayaki*. History was repeating itself, for Alladiya had been decisively attracted to the style of a musician (Mubarak Ali Khan) not of his own *gharana*. But Alladiya had no patience with his son's waywardness, and the two quarrelled with great enmity. Manji ceased singing for seven years and became a forester in Kolhapur state. Then he broke his contract and moved to Bombay, where he resumed musical practice and began to perform again (Garg 1957: 274–5). He sang *dhrupad* and *dhamar* (with *boltan*s in the style of Natthan Khan of Agra), *khyal*, *hori*, and *git* – and *thumri* and *ghazal*, which his father would not sing. He did not care for *tarana* (though he sang one in Rag Nat Narayan). From 1930 to 1935 he delighted audiences in Bombay. When he died in 1937, Alladiya was so disconsolate that he stopped singing for a time.

Bhurji Khan devoted his life to teaching. He outlived his father by only four years.

Mallikarjun Mansur

The most outstanding student of Manji and Bhurji Khan was Mallikarjun Mansur, who worked with both of them. Born in 1910 in Mansur village in Dharwar district, he was not from a family of musicians, though his brother Basavraj was a dancer. Nor was music Mallikarjun's sole pursuit; he studied Kannada literature as well. He was sent from the village to Dharwar for his education, but soon relinquished formal schooling for the musical training that was arranged by his brother (Garg 1957: 280). From the age of twelve to eighteen he studied with a Gwalior *gharana* singer, Nilkanth Buwa Alurmath (a disciple of Balkrishna Buwa Ichalkaranjikar), but descriptions of his performances place his style squarely in the Alladiya Khan tradition. For some time Mallikarjun held the important post of music director of His Master's Voice Co. in India. He has been attached to the Dharwar station of All-India Radio as music adviser. In recognition of his artistry, he was given the prestigious Padma Shri award (1970).

Among the relatively small number of disciples of Alladiya Khan himself, the two who achieved national prominence make this *gharana* exceptional – Kesarbai Kerkar and Moghubai Kurdikar – both women, who persevered in a musical world dominated by men. Since they played major roles in the cultural and social changes in twentieth-century India, they are given special prominence in the discussion of this *gharana*.

Kesarbai Kerkar

'There is something queenly about her. Aloof, gracious, demanding . . . It is not often that one meets a reticent, imperious and self-sufficient introvert of the stature of Kesarbai who has the unique distinction of being the most perceptive exponent of the khyal style of singing in India today' (Raman 1971: vi). With that introduction, A. S. Raman began a newspaper article recounting an interview with Kesarbai Kerkar. She was eighty-two at the time, and no longer singing publicly:

K: . . . I knew when to retire. When I realised that I could no longer sing as I should, I just withdrew myself from the scene . . .

R: When was your last concert?

K: I have a bad memory for dates. I think it was in 1965. But I am not sure . . .

R: Kesarbaiji, what is in music to deserve your total dedication?

K: What is not in it? . . . Music is yoga, a sort of tapasya (penance). No wonder that in those days, according to legend, a master who could render the rag Megh Malhar could induce a torrential downpour of rain . . . Throughout my career I have tried to be consistent and conscientious. And punctual too. I think I have never disappointed my audience. I was not always at my best. But I was never below the expectations of the public. Also I have brought a certain amount of prestige and dignity to music as a career. No lobbying, no canvassing, no name-dropping. If I sang at concerts, I sang on my own terms.

Convinced that Indian music today has ceased to be an aesthetic means to a spiritual end, and has become a 'free-for-all', Kesarbai chooses to remain aloof. She does not even devote herself to teaching (V. H. Deshpande 1973: 96).

Kesarbai was born in Goa in the small village of Keri, about seven miles from Panaji (the capital of Portuguese Goa), on July 13, 1890 (or 1892 or 1893). As to her genealogy:

K: Don't ask for details about my grandparents, parents, uncles, aunts, and so on. I don't think one should romanticize one's past . . . . Please don't remind me of my ancestors. Let us not disturb them. They are happily resting in heaven.

Her earliest experience with music came through the temple:

K: In those days, the only source of music was the temple. You know what I mean. Kirtans and bhajans . . . At the time of the evening arti [worship] at the temple of Santha Durga, I used to listen carefully to devotional music and on reaching home found myself humming the tunes I had heard earlier. Just like the boys and girls who are so crazy about film music today.

   My mamu, that is, my maternal uncle, encouraged me in this. Forget about his name, it's not important. He was a lover of classical music. He had some business interests in Bombay where he had opportunities of coming into close contact with music and musicians. He at once decided that there was music in my blood. I was seven then.

Kesarbai's uncle tried to find a teacher for her at the nearby Mangesh temple, but there was no-one with sufficient knowledge. According to Garg, when she was eight she began her musical instruction in Kolhapur, with Abdul Karim Khan (of the Kirana *gharana*); for about ten months he taught her many exercises, along with one or two *ciz*. The instruction ended when he left Kolhapur for Poona (Garg 1957: 128). Kesarbai apparently did not mention this in her interview with Raman (or he neglected to include it in his published article).

K: About four miles from my village, in a zamindar's house, lived the famous singer, Ramakrishna Buwa Vaze [Gwalior *gharana*]. I was taken to him in my thirteenth year. He used to be away for about six months in a year on his concert tour. So there were frequent interruptions, but I managed to stay on for about three years learning from him the rudiments of voice culture. When he left for good at the end of the third year to further his own professional interests, I found myself back home. At last, in my 18th year – in 1908 – we all reached Bombay: my mother, mamu and myself.

We decided to settle down here. But our search for the ideal guru continued. We had heard a lot about Barkatullah, the well-known sitariya (sitar virtuoso) of the Mysore and Patiala durbars. For six years I took lessons from him. I learnt a number of ragas from him: some completed, some left unfinished (cf. Garg 1957: 128; Bhagvat 1972: 5).

The Garg article supplements detail at this point in the narrative of Kesarbai's training. In 1912, when Alladiya Khan resided in Bombay for eight months, Kesarbai asked to take instruction with him. To this the *ustad* assented, but 'she could not master his *gayaki*'. Alladiya's health deteriorated and subsequently he left Bombay for Kolhapur (Garg 1957: 128). Kesarbai's story of her life does not mention that interlude; instead, she proceeds directly from her sixth year with Barkatullah Khan when his professional commitments prevented him from conveniently teaching her:

к: Again, at the end of the sixth year, the problem of the guru arose. Pandit Bhaskarbua Bhakhale, who had been the disciple of Nathan Khan and Ustad Alladiya Khan Saheb, offered to teach me for some time. But I could learn very little from Panditji, because I could stay with him only for a few months. Barely for a year. He then had to leave for Poona where he was later to busy himself with the affairs of the Bharat Sangeet Sabha.

Garg asserts that upon the departure of Bhaskar Rao Bakhle (1913?) from Bombay, Kesarbai studied again, perhaps intermittently, with Ramkrishna Buwa Vaze, and that her training continued in that inconsistent way until 1917 (1957: 129).

к: By now I really got tired of the guru hunt! I decided to learn only from Ustad Alladiya Khan Saheb and from no one else. My mind was firmly made up once and for all.

But he would not respond at all to my repeated pleadings. He had no sympathy for my musical urges for one reason or another. He was then at Sangli for reasons of health, though employed as Kolhapur's court musician: His Highness used to be very fond of him.

According to Bhagvat, Kesarbai approached the Kolhapur ruler Shahu Maharaj for help:

She begged him to intervene on her behalf and permit Alladiya Khan to teach her. Shahu Maharaj was quite sceptical. 'You are asking for too much. It is like being tied to an elephant. How will you manage to cope with the burden?' But Kesarbai was adamant and Shahu Maharaj granted Khan Sahib permission to instruct her in music. But the battle was still far from won. Alladiya Khan Sahib himself was not too enthusiastic and it was the plea of one of his most intimate friends that persuaded him to accept Kesarbai as a pupil (Bhagvat 1972: 6).

The 'intimate friend' must have been Seth Bitthal Das of Bombay; according to Garg, Das called Alladiya Khan to Bombay and requested that he instruct Kesarbai. Alladiya is said to have responded that in 1912, when he had taught her for three months, she had not been able to acquire his *gayaki*, and consequently he would not teach her again. On Bitthal Das's persistence, however, Alladiya agreed to give her *talim*, but with stipulations that were actually put into writing (Garg 1957: 129).

к: At last, after a long and painful wait for 3½ years, I found myself in a very enviable situation: for he accepted me as his disciple, though reluctantly and on one condition.

R: That you should not sing publicly while he was alive? Our ustads are often very jealous of their pupils.

K: Not Khan Saheb. On the contrary, he insisted that I should always sing with him at concerts. Always: that was the condition he stipulated.

They also agreed that she would commit herself to him as *sisya/shagird* (disciple) in the traditional *gandha bandh* (initiation) ceremony and present him with a certain sum, as was usual. She was to continue *talim* with him for about ten years; if he had to leave Bombay, even to reside elsewhere, she would go with him for instruction. She would pay him a monthly stipend, even if his health was not good or if he had to travel for some work. Agreeing to those stipulations, Kesarbai did *gandha bandh* in January 1921 and began the long-sought *talim* with Alladiya Khan (Garg 1957: 129). Kesarbai gave the date as a year earlier:

K: In 1920, I started learning from him. To be precise, January, 1920. I remained his disciple till his death in 1946. Twenty-six years of rigorous training. Each day more than ten hours of hard work . . . Each day, my practice under his guidance would begin at eight in the morning and go on until one in the afternoon. Again from four to a very, very late hour.

I used to travel with Khan Saheb and sing with him at concerts, as I have already told you: this sort of professional experience gave me immense self-confidence.

After his death, my concert career began. I mean solo singing.

One highlight of Kesarbai's career came early – 1938 (before she had begun her solo singing career in earnest) – in the form of a note from Rabindranath Tagore written after an evening's performance: 'The magic of her voice with the mystery of its varied modulations has repeatedly proved its true significance not in any pedantic display of technical subtleties [that are] mechanically accurate, but in the revelation of the miracle of music only possible for a born genius' (Raman 1971: vi). Tagore conferred on her the title 'Sur Shri' ('Queen of Music'), by which she came to be known.

Kesarbai was invited to sing in many places, among them Kashmir. As described by Karan Singh, a son of the late *maharaja* of Jammu–Kashmir, formal *darbar* was held twice a year; all courtiers came to bring a gift. The *maharaja* sat on his throne at the far end of a long rectangular hall, and the ministers sat, placed down the hall according to rank. One to one-and-one-half hours were consumed as each in turn made a presentation. At the opposite end of the hall stood a singer and the accompanists, performing during the proceedings.[1] While it was an honor to provide music for such occasions, the music itself fulfilled a background entertainment role. There were also informal occasions 'at home' when musicians performed. The *maharaja* of Jammu–Kashmir 'called' Siddeshwari Devi and, especially, Kesarbai to sing on such occasions.

In 1953 Kesarbai received the President's Award for Hindustani Vocal Music from the Sangeet Natak Akademi, and in January 1969 she was awarded Padma Bhushan by the President of India. In her view she was also the only legitimate heir to the tradition of Alladiya Khan, despite the 'presence' of Moghubai Kurdikar:

R: Did he [Alladiya Khan] have any other disciple?
K: In his lifetime, none. After his death, many! I mean, the sort of *sadhaks* [devoted disciples] he had in mind, none.

---

[1] Information from an interview with Karan Singh, May 5, 1978 (airline flight, Agra–Delhi). Karan Singh watched the proceedings as a young prince with his mother in the *zenana* (women's balcony) from above. Formal *darbars* were discontinued in Kashmir in 1947.

Moghubai Kurdikar

Though she did not assume the role of substitute for a son which Kesarbai Kerkar took, Moghubai Kurdikar, like Kesarbai, mastered the Alladiya Khan style and received the highest honors. Moreover, with her devotion to teaching (which Kesarbai eschewed), she has assured, at least for a time, the continuation of the tradition of her *ustad*.

Moghubai was born in 1904 and spent her childhood in Goa, in a village called Kurdi. Her first training was in dance, as she spent five or six years with the Parvatkar Natak Mandali, a touring drama company. There she studied dance with Ramlal Kathak, working with the *tabla* player Layabhaskar Karumama, and she studied the music for several dramatic roles with Chintabagurav, developing a sense of the dramatic art as well as expertise in rhythm (V. H. Deshpande 1974: 12).

As related by one of her disciples, when Moghubai was fifteen or sixteen years old she was in Sangli with the company and happened to be staying in a house next to where Alladiya Khan was staying. Every day, as she practiced a song for the role of Vasantasena, Alladiya heard her as he passed by. Wondering who the singer was, he went up the stairs to see; naturally Moghubai was startled when a stranger walked in, and she stopped singing. Explaining that he had heard her from the street and wanted to hear her properly, he asked the young girl to continue singing. Impressed, he explained who he was and offered to teach her. Only after he had begun instruction, when Moghubai happened to attend an important private concert by Alladiya, did she really understand who the *ustad* was (V. H. Deshpande 1974: 13).

The account of the student–teacher relationship of Moghubai and Alladiya which is given in Garg (1957: 304) differs in an important respect from that related by her disciple V. H. Deshpande. The Garg article pictures a somewhat adversary relationship. After studying with Alladiya for some time, it says, Moghubai went to Bombay, curtailing her training with him, a move which Alladiya did not appreciate, since he expected devotion from those he agreed to teach. In order to continue her musical training in Bombay, Moghubai began studying with Bashir Ahmed Khan of the Agra *gharana* (V. H. Deshpande 1973: 82) and with Vilayat Hussain Khan, also of Agra (Garg 1957: 304). That had persisted for a while when Alladiya Khan too moved to Bombay (possibly c. 1929). In telling us that when Moghubai wished to return to *talim* with Alladiya he was reluctant, saying that she had changed her *gharana* and that it would be difficult for her to change her *gayaki* once again, the article in Garg implies that Moghubai had studied with others without Alladiya's permission. Eventually, though (we are reassured in Garg), she convinced him, and began to receive instruction with him. She worked under a disadvantage, but gradually received the confidence and trust of the *ustad*. 'With a child in her lap and tambura in one hand, she practiced, and at home everyone did all the household work to leave her time for musical instruction' (Garg 1957: 304).

Deshpande's account enumerates the same teachers for Moghubai, but clearly states that she was acting on the advice of Alladiya Khan. She also studied with Alladiya's younger brother, Hyder Khan, and 'for a while also, [did] a bit of talim' with Inayat Hussein Khan of the Sahaswan *gharana*. Moghubai's preference was for study with Alladiya, however, so from 1920 to 1946, when the *ustad* died, she got rigorous instruction from him.

Kesarbai Kerkar's statement, cited earlier, that Alladiya had no other disciple than herself is recalled by a paragraph in Deshpande's article (1974: 13): to Moghubai's surprise, during the period of study with Alladiya, someone spread the rumor that she was not his 'official disciple'. When she complained to the *ustad* about it, he announced in a *mehfil* (private concert) that she *was* an 'official disciple' and that 'there should be no mistake about it'. Moghubai considered the matter closed after that.

Like Kesarbai, Moghubai was honored with the President's Award for Hindustani Vocal Music, conferred by the Sangeet Natak Akademi in 1969. Assisting her in the concert on that occasion – in the traditional role of student of the soloist – was Moghubai's daughter, Kishore Amonkar.

Kishore Amonkar

Kishore Amonkar, the 'baby in the lap' during her mother's years of study, has now become one of India's leading vocalists, carrying on the tradition of her mother's stern *ustad* Alladiya Khan. After training with her mother, she studied under Ramkrishna Buwa Parvatkar and Mohanrao Palekar (*Program of the Shankar Lal Festival of Music*, 1978).

Musical styles of Alladiya Khan *gharana* musicians

Alladiya Khan

Described in general terms, Alladiya's *khyal* style, combining elements from both *dhrupad* and *khyal*, was well-proportioned, majestic, and serene, with restrained expression yet lilting rhythmic patterns, neat and methodical in presentation yet with flights of imagination, and cultivating both *svar* and *laya* – every element was fully developed and happily blended into a balanced whole (V. H. Deshpande 1973: 17 and 1972: 3).

The two descriptions of Alladiya's *khyal* style that recur most frequently are 'close to *dhrupad*' and 'difficult'. 'Close to *dhrupad*' meant several things. He would develop the *sthai* of the composition for a long time (relative to *khyal*), without *khatka* ('jerks') or anything resembling a *tan*. As explained by Shukla, an important element here was his effort to keep both the textual and the musical composition intact, so that through the development of the *sthai* the form of the whole *khyal* would evolve. Alladiya also kept the entire *sthai* text, rather than just allowing pieces of it to recur throughout the improvisation. After developing the *sthai*, he would slowly sing *alap*, both with '*svars*' and with *bols* in a vocal style that was simple, grand, and open-throated, without any guttural or nasal sounds. True to *dhrupad* style, he excelled at *boltan*; he knew many *pakhavaj padhants* (recitation syllables for drumming), and he would create a *boltan* or *tan* to match the rhythm, instantly, in any *raga* (1971: 21, 15, 24; surely Shukla is here referring to *bolbant*).

Typically of *khyal* singers, he cultivated a voice sweeter, more mellow, and more elastic than would be expected of a *dhrupad* singer. And he cultivated rippling and rolling *tans* 'in the way of Jorh [pulsating], full of Yatis [contours]'; Ratanjankar notated an Alladiya Khan *tan* in Rag Purvi, as shown below (1966: 30).

Alladiya's basic tempo was fairly slow (the slowest among those *gharana*s that value *layakari*), and his acceleration was slight, leaving time for intricate designs and lightning-fast subdivisions of the beat. Most strikingly, he sang only *bara khyal*, eschewing presentation of a fast composition (V. H. Deshpande 1973: 77–8). He could, however, achieve the acceleration effect of a fast *khyal*, through increasing rhythmic density.

Alladiya usually sang in *vilambit tintal*, a balanced *tala* that permits of much rhythmic play. Lest one consider it unchallenging for an artist to sing *khyal* usually in only one *tala*, it is important to note that he performed a variety of other *tala*s when he performed other genres. For *dhrupad* the choice of *tala*s is varied; he need not have cultivated *ektal* in *khyal* as many singers do, because he sang that *tala* (as *cautal*) in *dhrupad*. His use of *dhamar tal* (fourteen counts, $5 + 2 + 3 + 4$) for *dhamar*, and *jhaptal* for *khyal*-style *sadra*, accounted for further variety.

As analyzed by V. H. Deshpande, Alladiya carefully structured each *avart*, building the tension slowly up to a point just preceding the *mukhda*, which constituted its resolution. (He was adept in the art of joining up the extempore elaboration to the first cadence of the song: Ratanjankar 1966: 31.) The tension of each *avart* was higher than that of the preceding, and the highest was at the end, with a grand resolution (V. H. Deshpande 1972: 4 and 1973: 52).

The word 'difficult' used in descriptions of Alladiya's style refers to the difficulty of his singing style (*gayaki*), of his choice of *raga*s, of his rhythmic play (*layakari*), and of his *tan*s. An aspect of his *gayaki* was breath control, which he cultivated so as to be able to produce *tan phirat* (twisting, turning *tan*s) of unusual length, following one after another quickly and terminating with an unexpected twist before *sam* (V. H. Deshpande 1972: 4). He also needed well-controlled breath for sustaining tones in Dagar-style *alap*. He sang *raga*s unknown in his day (and therefore 'difficult') which had structures that were difficult to sing – many combinations of two *raga*s, the clarification of which proved to be a challenge (for lists of his *raga*s see Nadkarni n.d.; Garg 1957: 95, 275; Raman 1971).

Alladiya also cultivated the general principle of contrast, another element of a 'difficult' style. Three examples of contrast may be noted: a special accent placed unexpectedly on a pitch to heighten its effect; a single pitch sustained for a longer time in the midst of a fast, complex *tan*, to make the listener expectant about the next pitch; and pauses between notes (V. H. Deshpande 1973: 37, 52).

When one considers that Alladiya sang only *bara khyal* without proceeding to a fast composition, pioneered the singing of *sadra* in *khyal* style, and sang *raga*s that no one else sang, one has a picture of an individualistic musician. Critics of his style have stressed that his musical creativity was far more intellectual than emotional. It was said that he would work out intricate patterns and reproduce the same ones in any *raga* he sang, so that all *raga*s tended to sound alike (Deodhar in V. H. Deshpande 1973: xiii). Enthusiasts of his style effusively deny this, of course.

Mallikarjun Mansur

Some differences from the style of Alladiya Khan can be noted in Mallikarjun's recorded performances (GCI ECSD 2402 and ECLP 2384). The description 'close to *dhrupad*' does not seem pertinent here. While he does develop the *sthai* for 'a long time', the improvisation is neither *alap*-like nor tuneful; *vistār* (i.e., 'melody') seems the best word for it. While the text is there, most *vistar* is done to one or two words. Although *boltan* and *bolbant* do come into these performances, *tan*s predominate: Alladiya-style *tan*s, but ornamented with a heavy *gamak*. Whereas Alladiya was said to have accelerated the *tala* counts little, Mallikarjun speeds up considerably. Like other disciples in this *gharana*, he extends the *bara khyal* to a *chota khyal*.

Remarks made about Mallikarjun Mansur's concert performances, on the other hand, are very similar to those made about Alladiya's style. Three reviews of a single concert should convince anyone who doubts the existence of a style tradition. 'Mallikarjun, featured in the [AIR] National Programme tonight, has a unique distinction: he sings only to the vilambit laya and not to the drut. But he makes up for this drawback by working out melodic variations at bewildering pace. All this calls for remarkable voice control, which he possesses' (*Hindustan Times* 1969, by a critic unaware of the tradition). Adhering to Alladiya's preferences as regards *tala*, both compositions were in *tintal*, which prompted the unaware critic to quip: 'Could he not have chosen another time-cycle for the sake of variety at least?' (In view of this *gharana*'s preference for *tintal* it is noteworthy that on the recording GCI ECLP 2384 Mallikarjun performs *rupak tal* as well.)

A second review of the same National Programme noted the fast pacing of *tan*s, and also the rhythmic play with the text: 'He was entirely happy while shaping the word-setting of the khayal into rhythmical figures which he projected with great unction and celerity' (*Sunday Statesman* 1969a).

In the same concert Mallikarjun sang Hem Nat and Nayaki Kanhra – both *raga*s that are associated with Alladiya. The reviewer for the *Times of India* noted his love of complex *raga*s: 'Mallikarjun's genius seems to favour ragas which allow the lusty vocalist to "hop, step and jump" over musical spaces. Sawani Kalyan, Kedar Nat, Rageshwari, Jait, Bihagada sung by him in the previous programmes particularly agree with his creative temperament' (1969a). That critic noted his 'lovely return to the "som" after elegant and measured sorties', and *tan*s that 'zigzagged' through the notes but were always true to the *raga*.

Kesarbai Kerkar

The recording of Kesarbai Kerkar issued by the Gramophone Company of India (EALP 1278) is a compilation of nine short selections (one a *thumri* in *dipchandi tala*, fourteen counts). Of particular note is the solemn selection in *jhaptal*, 'Hā re daiyā', in the light of the remarks made earlier about Alladiya Khan's singing of *sadra* in *khyal* style. Other than this, all the *khyal*s are indeed in Alladiya's favorite *tala tintal*.

While it would be unwise to draw many conclusions about Kesarbai's musical style from this recording, two generalizations can be hazarded. One is that *vistar* is as appropriate a term for the slow improvisation in these *khyal*s as it was for Mallikarjun's. The second generalization concerns the *tan*s; they are the roller-coaster-shaped *tan*s for which the Alladiya Khan *gharana* is so famous. In these short recorded selections, there is little emphasis on rhythm. Even in *vistar* Kesarbai prefers to sing on the vowel 'ā' to the extent that the word or two in the *mukhda* provides a sharp contrast. On the recording, the selection in which she uses the most text is 'Mhāre dere āo' in Rag Desi (familiar from Chapter 3; see Exx. 3–1 to 3–4); she draws particularly on the phrase 'āvojī Maharājājī'.

Moghubai Kurdikar

The one recording available for Moghubai (GCI ELRZ 17) consists of *tarana*s in two fairly unusual *talas* (*yog tal*, fifteen and a half counts; *savari*, fifteen counts), *sadra-khyals* in *jhaptal*, and, of course, *tintal khyals*.

All the short selections show in her performance style a gracious blending of melody and rhythm, as V. H. Deshpande leads us to expect (1973: 47). Although much of the improvisation in this *khyal* is sung *akar*, her enunciation of the text, when it is there, is fine and clear. In the Rag Sohoni [Sohani] *jhaptal* piece, she created double-speed pulsation with the text which was followed by a triplet-rhythm figure. In the Jaijaiwanti *jhaptal* piece, her *bolbant* included quadruple subdivision of the beat.

For Moghubai, being mindful of rhythm also means making a careful approach to *sam*: 'Here, the accompanying rhythm is not put to slumber to wake up fitfully when the "Mukhra" or the closing stem of the main strain comes, as is the case with the Khayal rendering in other vocal styles' (*Times of India* 1969d).

According to V. H. Deshpande (1974: 14), it was Moghubai who added the singing of a fast composition (following the slow *khyal*) to this *gharana* style. The selections recorded on ELRZ 17, however, are for the most part medium-speed, by present-day standards.

Improvisation (*vistar*) is sung *akar* by Moghubai as well as by Kesarbai. And *akar tans* of the Alladiya Khan style are plentiful. In both *vistar* and *tan* she uses her voice to sustain 'pure' pitches and then lets her natural vibrato creep through, or else she turns the vibrato into a *gamak* – an attractive element of her style. The technical polish of a thorough training in Alladiya's style has been noted by reviewers for Moghubai, as for all his students, and she has attracted the attributions 'pristine purity', 'depth', and 'dignity'.

Kishore Amonkar

Kishore Amonkar draws large admiring crowds for what are often dubbed 'thrilling vocal recitals'. She is a 'star' in every sense of the word. She sings with 'sweet strength', using her voice to express emotion, yet retaining her dignity.

Illustrious daughter of her illustrious mother Smt. Moghu Bai Kurdakar, Kishori Amonkar is one of the most outstanding of the women melody-makers in this country . . . 'The lean lady with a big heart' would be one way of describing this fiery and highly imaginative artist. The probing and pincer-like voice penetrates deep . . . And how courageous of the wiry vocalist to perfect her training under her mother, to master her style and gayaki and having done so, break away from it and launch on pastures new and new moorings! That is the way of an original genius (Program of *Festival '75: Women Music-Makers of India*, Wadhera 1975: 9).

However 'new' her style might be, the progression of events in a *bara khyal* sung by Kishore is like that described for Alladiya Khan. It is demonstrated below, with transcriptions from her *madhya laya tintal* performance in Rag Jaunpuri, recorded on GCI ECLP 2326. First, the complete *ciz sthai* and *antara* are sung, taking two to four *avarts*. Like Kesarbai and Moghubai, Kishore sings *vistar* on 'ā' or 'nā', with text only at the *mukhda*. The *vistar* progresses gradually upward in pitch register, through *antara* range. In Ex. 6–1 the last *avarts* of *vistar* are shown. *Avart* 11 began with a pulsating rise on 'ā', as did *avart* 12 (from count 2). Toward the end of each of those cycles the melody became more rhythmically persistent. In *avart* 13 rhythmic movement was emphasized, leading to *avart* 14, which culminated in *bolbant* that served to mark off the end of the *vistar*.

Plate 9   Kishore Amonkar of the Alladiya Khan *gharana*, with *tambura*

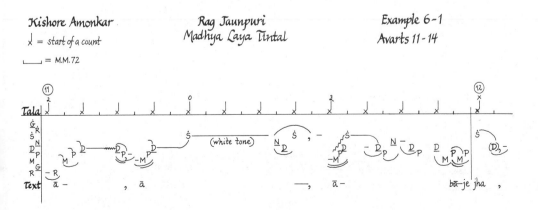

After the '*alap*' Kishore sang *boltan*s (Ex. 6–2), which were both melismatic (*avart* 19, counts 5–7) and rhythmically purposeful (the rest of *avart* 19).

The *tans* that followed ranged widely and proceeded at different speeds. In an *avart* of *akar tans* she first built up motives – as pitch areas – and then launched into a *tan* that went on and on (as shown in Ex. 6–3). Once she began the *akar tans* in earnest, she devoted herself to them to the end of the performance, without reverting to other textures for contrast.

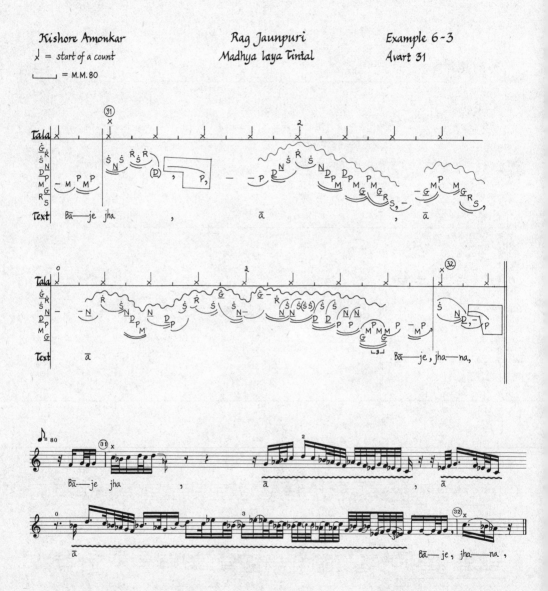

Kishore Amonkar   Rag Jaunpuri   Example 6-3
⌐ = start of a count   Madhya laya Tintal   Avart 31
└──┘ = M.M. 80

The 'roller-coaster' *tans* for which the Alladiya Khan style is so famous can be heard in all of Kishore's performances. A sample from a Rag Bageshri performance (GCI ECSD 2702) is shown in Ex. 6–4.

Kishore Amonkar   Rag Bageshri   Example 6-4
                                   Vilambit Tintal   Avarts 26-7

♩ = tabla strokes
⌊____⌋ = M.M. 66

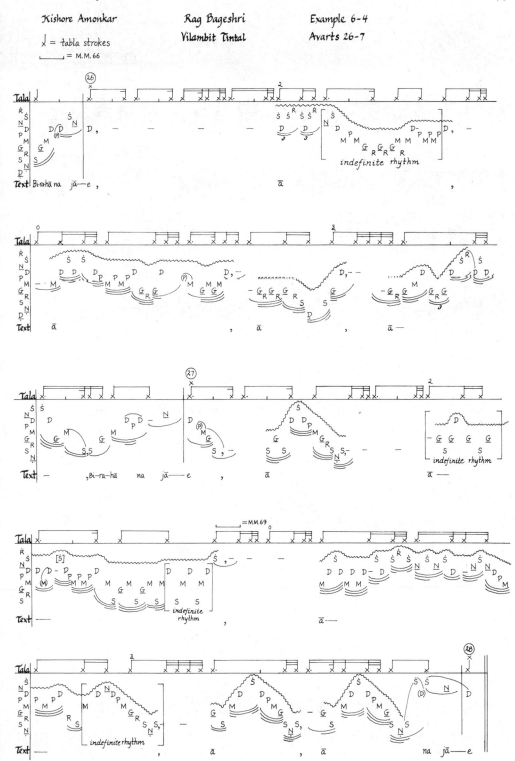

When abstracted into a graph of the pitch curves, the shapes of those famous *tan*s are clearly revealed, as shown below.

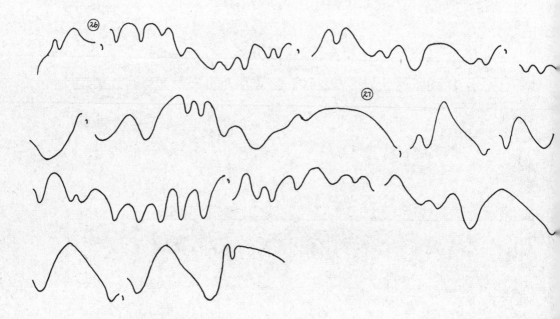

Exx. 6–2, 6–3, and 6–4 also serve to demonstrate the smooth manner in which the Alladiya Khan singers are said to integrate the *mukhda* into the passage which precedes it. The *mukhda*s of the Jaunpuri composition shown in Exx. 6–2 and 6–3, 'Bāje jhana', begin on the pitch Pa (notated as G); accordingly the *boltan* and *tan* which Kishore sang just before the *mukhda* were melodically conceived to join it with conjunct motion. The Bageshri composition *mukhda* shown in Ex. 6–4, 'Birahā na jāe' ['Virahā na jāla'] begins on pitch Sa (notated as C); thus the preceding *tans* resolved to Sa.

Nom-tom-like *akar* passages are particularly distinctive in the Alladiya Khan style. They may be described as a pulsating effect created by a definite rhythmic placement of 'ā'. This important style element is shown in Ex. 6–5.

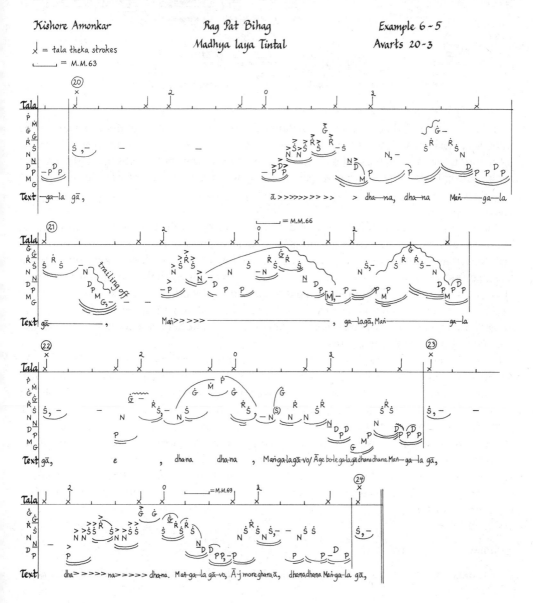

It has been noted that Alladiya accelerated the speed of the *tala* counts relatively little. Likewise, Kishore usually accelerates relatively little throughout any one *khyal*. Points of acceleration are predictable and noticeable. In *bara khyal* the speed picks up slightly as she begins to emphasize rhythm, then it again picks up when she sings *akar tans*. The *tabla* player is likely to accelerate gradually during *tan*s; this is peculiar neither to Kishore's playing nor to this *tabla* player.

Kishore's exploitation of her voice, particularly in the *alap* portion of her performances, has her audiences in thrall (it is not unusual to hear expressive responses from them). She makes delicate use of sustained, pure tones pulled down into a *mind*, with a narrow vibrato creeping into the pitch on which the *mind* ends; a sweet, slow, slight vibrato on prolonged pitches; and pure tones on high, prolonged pitches, merging into a sustained, narrow vibrato (see Ex. 6–1 above). Though she exploits mainly the middle and upper parts of her vocal range (i.e., not the lower register), Kishore knows how to take her audience high emotionally, and then drop them to the depths.

Kishore's relationships with her accompanists vary from performance to performance. At the Shankar Lal Festival (New Delhi) in 1978 she sang with *tabla* and *sarangi*, but also with harmonium and with a supporting singer who played *tambura*. Kishore herself played *tambura*. At the outset of her performance, she directed their placement on the stage in a commanding manner. She interacted with the *sarangi* player a great deal, waiting for him to repeat passages she had just sung; at other moments the supporting singer filled that role. When she wanted to speed up suddenly in the fast *khyal* Kishore actually snapped her fingers at the *sarangi* player. On that occasion she gave the *tabla* player opportunities for brief solos in the fast *khyal*. Such solos can also be heard to her Bageshri recording (but not in the Bhup or Jaunpuri recordings).

Summary

Like the style of the Agra *gharana*, that of the Alladiya Khan *gharana* is described as 'close to *dhrupad*'; like the early Agra *gharana* singers, Alladiya Khan was first a *dhrupadiya*. Correctness and vocal control were important to him, and mastery of technique was primary – all of those remarks are often made about *dhrupad* singers.

As was noted with musicians of the Agra *gharana*, a *khyal* style that is 'close to *dhrupad*' involves greater attention to the elements of text and metered rhythm. In Alladiya's style, attention to the text apparently meant using more of the *ciz* text than most performers do; this he shared with singers of the Agra *gharana*. In *dhrupad*, it also means using the text in *bolbant*; in *khyal*, *bolbant* is most likely to be cultivated by artists such as Alladiya who have studied *dhrupad*. (The decrease in *bolbant*, and also *boltan*, among *khyal* singers throughout the twentieth century is probably due to the decrease in training in *dhrupad*.) In *khyal*, attention to the text and its rhythmic implications can also be manifested in the cultivation of *boltans*, and this is indeed a type of improvisation one is likely to hear from an artist of the Alladiya Khan *gharana*.

Nom-tom-like, rhythmically pulsating melody is also a characteristic of the Alladiya Khan style that could be seen as 'close to *dhrupad*'. Compared with the style of Agra *gharana* singers such as Faiyaz Khan and Latafat Husain Khan (see Chapter 4), however, *nom-tom* as performed by Alladiya Khan *gharana* artists bears only a slight resemblance to that type of improvisation in *dhrupad*.

Three characteristics are particularly distinctive to the Alladiya Khan *gharana*: the preference for *tintal*, even for *vilambit laya* performances; emphasis from generation to generation on a particular repertoire of *ragas*, particularly complex ones; and, last, the propensity for *tans* with a 'roller-coaster' configuration. The proportion of performance time devoted to *tans* is relatively large. It is noteworthy that commentaries on Alladiya Khan and Mallikarjun Mansur stress technical mastery, noting 'severity of expression'. Kishore Amonkar's style, on the other hand, is noted as emotionally expressive, as well as musically correct.

7 Kirana

The context

Situated in the modern state of Uttar Pradesh, Kirana (Kairana on the highway markers) appears on approach to be a large village, dominated by the signalling shape of a Muslim mosque – a striking scene in a North Indian village today. Kirana is one of a cluster of villages in the Delhi area where a complex network of families of musicians have lived and inter-married for numerous generations. Among those villages are Panipat (the scene of several decisive battles in the subcontinent's history), Sonipat, Hussainpur, Ambeta, Chhaprauli, Kandhla, Merath, and Kirana. Hussainpur, for example, was the ancestral home of musicians who became associated with Gwalior – Shakkar Khan, Makkan Khan, and Haddu and Hassu Khan (Jariwalla 1973: 8). C. L. Das (1958: 47) explains the presence of so many families of musicians in Kirana as follows: during the Mughal period disciples of the great singer Gopal Nayak were living in the town of Gatahi, which disappeared in the flooding of the Yamuna river, and the musicians were resettled in Kirana by the Mughal emperor Jehangir.

For the history of the Kirana *khyal gharana* in terms of families of musicians, one has to consider this clustering of families and look beyond *khyal* to musicians with other expertise – *bin*, *sarangi*, and *sitar* players, and singers of other types of music. The clustering of families of musicians helps to explain the association of Bande Ali Khan, a famed *bin* player, with the Kirana *gharana* of *khyal* singers, for in 1870 his father, the distinguished *bin* player Saduq Ali Khan, was living there, and so his son Bande Ali Khan, *bin* player at the Indore court in 1899, became associated with Kirana. While the name of Bande Ali Khan is frequently cited in historical accounts of the Kirana *gharana*, there is no blood relationship between him and the great vocalists Abdul Karim Khan and Abdul Wahid Khan (see Chart 7–2). Because this is a matter of constant confusion, a variant genealogy for Bande Ali Khan, compiled from Agarwala (1966: 34) and Wadhera (1954c), is shown in Chart 7–3. Yet another tracing of Bande Ali Khan's relations is found in Neyman (1980: 246).

For an explanation of the Kirana *gharana* style of *khyal* singing it is necessary to look in particular at two *upstads*, cousins, who came from the village of Kirana itself, Abdul Karim Khan and Abdul Wahid Khan.

Musicians of the Kirana *gharana*

Abdul Karim Khan

Abdul Karim's *gharana* traces its musical history back to the period when the Mughal emperor Humayan was beginning to spread his power over the great kingdoms of Hindustan, that is, to the time of the Tomar dynasty of late sixteenth-century Gwalior and, specifically, to Nayak Dhondu and Nayak Bhannu, disciples of Gopal Nayak (Vasistha 1966). More recently, about 200 years ago, the names of 'Hingarang' (Hussain Ali) and 'Sabaras' (Ghulam Maula) of the Delhi court are cited, as *dhrupad* and *khyal* singers in the same line. In the nineteenth and twentieth centuries, musicians in Abdul Karim's extended family were patronized in various places, among them Lucknow, Bidar, Hyderabad, Mysore, and Kolhapur.

Much has been written about Abdul Karim Khan. On the centenary of his birth his disciple Balkrishnabuwa Kapileshwari published an exhaustive study, in the Marathi language (1972). Subsequent to that, and drawing copiously on it, Jariwalla issued his own, shorter, more personal account of the *ustad*'s life and music (1973), which was also published by Balkrishnabuwa Kapileshwari. Because of these thorough studies, only the barest essentials about Abdul Karim's life are given here.

Abdul Karim was born in Kirana on November 11, 1872, and grew up in the home of his mother (a spirited person and talented *lathi* player), with his paternal uncles and brothers; his father, Kale Khan, was at the Bharatpur court with Shende Khan for a time (see the genealogy according to Jariwalla, Chart 7–2). Abdul Karim's first musical training came from his 'cousin brother' Nanne Khan who, when retiring from service at Bidar–Hyderabad, returned to Kirana at the time the young boy was ripe for teaching. Abdul Karim's father, Kale Khan, taught him as well. Both teachers found the boy intellectually inquisitive and wanting to know the reasons for things. In this extended family where music was being made constantly, the learning process 'in the *gharana*', osmosis, was undoubtedly important for his musical education.

As a boy, Abdul Karim sang at the Yamuna concerts where would-be artists contended on what appears to have been a fairly regular basis. At the age of eleven, supported by his brother Abdul Latif Khan, he sang before a gathering of musicians at Merath, and at about seventeen he performed in Mysore under the sponsorship of his kinsman, the *sarangi* player Hyder Baksh, when the music-loving Chamaraj Wadiyar was the ruler there. Thus, Abdul Karim was nurtured on performing. However, it is striking that Jariwalla (1973) does not mention that Abdul Karim assumed the supportive role for his father that was a traditional option. Also, a curious comment made by Jariwalla is that the Kirana singers did not learn to sing with the support of *sarangi*; this is intriguing because many Kirana musicians were excellent *sarangi* players, and it seems that *sarangi* support would have been readily available, even for casual practice.

In 1889–90 Abdul Karim was married to a girl of his family's choice. Shortly afterwards he, his father, and his brother Abdul Latif began a tour of concerts arranged by various relatives and other supporters. These led to a succession of short-term employments at several courts. In about 1894 (when he was twenty-two) Abdul Karim and his younger brother Abdul Haque travelled to Baroda, a court which was to become associated with memories of Abdul Karim. There the young boys were hired by the *maharaja* to teach music to the women in the household. By a sequence of events they gradually became better known to the court musicians, among them the renowned Gwalior *gharana* singer Faiyaz Mohammad Khan. Jariwalla relates (1973) that two musical factors made a novel impression in the musical circle. One was their choice of a Pahari Mand *Dhun* (a non-classical regional song) as a closing number, and the other – which seems to be distinctive of Kirana musicians – was their tuning of the *tambura* to Ni rather than to Pa for those *ragas* for which it is appropriate.

Chart 7-1: Kirana Gharana Teaching Lines

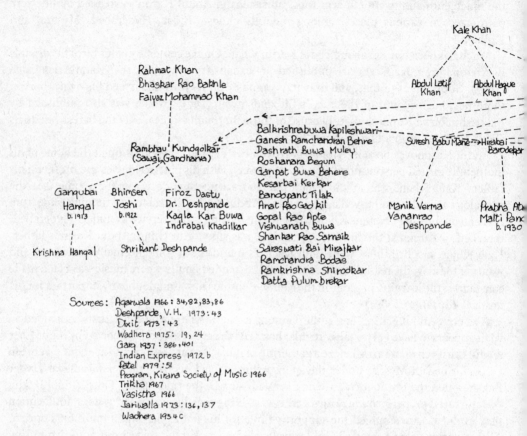

Sources: Agarwala 1966 : 34,82,83,86
Deshpande, V. H. 1973 : 43
Dixit 1973 : 43
Wadhera 1975 : 19, 24
Garg 1957 : 386,401
Indian Express 1972 b
Patel 1979 : 51
Program, Kirana Society of Music 1966
Trikha 1967
Vasistha 1966
Jariwalla 1973 : 136, 137
Wadhera 1954 c

On one occasion Aliya–Fattu, the famed pair of *khyal* singers from Pariala (see Chapter 8), visited Baroda to sing, on the recommendation of the Maharaja of Patiala. At the *darbar* concert Aliya Khan sang, and was greeted with thunderous applause. The ruler of Baroda then inquired which of his state musicians could 'answer' Aliya, and his best musicians, Maula Baksh and Faiyaz Mohammad, replied that it would be disrespectful to the fame of the pair Aliya–Fattu to sing after them as a rival. The *maharaja* (Jariwalla 1973: 37–9) was not pleased that this custom among musicians was given precedence over his wishes, and he called in the young pair Abdul Karim and Abdul Haque who – either because they were young and had less to lose, or because they were in court employ, though not as *darbar* musicians – agreed to sing, and did so beautifully, much to the anger of the musical establishment. This brought them immediate fame, and infamy, and shortly a better position at court, although it did not bring them the good will of established musicians, who objected to them in several ways. One serious objection sprang from the fact that the boys had been born into a *gharana* of *sarangi* players. Jariwalla (1973) refers to a gradual softening in this attitude.

The period when the brothers from Kirana were in Baroda was the time when the Maharaja

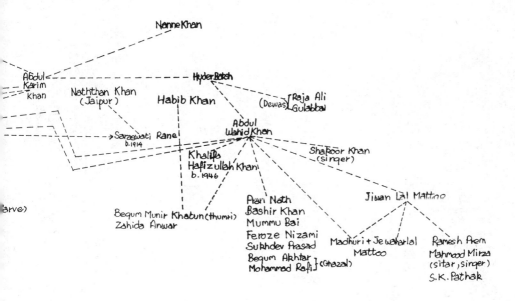

Sayaji Rao had become fascinated with musical notation, with the prospect of Indian music being played in ensemble in the manner of western orchestral music, and with systematic teaching of music in institutions rather than by the traditional *gurukula* system. The influence on the *maharaja* seems to have come from Westerners, primarily a Mr Fredilis. When he left Baroda Abdul Karim, too, became involved with institutional teaching in the *gurukula* style and with the problems of notating Indian music, but while in Baroda he was not a particularly cooperative party in the activities.

In 1902 (Garg 1957: 86) Abdul Karim left Baroda suddenly, at the request of and in assistance to a spirited young lady named Tarabai, who had been his student in Baroda and now became his life's companion. Tarabai's mother Hirabai had died and her father, Sardar Marutirao Mane, had begun drinking, which resulted in violence (Jariwalla 1973: 43, 109); so with Abdul Karim and his brother, Tarabai fled to Bombay. After a few concerts in Bombay arranged by friends, the party went to Miraj, where Abdul Karim went to worship at the tomb of Kwaja Shamna Mira, to whom he had long paid respect. In Miraj he and Tarabai were married. His earlier marriage to the girl of his family's choice had been ritualized but it was

188

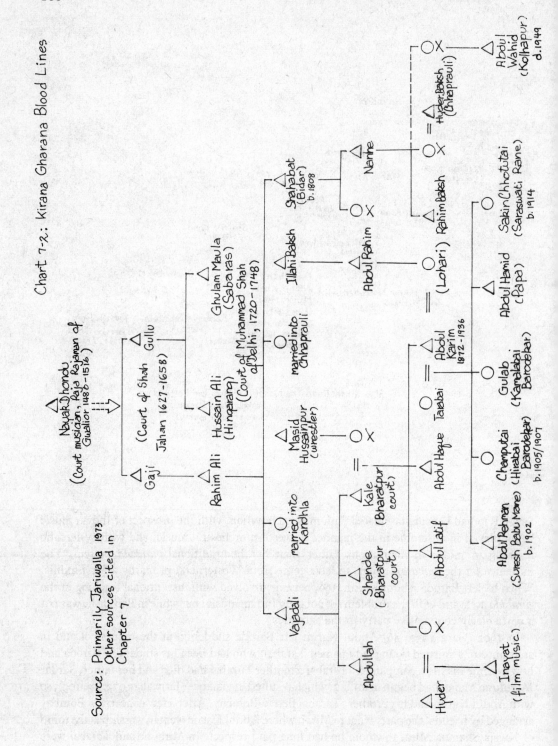

Chart 7-2: Kirana Gharana Blood Lines

Source: Primarily Jariwalla 1973
Other sources cited in
Chapter 7

Chart 7-3: Bande Ali Khan: Genealogy

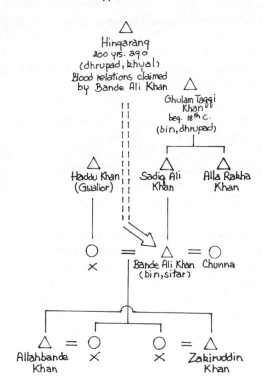

apparently never consummated. His mother tried to make him behave like a proper husband to her, but he never did, considering marriage to be a matter of personal preference and love to be like an art, above *gharana* (Jariwalla 1973: 196).

Abdul Karim's next professional activities included a tour of Maharashtra and Karnatak, two to three years in Sholapur, and one year in Kolhapur. During this period two important future Hindustani singers were attracted to his music; Kesarbao Kerkar (later of the Alladiya Khan *gharana*) began studying with him in Kolhapur, and at Kundgol in Karnatak the young Rambhau Kundgolkar (Sawai Gandharva) heard his future *ustad* for the first time.

Between 1902, when their first child Abdul Rehman (later known as Suresh Babu Mane) was born, and 1914, Abdul Karim and Tarabai had five children (see Chart 7-2; Hirabai Barodekar, their second child, is discussed below). Also at approximately that period, Abdul Karim's systematic bent led him to work with Ernest Clements and Rao-Bahadur R. G. Deval, who were making a systematic attempt to discover the basis of scale-building in Indian music. According to Jariwalla:

under British rule a commission was appointed under the chairmanship of Mr Ellis to go into the question of systematizing Indian music. But its report failed to achieve the object and, in the process, Indian music suffered a humiliation amidst so many conflicting interpretations of the texts . . . it came to be thought that Indian music had no scientific basis at all (1973: 128).

Maintaining that the rules of music are implicit in the music that is sung, Abdul Karim sang for Deval, leaving Deval to deduce the theory from it and compare it with the writing in ancient texts. Concentrating on the problem of the twenty-two *srutis*, Deval published his findings in *Hindu Musical Scale and Twenty Two Srutis* (1910). In this effort he was joined in 1910 by Ernest Clements, district judge of Satara, who was a scholar of Western music. With the help of Abdul Karim, Clements published his *Introduction to the Study of Indian Music* (1912–13), but when Clements began experimenting with a fixed-*sruti* harmonium Abdul Karim lost sympathy with the project: 'The shrutis cannot be separated from the swaras which alone remain the unit of our singing. The shrutis cannot be sung independently of the svaras in which they inhere' (Jariwalla 1973: 130). Deval and Clements continued to pursue their work, however, with the help of V. N. Bhatkhande (see Chapter 5), holding conferences at Baroda, Benares, Lucknow, and Delhi. What Abdul Karim saw was a growing movement of agitation for the de-Muslimization of Hindustani music, with insults and indignities heaped on Muslim singers, but he tried to remain aloof from it. It must have been more difficult for him than for some Muslim artists, because he had been cooperative in the initial studies.

Upon leaving Sholapur, Abdul Karim decided with Tarabai to begin a music school; choosing Belgaum as a location, they opened their Arya Sangit Vidyalaya in 1910. It operated on the basis of the old *gurukula* system of individual rather than class training, and each student had to commit himself to eight years of study. Among his first group of students were two brothers named Kapileshwari and others who remained important in Abdul Karim's life and in the transmission of his art. Balkrishnabuwa Kapileshwari continued Abdul Karim's work on music theory, producing in 1967 a report which was distributed to the Sangeet Natak Akademi and to universities with music departments (he is also the author of the Marathi biography mentioned above).

To permit expansion, the school was soon moved to Poona (1913, according to Garg 1957: 86), where Abdul Karim's cousin Abdul Wahid Khan (nephew of Hyder Baksh) lived with them and helped with the teaching. While Abdul Karim was away on concert tours, Tarabai proved herself a spirited taskmistress at the school, even to the point of driving students away. In 1916–17 Abdul Karim opened a branch of his Vidyalaya in Bombay and moved his family there. In order to compete with the Gandharva Mahavidyalaya of Vishnu Digambar Paluskar, at the insistence of Tarabai and others, he gave up the bond-*gurukula* system of assuring consistency among students and charged them for tuition on a collective basis. Six months later, in 1918, while Abdul Karim was again away on tour, Tarabai left him, taking the school's money with her; in everyone's view this was a shocking action, for they had risked so much to be together and shared so much in their years together. Abdul Karim moved to Mysore.

In Jariwalla's biography (1973) one aspect of Abdul Karim's personality mentioned frequently is his catholic spirit; the social or religious community or caste to which a person belonged did not matter to him. In return, he astounded many by his ability to chant *mantras* in Sanskrit and was, on several occasions, permitted to sing in Hindu temples. The pinnacle of this attitude came when he appointed Balkrishnabuwa Kapileshwari his heir in the Kirana *gharana* – a Hindu heir of a Muslim *gharanedar*!

In 1927 Abdul Karim settled permanently in Miraj. His life consisted of giving concert tours and teaching pupils, including the young Roshanara Begum, whenever he was in Bombay. He apparently was generous to a fault, open in giving music to anyone who wished to learn. He himself lived frugally and treated his students with personal care. His health deteriorated and, on October 27, 1936, he passed away on a railway platform en route to Pondicherry.

Among the disciples of Abdul Karim, three are highlighted here to show up the different perspectives of the *ustad*'s legacy.

Roshanara Begum

There are two contrasting stories about the discipleship of Roshanara Begum, the great Pakistani singer who was born in Calcutta in 1922. Jariwalla relates that Chandra Begum, Roshanara's mother, had been trained by Abdul Karim's brother Abdul Haque and wanted her daughter to study with Abdul Karim. Since she had no money to offer Abdul Karim at *gandha bandh* (the initiation ceremony), she was hoping to find employment for her daughter in Bombay as a playback singer for films and took her there in 1935–6 with that in mind. Abdul Karim agreed to teach her free of charge during the days when he was in Bombay each month. Since Roshanara had already 'had the Kirana *gayaki* in her blood through her mother, she could pick it up quickly' (1973: 204–5).

In an interview in Delhi in 1978, during her first visit to that city after she had migrated to Pakistan in 1948, Roshanara recounted how she first began with music, in the lap of her 'singer-aunt' in a Patna neighborhood. She first heard Abdul Karim in Bombay. She reminisced: 'The soft and delicate style of Khan Saheb was enticingly sweet in intonation and alluringly silken in tonal embroidery. I was simply charmed. His *alap* elaboration was studded with subtlest swara variants. Indeed it was a magic spell' (Patanjali 1978). Abdul Karim was reluctant to take her as a pupil, saying that she would only leave music after her marriage; however, he finally accepted her. Whenever he was in Bombay for concerts or radio recitals – usually for about ten days – Roshanara would go to his flat in Kalbadevi every day, and the *ustad* would sing with her: 'Multani was the first raga I learnt. He would teach the rudiments of a raga for six months' (Patanjali 1978). He stressed the need for a scientific foundation for great music, and for close attention to voice culture and *swara* drill.

The day for her debut came in Kolhapur when Roshanara was in her early teens. Abdul Karim himself tuned the *tambura* for her, and she sang a *bandish* for which he was known, 'Ā Piyā gunavanta' in Rag Puriya. There was a terrible moment when the audience demanded that she end the concert with a *thumri* which she had not learned and which Abdul Karim insisted that she then sing. An intermission was announced, during which he taught her the text and melody, and she then sang the song for an hour! By the time of the Partition (1947) Roshanara Begum had established an excellent reputation as an artist. While it was a great loss to India when her husband opted to migrate to the new state of Pakistan, it was a great loss to all of South Asia when she died on December 15, 1982.

Ganesh Ramchandran Behre (Behre Buwa)

The singing of Ganesh Ramchandran Behre, popularly known as Behre Buwa, reminded listeners of the sad, doleful, very emotional air with which Abdul Karim could sing. Born in 1890 near Bombay, the young Behre Buwa was of a poor Brahmin family (cf. Wadhera 1955). His propensity for music showed at an early age and, at fourteen he left home in search of a suitable arena for his interests. Since that was a period when the Marathi stage flourished, he soon got a place in the Natya Kala Paravartak, a drama company in Bombay.

He met Abdul Karim Khan when his troupe appeared in Sholapur, and when the *ustad* agreed to accept him as a pupil he left the troupe to study singing. His training was periodic, depending on the vicissitudes of his *ustad*'s professional career, so he also studied with Rajab Ali Khan of Indore and for one year with Bhaskar Rao Bakhle. When Abdul Karim opened his Arya Sangit Vidyalaya in Bombay, Behre Buwa joined the teaching staff. In 1932 his beloved wife died: never really recovering, he adopted a life of renunciation, living in a lonely spot in the Ratanagiri district where he had been born and where he built a temple of Shri Dattatraj. Most of his time was spent in praise and worship of the deity, not in an active musical career, but he was brought out of retirement to sing two National Programmes in the 1950s.

Sawai Gandharva (Rambhau Kundgolkar)

Sawai Gandharva was also a disciple of Abdul Karim and was associated with the Marathi theatre. In fact, in the heyday of his art he received nearly unrivalled acclaim for his acting and singing abilities. Like his *ustad*, Sawai Gandharva was praised for his intensity of feeling, the pathetic and devotional appeal of his *vilambit khyal*s. To achieve the fluid, ornate style of Abdul Karim, Sawai had to work diligently because his voice was not naturally suited to it; his success can be measured by the consistency with which reviewers commented on the pupil 'singing with his master's voice'. On the other hand, Sawai was an avid learner and he 'borrowed' from the styles of such musicians as Rahmat Khan, Bhaskar Rao Bakhle, and Faiyaz Mohammad Khan (M. D. Nadkarni 1948b). Among his most accomplished students were Gangubai Hangal and Bhimsen Joshi. Also mentioned in Garg are Firoz Dastu, Dr Deshpande, Kaglakar Buwa, and Indrabai Khadilkar (1957: 386). For the last ten years of his life, Sawai Gandharva suffered from paralysis and was unable to sing – a tragic and prolonged end to a brilliant career. He died on September 12, 1942, in Poona, at the age of sixty-seven (Garg 1957: 386).

Gangubai Hangal

With Gangubai Hangal, there is a refreshing change from musical encouragement and training from father to son, for it was her mother who initiated her training and, among Gangubai's children, it is her daughter Krishna who has chosen a musical career.

Gangubai Hangal was born in February 1913 at Dharwar, to Chikku Rao and Ambabai (Garg 1957: 133), a Kannarese-speaking South Indian family. Ambabai was an accomplished Karnatak musician (Garg 1957: 133), but she also had a fascination for Hindustani music (Vasudev 1959: 42). She did not want her daughter to learn Karnatak music, and in initiating her into the study of music she concentrated on 'straight *sargams*' until she could find her a proper *guru*. Gangubai seems to have made her first public appearance as a singer before she had a proper *guru*, however, for she sang in Belgaum in 1924 (Garg 1957: 133).

Gangubai's first formal study of Hindustani music was in Hubli at Krishna Acharya's school (Garg 1957: 133); her mother took her there in 1926 when Gangubai was thirteen. 'I learnt 60 compositions in drut laya within a year', recalls Gangubai, 'after which there was again a break in my musical instruction' (Vasudev 1959: 42). Three years later she became a disciple of the famed Sawai Gandharva, but her study with him was not constant; she could study with him for only fifteen days a year, when he returned to his village to look after his land (*ibid.*). The rest of the time she practiced under the tutelage of her mother and Dattopant Desai, a family friend (*ibid.*) or maternal uncle (Garg 1957: 133).

In 1932, when Gangubai was nineteen, Amabai passed away. In great distress Gangubai gave up singing, returning to it only at the insistence of an uncle and of Desai (Vasudev 1959: 42). Soon after, in 1934–5, she made recordings (78 rpm) for several companies (Garg 1957: 133). 'Three minutes then seemed a terribly long time. Now, of course, I do not think I could go beyond a few notes within that time limit', she remarked in 1959 (Vasudev 1959: 42).

More intensive training with Sawai Gandharva became possible at about the time Gangubai's reputation began to spread, through performances outside Hubli – in a Calcutta music gathering in 1938, for example (Garg 1957: 133). In that year Sawai settled in his village of Kundgol in the Dharwar district, eleven miles from Hubli (*ibid.*), and Gangubai assumed a routine of travelling there by the evening train, to return late at night (Vasudev 1959: 42). This she did for three years, until 1941 when Sawai Gandharva's health began to deteriorate; until his death in 1942 her *talim* was occasional. By that time, however, she was travelling throughout India on performing tours as an established and respected musician, specializing in *khyal*. She also broadcast for the All-India Radio stations.

As late as 1945, Gangubai included in her performances such lighter genres as Marathi *pad*, *bhajan*s, and *thumri*s. Vasudev's article on her (1959: 42), which resulted from an interview, explained that her disillusionment with those forms arose not

from the presumptuous reactions of a classicist but from the mundane and rather vexing problem that radio fees presented. For every light song broadcast, the already limited fee was depleted by a further

Plate 10   Gangubai Hangal of the Kirana *gharana*, with accompanists (photo by permission of the Sangeet Natak Akademi, New Delhi)

fifteen rupees which went to the composer. Monetarily, it became a dubious proposition. Those days (the early 'thirties) the radio was considered a fashionable and sustained forum of expression for musicians – an attitude formed on its account tended to condition practice in general, it seems. For Gangubai, all this meant giving up singing *bhajans* and *pads*. 'I really can't say why I neglected the *thumri*, however', she ruminates. 'It just slipped into the background and I never bothered to pick up the threads again'.

She may have resumed singing *bhajans*, however, for the program for *Festival '75: Women Music-Makers of India* cited her 'own inimitable style of bhajans which unfailingly echo the mystic mind and music of Abdul Karim Khan' (Wadhera 1975: 24).

Vasudev, who is adept at describing the physical appearance and personal impression created by great Hindustani musicians, tells of a small, thin, rather insignificant-looking woman less than five feet tall, who dresses simply, 'does not seem to expect any extraordinary favours for being able to sing well', and stands almost in awe of the organizers and patrons of music (1959: 42). Commenting along the same lines about herself, Gangubai described how, when she first went to the Delhi All-India Radio station to broadcast in 1938, she had to undergo 'a sorry experience':

'I was so thin and dark and meek, lost in a nine-yard sari', she said, 'that nobody could imagine that I had come to sing. When I enquired for the person concerned at the studio, I was told to sit on the peon's stool outside and await my turn. I did not know what to do, so I just sat'.

Two months later, practically the same thing happened when she went to sing at a conference in Calcutta. Her first call was to go to the temple. When she returned, she was told that the organizer of the conference, Nahar Babu, was rather nervous after having seen her; he wondered if she could sing at all! And so, to allay his fears, she had first to sing at an exclusive private gathering at his house! At that same conference, she was singled out for eight medals! 'It was a fashion those days for men of means to bestow medals upon the singer they liked best. Eight medals were announced for me, though I got only one or two in hand!' (*ibid.*).

Honors of a more modern nature were bestowed upon Gangubai Hangal in later years. She was recipient of Padma Bhushan, from the Government of India, and of the Sangeet Natak Akademi Award for Hindustani Vocal Music.

Bhimsen Joshi

Bhimsen Joshi, the most prominent male disciple of Sawai Gandharva, was born in the Dharwar district, at Rom, on February 14, 1922 (*Program of the Shankar Lal Festival of Music*, 1978); he too has been one of the 'superstars' of Hindustani classical vocal music. His family was said to have 'cherished and nourished traditional values for several generations', with none of the customary references to a supportive member of the family who might have helped him get started in music. Instead he left home several times in search of a *guru*. Since Sawai Gandharva was from the Dharwar district and settled on his land there in the late 1930s when Jashi was a teenager, it is not surprising that Sawai became that *guru*.

While his style is unmistakeably that of the Kirana *gharana*, Joshi is an imaginative musician and has not hesitated to learn from others. He apparently took some instruction from Mushtaq Hussein Khan of Sahaswan/Rampur (*Sangit Natak Akademi Award Booklet*, 1976), and was so enamoured of the *bolalap* and *boltans* of the Agra singer Vilayat Hussain Khan, and of the Rag Shudh Kalyan *tans* of the Gwalior tradition (Karnani 1976: 91), that he adopted these into his style.

Abdul Wahid Khan

The second of the great *ustad*s with whom credit for the Kirana *khyal gayaki* lies is Abdul Wahid Khan. Though his contribution to the *gharana* is invariably cited in glowing terms, he personally seems to have been overshadowed by his elder cousin Abdul Karim. They were related through a complex of intermarrying families, but not as closely as uncle and nephew, as the article in Garg claims (1957: 341).

Abdul Wahid was the son of the brother of the great *sarangi* player Hyder Baksh or the son of his sister (Trikha 1967 and notes to GCI ECLP 2541). He lived with Hyder Baksh in Kolhapur where his uncle was employed as a musician, and received his musical instruction there. Very little detail has been written of his life. Significantly, he is mentioned only once in the Jariwalla biography of Abdul Karim Khan, as the teacher of Abdul Karim's daughter Hirabai Barodekar (1973: 197). After teaching Hirabai for about five years, Abdul Wahid left Bombay to live in Lahore, where he made an independent career until his death in 1949.

Prakash Wadhera (1954c) described Abdul Wahid Khan's temperament as 'inclined towards self abnegation', with a most religious and pious attitude to life. He paid homage all his life to Hazarat Ali Naki, a saint living in Multan in the Punjab (now in Pakistan), and according to his students even sought the approval of the *pīr* (spiritual guide) for all his engagements to sing. Another aspect of Abdul Wahid's personality was described by his most famous disciple Hirabai Barodekar: 'Khan Sahib Abdul Waheed Khan was a very moody teacher whose wrath could be stirred by the slightest error. But he was the best teacher I have come across' (Wadhera 1953c).

Hirabai Barodekar

Hirabai Barodekar was born in Miraj (Mangekar 1964[1]) in 1905 (Jariwalla 1973: 127), or on May 29, 1907 (Garg 1957: 401), the second child of five of Abdul Karim Khan and Tarabai. One newspaper article about her recounts how the newborn infant was left unattended in a corner of the hospital room, assumed stillborn, until she let out a very shrill cry.

Although Hirabai and her siblings were left with their father when Tarabai fled in 1918, Hirabai never seems to have taken formal training with her father, probably because fathers did not prepare their daughters to be professional musicians. According to her own account, Hirabai absorbed some of her father's art, for she copied what he was teaching her older brother Suresh Babu Mane (Abdul Rehman). Both children, however, studied with Abdul Wahid Khan; Hirabai took intensive training with him from about 1919 or 1920 to 1924–6.

In 1923 Vishnu Digambar Paluskar had Suresh and Hirabai sing at a public performance he organized (Jariwalla 1973: 197). Thus the struggling young artists were given recognition and encouragement by one of the leading Hindustani musicians who was involved in the movement to bring classical music to the public and break the prevailing social barriers of musical performance (see Chapter 3 above).

Hirabai played a leading part in another cultural 'revolution' – the Maharashtrian revival of theatre with its concomitant arts, classical music and dance. As has been seen earlier, young male Maharashtrian artists found this a superb outlet, but, as related by Mangekar (1964), Hirabai 'broke the century-old ban on women appearing on the professional stage in

---

[1] The information in this Mangekar article seems to be the precise source for Dolly Rizvi's article on Hirabai in her accounts for children of the lives of great musicians of India (1968).

Maharashtra. She heralded a revolution by [taking part in] plays with mixed casts, and herself acting on the stage opposite famous male stars'. The male stars included her brother Suresh and the famed Sawai Gandharva, a student of her father. In the early 1930s the troupe was fairly successful and maintained a touring and performance schedule with a number of plays. In 1936, with the advent of the 'talkie' movie, such troupes as Hirabai's either waned in influence or ceased functioning.

When the troupe disbanded Hirabai took part in another aspect of the continuing process of introducing art music to the non-court world in North India: theatre concerts, which brought classical music – *khyal* and *thumri* – to the theatre-going masses, who were more accustomed to hearing *bhajan*, light music such as *ghazal*s, and other forms often accompanied with dancing by a singing actress (Mangekar 1964).

As her reputation as a fine musician grew, Hirabai travelled extensively to perform, sang from radio stations, and made numerous commercial recordings. In 1949 she performed in Africa, and in 1953 travelled to China under government auspices. In 1965 she received due recognition through the Sangeet Natak Akademi Award for Hindustani Vocal Music, then in 1970 the Padma Bhushan. Hirabai now lives and teaches at the Sangeet Research Academy in Calcutta.

Hirabai performed often with her sister Saraswati Rane (b. 1914). Younger by seven or nine years, Saraswati looked to Hirabai for her musical training. She also had considerable training from Naththan Khan of Jaipur, but, according to V. H. Deshpande at least, only occasionally can a resemblance to the Jaipur style be heard in her singing (1973: 86). Saraswati is known not only for singing *khyal* but also for a type of song in Marathi called *bhav-git*.

Pran Nath

Pran Nath, a Punjabi, studied with Abdul Wahid Khan in Lahore. A devoted disciple, Pran Nath lived with Abdul Wahid and served him in the traditional *gurukula* manner, helping with kitchen duties, giving him massages, and so on. Once when Abdul Wahid was sitting on a *charpai* preparing his *hookah*, moving the coals with iron tongs, Pran Nath was at his feet playing *tambura* and singing. When the disciple made a mistake, the *ustad* pulled his earlobe with the hot tongs. Pran Nath dismisses those acts of discipline with understanding and remembers his *ustad* with warmth, respect, and gratitude. Their *guru–sisya* relationship was a long and sincere one, and Pran Nath is lauded by other musicians, including Hirabai Barodekar (in 1978), for having set a good example in the traditional manner.

Pran Nath settled in India and became a radio artist for the New Delhi station. In the 1960s he was a teacher of Hindustani vocal music at Delhi University, the Shri Shankar Lal Institute of Music, of Delhi University, and, in addition, he attracted several Western students of Indian music. In the 1970s he moved to the United States under the sponsorship of one of his disciples, the composer Terry Riley of Mills College, Oakland, and is now teaching, recording, and performing, primarily in northern California.

Musical styles of Kirana *gharana* musicians

For the most part, the musical characteristics listed by sources for the Kirana *gharana* are attributed to the style developed by Abdul Karim Khan, the 'founder' of the *gharana* in terms of *khyal* singing. Therefore, the characteristics of his style are discussed here first, then other generalizations about the *gharana* style follow, and then a closer look will be taken at Gangubai Hangal and at performances by Bhimsen Joshi, the leading female and male third-generation Kirana *khyaliya*s in the direct line from Abdul Karim Khan. The second part of this musical analysis focuses on Abdul Wahid Khan and his disciples Hirabai Barodekar and Pran Nath.

Abdul Karim Khan

The available recordings of Abdul Karim offer short selections from the early days of discs, compiled and reissued. Comparing written and spoken comments about the *ustad*'s music with those recordings, one is inclined to agree with Dixit when he speaks of one rare disc by the *ustad*: 'One can hardly place the musician as Abdul Karim Khan even after ten guesses' (1973: 42). On GCI 33 ECX 3253 he sings four brief, medium-speed *khyal*s, two in *tintal*, one in *ektal*, and one in *jhaptal*, featuring *raga*s Basant, Jogiya, Bhimpalasi, and Shankara. The other side of this recording has three *chota khyal*s in fast speed (but the singing seems *madhya laya*) and his famous *thumri* 'Piyā bin nahīn āvat'. On his other recordings as well the fare is an assortment, including *hori* and *tarana*. Since it would be hazardous to generalize from these recordings about his *khyal* style, particularly *bara khyal*, emphasis is laid here on statements that have been made about his singing.

Two adjectives have been universally used to describe Abdul Karim's voice: 'sweet' and 'pliant'. To these can be added 'high', for his natural pitch lay in a range that Western practice would call tenor. He produced an effect that was the opposite of, for instance, the powerful, forceful Agra *gharana* voice.

While it would be reasonable to assume that a Hindustani singer with a sweet voice would cultivate sensuous feeling, Abdul Karim did the opposite. While he sang with great tenderness and depth of feeling (Garg 1957: esp. 86), the feeling expressed was more spiritual than sensual. Like his blood relations in the Kirana *gharana*, Abdul Karim was deeply religious in his daily life. For instance, he would always return to Miraj at the approach of the annual festival of Urs of Mira Sahid, wherever he might be, and distribute food to the needy.

Although one might reasonably expect a Hindustani singer with a pliant voice to cultivate fast-moving passages, the opposite was the case with Abdul Karim. He cultivated elongation of pitches (V. H. Deshpande 1973: 75), taking extreme care about intonation (*ibid.* 41), and creating subtle shades – *kāns* (*ibid.* 75 and Garg 1957: 86). As explained by Deshpande, *kans* are 'note particles' above or below the precise *svara* line, subtler even than *sruti*s or microtones, but belonging to the specific region within a pitch. In Deshpande's opinion, there is a direct relationship between the use of *kans* and the emotional content of music; they are most likely in prolonged pitches, and as the use of *kans* decreases the style becomes increasingly oriented to *svara* patterns rather than to *svara*s themselves, and is more intellectually (rather than emotively) appealing. Govindrao Tembe is of the opinion that it was Abdul Karim who started the vogue of such profuse and varied use of *kans*, at least in Maharashtra (V. H. Deshpande 1973: 75).

According to Dixit (1973), Abdul Karim could reproduce all twenty-two *sruti*s in a *saptak*. This seems like something he would have done as a demonstration, rather than build it into an emotive performance. The article on Abdul Karim in Garg tells us as well that he cultivated *mind*, a pulling legato connection between two pitches (1957: 86); that is also cultivated in slow, expressive singing. The explanation most frequently offered for the Kirana propensity for subtlety of intonation and for *mind* is that the family has a history of being instrumentalists (as well as vocalists), and it is easier to produce *kan*s on stringed instruments than with the voice. It is tragic that none of the selections recorded by Abdul Karim gives us a glimpse of this, but it can be heard in the music of other Kirana musicians.

These attributes of the *ustad*'s style, emphasizing *svara* as they do, led him to de-emphasize *laya*, and led V. H. Deshpande to describe his style as almost devoid of rhythmic play. Emphasizing *svara* also meant paying little attention to fast speed. (The recorded selections that are available commercially, being in *madhya* and *drut laya* and including *tarana*, give a distorted picture of his emphases.) Critics of Abdul Karim found his music lacking in dramatic contrast and therefore monotonous, and also – a serious charge – lacking in formal structure (1973: 41). For those who enjoy emphasis on *svara* and on *alap*, however, the music of Abdul Karim was a pinnacle.

Kirana style in general terms

From Abdul Karim Khan's style, then, the Kirana style is expected to display slow, expressive singing – the slowest of all the *gharana*s, according to V. H. Deshpande (1973: 77). The slow speed and expressiveness are associated with elongation of notes, 'caressing of notes', and 'sweetness of melody due to the tonal quality, which imbibes a gradual, subtle use of semitones in the main note' (Dixit 1973: 38). Added to this is a minimum of rhythmic play, for as adherents to the *gharana* say, 'You miss a trifle if you miss tal, but if you miss svara you miss all' (V. H. Deshpande 1973: 42). The overall effect is of quietness and peace (Agarwala 1966: 35).

Dixit has acknowledged the criticism made of Abdul Karim Khan and his followers that their performances lacked formal structure:

The Kirana musician seems to have all the time in the world once he has started and closed his eyes to mundane things like the audience . . . This has provoked derisive, and wholly unjustified, remarks from listeners. They say if one Kirana gharana musician takes half an hour to reach *gandhar* [Ga of the middle register], another musician of the same gharana will take one hour to do so (1973: 39).

To counter the opinion that the Kirana mode of presentation lacks 'form' because of this, Dixit puts forward the following argument:

As we know, apart from (a) the composition in two parts of a khyal (b) the melodic structure (that is the raga) as accepted in its general structure and (c) the tala, governing or accommodating the melody, there are no norms, no invariables, which can be enumerated about the singing of khyal . . . The appearance and existence of so many gharanas is proof enough that what is termed 'form' is an elastic, accommodative arrangement and not a fixed principle of scientific rigidity (1973: 40).

V. H. Deshpande (1973: 75), however, found the styles of Abdul Karim's successors to have 'honoured the principles of organization to a much greater extent' than did the *ustad*.

The use of the *khyal* text in Kirana performances is mentioned by commentators in two ways: first, to reiterate that the artists have not developed *boltan* or *bolbant* in eschewing *layakari*; secondly, Dixit informs us that *sargam* elaborated in 'an ingratiating manner has become one of the notable and accepted ingredients of Kirana *gharana* performance' (1973: 41).

With respect to *tans* – another element of speed – the practice of each Kirana artist would appear to be an individual matter, at least according to Chandrakant Lal Das (1958: 48). Abdul Karim, he says, was 'indifferent to the long intricate and obtrusive tans'; rather, he produced 'short, simple and consistent pieces of tans rendered with spontaneous ease'. On the other hand, Abdul Wahid, in his richly sober voice, displayed the glamor of *tans* in fast tempo. Bhimsen Joshi, says Das, has been able to achieve a fusion of the two styles: 'The slow tempo . . . evokes a profound depth and sobriety which gets enhanced effect through the highly intricate tans (Variation) meandering over the fast tempo' (1958: 48). Dixit general-izes: 'The Kirana musician's *tan* or swift note presentation is simpler than that of the musicians *of other gharanas* . . . His style is lucid and delightful but not florid' (1973: 41).

Lastly, comments are offerred on repertoire and *ragas*: 'The Kirana school presents the established *ragas* and the repertoire of these musicians is limited compared to that of the Agra or Jaipur school' (Dixit 1973: 42). According to Jariwalla, Kirana musicians take particular pride in singing the compositions of their ancestors 'Hingarang' and 'Sabaras', which only they sing (1973: 12). It could be expected, however, that the Kirana repertoire would be limited in comparison with that of the older *gharanas* and particularly those in which musicians have enjoyed composing for several generations.

Dixit has pointed out that Kirana musicians do not care to mix *ragas* – as in combining attributes of two traditional *ragas* to form a new one (1973: 42). He has suggested that this is because their preference for exploring the emotional or aesthetic conception of a *raga* would be hampered in such mixed *ragas*. In Jariwalla's biography of Abdul Karim Khan, in fact, Kafi Sindhura and Pahari Mand (two *ragas* derived from Bhup), in which he sang regional songs rather than *khyal*, are the only two mixed *ragas* among the numerous *ragas* mentioned in the discussion of songs the *ustad* performed. Abdul Karim once sang a new *raga* – Rasikranjani – in order to mystify his listeners (1973: 104).

A number of years ago, Prakash Wadhera generalized about the choice of *talas* on the part of Kirana musicians, finding that the predominant style continued to use slow *talas*, *jhumra* and *tilwada*, with the younger exponents of the style who were 'desirous of popularity' taking to fast compositions in *jhaptal*, *ektal*, and *tintal* (1954c). If the recent releases of recordings by Abdul Karim Khan are any indication, the example for the 'younger exponents' was set some years earlier by the master.

Gangubai Hangal

Comments on Gangubai Hangal's voice make one wonder how she could have adjusted to study in a line of musicians noted for achieving 'facile sweetness'. The description of her voice as 'masculine' is one she had had to become accustomed to even by 1959, for in an interview with Gangubai, Uma Vasudev discussed it with her: 'Even Gangubai herself laughs about it and relates how the famous Kannada poet, Bendre, teased her: "Surely your voice is like a man's. Maybe it is the soul of some frustrated ustad who could not sing who has found his expression through you!"' (1959: 42). Vasudev then asked her how her voice changed from a 'thin, reedy, hesitant voice' in the 1930s to a voice of extraordinary power and vigor:

She said she did not know how it had happened – the change had been gradual. Did she practice any particular way? No, except that Sawai Gandharva, her *guru*, dinned it into her ears that one's methods of forming the sound 'Aa' – the point from which all music emanates – should be uttered so uninhibitedly that it almost hurt in the stomach (*ibid.*).

On the effect of her singing, critics seem to agree on descriptive phrases such as 'majesty', 'rugged grandeur', and 'overbrimming emotion'. Particularly descriptive was this by Uma Vasudev, speaking of her rendering of specific *ragas*:

The *Malhar* [a melody supposed to invoke rain] by Gangu Bai . . . would never portray the soft patter of rain, but a torrential, tropical downpour. The *Marwa*, with its ascetic, lonely spirit, which she sang recently in Delhi, did not, and would never, convey the gentle loneliness of a melancholy setting, but the wind-swept desolation of a barren plain (1959: 42).

Contrast through ornamentation and vocal production is one of Gangubai's stylistic accomplishments. Dramatic contrast is created, for example, when an interval such as Ma to Dha is produced first as a detached step from pitch to pitch, then as a unit with *mind* connecting the two pitches. In addition, she uses subtle dynamics on the text syllable 'ā', opening and closing the sound as she prolongs the pitch. That, followed in succession by prolongation of the same pitch with *kan* (subtle oscillation within the pitch), or by a pitch prolonged with a series of subtle slow dips away from and back to the pitch, is subtly powerful. A pitch prolonged with *kan* leading to another rendered without fluctuation is equally effective.

In Ex. 7–1, from a performance by Gangubai of Rag Asavari, several contrasting effects are demonstrated. In *avart* 18 a pitch-plateau ascending *gamak tan* was balanced by a descending *gamak tan* with greater variety of pitch contour. The *gamak* was eliminated for a legato rendering of the *mukhda* 'Ye mātā bhavānī'. In *avart* 19 a connected leap from R̲e to R̲ė prepares the listener for the 'dipping' rhythmic motion on R̲e in counts 7–9, which was followed by the legato descent to meet the *Mukhda* 'bhavānī'. In *avart* 20, count 4, the attention to detail in ornamentation is shown by discrete treatment of two successive pitches, first the slight oscillation on Pa, then the slur upward into Dha. In count 11, Gangubai threw out the pitch R̲ė and leaned into the cascading descent of a rapidly ornamented *tan*; this is so distinctive and so reminiscent of moments in performances by Bhimsen Joshi that the possibility arises of their having inherited it from their teacher Sawai Gandharva.

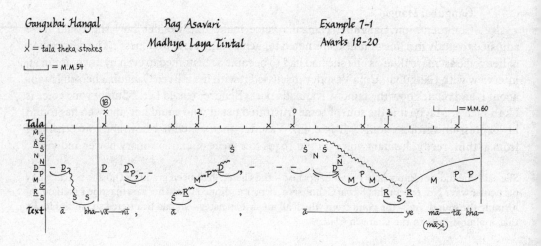

Gangubai Hangal   Rag Asavari   Example 7-1

✗ = tala theka strokes   Madhya Laya Tintal   Avarts 18-20

└──┘ = M.M.54

In a performance at the Tansen Festival (Gwalior) in 1968, Gangubai presented a *jhaptal khyal* in Rag Abhogi. She sang a pre-*ciz alap* on the vocables 'da' and 'na' which resembled the beginning of a true *alap*. The *ciz sthai* and improvisation, followed by *antara* and further improvisation, was rhythmically so smooth that it was not very noticeable when she sang the *mukhda*. The first noticeable rhythmic melody came as she improvised in *antara* range, in the form of a near-*tihai*. Again in the following *avart*, she enunciated the text syllable 'a' three times in marcato fashion as the *mukhda* approached; in such an otherwise floating perform- ance, that rhythmic enunciation alone was sufficient to provide what seemed in that context an enormous contrast. When she had finished her *alap*, Gangubai's supporting singers performed; that, and a *tabla tihai*, marked the end of the initial part of the performance.

A number of Gangubai's *tan*s circulate around three or four pitches, and they are usually slow enough for the pitches to be distinguished upon close listening. A cycle of *gamak tan*s ending with the *mind*-rendered *mukhda* can be very striking. Although the final *avart*s of that Abhogi performance featured increased rhythmic emphasis, the textual material she used was minimal, as in 'aye ayeri a a a'. Through her cultivation of ornamentation and different methods of vocal production, with this minimal use of textual material and very little emphasis on rhythm, her style appears to be consistent with that of the Kirana *gharana* in general.

Bhimsen Joshi

From this statement given by V. H. Deshpande, we can expect Bhimsen Joshi to display the basic Kirana musical characteristics: 'Those who have been fortunate to hear Abdul Karim Khan, Sawai Gandharva and Bhimsen Joshi must have noticed how at each generation new ideas were imported into the gharana and yet the basic gharana remained unviolated' (1973: 14). On the other hand, he says: 'Sawai Gandharva's disciple Bhimsen Joshi has a remarkably wide outlook and receptivity. He has striven hard to hear and study various styles to enrich his own' (*ibid.* 85).

In his recent book *Listening to Hindustani Music* (1976), Chetan Karnani of the University of Rajasthan (Department of English Literature) included a chapter on Bhimsen Joshi which is an excellent detailed analysis from Joshi's commercial recordings. The discussion below transmits Karnani's major points and supplements them with precise examples and additional observations.

Karnani finds that the melodious voice of Bhimsen Joshi reminds him of the voices of Abdul Karim Khan and of Joshi's *guru* Sawai Gandharva, and that there is also a 'certain meditative, introspective touch about his vocalism' which was characteristic of the two earlier Kirana *ustad*s (1976: 90). Others have described Joshi's voice as 'rich', 'resonant' and 'sonorous'. Additional phrases that have been applied to his voice, referring more to vocal production and less to his natural voice, are a 'sobbing voice' (*Times of India* 1970e) and 'crooning tone in more rapid utterances' (*Sunday Statesman* 1968). Printed programs heralding Joshi's appearances in major festivals proclaim his 'serenity' and 'devotional approach' (*Program of the Shankar Lal Festival of Music*, 1978), and his 'warmth and sensitivity' (*Sangit Natak Akademi Award Booklet*, 1976).

Of utmost importance in the Kirana style is subtlety in intonation, and Joshi has cultivated this. In listening very carefully to his Lalit recording (GCI ECLP 2264), for example, one hears *kans* even in the pre-*ciz alap*, on the sustained pitches such as Ma' and Ma. The oscillations within the pitches are so slight and subtle that one wonders if they are really there – until the harmonium player in the recording prolongs the steady pitch slightly longer, at which point the vocal oscillation sounds exceedingly wide. In addition, vocal vibrato is used to full effect, particularly contrasting with *mind*, for which Kirana is well known – all in the short span of, for example, one phrase in the Lalit pre-*ciz alap*:

Another example of discriminating intonation is his very low <u>Re</u> in the Puriya Kalyan recording (GCI ECLP 2253).

One subjective remark on the *mind*s of Joshi is in order. Unlike the sustained, relaxed, legato sound of the *mind*s of Abdul Wahid Khan and Pran Nath (discussed below), Joshi's *mind*s sound (to me) like a tense, pulling legato. Karnani refers to them as 'matchless glides' (1976: 93).

Karnani finds Joshi's use of dynamic contrast particularly striking, citing his full-throated *tar Pa* which creates a very loud effect and remarking that 'he occasionally turns his head sideways and whispers a low trill or renders an intricate pattern of notes' (1976: 94). Compared to other artists, Joshi moves a great deal while he sings, and this seems to be increasing as the years pass. One reviewer referred to 'Bhimsen-like contortions, physical gestures' (*Times of India* 1970e).

Joshi also achieves dynamic contrast through manipulation of vowel sounds. In the Lalit pre-*ciz alap* sung to the *ciz* text 'Rain kā sapanā', he kept all the vowel sounds closed until near the end when he opened up the 'ā' of 'sapanā' in this manner:

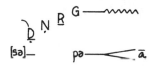

Later in the Lalit recording, in *avart* 13, where he arrived in his *alap* at *tar saptak*, he gave out Sȧ with considerable dynamic volume but on the vowel 'ī' of 'rī' rather than on 'a', as is more customary. On that vowel 'ī' he made a decrescendo to a point of almost no sound, and extended the melodic phrase similarly quietly. Then in two successive *antara avarts*, shown in Ex. 7–2, he exploited dynamic contrasts, utilizing to dramatic effect the vowels 'ī' and 'ā'. In *avart* 16, he sang almost without sound on 'ī', until he reached the *antara mukhda* 'Sovata rī' which he sang full voice. In *avart* 17, the syllable 'a' was his vehicle for the most part, in the words 'jaba', 'pāya', and 'apanā'; the *sthai mukhda* which ends this cycle features 'a' vowels as well. The effect is most dramatic. In Ex. 7–3, *avart* 17 of his Miyan ki Todi recording (GCI EALP 1280), he brought dynamics into play even in a rhythmic context (see counts 5 and 6, where three successive motives lead to Sȧ, which he prolonged a little and leaned into with a crescendo).

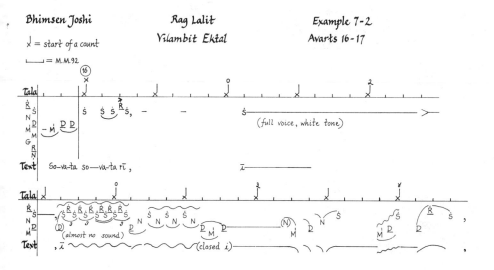

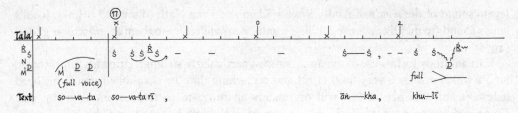

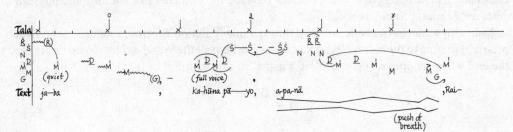

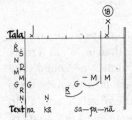

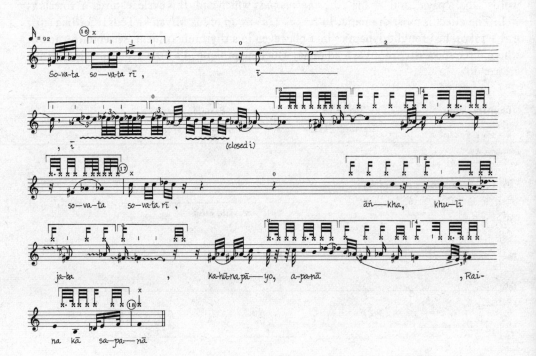

Bhimsen Joshi   Rag Miyan ki Todi   Example 7-3
♩ = start of a count   Vilambit Ektal   Avarts 13-17

⌐___⌐ = M.M. 58

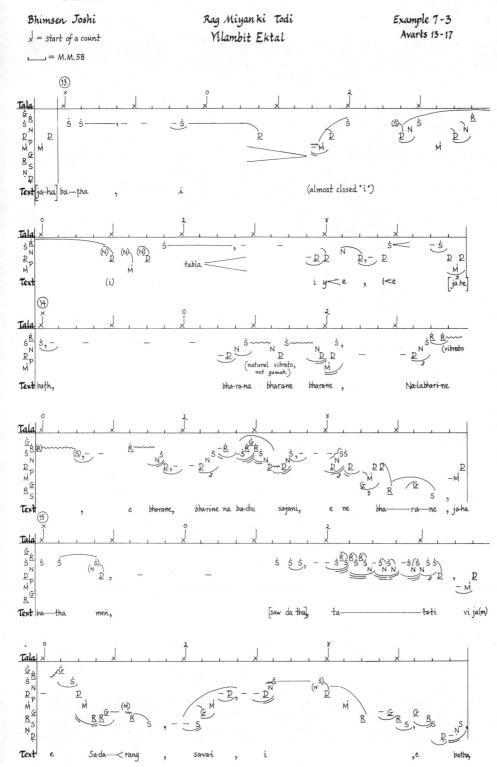

Joshi's placement of 'i' on the prominent *antara* pitch Så is a characteristic detail of his style. A good deal of higher-pitched melody in his Miyan ki Todi performance was sung to the vowel 'i'. Ex. 7-3, *avart* 13, is just one instance of that.

In the context of Joshi's romantic fondness for 'srutis and quavers', Karnani (1976) praises him for giving semantic content to Indian music, and cites his interpretation of the text in the Lalit recording. While Joshi is unusual in singing pre-*ciz alap* to the *ciz* text, he sings *bolalap* mostly on the first phrase of the *sthai*, as most singers do. One unusual instance of his use of the text in *boltan* is shown in Ex. 7–4, from his Shudh Kalyan recording (GCI ECLP 2264). Accumulation of meaning of the text is achieved in one cycle of the *tala*: first he sang a *tan* (on 'ā', without textual meaning); then a *boltan* on 'tuma' ('you') and a second *boltan* on 'bina' ('without'), forming 'without you'; then he climaxed with the textual phrase in the *mukhda* 'tuma bina, kaun' ('without you, what?').

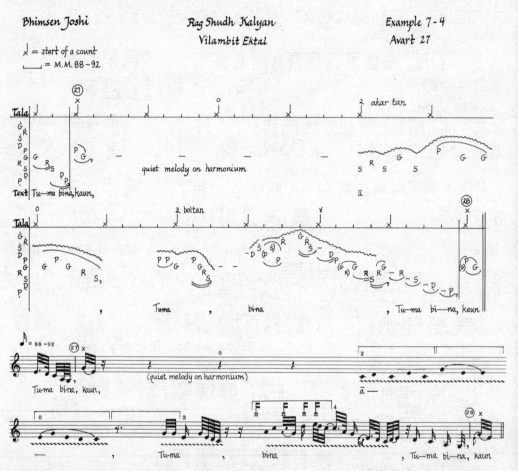

Bhimsen Joshi   Rag Shudh Kalyan   Example 7-4
                  Vilambit Ektal   Avart 27

Karnani sees Joshi's singing of *bolalap* and *boltan* as *layakari*, speaks of his 'reliance on *layakari* as one of the important elements of his vocalism', and points out that the artist has borrowed many of his patterns in *bolalap* and *boltan* from Vilayat Hussain Khan:

But, as he [Joshi] once told me [Karnani] with a twinkle in his eye, he had processed all these borrowed commodities in his Kirana factory – he has added to this borrowed stuff a certain emotional aura and meditative touch. The difference between Vilayat Hussain and Joshi is that while the former sang in a bold, bull-throated voice, the latter sings in a subdued and soft way (1976: 91–2).

In more obvious rhythmic play, Joshi sings *bolbant*; this is most untypical of Kirana. An instance of his *bolbant* is shown in Ex. 7–3, *avart* 17, counts 3–11. He is likely to repeat single words rather than text phrases in *bolbant*, and he might combine words of the text out of the order in which they appear in the composition. Joshi also enjoys *tihai*, which are a type of *bolbant* (see, for instance, Ex. 7–3, *avart* 16). For brief moments of *bolbant* his favorite spot in slow-speed *ektal* seems to be during the 'tirakita' pattern of strokes in the *tabla theka* in counts 4 and 10, which is usually drummed very clearly and sparsely relative to the 'filled-in' *theka* surrounding it (see, for instance, the *theka* rhythm notated in Ex. 7–4). The choice of that moment for *bolbant* makes the rhythmic play blatant, and utterly clear to any listener.

Two other traits distinguish Joshi's performances from those of the earlier Kirana *ustad*s. With respect to 'text', it must be pointed out that Joshi, unlike Abdul Karim Khan, plays down *sargam*, featuring it rarely (if ever) in his performances. The slow tempo in which both Abdul Karim and Abdul Wahid rendered their expressive performances is not a trait associated particularly with Joshi.

The lack of a sense of formal structure which put Abdul Karim Khan supporters on the defensive is not a problem for Joshi, according to at least one critic: 'The slow exposition was knit in a compact, coherent design in which the raga unfolded itself methodically, note by note, and yet not becoming ponderous as in some other Kirana exponents' (*Times of India* 1970e). Analysis of five *bara khyal* performances reveals that while (on recording) Joshi might sing the more usual less-than-a-minute pre-*ciz alap*, he might also sing a longer one (for instance 2:27 in Puriya Kalyan). He is likely to place this mostly in *mandra saptak*.

Joshi sings only the *ciz sthai* at the outset, waiting until after his *raga* exposition to sing the *ciz antara*, if he sings it at all. Rhythmic emphasis is likely to come relatively early in the exposition, however, as he uses it for variety when he is presenting similar melodic material in two successive units of *alap*. He is not likely to dwell long on the lower *sthai* range and he would compress his presentation of the upper tetrachord of the middle register; conversely, if a generalization were to be hazarded, it would be that he handles the two *madhya saptak* tetrachords equally, if anything prolonging Dha or Ni (depending on the *raga*) to create the climax to Sà. In his excellent Puriya Kalyan recording, the *alap* was exemplary, with a delightful twist as he ascended gradually to Dha, to Ni (two *avart*s, one with *bolbant*), and then, avoiding Sà to Rè and then Sà. Further suspense came with a rhythmically pulsating *avart* (10) in *sthai* range; Sà finally came in *avart* 12, introduced by the *ciz antara*.

Karnani points out another distinctive structural feature that one is likely to hear in a Bhimsen Joshi performance: 'In his recorded slow khayals, he always renders an antara and thereby changes his sam after fifteen minutes or so' (1976: 95). Indeed, in his Shudh Kalyan recording Joshi utilized the *antara* text and *mukhda* for an extraordinary length of time – from *avart*s 12–13, when he sang the *ciz antara*, through to *avart* 24. On close transcription, however, it appears that the complete *ciz antara* is not always there. Ex. 7–3, from his Miyan ki Todi recording, lacks only the initial *avart* of *antara* (which textually was mostly sung to 'i'). *Avart*s 12–13, 13–14, and 14–15 ended in *antara mukhda*; in *avart* 15 came most of the *antara* text, and it can be compared to the complete text of the composition given in Chapter 2 (Text 1). The improvisation is clearly *antara* improvisation, however, and it is refreshing to hear an artist utilize an *antara mukhda*.

Karnani commends Joshi for the contribution that he made to the Kirana school by imparting to it the dazzling brilliance of *tans*. 'He has specialized in uljatti taans – these are usually woven round three or four notes, then there is a sudden tetrachordal or parallel octave jump' (1976: 92).[2] In addition to leaps and (therefore) quick changes of register in his *tans*, Joshi varies his *tans* by means of a sudden, rhythmic vocal thrust, followed by a volley of pitches, as shown below.

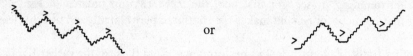

The accented thrust gives way to a very lightly produced *tan*. He uses *gamak* in *tan* to tantalizing effect – a slow *gamak* on the *tan* pitches sounding very different from a fast one. A *tan* can be made to sound fast by virtue of the *gamak* rather than by the number of pitches traversed. These uses of *gamak* in *tan* are not unique to Joshi, but he uses them effectively. He also sings *alankarik tans*; there is one notated in Ex. 7–3 above, the second half of *avart* 16. When he renders his *tans* with a very fast, vibrato-type *gamak* it is very difficult to pinpoint the pitches; his *tans* are far more intricate rhythmically and melodically than one can easily hear as they fly past.

Two further characteristics of Joshi's performance should be pointed out. One is that he sings very long melodic phrases in one breath. Note, for example, the long, quiet melodic phrase in Ex. 7–2, *avart* 16, counts 3–10, which he sang in one breath. The sudden silence following the *mukhda* which closed off that phrase at the beginning of *avart* 17 demonstrates the second characteristic: the dramatic use of vocal silence. Since Joshi performs on his recordings with harmonium accompaniment, which is very quiet, the effect of vocal silences is very dramatic; it is the beautiful *tambura* resonance which comes through at such moments. He is also likely to leave time (therefore moments of relative silence) between *tans* within an *avart*, as in Ex. 7–3, *avart* 14, count 5, and *avart* 16, counts 4–6.

To conclude this discussion of Bhimsen Joshi, it seems fitting to refer to two remarks made by Karnani about this great Kirana artist, which will sound familiar from the discussion of Abdul Karim Khan above. First, 'Joshi has always preferred traditional compositions to new-fangled ones . . . Most of Joshi's recorded compositions have been borrowed either from Adarang or Sadarang' (1976: 93–4; for instance, 'Daiyā baṭh dūbhar bhaī' in Rag Miyan ki Todi is attributed to Sadarang). Secondly, 'The ragas he has mastered can be counted on one's finger-tips' (1976: 95; this is an exaggeration because Karnani himself lists the twenty-five *raga*s on Joshi's recordings). While that seems to vex Karnani (1976: 96), who otherwise admires Joshi greatly, it is nevertheless in keeping with Joshi's Kirana background.

Thus, Bhimsen Joshi is an example of a Hindustani artist who has cultivated both of the expectations of his musical cultural tradition – by sustaining and maintaining the 'old' while making individual contributions to the 'new'.

Abdul Wahid Khan

The second of the great *ustad*s of Kirana was Abdul Wahid Khan. While accounts of Abdul Wahid speak of his music in adulatory terms, remarkably little detail can be gleaned

---

[2] Karnani continues: 'He has introduced a new commendable innovation. Towards the end of his bada khayal, he starts a volley of brilliant tans in slow Ektala. This is unlike many other artists who sing their taans in fast Teentala only'. Why Karnani asserts this is unclear to me, because *tans* are sung by most artists toward the end of their *bara khyal*s, as a basic ingredient in improvisation, no matter what *tala* they are utilizing.

about it from printed sources. What is said here will sound familiar in terms of Kirana. The most striking aspect of his performance was apparently his *alap*. The time he took, and the care, to elaborate the *raga* was exceptional among *khyal* singers: he might take an hour on one *raga*. Among his favorite *ragas*, according to the article on him in Garg (1957: 342), were Malkosh [Malkauns], Miyan Malhar, Multani, Lalit, and Darbari Kanhra. Among *talas*, he particularly enjoyed *jhumra* (Joshi 1976).

V. H. Deshpande commented that Abdul Wahid's method of melodic elaboration was 'purely Kirana'; he paid close attention to chastity of *swara* intonation 'and accentuated its rich soporific effect' (1973: 66). This is counter to the charge made against Kirana by critics who say the *swara* of Kirana is *besur* ('out of tune') (1973: 74). Another comment about Abdul Wahid concerns his slow speed in *khyal*, which, when sung in his full-throated voice, gave an impression of 'serenity' (V. H. Deshpande 1973: 66). When questioned about her *ustad*'s tempo, Hirabai Barodekar is said to have remarked that 'only Ustad Abdul Waheed Khan could manage a slow tempo with grace. Others made vain and clumsy attempts to imitate that tempo' (Wadhera 1953b). In addition, as Joshi put it, Abdul Wahid was not particularly fond of *drut khyal* (1976).

He did not cultivate *layakari* in his music (V. H. Deshpande 1973: 66; Garg 1957: 342), as is to be expected from an artist who emphasized *alap*. The article in Garg (1957: 342) points out, however, that his *tan*s were intricate and moved at quadruple speed. The distinction made between speed and rhythmic play is clear. Joshi, too, mentioned his *tan*s, and also his use of *sargam* (1976). Amar Nath, whose *guru* Amir Khan was greatly influenced by Abdul Wahid, pointed out Abdul Wahid's use of silence, in pauses between improvisations.

Little music recorded by Abdul Wahid is available, because he could not be persuaded to record until 'he was on the wrong side of seventy' (notes to GCI ECLP 2541). His one record, 'Ustad Abdul Waheed Khan: Great Master, Great Music', includes portions of three *bara khyal* performances – all in *jhumra tal*. The second side is devoted to one of his favorite *ragas*, Darbari Kanhra.

Abdul Wahid established a slow speed (♪ = 84) for the Darbari Kanhra performance. This may have been slow at that time, but more recently Amir Khan sang considerably slower. In the 25:24 minutes on the disc, Abdul Wahid did not increase his speed by increasing the rate of the *tala* counts (but most artists do not accelerate greatly until the *alap* portion of a performance is completed). In keeping with comments about his music, all the time on the disc is devoted to *alap*, to progressive delineation of the *raga*, to exploring pitch areas in *merkhand* style. At the end of the 25:24 minutes, where the performance has been cut, he has ascended to *madhya* N̲i, but no glimpse of Sȧ has been given. Furthermore, in the sixteenth minute of the performance on this record, a splice seems to have been made (or the machinery on which he was recorded slowed down), because there is a drop in pitch of about a half-step), so the real performance time taken to reach Sȧ is unclear. In the matter of length of *alap* alone, one of Joshi's remarks seems accurate: 'He had little use for the gallery and even less for gimmicks. His music was too esoteric for the uninitiated, and was more educative than entertaining' (1976).

In this Darbari Kanhra recording Abdul Wahid sang only 52 seconds of pre-*ciz alap*, and then sang the *ciz sthai* ('Gumānī jāga') clearly, followed closely by the *ciz antara*. In those first three *avart*s of the performance, devoted to the *ciz*, three characteristics stand out: his text enunciation was clear, but not rhythmically 'punchy'; oscillations such as those on D̲ha and

Ga in this *raga* were beautifully exploited in his style of cultivating correct, subtle intonation: and he joined pitches in luxuriant, pulling *mind*s.

*Avart*s 5–12 of his *khyal* explore the same pitch material: G̲a Ma Pa Dha Ni Sa, with the *mukhda* also taking in Re Ga and Ma. *Avart*s 5–9 are shown in Ex. 7–5. By following each melodic phrase which begins with Ma Pa D̲h̲a, for example, one can see the means by which variety is achieved, even in phrases using essentially the same pitch material.

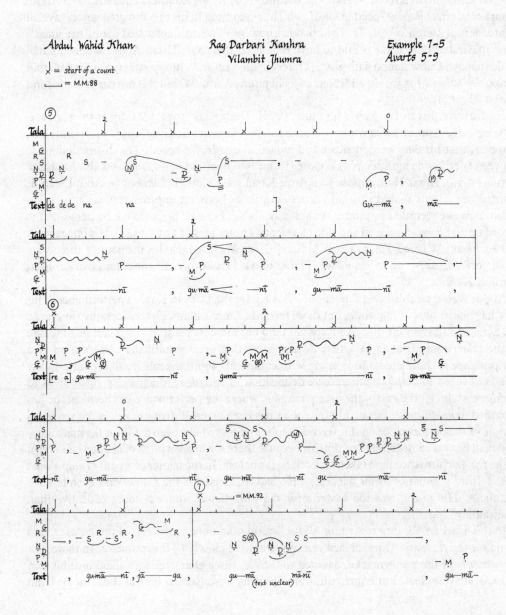

Abdul Wāhid Khan · Rag Darbari Kanhra · Vilambit Jhumra · Example 7–5 · Avarts 5–9

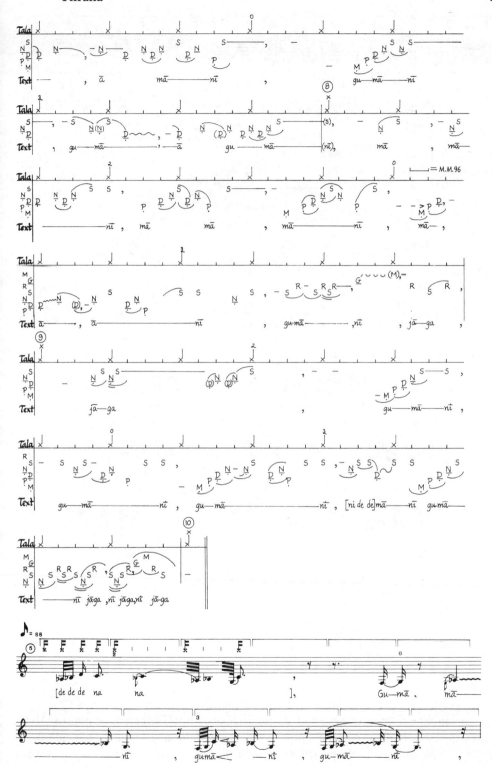

One detail which appears here and through most of this Darbari recording is Abdul Wahid's completion of the *mukhda* before *sam* (*atit*), without any feeling of having missed *sam*. (In the Rag Multani performance on the other side of this disc, he resolved the *mukhda*

on *sam* most of the time.) An ornamentation pattern that appears in these *avart*s also appears elsewhere – a dip to the next lowest pitch, enunciated in *avart* 6.

Another significant moment is shown in Ex. 7–6 – the mixing of *sargam* with text phrases in the same *tala* cycle. Abdul Wahid was 12:50 minutes into the performance at this point, having reached G̲a in his ascent, and these *sargam* passages remain in character pitch-wise. He used *sargam* elsewhere in the performance (*avart* 27, just after the splice) in a rather sultry vocal style, again mixed with *bol*s. At 21:44 he used *sargam* to sustain the interest in the Pa region; a slight rhythmic difference is created there by hitting the pitches directly rather than approaching them 'obliquely'.

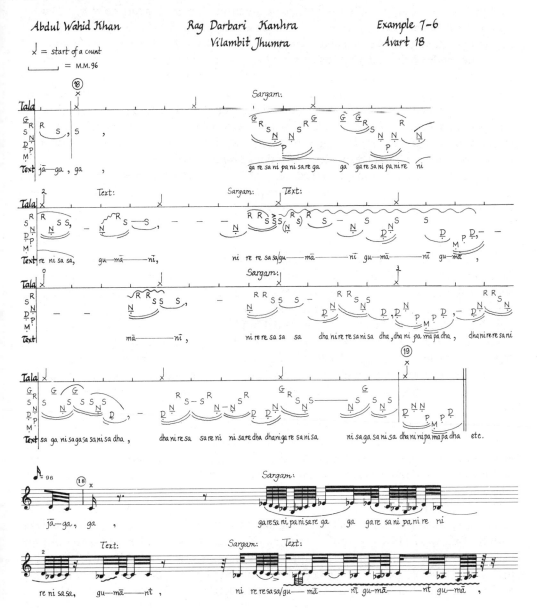

Abdul Wahid Khan   Rag Darbari Kanhra   Example 7–6
                          Vilambit Jhumra   Avart 18

While Abdul Wahid did not obviously cultivate *layakari* (rhythmic play), it is striking that his slow *alap* has purposefully rhythmic movement in it. Beyond *avart* 12 of this Darbari Kanhra performance the *alap* is not reposeful or serene; rather, it is restless, due to play with rhythmic grouping through syllable change.

The first side of the disc gives us extracts from pieces, beginning well into the performances: he had reached Dha in Rag Patdip and was thoroughly into *antara* range in Rag Multani. In Patdip we hear *sargam* and, just once, a *tan* repeated in *sargam*. While Abdul Wahid left moments of silence between his *tans*, I would hesitate to suggest that this is the same use of silence as that commented on by Amar Nath. There is no consistently clear instance of that characteristic in any of these selections. Nor is it possible to point to remarkable, intricate, fast *tans* in these selections, as is to be expected from an artist 'on the wrong side of seventy'. One has to be grateful to All-India Radio and agree with D. T. Joshi's notes for the disc: 'That we have been able to preserve some of the Maestro's music against such odds, is an achievement of which we can be justly proud'.

Hirabai Barodekar

As with her *ustad*, Hirabai Barodekar has been praised most frequently for her *alap* (*svar vistar*), and therefore particularly for her *vilambit khyal*, although she sings *tarana*, *thumri*, *bhajan*, and Marathi *pad* as well (Mangekar 1964; Garg 1957: 401). Descriptions of her voice include 'liquid, flowing', 'the feel of velvet', and 'the grace and poise of a bird in flight'; to those I would add 'light', even 'delicate'.

Although slow speed does not seem to be an attribute used by critics to distinguish her style, Hirabai does begin her *vilambit khyal* in the same slow speed-range as Abdul Wahid; and she does not speed up as much as many performers do in *vilambit khyal*. Perhaps it is because she does not eschew *drut khyal* that her performance is not noted as 'slow', as her *ustad*'s was.

It is assumed that when V. H. Deshpande said of Hirabai 'In neatness of arrangement, proportionality and overall shapeliness Hirabai's achievement is truly remarkable' (1973: 75) he was referring to her *raga* exposition, for that is the element which dominates her *bara khyal* performances. Sustained contrast to *alap* comes in the *chota khyals*, which are dominated by *tans* and reiteration of the *ciz*.

Particularly striking in Hirabai's performances are pauses lasting for an *avart* that subdivide the performances into sections. It is not uncommon for artists to finish the *mukhda* with the first two or three beats of an *avart* and then rest for several beats in that *avart*, but usually they begin the next phrase of improvisation at some point toward the middle or end of the cycle. Hirabai's pauses are perceived as very long by comparison (this is what I had expected to hear, but did not, in Abdul Wahid's selections). What distinguishes Hirabai's performances even further, however – a consistent individualistic characteristic of her *khyal* style – is what happens during those pauses: she has the *tabla* player take solos. For such a thing to occur in the fourth *avart* of the slow-speed performance (as in her Ramkali recording) and after the fourth *avart* (as in her Yaman recording, GCI ECLP 2275) is indeed distinctive. Those *tabla* solos definitely function as period markers, but toward the end of her *vilambit* performances they also seem to be *tabla* solos for their own sake, perhaps because she wanted to rest. In Hirabai's *chota khyal* the *tabla* part remains unusually active in accompaniment, as well as occasionally providing solo material. The Yaman recording ends in a voice–*tabla* relationship that resembles the simultaneous improvisatory relationship between voice and *pakhavaj* in *dhrupad*.

A distinctive characteristic of Hirabai's vocal phrasing is her way of sustaining a tone to the extent that one thinks the melodic phrase will end with it, and then continuing with more of the phrase afterwards. An instance of that is shown in Ex. 7–7 (see the arrows).

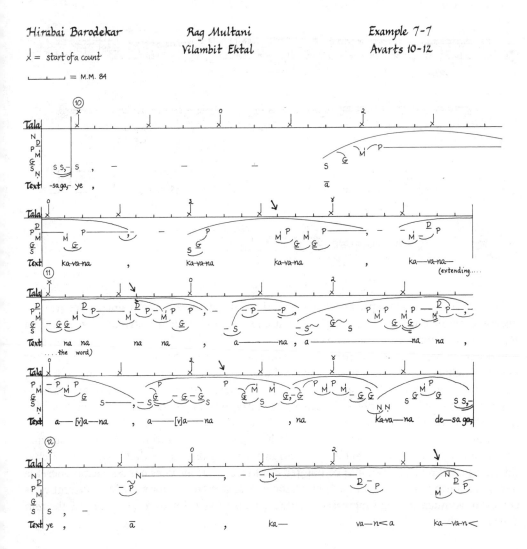

Hirabai Barodekar Rag Multani Example 7-7
Vilambit Ektal Avarts 10-12

𝄆 = start of a count

= M.M. 84

Hirabai also gives a glimpse at *bolbant*-type rhythmic enunciation, but since it occurs only once in each recorded performance (or not at all in some) it provides striking contrast. In a Rag Yaman performance (see Ex. 7–8) *bolbant* succeeds *tan* in the same *avart* (24). *Bolbant* also occurs in her Multani recording, in the fourth *avart* from the end of the *bara khyal*, but her vocal delivery was so smooth that the rhythmic effect was minimized. Since she ended the Multani *bara khyal* shortly after that with a *tihai*, there was an impression of attention to rhythmic play, but on the whole the same generalization can be made about her style as was made about Abdul Wahid's: she does not cultivate *layakari*.

Hirabai's *tan*s, as demonstrated particularly in Ex. 7–8, tend to include both leaps and curvaceous melodic motion. She sings them in a 'loose' *gamak* style that makes the pitches difficult to distinguish. It should be pointed out as well that she does not noticeably increase her speed during the *tan* portion of her performance, as many performers do; acceleration is achieved as much through increased rhythmic density as through acceleration of the *tala* counts.

Hirabai Barodekar

Rag Yaman
Vilambit Ektal

Example 7-8
Avarts 24-5

x = start of a count
⌐___⌐ = M.M. 104

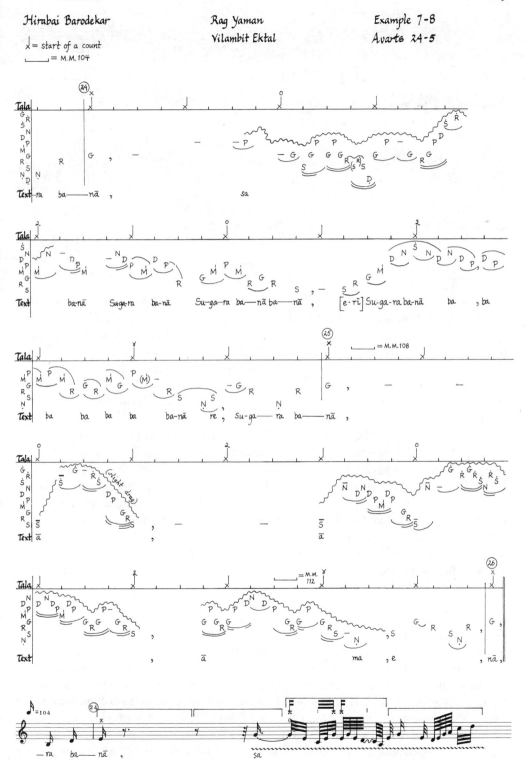

Pran Nath

Pran Nath, who was devoted to Abdul Wahid Khan, has patterned his *khyal* style closely on that of his *ustad*. In matters of *alap* style, clear intonation, slow speed and avoidance of fast speed, use of *sargam*, and lack of attention to *layakari*, we hear in Pran Nath's performances what the descriptions of Abdul Wahid's performances led us to expect in his. This was recognized in a review of Pran Nath's first concert in Bombay: 'Pran Nath belongs to the Kirana tradition and the impress of Abdul Waheed Khan reveals itself in ample measure in his singing more especially in the smooth, placid flow of *alap*, as also in the judicious use of *sargams* and *taan* patterns' (*Times of India* 1968e).

The similarity of *alap* style can be seen in Ex. 7–9, from a performance of Rag Bageshri. Six cycles are devoted to essentially the same melodic material; this process of exhaustive exploration of the possibilities of a pitch area relies on rhythmic detail as much as melodic. Improvisation in *avart* 2 encompasses M D N S, D P D N D; the pitches in the *mukhda* (last two counts) are not considered part of the *alap* material. *Avart* 3 adds middle-register Re and Ga. From there to the end of the example the same melodic material is explored, obvious repetition is avoided, and subtle change is made the musical challenge. To the greatest possible extent the *mukhda* is embedded into the *alap*, by continuing the phrase well beyond *sam* and singing it with the same rhythmic and melodic style as the *alap*-type improvisation which precedes and succeeds it.

Pran Nath continued this Bageshri performance with pitch Ga and the unit Ma-Ga being more prominent in *avart*s 9 and 11, after which he sang the *ciz antara* for one *avart*. The *ciz antara* and the long *avart* of rest (*avart*s 12–13) subdivide the performance, as in Hirabai's Ramkali performance, marking off the improvisation in *sthai* range. Unlike Hirabai, however, Pran Nath did not relinquish such *avart*s of rest to the *tabla* player. After the 'break' he improvised in *antara* range, with Rė his highest pitch. The *alap* character of his improvisation did not change before the end of this *vilambit* selection. The structuring of Pran Nath's *bara khyal*s, then, resembles that of Abdul Wahid's Darbari Kanhra described above.

Also like Abdul Wahid's is Pran Nath's tendency to combine *sargam* and text in the same unit of improvisation. He occasionally sings *boltan*. Unlike Abdul Wahid, however, Pran

Pran Nath   Rag Bageshri   Example 7-9
                   Vilambit Ektal   Avarts 2-8

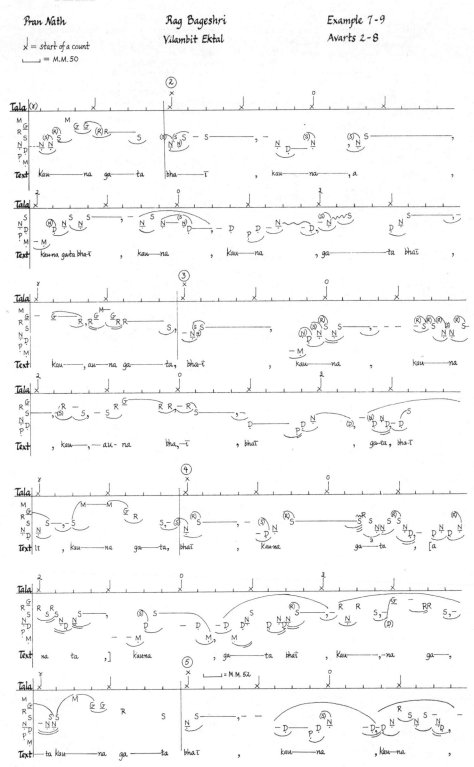

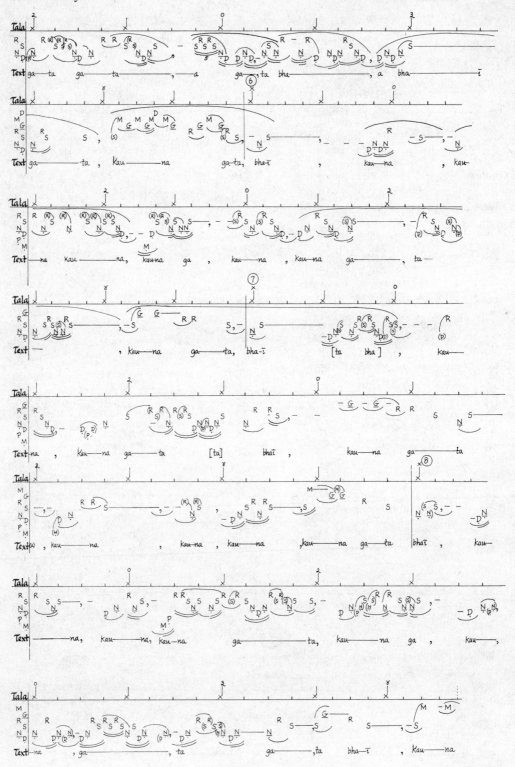

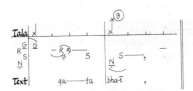

Nath sings strikingly few *tan*s; those that he does sing are very slow, with a loose vibrato that tends to hide the pitches.

Pran Nath's espousal of slow speed and eschewance of fast speed are seen in the minimal acceleration pattern – practically none at all – that he follows in his performances, and also in the speed of his *chota khyal*s. They are not *drut* speed, but *madhya laya*.

One of Pran Nath's individual achievements as a singer is his *mind*s, which he has kept within the Kirana tradition, but he has mastered them more than any other Kirana musician I have heard. He clearly prefers slow, sustained singing, with primary attention given to the *raga* in *alap*, subtleties of intonation, and connections between pitches. He carries out his preferences with superb artistry.

Summary

In the enumeration of characteristics of Kirana style, as culled from various commentaries (pp. 198–9ff.), the first item mentioned was tempo, which was reputed to be unusually slow. The performance speeds of these Kirana musicians are not in fact slower than those of other *gharana*s. A comparison of numerous performances by many performers shows Kirana on the whole to be generally slower than Gwalior, but a bit faster than Agra. Acceleration of the *tala* counts takes place within a very small range.

The types of vocal qualities, natural and studied, vary widely among Kirana artists, if the descriptions reveal anything: 'melodious and sweet voice' for Abdul Karim Khan (Garg 1957: 86); 'rugged grandeur' for Gangubai Hangal; 'sobbing voice' and 'crooning tone' for Bhimsen Joshi and the like. There is a consensus in commentaries about performances by these artists, however, in the matter of using the voice with emotive expressiveness. Use of *kan*s – subtle intonation within a pitch – exquisite *mind*s, controlled degrees and placement of vibrato, are examples of this. The variety sought in a Kirana performance consists, to a great extent, of this use of the voice, rather than of the use of essentially different musical elements (melody and rhythm). The utilization of various vowels, different speeds of *gamak*, and play with vocal dynamics (particularly for Gangubai Hangal and Bhimsen Joshi) are other examples of this.

Melody reigns supreme in Kirana style, and the *raga* is explored at very great length by some Kirana artists relative to other singers of *khyal*.

The statement has been made that the text is kept clear by Kirana artists. This seems to be largely true, but very little of any single *khyal ciz* is used. *Bolbant* is sung very seldom (mostly by Bhimsen Joshi), and it is not intricate rhythmically. *Boltan*s occur in Pran Nath's *chota khyal*, and Bhimsen Joshi sings them in *bara khyal* as well (he is said to have borrowed them).

Sargam, rather than text, seems to be a route Kirana musicians take to achieve rhythmic emphasis. In Abdul Karim Khan's medium-speed and fast-speed performances the *sargam* passages are highly rhythmic and prominent – and delightful; among his disciples, Gangubai and Joshi both use *sargam* minimally. Abdul Wahid Khan used *sargam* in slow *alap* as well, and his disciples sing *sargam* quite a bit.

The *tan*s of Kirana musicians do not seem to constitute an element of *gharana* characterization. They may be slow or fast, simple or intricate, clustering around three or four pitches or encompassing many pitches, and so on.

Several other elements of structure or style require mention, although they are not matters of consensus among Kirana artists. Abdul Wahid Khan presented his *sthai* and *antara* together right at the beginning of his *vilambit khyal* performances; this was seen in the Alladiya Khan tradition, as well. Hirabai Barodekar sang the *antara* at the beginning in one performance, though she sang it later in a different performance. Pran Nath sings *antara* later (or not at all), while Bhimsen Joshi sings it later, and might dwell on it for *mukhda* purposes, or he might not sing it at all. Nor is there consensus about what to do with the pre-*ciz alap*, as regards length, melodic nature of the improvisation, or text – whether to sing it to vocables or to *ciz* text. This and other matters seem to be up to the individual artist in the Kirana *gharana*. Gangubai Hangal and Pran Nath enjoy working the *mukhda* into the melodic and rhythmic context of the preceding *avart*. Bhimsen Joshi sings long phrases in one breath and also cultivates the dramatic use of silence; he features quick thrusts in his *tan*s. Hirabai Barodekar waits a relatively long time after the *mukhda* before she begins her next melodic unit, and she is the only Kirana artist I have heard who has the *tabla* player take an active solo role in the performance.

It appears that in structuring the *khyal* performance, the Kirana tradition admits of flexibility with regard to the nature of the pre-*ciz alap*, the presentation of the *ciz*, the proportions and melodic nature of the *alap*, the inclusion of *boltan* and *bolbant*, and the inclusion of *chota khyal*. The flexibility is itself a *gharana* characteristic. The general emphasis on melody – whether in terms of form or style – is the shared feature, and that is played out in ways that may be shared (*alap*, *mind*, *kan*, and other means of vocal expressiveness) or individual. As to their repertoire of *raga*s, *tala*s, and *ciz*, the singers partake of the body of traditional materials, as well as offering one particular 'family' set of compositions.

8 *Patiala*

The context

On the highway from Haryana state, close to the city of Patiala in the Malwa district of the Punjab, one passes a formidable fort with the old defensive form of double, inward-slanting walls encircled by a moat. One is reminded of the militant past in an area of constant warfare, and of the glories of Sikh fighters renowned for their fierceness and valor.

Patiala, which held primacy of place among the Sikh states, rated as a separate political entity from 1762 to 1763 under the leadership of *rajas* of a family of Sidhu Jat Sikhs, who trace their ancestry back at least to the Rajputs of the twelfth century and to the area of Jaisalmer in Rajasthan state. The Patiala line came first under Raja Ala Singh (d. 1765), then his grandson Amar Singh (1765–81), and then passed to Amar Singh's son Sahbin Singh (1781–1813), and to Sahbin Singh's son Karem Singh (1813–45). Karam Singh's son Narindra Singh (1845–62) was in control, and was the acknowledged leader of the Sikhs, in 1857 when 'mutiny' against the British was attempted by several North Indian rulers.

Narindra Singh chose to back the British, thereby placing the Patiala rulers in a favored position. They ranked as first among the chiefs of the Punjab and, as such, were accorded the rank of *maharaja*, which entitled them to a salute of seventeen guns in the British system of according status. Narindra was succeeded by his son Mohindra (who died suddenly in 1876), and then by his grandson Rajindra (ruled 1876–1900), who was an enthusiastic patron of the arts. Rajindra's eldest son Bhupindra Singh (1891–1938) and Yadavindra Singh (b. 1913) were the last rulers of the princely state of Patiala.

Patronage of music at the Patiala court is said to have begun with Raja Ala Singh (Bajwa 1969: 30), but for the beginning of the history of the Patiala *khyal gharana* the important period was the reign of Maharaja Narindra Singh and specifically the time of the 1857 'mutiny'. During the 'mutiny' one of the greatest of *khyal* singers, Tanras Khan, fled the Delhi court of the last Mughal emperor Bahadur Shah and sought refuge at the Patiala court. Although Narindra Singh was on the opposite side in the 'mutiny' from Tanras Khan's erstwhile patron, he received the singer at the Patiala *darbar*. At least the physical surroundings must have seemed familiar to the estranged artist, for the Patiala ruler was residing in his Motibagh Palace, designed after the Mughal-style Shalimar garden in Lahore (Bajwa 1969: 7).

The 'new' city of Patiala, built when the British were consolidating control of the nation, shows a shift in architectural style which was appearing in various parts of India. Many buildings, including the palace built by Rajindra Singh, have the design of early Indo-colonial style; the royal palace (which now houses the Punjab State Archives and Historical Museum) is a large but not imposing home that faces onto a British-style garden. Nowhere is there a suggestion of military preparedness. The city is open to the countryside, surrounded by lush grain fields. The old fort close by is now occupied by Indian military forces, and across the road is the modern Punjab University. At present the area exudes an impression of orderliness, industrious agricultural activity, and prosperity.

Musicians of the Patiala *gharana*

The early musicians

While Tanras Khan was at Patiala he took as his disciple a member of the Anandpur *rababi gharana*, Bhai Kalu Rebabi. 'His [Kalu's] two sons, Ali Bux [Baksh], along with Fateh Ali, a friend of Ali Bux, also became disciples of Ustad Tan-Ras-Khan of Patiala' (Bajwa 1969: 30).[1] From Ali Baksh [Bux, Bax] and Fateh Ali Khan (who may have been distantly related cousins as well as friends) dates the *khyal* tradition of Patiala, but their training process took them to Jaipur, Gwalior, and Delhi before they returned to Patiala.

According to Sharma, both Ali Baksh and his friend Fateh Ali received their initial training from Miyan Kalu Khan in Jaipur (B. L. Sharma 1971: 41). Miyan Kalu took them to Behram Khan, the famed *dhrupadiya* of the Dagar tradition who was court musician to Maharaja Ram Singh (1835–80) of Jaipur, for it was important for *khyal* singers to have *dhrupad* training as well (see Charts 8–1 and 8–2). After studying with Behram Khan, Ali Baksh and Fateh Ali went to Gwalior to study with Haddu Khan (Munnawar Ali Khan, Interview: 1978, and V. H. Deshpande 1973: 82). Thereafter they studied in Jaipur with *khyaliya* Mubarak Ali Khan, a court musician to Ram Singh and son of Bade Muhammad Khan (of Gwalior and Rewa fame). Finally, Ali Baksh and Fateh Ali travelled to Delhi to study with Tanras Khan, who had returned there. Having studied for twenty years, the two young *khyaliyas* were considered accomplished musicians who had shaped an appealing style of *gayaki* – *madhya laya* from Haddu Khan, speedy and complex *tan*s from Mubarak Ali Khan, some style of *vilambit* and rhythmic variations from Tanras Khan, and correct form of *raga* from Benram Khan (Munnawar Ali Khan, Interview: 1978).

Invited to be court musicians for Rajindra Singh in Patiala, Ali Baksh and Fateh Ali travelled from Delhi in the company of the famous female singer Gokhi Bai (Bajwa 1969: 30).[2] On the death of their patron Maharaja Rajindra Singh, in 1900, the two singers – then known as Aliya-Fattu – were forced to leave the Patiala *darbar*, as the heir was a minor and all patronage was suspended until he came of age. Ali Baksh went to Tonk, near Jaipur, to be court musician for the *nawab*, who presented him with the honorary title 'General'; the artist was known thereafter as Ali Baksh General. He returned to Patiala when Bhupindra Singh (d. 1938) assumed the throne. As *maharaja*, Bhupindra Singh was a most enthusiastic patron of performers; he opened a new department of music and dance and had artists accompany

[1] There seems to be some confusion about the identities of two musicians with 'Kalu' in their names – Bhai Kalu Rebabi and Miyan Kalu [Kaloo] Khan, both of whom are said to be the father of Ali Baksh (Bajwa 1969: 30 and B. L. Sharma 1971: 41). With trepidation, I put them both on Chart 8–1 in the same genealogical position. Sharma confuses the situation further in another paragraph in his 1971 article when he describes 'Miyan Kaloo and his sons Akbar Khan and Sadoo Khan' as disciples of Gokhi Bai.

[2] B. L. Sharma (1971: 41) asserts the commonly accepted 'fact' that they received training from Gokhi Bai and then became disciples of Tanras Khan. It would have been unlikely for male musicians to take training from a female musician; in any case, this is contrary to the information given by Munnawar Ali Khan and by the *dhrupad* singers N. Zahiruddin and N. Faiyazuddin Dagar. Gokhi Bai was a well trained artist; she studied with Behram Khan in his home, and, like all male disciples, she had to shave her head and undergo strict discipline.

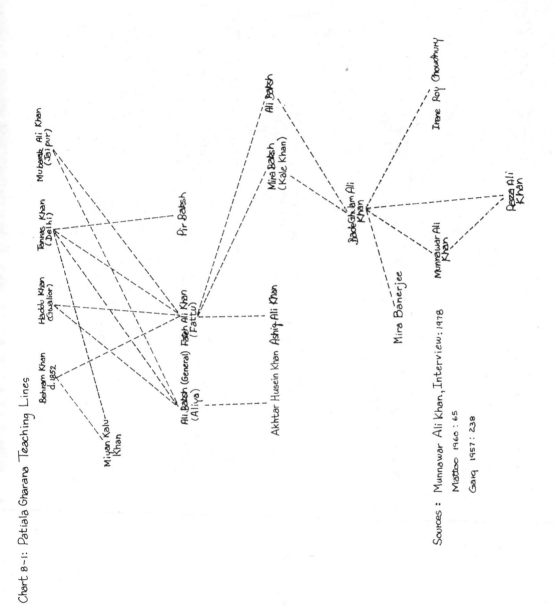

Chart 8–1: Patiala Gharana Teaching Lines

Sources: Munnawar Ali Khan, Interview: 1978

Mattoo 1960: 65

Garg 1957: 238

229

Chart 8-2 : Patiala Gharana Blood Lines

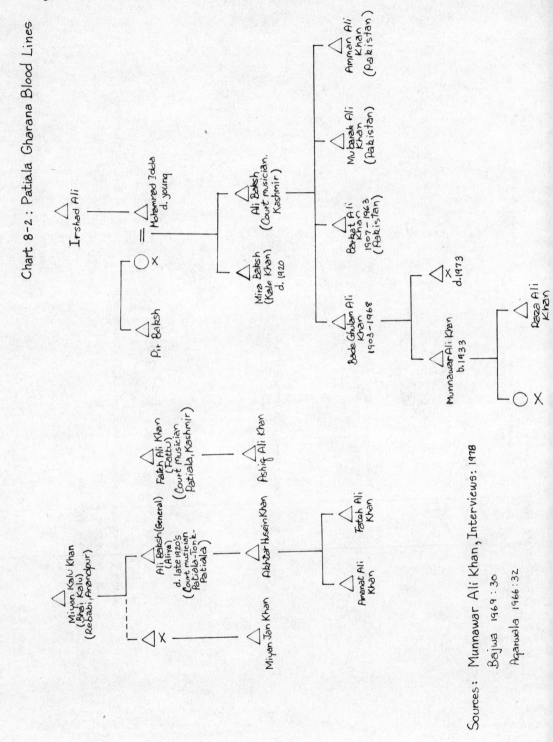

Sources: Munnawar Ali Khan, Interviews: 1978

Bajwa 1969 : 30

Agarwala 1966 : 32

him wherever he went (Bajwa 1969: 30). Ali Baksh's son, Akhtar Husein Khan, remained at the Patiala *darbar* until 1947 – the year of Partition – when he moved to Lahore, Pakistan (Munnawar Ali Khan, Interview: 1978; cf. Agarwala 1966: 32). Akhtar Husein had at least two sons, who became good singers of *khyal* (and of *ghazal*), but there is sparse audience now in Pakistan for *khyal*.

When Ali Baksh and Fateh Ali left the Patiala *darbar* in 1900 Fateh Ali joined the Kashmiri *darbar* of Maharaja Pratap Singh. Fateh Ali had a son, Ashiq Ali Khan (Agarwala 1966: 32), who, according to Munnawar Ali Khan, remained unmarried (Interview: 1978). He is very likely the 'Ashik Ali Khan' (mentioned in B. L. Sharma 1971: 34) who was court musician to Madho Singh (1880–1922) of Jaipur. Sharma also includes an 'Ashik Ali' in the list of musicians who served the *nawab*s of Tonk – along with Ali Baksh (and Fateh Ali?), Miyan Jan Khan (nephew of Ali Baksh, according to Agarwala 1966: 32), and Kale Khan – all members of the same musical group (1971: 34). Thus, the Patiala–Tonk–Jaipur–Kashmir circuit flourished through another generation after Fateh Ali.

The voice-culture developed by Aliya-Fattu of Patiala was taught to two disciples from the Kasur *gharana* of *dhrupad* singers, near Lahore – Ali Baksh and his brother Mira Baksh (known as Kale Khan). Through them the Patiala style was continued in India.[3] Since the style of Fateh Ali was more appealing than that of Ali Baksh General to the brothers Ali Baksh and Kale Khan, they studied with Fateh Ali. And, like his teacher, Ali Baksh became court musician to the Maharaja of Kashmir.[4]

Kale Khan chose to remain an independent musician, a difficult choice for the time.[5] As described by Munnawar Ali Khan (Interview: 1978), the British period was very difficult for non-court musicians; they were usually very poor, but they were diligent in preserving their music. There were several thousand of them and, by comparison, a relative handful of court musicians, who tried to prevent the former from acquiring appointments at court. In addition, the British discouraged performances of the arts in public.

Bade Ghulam Ali Khan

Following the example of his *ustad*, Kale Khan's famous disciple Bade Ghulam Ali Khan also remained an independent musician. Called 'Bade' ('the Great'), Ghulam Ali was the son of Ali Baksh and had three brothers, all of whom were musicians: Amman Ali Khan, Mubarak Ali Khan, and Barkat Ali Khan, famed for *ghazal* and *thumri* (these three remained in Pakistan after Partition). Ghulam Ali was born in 1903 (or 1901, Misra 1954: 50; or 1902, Saxena 1956b: 7) in Lahore, where he spent his childhood.

There are two basic versions (with variants of each) of Ghulam Ali's childhood and musical training. According to one version (Maudgalya 1968a: 35), his mother died during his early

---

[3] This family history was recounted by Munnawar Ali Khan (Interview: 1978). Of the Kasur *gharana*, Irshad Ali, the grandfather of Ali Baksh and Kale Khan, had been a court musician to Ranjit Singh (1799–1839) in the Punjab. Irshad Ali's son Mohammad Idda died at a young age, leaving Ali and Kale (see Chart 8–2). Pir Baksh Khan, the boys' maternal uncle, was Tanras Khan's first disciple; he was court musician to a succession of kings of Afghanistan and died during the rule of Aman Rakhan Khan (who had become his disciple).

[4] B. L. Sharma lists an 'Ali Bax' as court musician to Madho Singh II (1880–1922) of Jaipur (1971: 34). According to Munnawar Ali Khan (Interview: 1978), Ali Baksh General died in the late 1920s, so it could have been he; and Munnawar Ali did not mention his grandfather having been a Jaipur court musician.

[5] This authoritatively contradicts an article in *The Hindu* (April 26, 1968), which stated that Kale Khan was a musician in the Jammu *darbar*.

childhood and his father had to leave him to take his position as court musician in Kashmir. Because of difficulties with his stepmother, Ghulam Ali stayed for several years with his uncle Kale Khan, who took him to Bombay in search of a livelihood. Until he was twenty-one, Ghulam Ali made little progress in his study of music. Then Inayati Bai, one of his father's pupils, helped him; he learned *sarangi* and voice, but gave up *sarangi* when it became clear that vocal music was his forte.

According to the other version (Garg 1957: 227, and Wadhera 1956 and 1957), Ali Baksh took a second wife (which was possible according to Muslim custom) before his first wife died, when Ghulam Ali was twenty years old. By that time Ghulam Ali had finished his training with Kale Khan and was living in Lahore. His mother and the second wife of his father did not get along, and one day Ghulam Ali's mother said to him: 'Go out and learn to play *sarangi* somehow, because now you must earn a living to support me and your younger brother'. He did, but he did not stop his vocal practice. Since Ghulam Ali had completed years of study by that time, he perhaps did not try to earn his living by singing because it would have been disrespectful to his father. Sons or disciples did not usually become independent vocalists until their father or *ustad* had died.

The story of Ghulam Ali's having studied the *sarangi* was somehow magnified into a story of his having been first and foremost a *sarangi* player who switched to singing at a late age. This (denigrating) rumor he felt called upon to deny: ' "Vocal music was always my first love", he says, "though I have sung and played on instruments to earn a living. To know an instrument intimately, however, is a great help in initiating one into the profundities of notes" ' (Vasudev 1958: 51).

Ghulam Ali began studying with his uncle Kale Khan at about five (or possibly seven). According to Saxena, the *gandha bandh* ceremony was attended by such well-known musicians as Miyan Jan Khan (nephew of Ali Baksh General), Chajja Khan (perhaps the one employed at Uniara in Rajasthan; B. L. Sharma 1971: 34), Nazir Khan, and Khadim Husain (Saxena 1956: 7). When he was about twelve Ghulam Ali had the honor of performing in the *darbar* held by the Prince of Wales in Lahore on the occasion of the prince's first visit to India (c. 1915) (Saxena 1956b: 7). A majority of sources agree that he studied with Kale Khan until Kale Khan died, when Ghulam Ali was seventeen (c. 1920).

An often-repeated anecdote about Ghulam Ali concerns the death of Kale Khan:

'With Khan Saheb Kale Khan, music has also died in his family', lamented a fellow musician.

'I was determined to show him that he was utterly wrong', Ghulam Ali reminisced, emotionally. 'I would see to it, said I to myself, that music would live as gloriously as before in our family' (Vasudev 1958: 51).

'From the age of seventeen to twenty-two,' he states, 'I practiced hard day and night, at the cost of my sleep. Music became my sole life. All my miseries and happiness lay engrossed in my music' (Misra 1954: 50).

'Three years later [c. 1923], the same person asked me to sing with him. He was treating "Kaliyan Sang Karat Rang Ralian" in Bahar. Everyone was struck with wonder as I went through a few phrases in an elegant, finished style' (Wadhera 1956).

According to the article in Garg, at about this same time Ghulam Ali went to Bombay to study with Sindhi Khan of the Gwalior *gharana* (1957: 228) and learned a number of compositions (Misra 1954: 50). He first performed in public when he was twenty-three, appearing as supporting artist for his father at a music festival in Lucknow (Mannawar Ali Khan, Interview: 1978).

When success came to Ghulam Ali it came like a fast, rippling *tan*, described beautifully by the Gwalior *gharana* musician Vinay Chandra Maudgalya:

During the 1940 session of the All India Music Conference at Calcutta a huge person of dark complexion was seen on the stage getting ready for his 'maiden' performance in the Conference. The doubting listeners had a pleasant shock when a voice sweeter than honey reached their ears. They had seldom heard such an aesthetical interpretation of classical music. Singing the fastest and most intricate *tāna-s* in a perfectly easy and tuneful way was something beyond their expectation. The *Thumrī* that followed the *Khayāl* created a perfectly romantic mood, and the *Bhajan*, which came after, an atmosphere of extreme devotion. Eve the critical type of listeners who are not easily pleased became ardent admirers of the musician, and the masses went mad after him.

Until then the musician was little known outside his own province of Punjab. From that day onwards, Bare Ghulam Ali's name and fame grew like wild-fire, throughout the whole country (1968a: 35).

Thereafter, Ghulam Ali was in constant demand for concert performances and for radio broadcasts. He even sang for a few films, among them 'Baiju Bawra', and also 'Mughal-e-Azam', in which his singing was used for the character of Tansen (Rizvi 1968: 46).

Ghulam Ali sang twice for Mahatma Gandhi in Bombay in 1945, and Gandhi presented him with a letter of adulation (Garg 1957: 228). Unlike many of his fellow musicians (particularly Hindu musicians of the Gwalior *gharana*), however, Ghulam Ali did not become involved in the political turmoil of the times. When anyone spoke of politics and of India and Pakistan, he exclaimed 'Talk to me of the purity of the note. I am interested in little else' (Vasudev 1958: 51). Partition must have been a painful time for Ghulam Ali, for his ancestral home in Lahore was subsumed into Pakistan, while his audiences remained in India. All his brothers remained in Pakistan, but after several years in Pakistan, Ghulam Ali chose to take Indian citizenship. 'When everyone left Lahore it became a cultural desert. And when life is unquiet, people do not want to listen to music', explained Ghulam Ali's son Munnaware Ali. 'It was difficult for Indians to settle in Pakistan but easy for Pakistanis to settle in North India' (Interview: 1978).

In 1953 Ghulam Ali had been taken to South India by G. L. Balasubramanyam for an extensive performing tour. The receptivity to Hindustani music was not very high at that time, but the singing of Ghulam Ali was very successful. Munnawar Ali Khan relates that when his father first appeared onstage in South India, the audience laughed because he was such a big man, with a mustache (rare in Hindu South India). When he sang they were surprised: 'On the second day they wanted to worship him as god of music'. After becoming an Indian citizen, Ghulam Ali was based in both Bombay and Calcutta, but he travelled extensively to perform and to attend various conferences and seminars throughout the country. The seminars frequently focused on music theory, but Ghulam Ali was impatient with theorizing. 'At a seminar once, when discussion between two learned theorists became terribly involved over the rendering of certain shrutis, Ghulam Ali stood up, and said, "Nobody can understand you like this. Why don't you give a practical demonstration? That is what matters." He illustrated the point with a swiftly soaring *taan* and stalked out of the room' (Vasudev 1958: 51).

As his son noted, Ghulam Ali was not only a 'great' (*bade*) musician, but a 'large' (*bade*) man. (The article in Garg 1957: 227–9 devotes an inappropriate amount of text to his life and

Plate 11   Bade Ghulam Ali Khan of the Patiala *gharana*

eating habits.) Descriptions of him tend to phrases such as 'huge person' or 'massive frame', and refer to his fantastic handlebar mustache. They also invariably speak of him as generous and feeling, open-hearted, and beloved by all who knew him. He was apparently a person with a bent for spontaneity, for many anecdotes are told about his musical reactions to events around him. One morning in Delhi, as Ghulam Ali was finishing a concert with a Bhairavi piece, all present seemed to be spellbound, when suddenly the shriek of a railway engine pierced the morning air and threatened to break the spell. Ghulam Ali at once let his voice fly up to *tar saptak*, merge into and linger at the pitch of the shriek, and then 'with that high note as a base, executed a beautiful, fluent pattern which cancelled the otherness of the noise completely and made it appear as an integral accent in the beauty of the tan' (Saxena 1956b: 7).

Another distinctive feature of Ghulam Ali's performance was his use of the *svarmandal*, as well as the *tambura*. A. D. Ranade (1981: 21) suggests that this use of *svarmandal* was related to Ghulam Ali's understanding of and desire to reach 'the layman'. While Ranade suggests the layman 'likes to have his "ears" filled while he is listening to music' (1981: 20), paintings from the Mughal period suggest a long tradition of *svarmandal* as an accompanying instrument in court circles; it is used by other Punjabi singers, including Salamat Ali Khan of Pakistan.

One manner in which Ghulam Ali 'played to' his uninitiated audiences was to repeat what he had already popularized in his recordings, thus 'taking no creative risks whatsoever. On

Plate 12   Male court musicians, including a *svarmandal* player, presented in royal procession (painting in *Shah Jahan Nama*, c. 1650–60, Windsor Castle, f. 120 v. p. 238; reproduced by gracious permission of Her Majesty the Queen)

the other hand, in smaller *mehfil*s, he was a totally changed musician. Then he exhibited an earnestness of purpose that transformed his music' (A. D. Ranade 1981: 21). He preferred to specialize in a few *raga*s, thereby creating surprises within the familiar.

Risking criticism from the classical music elite, Ghulam Ali also charmed audiences with his rendering of the light classical genre *thumri*. By playing to a general audience, however, he contributed a great deal in the process of attracting them to the previously cloistered art-music tradition. In recognition of his artistry, in 1962 Ghulam Ali was awarded the honorary title Padma Bhushan by the Government of India and the President's Award for Hindustani Vocal Music by the Sangeet Natak Akademi. It could not have come at a more supportive time, for the great artist had suffered a paralytic stroke from which he was struggling to recover, with an indomitable spirit:

At one stage, Khan Sahib was advised to have massage to tone up his muscles. A well-known therapist was arranged for . . . Guruji never liked this treatment, but soon found a way to pass the two hours happily. It was an amusing sight . . . Whatever movement the masseur made, Khan Saheb translated into vocal sound: all the patting therapy he would copy in sargam, the massaging into glides (Gilani 1969: 23).

For two years the *ustad* worked to retain his voice by the method he had learned from his uncle and his father. Though still unable to walk, he was able to present a post-award concert for the Sangeet Natak Akademi and to give several more performances. His death came on April 25, 1968.

Munnawar Ali Khan

Bade Ghulam Ali Khan had two sons. Only one, Munnawar Ali, became a musician, and his reputation is growing. He began studying with his father in 1950, was initiated with *gandha bandh* and, when he had progressed sufficiently, began to sing with his father in the traditional supporting role.

The close association of son with father in training, in a supporting performance role and in sustaining a family musical tradition, was appropriate for a patronage system in which it was likely that the son would eventually fill the father's position as earning musician. The likelihood was strengthened when the musical style was associated particularly with a place, as in the case of a court. Ghulam Ali remained apart from that system of patronage, however – in any case it ended in his lifetime – and the close association of Munnawar Ali with his father in training, in a supporting performance role and in the sustenance of family musical tradition, made it in some ways more difficult for Munnawar Ali to succeed as an earning performing musician after his father died. Reminders of the father in a son's style are inevitable in such a tradition. But rather than emphasize the positive aspects of those reminders – including the fact that continuity of style has been achieved – music critics are more likely to demand from the start of a son's independent career the predominance of individuality over tradition.

Ali gave his first independent performance in 1957 when he was twenty-four years old, sponsored by the Sadarang organization in Calcutta, which had been established by his father, but he also continued to perform with his father. After his father died, and until 1976, Munnawar Ali felt he had a difficult time being appreciated in his own right. The press was always thinking of his father and comparing them, but 'by the grace of God Almighty, I changed their minds' (Interview: 1978). When he was forty-three his performances were finally credited in their own right.

Munnawar Ali lived in Calcutta until 1978 because he felt that music audiences there had long been very receptive to vocal music. He has been drawn to Delhi, however, to teach at Bharatiya Kala Kendra, one of the major performing arts institutions. As a singer, he finds Delhi changing daily into a vibrant cultural center, whereas even ten years ago instrumental art-music was preferred to vocal art-music, and light vocal forms predominated in audiences' taste. Munnawar Ali performs on radio, and on television – a new outlet for performing artists. Like musicians of an older generation he prefers the *mehfil* setting to all other performance contexts, but opportunities to sing in such a context are few.

Although Munnawar Ali has not said so directly, his remarks suggest that he finds people thinking about him increasingly in communal terms, seeing him as a 'Muslim musician' rather than as a 'musician'. The shift in the musical sphere back to recruitment from non-Muslims seems to be fairly complete; other than his son, all his students are non-Muslim. He feels that communal considerations should be beside the point. Asked if he felt strange singing *khyal ciz* about Krishna, he replied: 'If the text is devoted to God – anyone's God – it's okay; if it's not, it's not good' (Interview: 1978).

Munnawar Ali's association with Patiala is by tradition rather than by residence, and maintaining the tradition is important to him. He was quick to point out, for instance, that the son of the former Maharaja of Patiala had attended his concert in the Shankar Lal Festival. He called attention to his Punjabi 'identity' in another way as well, pointing out that on his phonograph recording (GCI ECSD 2750) he sang a Punjabi song in Sindhi Bhairavi because Punjabi classical music has its roots in folk music.

Munnawar Ali's son Raza Ali Khan is now performing with him in the traditional supporting role. Raza Ali was initiated into music by his grandfather Ghulam Ali, and then studied with his father. Munnawar Ali also has a daughter: 'Times are changing. She has got a good voice and is talented. If she wants to learn, I will teach her' (Interview: 1978).

Among non-family disciples of Ghulam Ali, it is necessary to distinguish between disciples by training and disciples by inspirational influence. While he is said to have influenced enormous numbers of musicians, both vocalists and instrumentalists, the number of those specifically and consistently mentioned in association with his style are few. Disciples by *training* are Ahmed Raza (*vichitra vina*), Mira Banerjee (*khyal* and *thumri*), and Irene Roy Chowdhury (*khyal* and *thumri*). The leading *khyal* singer *inspired* by Ghulam Ali is Parveen Sultana, and the leading *thumri* singer is Nirmala (Arun) Devi.

Irene Roy Chowdhury

Irene Roy Chowdhury is of the younger generation of musicians whose period of training spanned the shift from the traditional *guru–sisya* 'system' to institutional affiliation, and she experienced both. Her family were from East Bengal (now Bangladesh), and at the Partition they moved to Calcutta. She started learning music because her father was fond of it and encouraged her. Her first serious study was with the distinguished *tabla* player and teacher Jnan Prakash Ghosh in 1953–4.

One day she heard Bade Ghulam Ali Khan sing, and it was on a similar occasion that the *ustad* asked her to sing as well. She recalled: 'He was impressed and told me to be his disciple' (Interview: 1978). She was very young and at first went just to listen. Studying with him was difficult because he lived in Karachi and went to Calcutta only in the winter for conferences. She would then go daily from morning to evening; he would teach her when he was in the mood, otherwise she would just listen (this important process of osmosis is one element severely lacking in institutional training).

In 1955 Irene was placed first in *khyal* and *thumri* in an All-India Radio competition. She was interviewed by the Ministry of Education and selected for a three-year scholarship for musical instruction, for which she moved to Delhi. That was in 1957, and Ghulam Ali, who was still a Pakistani citizen, could not teach under the Indian Government scheme. So the Ministry arranged for her to study with the *dhrupad* singers N. Moinuddin and N. Aminud-din Dagar – *alap* and *khyal*, not *dhrupad*. After three years her younger sister Anita Roy Chowdhury received a scholarship to study the Sahaswan style, and the family moved to Delhi.

When Irene's scholarship ended and she finished her study with the Dagar brothers, she began to perform widely and went to London, Russia, Japan, Hong Kong, and Bangkok as part of government cultural tours. *Khyal* and *thumri* are her forte, but since she teaches at Kathak Kendra in New Delhi she is often associated (by others, not by herself) more with *thumri* singing.

Parveen Sultana

Parveen Sultana, disciple of Ghulam Ali by inspirational influence, was born in Nowgong, Assam. She received her initial musical training from the age of six from her father, Mohammad Ikramul Majid, who was a disciple of Gul Mohammad Khan of Karachi and later of Bade Ghulam Ali Khan (Notes to GCI ECSD 2480). From the age of ten she studied for six or seven years with Shri Chinmoy Lahiri in Calcutta. 'But she has always been under the spell of the ornate Patiala gayaki as expounded by Ustad Ghulam Ali Khan whom Parveen holds in high esteem and all along listened to fondly' (*Festival '75: Women Music-Makers of India*, Wadhera 1975: 22). She has the distinction of being one of the few Muslim women to sing *khyal*. Musically, she is praised for her rare emotional fervor in slow expositions and her rich, sonorous voice, enviable range, and skill in both melodic and rhythmic design, but she is criticized for excessive ornamentation and a tendency for a sentimental touch in *khyal* that is more appropriate in *thumri*. Like her Muslim *ustad* (by inspiration) she performs *bhajan* along with *khyal* and *thumri*.

Musical styles of Patiala *gharana* musicians

Aliya–Fattu

The vocal style of Aliya–Fattu was distinguished by a rich, clear voice and they had a marvelous command over powerful and very fast *tan*s (inherited from Tanras Khan). They included *tappa tan*s, a specifically Punjabi genre, in *khyal*, and composed *ciz* in Punjabi as well as in the more usual poetic dialect, Braj Bhasha (Agarwala 1966: 32).

Bade Ghulam Ali Khan

By contrast, the voice of Ghulam Ali is described as elastic and sweet (though such adjectives must be subjective). B. R. Deodhar, who made a systematic study of the voice-culture of many musicians found that of Ghulam Ali perfect:

His manner of voice production was so satisfying as to be almost ideal. His voice had a range which covered the three octaves and operated with equal ease in all the three. Moreover the voice was deliciously sweet. It was bright, silk-soft and had the pleasantness of a moonlit sky. It was a faultless voice . . . His voice, in the lower octave, had the brilliance of the resonating shadja string of the *tanpura*. In the middle octave it reminded one of the deep-toned notes of an organ (quoted from V. H. Deshpande 1973: 54).

While his vocal range undoubtedly could cover three octaves, Ghulam Ali more usually displayed it through two and a half, from Ma to Sä. Ex. 8–1, from his recording of Malkauns (GCI EALP 1258), demonstrates a span from Dha to Sä. His flights to the very high reaches were just as likely to be exposés in legato passages as glimpses in *tan*s, making them all the more impressive.

Bade Ghulam Ali Khan   Rag Malkauns   Example 8-1
                               Vilambit Jhumra   Avarts 12-14

♩ = tabla strokes
⌞⎯⌟ = M.M. 92

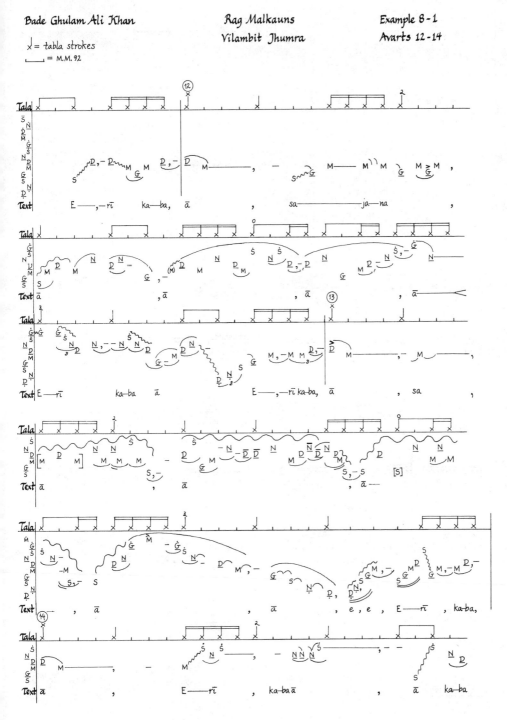

There were several other elements of 'correctness' in his singing and in his structuring of a performance. Another comment consistently made about his musicianship is that his intonation was perfect. Furthermore, he always sang both the *sthai* and the *antara* of every *khyal*, whether in slow, medium, or fast speed. And he kept the *sthai* text (at least the first line of it) clearly in the forefront by enunciating it and by avoiding long series of *avarts* of *akar* without reference to the text. He sang the *antara* where he felt it belonged, in the natural progression of the performance, when the *raga* development (*vistar*) had reached *antara* range, rather than immediately at the beginning with the *sthai* (Irene Roy Chowdhury, Interview: 1978). He did not cultivate the *ciz antara* using an *antara mukhda*, as he might have with his vocal range and his frequent trips to *tar saptak*; rather, he returned immediately to *sthai* text after presenting the *ciz antara*.

Despite all of the 'correctness' in important aspects of his voice-culture and structuring, Ghulam Ali was criticized for doing *khyal* an injustice in the way he sometimes structured his performances. Deodhar spoke frankly with him about it:

Because of our friendship I once made bold to tell him, 'Khansaheb, your music lacks order. You do *alapi* for some time, then go into notation-singing (*sargam*), then switch on to *tans* and come back to *alapi* again. Other musicians therefore complain that your music is un-gharana-like'. Khansaheb listened and said to me, 'I shall answer this charge only by singing. Listen to this Darbari'. He then rendered Darbari in such a manner for about an hour that I did not find the least disorderliness in his presentation. For the first twenty minutes he did *alapi* in such a sustained manner that the listener would not imagine that he was also capable of *tans*. He took only behelavas with *meend*: not a single *murki* nor even a small *tan* of two or three notes. Then he entered the *bol* part and ended with *gamak tans* which boomed like canon-fire. 'Why don't you always sing thus?' He answered my question by saying, 'It is not everywhere that one comes across listeners like you. I am a Punjabi and the general impression is that I employ the Punjabi graces (*harkats*) effectively and also excel in notation-singing. I am also known for my *tans*. If I sing *alapi* in the manner in which I did now I can read the disapproving expression on the faces of the listeners . . . When I realize this my concentration fails me and I begin to sing the way they want. Deodharsaab, my presentation is sometimes disorderly as you say but although I know this I cannot curb my mind (quoted from V. H. Deshpande 1973: 58–9).

Deodhar's criticism can be examined with respect to a selection of Ghulam Ali's recorded performances. These performances are of both *vilambit* and *madhya laya bara khyal* and *chota khyal*. Ghulam Ali was noted for singing comfortably in all speeds. He sang a variety of *talas* as well. In the four performances examined here, he included *vilambit jhumra*, *rupak*, and *ektal*, *madhya laya tintal*, and *drut tintal*. Within a performance he accelerated the speed relatively little in *vilambit khyal* (and did so gradually), while in *madhya laya* and *drut laya khyal* he was more likely to accelerate, and did so in sudden jumps.

The slow-speed Malkauns performance (GCT EALP 1258) is exemplary. The *ustad* explored the *raga* in *bolalap*, with minimal ornamentation at first: in the second cycle, joining two pitches with a slow, heavy oscillation; in the third cycle, gracing Ma in the *mukhda* and then waiting until *avarts* 8 and 9 to embellish the legato singing with more loose, slow oscillation. *Avart* 12, transcribed in Ex. 8–1, features more localized ornamentation. In *avart* 13 (also shown there) the first brief *tan* was allowed. With the *tihai* in *avart* 14 the *alap* portion was concluded. Then the real *tans* began in their proper place; the legato passages he used for contrast do not seem inappropriately *alapi*. This was not a performance that 'lacked order'.

The Gunkali medium-speed performance (GCI EALP 1258) follows that same format, but he also sang *sargam* once, seemingly as a bridge between improvisation that was *bolalap* tending toward *tan* and real *tan*s. He used very little ornamentation before the *antara*, other than slow, heavy oscillation, and there was very little even of that. It was a reposeful *vistar*, especially for a medium-speed performance.

Not the actual *vistar* of *alap* but the feeling of it was retained for a very long portion of the Darbari Kanada [Kanhra] recording (GCI EALP 1265), and it continued long after *tan*s were introduced, because of the rather frequent return to legato singing with a slow, oscillating *gamak*. This, I suppose, could be considered formally improper.

One of the characteristics of Ghulam Ali's style, as seen in the Gunkali performance and others, is the manner in which he eases toward *tan*. The wide, oscillating *gamak*s (undoubtedly the ones referred to as 'weighty' by newspaper critics) that were at first applied to emphasize one pitch and then to join two close but disjunct pitches, were gradually used to join pitches a sixth apart and then an octave apart, the pitches between being treated with the *gamak*. All he had to do was to increase the speed of the *gamak* for the same melody to become a *tan*.

Ghulam Ali's 'heavy' *gamak* was particularly prevalent in the Darbari Kanada performance where even *sargam* is ornamented with it. This is possibly due to the important part that ornamentation plays in Darbari Kanada with slow oscillations which come on Ga and Dha, and he made play with the idea of ornamentation. Pitches Ga and Dha are performed as follows: a *mind* leads down to the pitch from approximately the pitch above (often not quite), then there is a clear pitch, and then come the subtle oscillations 'within' the pitch. In a vibrato context the *mind* serves beautifully to say 'I am now approaching a proper Darbari Ga or Dha'; the *mind* is shown by the straight line in the units R⌐ᴹᴡᴡ⌐Gᴫ or M⌐ᴾᴡᴡ⌐Gᴫ,

or, in one dramatic case R⌐ᴹᴡᴡ⌐Dᴫ . In such instances, Ga or Dha are 'stood on', i.e., prolonged. (The accurate sense of pitch for which Ghulam Ali was applauded comes into play here.) In *tan*s and in fast legato passages in this performance he occasionally sang Ga and Dha without their distinctive ornamentation, and also included them in the vibrato from time to time; this is usual in any singer's performance of Darbari Kanhra.

The Kaushi Dhani performance (GCI EALP 1265), like the Darbari Kanada one, manifests some but not all the elements of structure that concerned Deodhar. Ghulam Ali did maintain the feeling of *alap* through most of the performance, even after presenting a *sargam* passage and, in fact, he used slow, expressive *sargam* amidst *tan*s very late in the performance (*avart* 105), which recalls the lyricism of *alap* in a way that could be considered formally improper. The two *sargam* passages in the performance are shown in Ex. 8–2 for comparison.

Bade Ghulam Ali Khan   Rag Kaushi Dhani   Example 8-2a
                                Rupak Tal   Avarts 57-62

♩ = start of a tala subdivision
⌐___⌐ = M.M.76

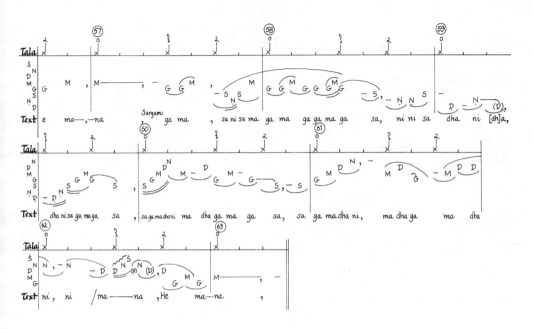

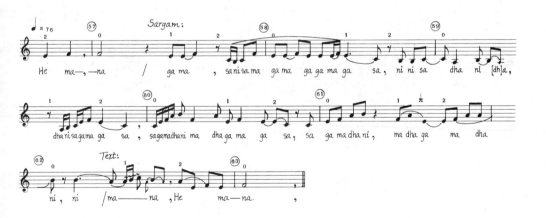

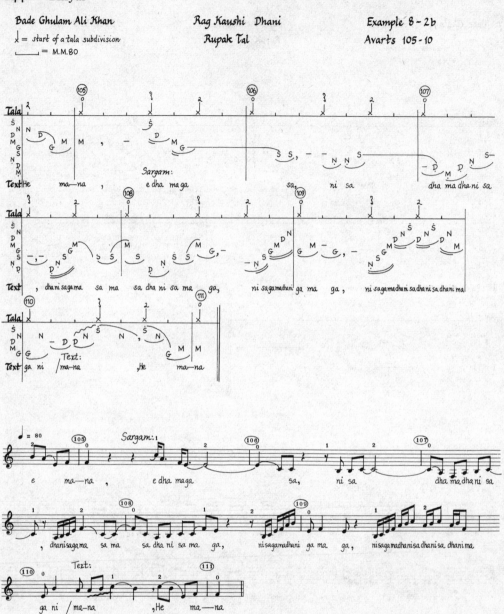

Bade Ghulam Ali Khan

Rag Kaushi Dhani

Example 8 – 2b

↓ = start of a tala subdivision

Rupak Tal

Avarts 105 – 10

└──┘ = M.M.80

Table 8–1 shows the overall structure of the Kaushi Dhani performance. Numbers in parentheses are the *avart* numbers on which sections begin after a *mukhda*; the bracketed information below such a number is the lapsed time. The numbers below the rules indicate the number of *avart*s between *mukhda*s (*avart*s are short in *rupak tal*).

Table 8–1 Structure of the Kaushi Dhani recording (Bade Ghulam Ali Khan, GCIEALP 1265)

(1) [0:30] sthai	(5) vistar:	(12) bolalap	(19)	(25)	(30)	(36)	
4	7	7	6	5	6	4	
(40) antara	(47) [4:18] sthai / mukhda						
7		I					
(48) wide range akar alap	(56) [5:06] sthai / mukhda						
8	I						
(57) sargam	(63) slow *gamak alap* tending to *tan*	(71)	(77)	(83)	(89)	(92) [5:58] tan / mukhda	
6	8	6	6	6	3	I	
(93) tan	(95)	(101)	(105) sargam	(111) tan	(114) [9:06] tan / mukhda		
2	6	4	6	3	I		
(115) [11:06] tan	(119) [11:34] x ⟶ to *chota khyal*						
4							

In this particular performance the introduction of fast *tans* so late in the *bara khyal* leaves to the *chota khyal* a function pleasantly and properly distinctive from that of *bara khyal*. (In many artists' performances the *chota khyal* is a fast piece that just continues the type of improvisation on which the *bara khyal* dwelled for a considerable time at the end.) Thus this performance (and the Darbari Kanada performance) presents the opposite of what Deodhar complained of: rather than presenting *tans* too early in the structure, Ghulam Ali left them until remarkably late. By creating a truly distinct *chota khyal*, he was living up to his reputation for taking each genre seriously in its own right (though this attribute was often couched negatively, for many musicians were displeased with his serious treatment of *thumri*).

Another comment offered about the structuring of Ghulam Ali's performances concerned his manner of *vistar*: 'His recitals conform to his belief that the real style of good khayal singing is "ekahri gayaki" – that is, patterns which go forward or backward, as distinguished from those that show the voice as first climbing up to a svara and then repeatedly reinforcing it with other flourishes that gather themselves up from below that note' (Saxena 1956b: 7). Saxena is referring possibly to performances like the Kaushi Dhani recording in which Ghulam Ali jumped between the pitch registers quite a bit, even in the first three minutes of improvisation.

It is difficult to generalize about the Ghulam Ali's *tans*. Unlike his Patiala predecessors Aliya–Fattu, he eschewed *tappa tans* in *khyal*: 'He is . . . emphatic on the point that khayal-singing should steer clear of "taans" of the "tappa" variety which, though difficult admittedly, are too restless to allow feeling to breathe, and too much involved to permit clarity of design and distinctness of effect' (Saxena 1956b: 7). Swiftness is a frequently cited attribute of his *tans*. But then again he excelled in sudden switching from slow to fast *tans* (Misra 1954: 50).

As to the shape of the *tans*, they were marked by variety. Saxena suggested that he preferred those with freely flowing, expansive movement to those intricately woven around two or three pitches (*uljhatti tans*) (1956b: 7), and indeed *tans* in his recordings are freely flowing and expansive. I hazard two further generalizations. (1) He sang both *vakra tans* (of many varieties) and straight, sweeping *tans*, but his straight *tans* were frequently characterized by breaks into short 'snips', separated either by a quick rest or by pausing to dwell on a pitch (or pitches) along the way. This may be what A. D. Ranade described: 'the distinctive feature of his tan-s was the use of speed in short, spiralling patterns, covering the whole range' (1981: 19). (2) The melodic boundaries of his *tans* were so clear and so well integrated into the musical context that the *tans* were not so much quick moments of virtuoso figuration as a contribution to the overall sense of ongoing melody. Close analysis reveals that Ghulam Ali varied his *tans* so greatly from performance to performance, and within a performance, that pinpointing a few details to support these generalizations must suffice.

The Gunkali recording (GCI EALP 1258) provides examples of several *tan* shapes and of a likely pacing of *tans* by Ghulam Ali. Ex. 8–3 presents *avarts* 26–31, which begin with the relatively slowly oscillating *gamak tans* which marked his style.

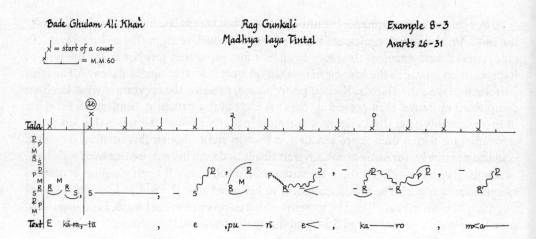

Bade Ghulam Ali Khan   Rag Gunkali   Example 8-3
                              Madhya laya Tintal   Avarts 26-31

♩ = start of a count
♩_____ = M.M. 60

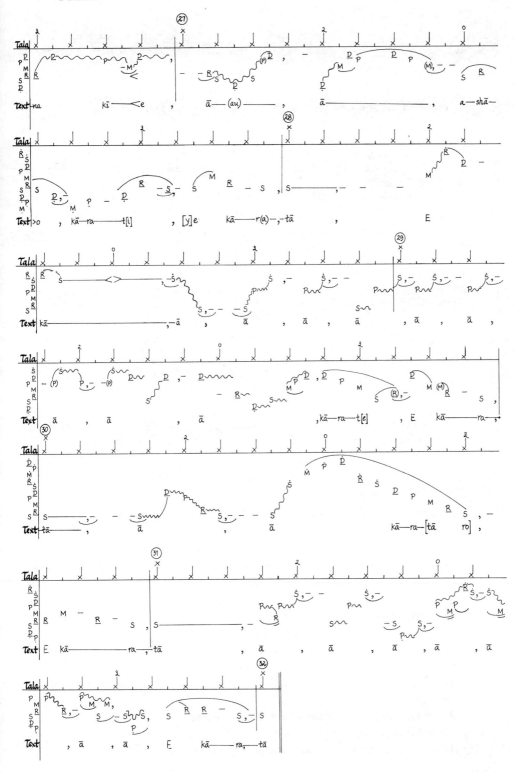

(a) *Avart* 26–7: a succession of slow *tan*s ascending from different pitches straight up to the same pitch (elsewhere, the opposite of this).

(b) *Avart* 28–9: straight ascent and descent (broken into separate units) with the same pitch boundaries, combined with (a).

(c) *Avart* 30: *tan* melding into legato singing, contributing to ongoing melody.

(d) *Avart* 31: straight *tan*s, covering a wide total range but with skips (therefore with both melodic and rhythmic breaks in the straight motion).

(e) *Avart* 32–3: contrasting passage of legato singing on *bol*s but continuing disjunctness (note use of voice).

(f) *Avart* 34: sweeping straight *tan*s without breaks.

(g) *Avart* 35: very high-range *bolalap*.

(h) *Avart* 36: mixture of *tan*s and sustained pitches.

(i) *Avart* 37: more of (a), (b), and (f).

(j) *Avart* 38–9: low range with *bol*s, to *tan* using a more forceful *gamak* for variety.

(k) *Avart* 40: fast *gamak tan*, sweeping over wide range. After these *avart*s, *sargam* followed.

In the Malkauns recording (GCI EALP 1258) there are two other shapes of *tan*s that are likely to occur in any performance of his. In *avart* 15, shown in Ex. 8–4, he used a wide range subdivided into small-range units, leading nicely to an all-encompassing *tan* to finish. In *avart* 16 there is a series of *tan*s starting from mid-cycle, in which each *tan* ends on a clear pitch and extends to legato melody rather than ending in a flash; this contributes to the general ongoing

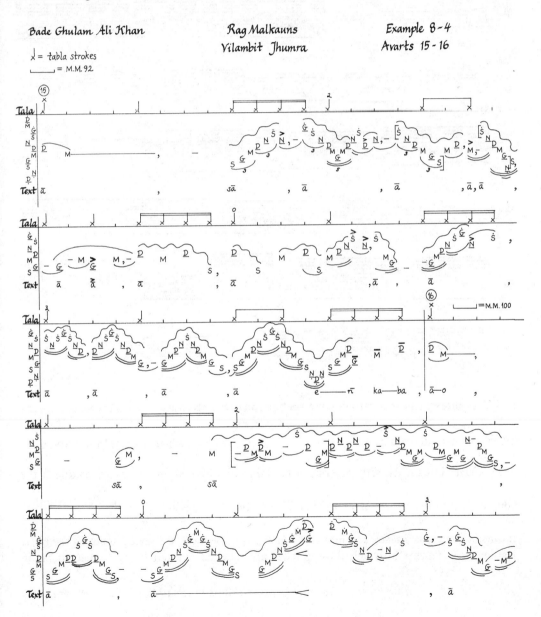

Bade Ghulam Ali Khan   Rag Malkauns   Example 8–4
Vilambit Jhumra   Avarts 15–16

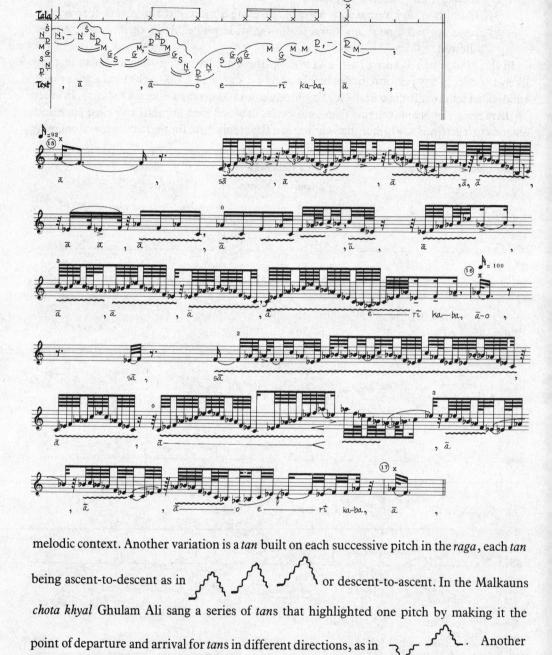

melodic context. Another variation is a *tan* built on each successive pitch in the *raga*, each *tan* being ascent-to-descent as in or descent-to-ascent. In the Malkauns *chota khyal* Ghulam Ali sang a series of *tan*s that highlighted one pitch by making it the point of departure and arrival for *tan*s in different directions, as in . Another means of variety is a *vakra tan* in ascent, that fills in between disjunct pitches in the *raga*, leading to a descent in which those pitches are touched without being connected, as in .. In the Darbari Kanada recordings the *tan*s are very diverse. *Vakra tans* of a sweeping nature are frequent, since *vakra* motion is characteristic of the *raga*. In the *chota khyal* each text-syllable is a take-off point for a *tan* – a series of *boltans*.

In V. H. Deshpande's important work on the *gharanas*, he characterizes the Patiala style (that of Ghulam Ali) as one in which *svara* and *laya* were blended – not the ideal balance of those two elements that Alladiya Khan achieved (in Deshpande's opinion), but a more balanced blend than that of the Kirana *gharana* (1973: 54). Ghulam Ali's use of *sargam* is an example of *svara–laya* blend. While most artists use *sargam* expressly for purposes of rhythm and speed, Ghulam Ali sang slow, expressive *sargam* that emphasized melody as well, placed in the *alap* for variety (Irene Roy Chowdhury, Interview: 1978); this was shown in Ex. 8–2a. On the other hand, he exploited *sargam* for *layakari*, as other artists exploit the text in *bolbant*; an instance of that is shown in Ex. 8–5 from the Malkauns *chota khyal* recording.

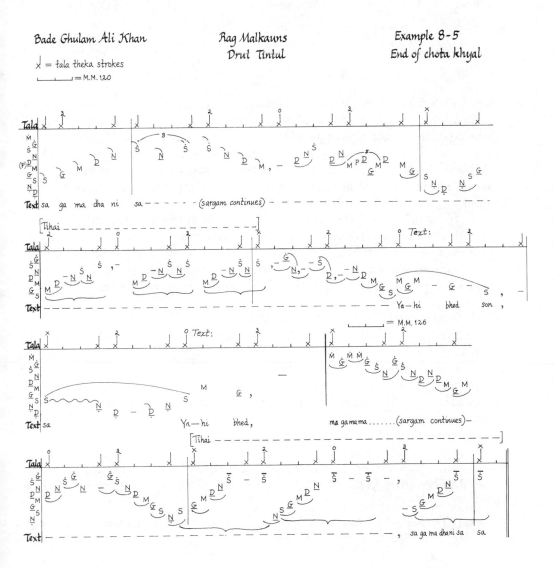

Bade Ghulam Ali Khan

Rag Malkauns
Drut Tintal

Example 8-5
End of chota khyal

Saxena points out two other characteristics of Ghulam Ali's style that could be seen as *svara–laya* blend. One is that the *ustad* always made certain that his *sam* came as a logical culmination to the musical phrase; the other is that he enjoyed creating *tihai* (1956b: 7). These two points are borne out in his recorded performances. He created *tihai* in which both the melody and the text were repeated three times; in one *tihai* a text phrase was repeated but there was no suggestion of melodic repetition. Not every performance included a *tihai*, however.

At the end of this analysis of some features of the music of Ghulam Ali mention should be made of his ultimate achievement, voiced by everyone who spoke of him – the intense sincerity and emotion with which he sang. The impression he created with his depth of emotion, expressive sensitivity, and facile musicianship attracted thousands of people to the newly burgeoning audience for the cloistered art of Hindustani vocal music.

Munnawar Ali Khan

As might be expected from his family heritage, Ghulam Ali's son Munnawar Ali is concerned with voice-culture: 'Voice culture used to be strong and loud, but that changed with microphones and p.a. systems . . . You must develop your voice so that you can sing all *raga*s; every *raga* must be sung with the same voice culture' (Interview: 1978). Of the voice-culture which he inherited from his father, Munnawar Ali stressed three aspects – full-throated voice, perfection of the notes, and control in the low voice. Indeed, 'full-throated' is the descriptive phrase likely to be offered about Munnawar Ali's voice (*Indian Express* 1972d), along with 'melodious, broad voice' (*Times of India* 1969b). As to control in the low register, it is noteworthy that Munnawar Ali begins his performance in a low register (rather than beginning in the middle and going low) with ease. His range is reasonably wide.[6]

---

[6] These and the following observations are made from his performance at the Shankar Lal Music Festival, April 9, 1978, and from discussion with him after that occasion.

Munnawar Ali sings compositions in all three speeds and in a variety of *tala*s, as did his father. Within one performance he sang *Vilambit jhumra tal* and *drut ektal*, as well as *madhya laya* and *drut tintal*. His first *khyal*(s) (Gujari Todi) in that performance lasted 55 minutes and his second (*madhya laya bara khyal-tarana* in Gaur Sarang) was a few minutes shorter. As he said later, 'I never sing more than 50–55 minutes. The audience gets bored; I get bored'. Munnawar Ali sang the *ciz antara* in the *antara* portion of the *bara khyal vistar* and also, like his father, retained the *sthai* (at least the first line of it) clearly through the *khyal*s.

The slow, expressive *sargam* that marked his father's performances was prominent in Munnawar Ali's performance as well. Ten minutes into the *vilambit khyal* it appeared – slow, in keeping with the *vistar* context, though at twice the rhythmic density of the *theka* subdivisions; it was an element of emotive expression rather than of rhythmic play. When queried about the slow, expressive singing of *sargam*, Munnawar Ali burst out with great pride that it was indeed distinctive of his family's style, that it had been the innovation of his grandfather Ali Baksh, and that his father had learned it from Kale Khan. 'At that time *ustad*s were against the use of *sargam*, but Ali Baksh began using it.'

Fifteen minutes into Munnawar Ali's *vilambit khyal* came *sargam* again, when *akar tan*s began to appear; this time the *sargam* was at four times the density of the *theka* subdivisions, and the range of single passages exceeded an octave. Amidst the context of *akar tan* two minutes later, *sargam* came in a highly ornamented passage. Five minutes before the end of that *bara khyal* (23 minutes into the performance) Munnawar Ali made *sargam* into an element of speed, with rippling density eight times that of the *theka* subdivisions, and he mixed that in an *avart* with legato prolonged phrases, as his father would have. Fast *sargam* was also part of the family style. Speaking of his father's tour in South India, Munnawar Ali recalled hearing that South Indian *sargam* at the time was slow, with many repeated pitches, and the Karnatak musicians who heard Ghulam Ali's singing were astonished by his fast *sargam*, which influenced them.

The proportion of attention to rhythmic play in Munnawar Ali's performance on that day was comparable to the proportion of rhythmic play in his father's recorded performances. While Munnawar Ali did not emphasize rhythmic play in these selections, he utilized it for striking and catchy contrast.

A notable difference between Munnawar Ali's performance at the Shankar Lal Festival and his father's recorded performances was one relationship within the ensemble: at one point in the medium-speed *khyal* Munnawar Ali set up a *sawal-jawab* relationship, in which he sang a passage and challenged the *sarangi* player to reproduce it precisely. This was remarkable, because he was performing with his son as supporting singer, and in such an ensemble repetition of phrases is usually done by the second vocalist.

In a review printed in the *Times of India* (1969b) Munnawar Ali was criticized for preferring dazzling effects, showing off his limitless virtuosity with 'external opulence' rather than 'the inner elusive essence of musical expression'. Nine years later, after the Shankar Lal Festival performance, a different critic belabored the same point (*Statesman* 1978), though it was not possible to detect any response of that sort in the audience on that occasion. One wonders if this sort of criticism is a lingering insistence on negative comparisons with Munnawar Ali's father, striking at that part of his art for which his father was so widely adulated but which is most subjectively judged.

Patiala *gharana* style is particularly characterized by its vocal technique, which emphasizes *mandra saptak* more than some other *gharana* styles do. This shows up not only in timbre but in the fair amount of *alap* time devoted to improvisation in *mandra saptak*.

Utilization of different styles of *sargam* also marks Patiala performances, especially the slow, expressive passages in *alap* style where the 'notation syllables' substitute for text syllables. *Sargam* is used for *bolbant*-type rhythmic improvisation and also to help achieve a faster speed (as with many artists who sing it). To a great extent *sargam* and text syllables are treated as interchangeable entities; both may occur in the same cycle of the *tala*, for example (as in the style of Abdul Wahid Khan of the Kirana *gharana*). The use of *sargam* does not seem to predominate over the use of the text, however. *Alap* is, for the most part, *bolalap*; text is, for the most part, enunciated clearly; and Patiala singers do, indeed, keep the *ciz* text present throughout a selection.

A variety of *tala*s, and a variety of *tan*s, are also characteristic of Patiala *gharana* musical preferences. For Bade Ghulam Ali Khan, one type of ornamentation – a heavy oscillation – was distinctive. While he occasionally sang *boltan*s, *tan*s were a never-ending source of creativity for him: they were expansive and freely flowing, with long lines broken up into 'snippets'; they were curvaceous; and they involved many shapes. A most significant feature of his *tan*s was his integration of them into the ongoing melodic context. In addition, it is significant that while he excelled at *tan*s he did not let them predominate in his *khyal* performances, as a less imaginative singer might have done.

9   *On individuality*

This chapter focuses on *khyal* styles associated more prominently with individual singers than with a particular *gharana*, although *gharana* styles have been important in shaping these individual styles. There are three very different situations here. The first – a pattern increasing in Hindustani classical vocal music – concerns artists who studied *gharana* styles formally but chose to remain independent of association with any one of them. The second involves a *gharana* (Delhi) in familial terms, but here the *khyal* style belongs primarily to one singer in each generation who has carved out his own specialization. The third is the case of a single artist – Amir Khan – who developed his own style without formal study with any *khyaliya* and whose style has been influential, although it is too soon to know if it will result in a *gharana* in stylistic terms.

Independent singers of *khyal*

While the preference to remain independent of a *gharana* might seem a recent trend in Hindustani music, the precedents for it from the beginning of the twentieth century are impressive. The performing lives of four independent musicians are discussed below.

Bhaskar Rao Bakhle
'To one of the most illustrious *khyaliyas* – Bhaskar Rao Bakhle (1869–1922) – goes much credit for cultivating the taste for classical music in Maharashtra and advancing the standard of its appreciation to a markedly high level, so that great savants like Alladiya Khan and Abdul Karim Khan made Maharashtra their permanent home' (G. H. Ranade 1967: 46–7).

Bakhle was born on October 17, 1869, in the village of Kathor in Baroda state to an impoverished Brahmin family (cf. Vedi 1969a and b). As a young boy he was left by his parents with an elder sister in Baroda, and thus his musical ability first naturally developed within the musical culture of that state. His first instruction was with the Hindu *dhrupad* singer of the state Vishnubuwa Pingle, with whom Bakhle first sang *kirtan*, in addition to classical music. When he progressed sufficiently to make an impression, the royal family arranged for his training at the Maula Baksh School of Music run by the state.

Even before his voice changed, Bakhle became a member of one of the music-drama troupes, the pioneer Kirloskar Natak Mandali, which had been founded in 1884. While with the troupe, he 'studied' with two *bin* players, one of whom was the noted Indore court musician Bande Ali Khan (from Kirana). When Bakhle's voice began to change he had to leave the troupe, and he returned to Baroda. The third in his succession of teachers, from 1886 to 1895, was the famous musician at the Baroda court Faiyaz Mohammad Khan, of the Gwalior *gharana*. His discipleship was a traditional one in that while he studied the fundamentals of *khyal* singing, he also performed such chores as tending sheep, sweeping the house, and overseeing the shopping (Vedi 1969a: 9). Bakhle accompanied Faiyaz at vocal recitals and performed independently at court. He also gave recitals in Bombay, with good response.

Bakhle then continued training under the Agra *gharana* stalwart Natthan Khan, remaining with him in Mysore and in Dharwar for five years. When Natthan Khan died, in 1900 or 1901, Bakhle settled in Bombay, and then returned to Dharwar, and at the age of thirty-two started teaching on his own. Many of his students were young actors of the Kirloskar Mandali. For a decade he performed widely both in the South (Mysore, Hyderabad, and Bangalore) and in the North, where he was supported by Vishnu Digambar Paluskar. He kept his connection with the Marathi theatre and 'produced' the great actor-singer Bal Bandharva.

Bakhle's final period of learning from a master came after he had settled (from 1911, permanently) in Poona. While running his own music school (the Bharat Gayan Samaj), he kept in close touch with Alladiya Khan, who was court musician at Kolhapur. From Alladiya he 'derived a deep knowledge of dhrupad singing and of many little known cheezas' (Vedi 1969a: 9).

Like the best musicians of his time Bakhle cultivated a wide range of genres – *dhrupad*, *khyal*, *thumri*, *tappa*, *hori*, and songs from drama. Thus he could offer his audiences a varied program at *kirtan*s, drama productions, and concerts for urban music 'circles'. Dilip Chandra Vedi credits Bakhle with shaping a new type of *thumri* (isolated from dance) for such recitals, and with cultivating in new listeners an eagerness even for 'pure glorious khayal' (1969b: 15).

Bakhle strove to make a reputation for himself at a time when the hegemony of Muslim musicians in North Indian courts was still firm. Citations in the *Bhaskar buwa Bakhale Birth-Centenary Souvenir* recall this:

The great master Rahimat Khan would not believe when he was told that a Hindu Pandit was singing at the Miraj Palace. He said that this music could only flow from one who sucked a bone for juice. He meant to say that only a Muslim could possess such a tuneful quality of voice (Anonymous 1969: 17).

Ramkrishna Buwa Vaze recorded: 'He (Bhaskarbuwa) sang very beautifully. Even the greatest Muslim musicians said that they had not heard a musician of his charm and grace' (Vedi 1969c: 31). Ramubhayya Date recorded the opinions of Alladiya Khan, Rajab Ali Khan, and Faiyaz Khan: 'They all unanimously said that the Hindus have produced only one singer whom we revere' (*ibid.*: 32).

A description of the manner in which Bakhle structured a *mehfil* is also given in the *Souvenir* (Anonymous 1969: 17, 19, 21). He would begin with a *raga* such as a variety of Kalyan or Kamod, Kedar, Bhup, and spend about an hour in a slow tempo on 'asthai' in that *raga* (*alap* in *mandra* and *madhya saptaks*, hinting at *tar saptak* – a method taught to him by Faiyaz Mohammad Khan), then about fifteen minutes on *antara* which brought into play *tan*, *boltan*, and complex *gamak tan* as the upper octave was developed. *Tan* patterns would be finished with delicate *mind*, *murki*, or other *gamak*s. With *antara*, too, came acceleration, reaching a climax at the end of the fifteen minutes.

After about a minute's break Bakhle would begin a second *khyal*, in a different but related *raga* (for instance, Dhani, Bageshri, Bihag Sohini, Jaijaiwanti, Kalawanti, Madhuwanti). The *tala* would also be different, and the tempo would pick up where the tempo of the first *khyal* left off. This second *raga* would get full though rapid treatment. (This sounds more like a *madhya laya khyal* than a *chota khyal* in fast speed, as presently performed.) Following it would come a light song of some variety.

The next part of the *mehfil* would feature a *raga* of *uttar anga*, like Malkauns. His renderings emphasized emotion and delicacy, without stressing rhythm (only a *tarana*, if one was offered in this part of the *mehfil*, would be particularly rhythmic). Such *mehfils* began at about 9 p.m. and ended at 5 or 6 a.m., with Bhairavi being the final item.

Bhaskar Rao Bakhle is particularly important as an example of one of the first performing artists to make his way independently of the courts, but, unlike others who achieved this, he was also independent of the support of one *gharana*. His memory has been kept alive through his students. Among the most distinguished have been the late Tarabai Shirodkar of Goa, Krishna Rao of Poona, Buwa Bagalkotkar and Bapu Rao Ketkar of Poona, Ganpat Rao Purohit of Bombay, B. R. Taale, Bal Gandharva, Bhai Lal Rababi, and Dilip Chandra Vedi (Saxena 1956a).

Dilip Chandra Vedi

While some will say that Dilip Chandra Vedi is a musician of the Agra style, Vedi himself said, when he was seventy-seven years old: 'I am not a blind follower of any gharana. God is not purchased by anyone. Music cannot be claimed by anyone. All artists take from all, but few admit it' (Interview: 1978).

Vedi was born on March 24, 1901 in Anandpur in the Punjab, to a family of Sikh businessmen (his father was a direct descendant of the great Sikh leader Guru Nanak). His mother died when he was two, and his father married again in 1906–7. Vedi related how a songstress was invited to sing as part of the wedding entertainment; he listened to her, and was able to copy it the next day, without knowing the meaning of the composition. Vedi said that when he was seven or eight his father sent him to study in Amritsar – painting, not music. This conflicts with the account in Garg (1957: 192). He was not allowed to attend music classes, so he would sneak in to listen. He asked the superintendent of his hostel to take him to a music competition. When he won first place without training he was permitted to join the music classes (1909 or 1910). His first teacher was Uttam Singh, a wealthy man who sang and taught at several schools for pleasure rather than for money; with him Vedi learned *dhrupad* and devotional songs.

His second teacher (from 1918 to 1922), and one from whom he imbibed ideas about the value of many *gharana*s, was Bhaskar Rao Bakhle. He thought Bakhle was the best of *khyal* singers. When Vedi began singing *khyal* he stopped singing *dhrupad* because, he said, *dhrupad* has to be sung by two people (since there is no accompanying instrument). When Bakhle died Vedi went to Baroda to study with the Agra *gharana* singer Faiyaz Khan, as his *guru* had done. In Vedi's opinion Bakhle and Faiyaz Khan were the best *bolbant* singers.

According to the article in Garg, Vedi was appointed court musician to the Maharaja of Patiala (in the Punjab) in 1924. And, like all good musicians seemed to be doing, he performed in the 1920s and 1930s at various conferences, in *sammelan*, and in princely states. He was honored in 1934 at the Sixth All-India Music Conference at Benares, being chosen as the judge for a scholarly discussion between Omkarnath Thakur and S. N. Ratanjankar. When Partition came (1947) he was in Lahore, living in an area where Christians and Muslims lived. Considering it dangerous, he fled one day to Delhi by train, with only one suitcase of possessions. He is proud to be one of those who never asked the government for compensation. He then had one short sojourn in the film industry, but he left at the insistence of Faiyaz Khan who was certain 'it would ruin his life'. Vedi returned to the Punjab to live, but he continued to broadcast for All-India Radio and to perform widely.

His most recent position has been in New Delhi, as senior professor of music in Bharatiya Kala Kendra, where he guides mostly advanced students; he also has worked with several Western students and been most open and helpful to them. Vedi has been a Fellow of the Sangeet Natak Akademi since 1964 and has served as examiner in music for several universities, for his knowledge of the theory, history, and practice of Hindustani music is formidable.

Manik Verma

Manik Verma is a woman whose training was with established musicians and who, like the men just discussed, had teachers from several different *gharana*s. She was born in 1926, twenty-five years later than Dilip Chandra Vedi, but still in a period when it was not easy for women to obtain training from traditional musicians. She was encouraged in music by her mother who was apparently also talented. Her early training was with Suresh Babu Mane of Kirana (son of Abdul Karim Khan) and with Inayat Hussein Khan of the Sahaswan *gharana*. Later she also trained under Jagannath Buwa Purohit of the Agra tradition. She is also reported to have been a student of Vedi (Garg 1957: 194). The very mention of the names of these teachers presents a clear but diversified set of expectations of what her *khyal* performances will be like.

Peculiarly, some attributes of her *khyal* performances suggest Gwalior *gharana* style, specifically her systematic structuring of the *khyal* with *alap*, *bolbant*, *boltan*, and *tan* in succession, and also her cultivation of the principle of musical contrast. One critic found traces of the Alladiya Khan style 'here and there' (*Sunday Standard* 1972). Thus, while it is important in traditional terms for us to know that Manik Verma's training was overseen by respected musicians, it is clear that the shaping of her *khyal* style has depended most heavily on her as an individual.

Omkarnath Thakur

Omkarnath Thakur was trained entirely in the Gwalior *gharana* and could be considered a Gwalior *gharana* musician. But he cultivated his own musical style to such an extent, and used his musical knowledge in such separatist endeavors, that he is just as frequently viewed as an independent musician.

Like his *guru* Vishnu Digambar Paluskar, Omkarnath Thakur had to overcome difficulties in childhood, though they were financial rather than physical. He was born in a village in Baroda state in 1897. His grandfather, Mahashankar Thakur, had taken part in the 1857 revolution on the side of Nanasaheb Peshwa. Omkarnath's father Gaurishankar was also military, in the employ of Maharani Jamunabai of Baroda, commanding 200 cavaliers (Neelkant 1964: 16). He moved the family to Broach in 1900. But Gaurishankar left the military life to become a *sannyāsi* (wandering religious mendicant), and his wife was left to manage the family. From the age of five Omkarnath helped in small ways, sometimes working as kitchen help, as a mill-hand, or as a small-part actor in Ramlila troupes (Neelkant 1964: 16). His father died when Omkarnath was fourteen.

Only by the good fortune of having a patron could the boy pursue the training in music for which he was clearly suited: a wealthy Parsi gentleman of Broach, Shahpurji Mancharji Doongaji, was so impressed by his singing that he took Omkarnath and his younger brother Ramesh Chandra (G. S. Desai 1968: 47) to Bombay in 1909 or 1910 and put them under the tutelage of Vishnu Digambar Paluskar in his Gandharva Mahavidyalaya. Omkarnath's accomplishments as a student must have been brilliant, for Paluskar took him with him to Nepal when he was invited there as a guest artist. In Bombay, Rahmat Khan, the son of Haddu Khan, would visit Paluskar. Omkarnath had the advantage of sitting behind and accompanying Rahmat Khan on the *tambura* on many occasions (G. S. Desai 1968: 47–8).

In 1916 Paluskar assigned Omkarnath the position of principal of the Lahore branch of the Gandharva Mahavidyalaya. There, in the Punjab, he met Ali Baksh and Kale Khan, the father and uncle of Bade Ghulam Ali Khan. On completing his assignment in Lahore in 1919, Omkarnath returned to Broach and started his own musical institution, the Gandharva Niketan (Wadhera 1954b: 13).

In the 1920s Omkarnath also was heavily involved with Mahatma Gandhi's non-cooperation movement (G. S. Desai 1968: 47). He even became the president of the Broach District Congress Committee. He was warned by musicians against becoming too involved: 'Patriotic statesmen there are many in the country', said Narayan Rao Khare to Omkarnath Thakur, 'but soulful musicians there are few' (Wadhera 1954b: 13).

In 1933 Omkarnath travelled to Europe and was among the first Indian musicians to perform widely there. On the occasion of the International Music Conference held in Florence, he gave a recital for two and a half hours, and he also had a private audience with and sang for Mussolini and is said to have moved him deeply. Between 1933 and 1954 he performed also in Rome, Milan, Asconia (Switzerland), Paris, Berlin, Hamburg, Budapest (where he recited the peace *mantra* from the Veda, in Parliament Square; G. S. Desai 1968: 48), Prague, Bucharest, Stockholm, Brussels, London, Wrexham (Wales), Moscow, Stalingrad (now Volgograd), Tashkent, Kabul, and Kathmandu (Neelkant 1964: 16).

After his wife Indira Devi died in childbirth in 1933 while he was in Russia, Omkarnath devoted his life completely to music. In the enthusiasm for an 'India for Indians', a wave of pride in ancient heritage swept the country during Omkarnath's maturing years and his natural interests in history and philosophy were perhaps heightened as he began to undertake research on the glorious ancient tradition of his country's music, decrying any foreign influences and even the contributions of Indian Muslim musicians. Mastering Sanskrit, he delved into the *Nātya Śāstra*, into the aesthetic theory of *raga*, and into works on the history of *raga*. The only unfortunate aspect of his work was a propensity (shared by other Hindu musicians) for ignoring the contributions of generations of great Indian musicians who were Muslim rather than Hindu, seeing them as 'corrupted present' rather than 'pure past'. In general, it was a difficult time for the Muslim musicians who had developed and sustained the very tradition which the Hindu musicians were performing.

Omkarnath Thakur became one of those rare individuals (formerly deemed a *nayak*) who was both musicologist and performing artist. One of the important achievements of his life was that he built a fine college of music at Benares Hindu University which incorporates both musicology and performance studies. In collaboration with his students Prem Lata Sharma (theorist) and Balwant Raj Bhatt (vocalist), Omkarnath produced volumes such as his textbook *Saṅgīt Anjalī*.

In the 1960s many honors were given to Omkarnath Thakur. In 1963, the year of his retirement as Professor Emeritus, he received the President's Award for Hindustani Vocal Music from the Sangeet Natak Akademi and was awarded an honorary Doctorate of Literature from Benares Hindu University. In the next year he received an honorary doctorate from Rabindra Bharati University, Bengal. He received the first Padma Shri title from the President of India.

Because an exhaustive discussion of Omkarnath Thakur's musical style is available in Hurie (1980), comments here are restricted to a delineation of those characteristics of Omkarnath's style which distinguish it from Gwalior *gharana* style and cause him to be regarded as an independent musician. The types of improvisation he included in his *khyal*s are very distinctive. While Gwalior *gharana* musicians cultivate *boltan* as a speciality, Omkarnath neglected *boltan*, relatively speaking. Conversely, he cultivated *tan* far more. While his *bolbant* was described as 'powerful' by Hurie, there was little of it other than *tihai*s; on the other hand, *bolbant* was relished by Gwalior *gharana* musicians of his generation. He would include *sargam*, albeit sparingly, while no Gwalior musician would. Nor did Omkarnath cultivate interplay with his accompanists as an element of form.

Omkarnath exploited dynamics and production of different vocal timbres, emphasizing the emotive content of music. He produced a type of ornament which might (inadequately) be described as a heavy jerk on each pitch. As described by Hurie (personal communication), it is a 'dropping into the throat, then jumping up'; Omkarnath's student Balwant Raj Bhatt referred to it only as a 'heavy gamak'. This *gamak* Omkarnath applied even in a relatively fast *tan* that included the renowned Gwalior octave leaps. Since types of improvisation and musical emphases are basic for distinguishing styles of *khyal*, it is clear that Omkarnath was indeed independent in important ways from his Gwalior *gharana* heritage.

The Delhi *gharana*

As stated succinctly by Neuman (1980: 155), the Delhi *gharana* is not recognized as an 'authentic *gharana*' by the more orthodox members of the musical world. A major reason he cites for this is a social one: that the *gharana* includes a number of *tabla* and *sarangi* players. The most significant reason is that it does not represent a truly unique musical style. The Delhi *gharana*, then, can be considered an area of musical individuality: while there have been the requisite three generations of disciples of vocal music, the *khyal* style of one leading singer in each generation has been individual. While the Delhi *gharana* is indeed a *gharana* in familial terms, the musicians have not developed a coherent and recognized style of performing *khyal*.

The members of this family (see Chart 9–1) have lived in the Delhi area for many generations. Included among the illustrious exponents of the Delhi *gharana* have been Umrao Khan, Shadi Khan, Murad Khan, Baba Nasir Khan, and also Tanras Khan, singer at the Delhi court of the last Mughal emperor Bahadur Shah II. In the early nineteenth century Ela Umra Khan, a musician at the court of the Maharaja Nahar Singh, ruler of Ballabhgarh near Delhi, was made a gift by the *maharaja* of four villages. One was Samepur, 'the village of melody'. During the 1857 'mutiny' against the British, the Ballabhgarh ruler was ousted, and Ela Umra's son, Sangi Khan, settled in Delhi (Wadhera 1954a).

Once, when Sangi Khan visited Samepur, he was shown all courtesies but one by other members of the *gharana* – he was refused the privilege of smoking the *hookah* with them.

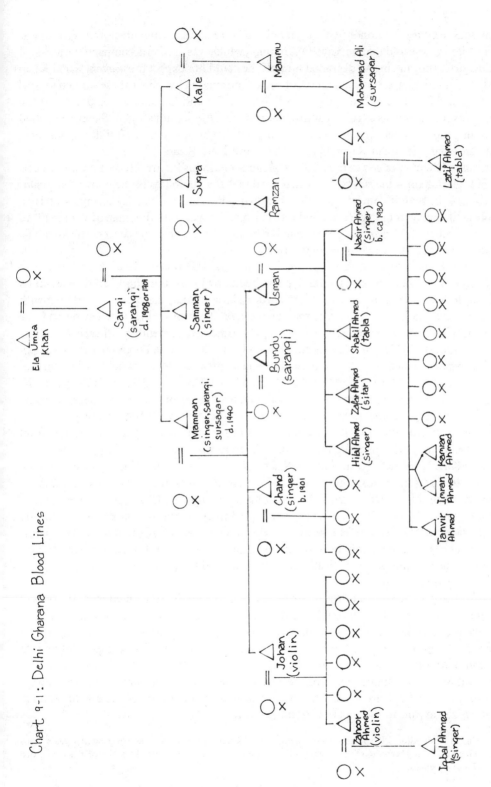

Chart 9-1: Delhi Gharana Blood Lines

261

Source: Nasir Ahmed Khan, Interview: 1978

When he asked why this honor (which symbolized acceptance as a member of the group) was refused him, he was told that he played the *sarangi*, which was used to accompany the music of dancing girls, and, having so degraded himself, he could not expect the *hookah*. Sangi Khan 'told the villagers that in that case they had better ban singing too, since these women sang as they danced. He then left the village and swore that he and his family would see that the sarangi was recognized as a truly beautiful instrument' (Anonymous 1963). Sangi Khan died in 1908 or 1909 (Wadhera 1954a), but the family felt that his mission was fulfilled by his sons, Mamman Khan, Samman Khan, Sugra Khan, and Kale Khan.

Mamman Khan was *ustad* to the next two generations in his family. He also invented a new stringed instrument – the *sursagar* – which combines the attributes of the *sitar*, *rebab*, *vina*, and *sarangi*, in that it can be bowed or plucked. (Because it has fifty strings and is so complicated to play, it has never been adopted by many musicians other than Mohammad Ali Khan, a member of the *gharana*.) Mamman Khan was a musician at the court of the Maharaja of Patiala, he died in 1940 (Anonymous 1963).

Mamman Khan's son Chand Khan was born in 1901 and was the leading Delhi *gharana* *khyal* singer of his generation. His training was begun by his grandfather, and then assumed by his father when Sangi Khan passed away. As was traditional, the young Chand sang with his father, even going on a concert tour at the age of seven or eight, when he had the opportunity to hear the greatest musicians of the time. He remembered hearing Rahmat Khan (Gwalior) in Madras and later Abdul Karim Khan (Kirana) in Poona (Wadhera 1954a). When he was a teenager, Chand was invited to sing at music conferences held in the courts of Hyderabad, Mysore, Baroda, and Gwalior. At the age of twelve (1913) he was employed at the Patiala court as his father had been earlier, and remained there for twenty-four years. Settling back in Delhi, Chand became music supervisor for the new Delhi broadcasting station in 1937; he had already sung for All-India Radio in Bombay (Wadhera 1954a). Now retired from active concert life, he enjoys the reputation of a good *khyaliya*.[1]

Chand Khan's nephew Nasir Ahmed Khan (born c. 1930) is the leading Delhi *gharana* singer of the present mature generation. Nasir Ahmed was trained by his grandfather Mamman Khan, his father Usman Khan, and his paternal uncle Chand Khan. He was also coached by his relations, Ramzan Khan (who opted to go to Pakistan at Partition) and the *sarangi* player Bundu Khan. His performance career began in 1955. By the late 1960s, reviewers of his concerts wrote in terms of 'assurance', 'poise', and 'purposefulness'. Two reviews in 1969 mentioned specifically his treatment of the *raga* (*Sunday Statesman* 1969b, and *Times of India* 1969c).

In performances broadcast in 1968–9 from All-India Radio, Nasir Ahmed spent the bulk of time in his *bara khyal* selections on the delineation of the *raga* in *badhat*-style *alap* (pitch-by-pitch elaboration). His pre-*ciz alap*s, sung to 'a' or 'na', resembled the initial moments of an extended *ragalap*. He seems to have been interested only in the *ciz sthai* text, presenting it to *sthai* and *antara*-like melody in the first slow cycle of a performance. Beyond that, his improvisation was on single words of the text such as 'gata', 'lala', and 'jaga'; those were usually pronounced indistinctly as if they were vocables, in order to emphasize melody and to deemphasize rhythm to the greatest extent possible.

[1] According to Nasir Ahmed Khan (Interview: 1978), Chand Khan has documentation covering fifty years of his performing life. From forty programs in Pakistan, for example, his son-in-law Salauddin Ahmed Khan recorded twelve hours of singing.

In Ex. 9–1, from a performance of Rag Bageshri, Nasir Ahmed's sensitive manner of introducing a new pitch is shown – in this case, Ma – in the *alap*. In the sixth cycle Ma was introduced lightly, without emphasis. In *avart* 7 Ga was still being emphasized and Ma oriented to it, until Ma was stressed slightly more in counts 9 and 10. In *avart* 8 Ma was clearly established as the focal point in the improvisation.

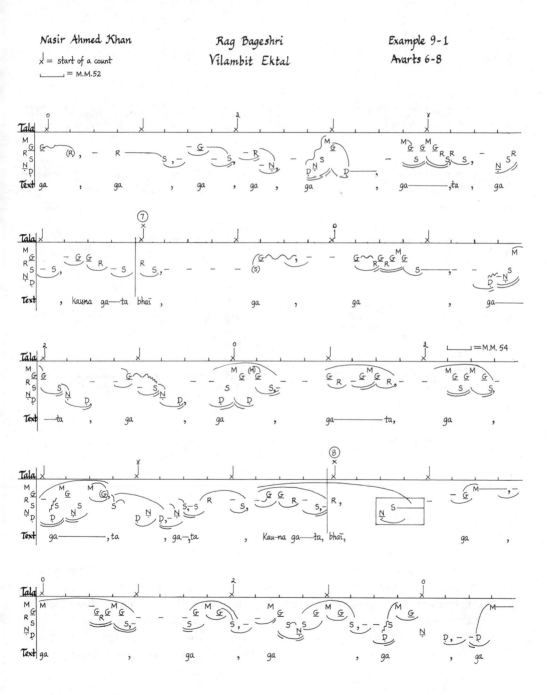

Nasir Ahmed Khan   Rag Bageshri   Example 9-1
                            Vilambit Ektal   Avarts 6-8

Sargam and *tan* are the two types of improvisation which dominate Nasir Ahmed's *bara khyals* beyond the *alap*, and they also constitute the bulk of his *chota khyal* improvisation. In many *sargam* passages he applies *gamak* to each pitch, as if the passage were a *boltan* or *tan*. He also creates contrast in *sargam* by singing first with *gamak* and then without it.

While reviews of the 1960s invariably mentioned Nasir Ahmed's skill in lightning-fast *tans*, it seems that in the 1970s *tans* became an increasingly important aspect of his *khyal* performances. He certainly stressed that himself, and added that he makes *sargam* into *tan*s (Interview: 1978). His skill in *tan*s was stressed repeatedly in tributes paid to him in the program of his Silver Jubilee Celebration (1978). He bears proudly the title 'Tan Samrat' ('Emperor of *tan*s'), which was bestowed upon him in 1962 by the Sangit Mitra Mandali of Jabalpur (Srinivas 1978).

A few general comments about Nasir Ahmed's presentation of three *khyal*s are made here (they bear testing with a larger number of performances than I have had available for study). First, there was scarcely a trace of *layakari* to be found in these performances; in reviews of the 1960s it was mentioned that he sang *tarana* (one in Rag Chandrakauns, specifically), so it is possible that he saves *layakari* for *tarana*. Secondly, he does not seem to emphasize width of vocal range, which was just over two *saptak*s in each of those performances. Thirdly, while he sings dramatically quietly in his presentation of *tar* Sa, there is relatively little dramatic exploitation of his voice. Fourthly, he accelerates the rate of the *tala* counts very little during *bara khyal*, using increasing rhythmic density as a means of acceleration. This contrasts with his *chota khyal* style, in which jumps in speed are easily apparent. He clearly views the purposes of the two *khyal* types as very different. Lastly, in the longer performances he enjoyed a sharing relationship with the accompanying members of his ensemble. Examples of this were breaks in *bara khyal* when he encouraged the *sarangi* player to 'repeat' his *tan*s. In the Bageshri performance the *tabla* player took a brief solo in *chota khyal*. However, this sharing relationship was the element sacrificed in the shorter performance, instead of, for instance, the *alap*, which might have been curtailed.

Plate 13   Amir Khan (center), Patna, 1956; note the harmonium (extreme right) in the accompanying ensemble (photo by permission of the Sangeet Natak Akademi, New Delhi)

Amir Khan

Amir Khan, born in 1912, was one of the greatest of India's musicians of the twentieth century. He was killed suddenly in an automobile accident on December 31, 1973. While his style was in many musical respects 'of tradition', in many other musical respects it was a manifestation of the best possible results of picking and choosing at will from the wide range of musical possibilities for singing *khyal*. Amir is spoken of by some in relation to the Indore *gharana* (e.g., V. H. Deshpande 1973), and by others in terms of being strictly his own person (e.g., Saxena 1974).

Amir Khan was born in Kalanaur, and spent his early childhood and the greater part of his adult life at Indore (Saxena 1974: 8). His father Shah Mir (Shamir) Khan was a *sarangi* player (of the Dhanadhtha *gharana* of professional musicians, and a court musician at Indore, according to Garg 1957: 89), and it was from his father that Amir received his 'formal' training. In Indore he grew up with the music of the vocalist Rajab Ali Khan, who was court musician at Dewas, about forty miles north of Indore, and the music of Murad Khan, the *vina* player (Saxena 1974: 8).

Amir was also impressed with the music of the vocalists Amanat Khan, who according to Amar Nath (Interview: 1978) enjoyed singing 'lots of sargam', and his brother Aman Ali Khan. Amanat and Aman Ali belonged to a group referred to as the Bhendi Bazaar group, consisting of three or four brothers from Moradabad who settled in that bazaar area in Bombay (cf. V. H. Deshpande 1973: 65). To this Bhendi Bazaar group Deshpande attributes the cultivation of the *merkhand* style of *alap* which was taken up by Abdul Wahid Khan of the Kirana *gharana* who, in turn, was another of the musicians who greatly impressed Amir.

Deshpande, who said that Amir 'is the only ray of hope in the surrounding darkness' (1973: 68), found the influence of Abdul Wahid Khan's *alap* 'so profound on Amir Khan that in a slow *khyal* he is almost a replica' (p. 66). He pointed out that like that of the Kirana *gharana* musicians, Amir's family tradition was *sarangi* playing,[2] and that musicians who are intimate with techniques of bowed stringed instruments seem to stress *alap* in their singing style.

Absorbing the musical characteristics he greatly admired, Amir infused them with his own personal musical artistry with such skill that it was possible for him to be successful in his own right. Unlike Nasir Ahmed Khan of the Delhi *gharana*, and unlike his independent 'predecessors' such as Bhaskar Rao Bakhle, Dilip Chandra Vedi, and Manik Verma, he achieved this without the formal training from recognized, established singers that is regarded as both a social and musical requirement. He was awarded the honor of being made a Fellow of the Sangeet Natak Akademi of Bihar and was given the President's Award by the (New Delhi) Akademi in 1967. In 1971 he was named Padma Bhushan by the President of India.

Amir had several students with diverse specialities: Munir Khan (*sarangi*), Mukund Gosvami (*bin*), and the singers Amar Nath and the husband and wife Pradyumna and Poorabi Mukherji. The brothers Surinder and Tej Pal Singh studied with him, but they have a style more of their own (Saxena 1974: 11). Amar Nath, in particular, is regarded as a disciple of the *ustad* who is carrying on his style. If, with the passage of time and events, Amir becomes considered the 'founder' of a *gharana* – and if, indeed, musicians still think in terms of *gharana* in another two generations – it will be a *gharana* in terms of music without ever having been a *gharana* in terms of blood relationships.

---

[2] Amir Khan's younger brother Bashir Khan is a *sarangi* player at All-India Radio Indore.

Amir was acknowledged to have absorbed Abdul Wahid Khan's style of slow singing (Saxena 1974; Amar Nath, Interview: 1978). Their slow speed is indeed comparable; furthermore, neither artist accelerated the pace of the *tala* counts very much within a selection. At such a slow speed the artist has options for sustaining musical interest, and in one of those options Abdul Wahid's and Amir's styles are similar: while the very first cycles of a performance have reposeful moments, there are soon successive cycles of melody with a certain restlessness, constant motion rather than the sustaining of pitches with subtle voice changes and play with intonation. Both artists seem to have used enunciation of the initial consonants of text words for clear phrasing of melodic units within long cycles in slow speed. Both found *jhumra tal* preferable for *vilambit laya* performance. These details are shown in Ex. 9–2, *avarts* 2–4 of Amir's Megh recording (GCI EASD 1331). Also like Abdul Wahid, Amir neglected *layakari* in slow-speed *bara khyal*. In such performances by both singers, almost the entire time was devoted to *alap*.

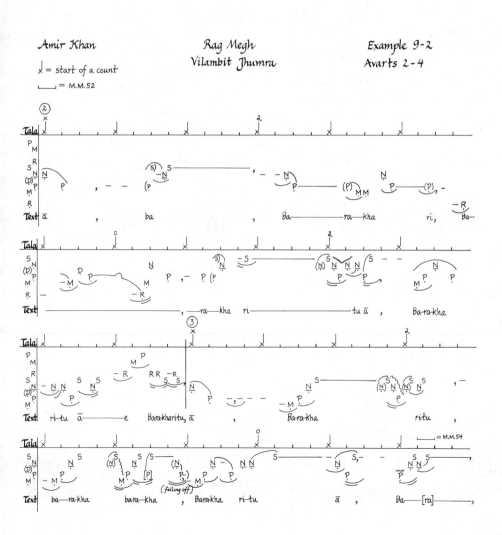

Amir Khan — Rag Megh, Vilambit Jhumra — Example 9-2, Avarts 2-4

Amir treated his listeners to 'unhurried evocation of the form of *sthayi* and reverential access as if with unshod feet, to the core of the *raga* being rendered' (Saxena 1974: 7). His relationship with his audience was similar to that of Abdul Wahid: 'I must mention . . . [Amir Khan's] absolute indifference, while singing, to the reactions of the audience. He would here heed only his music, and his own conception of it. *Our* response, or the lack of it, had just no effect on him – at least not visibly . . . *he never seemed to make a conscious endeavour to please the audience*' (*ibid.*: 6).

According to his disciple Amar Nath, Amir felt that, while the proper treatment of notes in *tar saptak* was desirable, the *mandra saptak* was more important for serious effects. Given the time allotted in a commercial recording, Amir clearly made the decision to spend more time in the low register (and consequently less time in the higher register) than is usual. His voice in the low register was beautiful, 'rich, mellow . . . with its husky umbra', resulting in depth and dignity (*ibid.*: 7).

One of the most distinctive stylistic features of Amir's slow-speed singing is a particular shaping of melodic lines. Rendered graphically, it would look (approximately) like

. The first important pitch of the phrase is approached from below (or above, or around) by a fast, vibrato-like *gamak* (*murki*), then that first important pitch is sustained, and then it gives way to one or more 'units' of sustained pitch followed by a more active descent–ascent melodic configuration. That sudden, fast *gamak* on a pitch in an otherwise relatively reposeful melodic context was frequently employed by Amir to 'announce' the beginning of the *mukhda*. This was particularly noticeable in his Darbari Kanhra, Lalit, and Megh recordings. He used his *murki* in other contexts as well, but none as consistent as the beginning of the *mukhda*.

Judicious use of other types of *gamak*s is also characteristic of Amir's singing, even in the slowest portions. Each note is treated in some meaningful fashion, whether with *gamak* or sustained, and this maintains the musical interest even at slow speed. A simple melodic ascent in Rag Darbari Kanhra is made to sound exquisite by the configuration .

Amir's *alap* is *bolalap*, and his text enunciation is laudable. One point about Amir's use of syllables which Amar Nath made to Saxena concerned the vowel on *sam*: 'So far as possible, the "sama" should be touched with an *akara-bol*, so that the "*sthayi*" may flower at the focus of rhythm' (1974: 11). Furthermore, as Amar Nath explained to me, *akar* (the vowel 'ā') on *sam* allows the singer to continue easily. Listening to Amir's recordings with this in mind, one hears the vowel function mostly as a vehicle for ongoing melody in slow speed, and as a point of rhythmic emphasis in faster speed. In his slow-speed Lalit recording, for example, the *mukhda* is treated primarily as a melodic phrase rather than as a point of rhythmic emphasis. The *sthai mukhda* 'Kahan jage rāt' came to *sam* on 'rā', but the melody is carried well into the next cycle: 'rā———t'. The *mukhda* 'Jai māte vīlamba' of his Hamsadhwani medium-speed *khyal*, on the other hand (GCI EASD 1357), hits *sam* on the vowel 'ī' of 'vīlamba', and the melody is continued into the next cycle with the remainder of the word.

What is noteworthy (and, in my listening experience, unique) is that Amir is meticulous about enunciating final consonants of words. If, for example, he has prolonged 'nā' of 'anāt', he ends the phrase with the closing 't'; more usually, singers would drop it, or make it 'ta'. Even words which end in the nasals 'n' and 'm' are usually closed equally carefully.

The types of improvisation Amir included in his *khyal* performances were *boltan*, *tan*, and sargam. *Boltan*s were occasional, as at the end of his Malkauns *bara khyal* and again near the end of that *chota khyal* (GCI EASD 1357), and they provided effective contrast with his *tan*s. Amir was praised for his *tan*s. Amar Nath pointed out that he used *tan* patterns that were used by the three musicians who so greatly inspired him (Rajab Ali Khan, Abdul Wahid Khan, and Aman Ali Khan); in addition, he had his own *tan* patterns. Descriptions of his *tan*s are expressive: '*drut taans* emanating from the *mandra* would often seem to up-gather themselves like a cloud' (Saxena 1974: 7n). The shape of his *tan*s varied. He sang them heavily, or he rippled lightly through them. Their speeds and ranges varied too: 'The agile voice enables the production of very fast tans and Amir Khan moves with encompassing ease in all the three octaves' (V. H. Deshpande 1973: 67).

According to Amar Nath (via Saxena 1974), Amir's opinion with regard to *tan*s was that whatever their design, their execution should always involve a measure of *gamak* (to give them depth), and *lahak* ('lightness', to temper the *gamak*). The 'measure of *gamak*' varied from *tan* to *tan* with Amir, and that was one factor that contributed to making his *tan*s interesting.

When Amir reached the *tar* Sa region, and after he had sung the *ciz antara* (if he did so) in a slow-speed *khyal*, one can expect him to have improvised with *sargam*. Vinay Chandra Maudgalya (Interview: 1978) remarked that Amir sang *sargam* in unique style – *alap*-like, in that more pitches were sung to a syllable than were enunciated by that syllable; I would amend Maudgalya's statement slightly to say that *sargam* passages in Amir's *bara khyal* were more like tuneful melodies. The tuneful *sargam* portion of his Rag Megh recording is shown in Ex. 9–3; it begins in *avart* 11. When asked why he deemed *sargam* so important, Amir would consistently answer that 'besides helping identification of notes – and so improvisation, too, without any risk of infringing the grammatical form of the "raga" – *sargam*s lend variety to singing by their own audible diversity' (Saxena 1974: 9). By 'audible diversity' he meant that Pa keeps the *akar* open, Ni shows the voice as subdued, and Ma holds a nasal resonance.

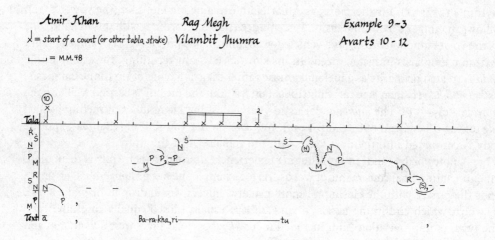

Amir Khan   Rag Megh   Example 9-3
x = start of a count (or other tabla stroke)   Vilambit Jhumra   Avarts 10 - 12
⌐——⌐ = M.M. 48

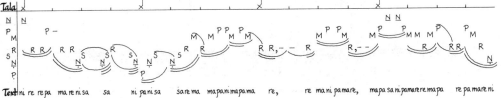

Vinay Chandra Maudgalya also pointed out (Interview: 1978) Amir's use of *gamak* on *sargam*. That is indeed a prominent feature of *sargam* style which Amir used quite purposefully, apparently for contrast, because some phrases are treated with *gamak* as a *tan* would be, while others are not. The penultimate cycle of his Megh *bara khyal*, for example, was double-speed *gamak sargam*, while the last cycle was quadruple-speed *sargam* without *gamak*, phasing into *sargam* with *gamak*. In the Darbari Kanhra *chota khyal*, he treated the beginnings of a succession of *sargam* phrases with a fast, vibrato-like *gamak*. Amir did not follow Abdul Wahid's practice of combining *sargam* with units of texted improvisation in the same cycle of the *tala*.

It was not uncommon for Amir to pair a medium-speed *bara khyal* with a fast-speed *chota khyal*. His recording of the Karnatak *raga* Hamsadhwani was an instance of this. Because his slow speed was so slow, his medium speed was distinctly *madhya laya*: and he occasionally sang a sequence of compositions in all three speeds, with a change of *raga* for musical interest. In April 1970 in Bombay, for example, he sang *vilambit* Basant Mukhari, and *madhya* and *drut laya* Gujari Todi (*Times of India*, 1970a).

Summary

The time is at hand in the history of *khyal* when young singers are thinking less and less in terms of *gharana*s. With the precedents set by such remarkable musicians as Amir Khan and others discussed in this chapter, it is possible to view somewhat more optimistically the loss of the sense of the importance of *gharana* as the next century approaches. It is important to realize that even in the halcyon days of *khyal gharana*s, when transmission of musical knowledge was tightly controlled, a significant number of fine musicians were learning from numerous sources and utilizing that diverse knowledge in the cultivation of their own styles.

10 *Conclusion*

The *gharana* system has been a positive force in the history of Hindustani art music insofar as it has ensured the continuity of the most fundamental characteristics of the Hindustani art-music tradition: the primacy of *raga* among all musical materials; musical structure based on clear and consecutive emphasis of the basic elements of melody, rhythm and meter, and on utilization of a recurring melodic motive to delineate musical units; and association of song text with composition and meter. In the eighteenth century, and probably through the nineteenth, those fundamental characteristics were manifested most thoroughly and superbly only through the vocal genre *alap-dhrupad*. Despite cries that the classical tradition was being dissipated, there does not seem to have been serious musical disruption with respect to the most fundamental characteristics of the tradition as *khyal* became the most prominent performance genre. *Khyal* itself now manifests those characteristics, just as *alap-dhrupad* also continues to do.

Although it is difficult to document, it is likely that, at the beginning of its existence as an independent genre, *khyal* did not fulfill one of those traditional requirements: it may originally have included minimal (or no) *alap*-type improvisation, which is the portion of the structure devoted to confirming the primacy of *raga*. Other characteristics of *khyal* which distinguish it from its predecessor *dhrupad* do not interfere with the fundamental set of characteristics indicated above. It seems that, from the beginning of *khyal*, the song texts have been more romantic and the compositions shorter than those of *dhrupad*; and the inclusion of *tan*s (and therefore *boltan*s) in *khyal* has distinguished the two genres in terms of types of improvisation (and, in living memory, the inclusion of *sargam* as well). The accompanying ensemble for *khyal* may have been different from that of *dhrupad* from the outset, although the widespread acceptance by male soloists of *sarangi* in the ensemble appears to date only from the 1930s.

The *gharana* system of organization of musicians and musical knowledge seems to have developed through the history of *khyal*, and most *khyal* singers have been part of the system. Therefore it has been musicians within the *gharana* system who have been responsible for developing *khyal* into the genre it is today, a genre which now encompasses even *alap*-type improvisation and therefore assures continuity of all the most fundamental characteristics of the Hindustani art-music tradition.

The contribution of the *gharana* system itself to this process is twofold: it provided a stable support system for musicians during periods of serious social and cultural disruption (as sketched in Chapter 1); and it assured cohesion and continuity of the musical tradition in the early twentieth century, when musical knowledge was being disseminated at a more rapid pace and to more diverse types of people than it had been for several centuries (if ever) in North India. It was important that those who were most capable as teachers, as well as those who were 'stars' in the performing arena, had a ready source for 'accreditation' when the system of transmission was changing so rapidly. Likewise, it was important that those who wished to study music could be certain of the 'pedigree' of prospective teachers.

The *gharana* system has also provided a source of cohesion in a cultural (and therefore a musical) system in which authority resides ultimately in the individual. *Khyal* has developed as a genre which admits of a remarkable degree of musical flexibility, which must owe its existence to individual creativity. The desirability and admissibility of individual creativity has been balanced in the development of *khyal* by the social fact of a group tradition rooted in the family system. Even though the family system has ceased to function in most *khyal gharanas*, the ideal of having a group tradition has remained, continuing to provide the musical factor against which individual creativity is balanced. The result has been one genre performed in distinctive group ways, while comprehending incredible diversity at the level of musical detail as cultivated by individual musicians.

In Table 10–1 characteristics of the styles of the six *gharanas* are displayed. The musical options enumerated in the extreme left column of the table are those which distinguish *khyal* among the improvisatory genres of North Indian vocal music, and those which might characterize the style of a group of *khyal* singers. The musical detail presented in this study, however, makes it clear that many musical options are available to *khyal* singers which do not necessarily characterize either the genre or a group tradition; rather, many are options from the Hindustani musical tradition in general, and all can be utilized in the development of individual style. With this larger set of options the factors of choice and capability, rather than heredity, become decisive more frequently.

In the sphere of 'emphasis on rhythm', which is one example of a characteristic of group tradition, one can find numerous musical options within each type of emphasis. In analyzing *tihai* in cadences sung by the *khyaliyas* considered in this study, for instance, I have found a sampling of options which only glimpses at a much larger number:

1 Repeating the text and melody three times.
2 Repeating the text three times but changing the melody.
3 Exact repetition.
4 Implying repetition, but manipulating it in some way.
5 Maintaining the nature of the improvisational unit which it completes: e.g., a *tan tihai* after a unit of *tan*, or *bolbant tihai* after a unit of *bolbant*.
6 Contrasting with the nature of the improvisational unit it completes: e.g., a *boltan tihai* after a unit of *tans*; or, more contrasting, a textually dense *tihai* (i.e., *bolbant*) after a unit of *boltan* or *tan*; or a *boltan tihai* after a unit of *sargam*.
7 Placement in *alap*, thereby adding contrasting emphasis on rhythm in a more melodic context.
8 Placement in the *mukhda*.
9 Placement before the *mukhda*.

The relationship of the soloist with the accompanist comes into play with respect to *tihai* as well, when the vocal *tihai* is matched by the *tabla* player, or the *tabla* player independently contributes a *tihai* when he senses a vocal unit coming to an end. Even this sample of options has not included the level of musical detail involved in the degree and type of rhythmic complexity used, ornamentation, dynamics, the melody itself, and other such points.

Table 10–1. *Khyal: characteristics of six gharanas*

Characteristics	Gwalior	Agra	Sahaswan/Rampur	Alladiya Khan	Kirana	Patiala
Vocal technique quality range ornamentation	Wide	Aggressive Powerful	Wide	Elasticity, flexibility Open	Long, sustained pitches *Kan, mind*	Emphasis on developing the voice Emphasis on lower register
Choice of *ragas*				Complex *ragas* Rare *ragas*	Traditional *ragas* No combined *ragas*	
Choice of *talas*				Emphasis on *tintal*		Emphasis on variety
Repertoire		Traditional and new compositions (i.e., emphasis on composing)	Large, including composing new songs		Traditional	
Performance speed level acceleration			Slight in *bara khyal*	Slow	Slowest De-emphasis on fast speed Slight in *bara khyal*	
General emphasis	Balanced emphasis on melody and rhythm Contrast	Rhythmic play Elements close to *dhrupad*	*Svara* (melody over rhythm)	Contrast Rhythmic play Close to *dhrupad*	Vocal expressiveness Emphasis on melody (*alap*)(i.e., minimum rhythmic play)	Balanced emphasis on melody and rhythm
Structure of *bara khyal* pre-*ciz* alap initial presentation of *ciz*	*Ciz*-like (tuneful) Slow speed: *sthai* → improv. → *antara*; Medium speed: *sthai & antara* → improv. OR *sthai* → improv. → *antara*	Might be lengthy Slow speed: *sthai* → improv. → *antara*	*Sthai & antara* → improv.			Might omit *antara*

Improvisation						
nom-tom		Nom-tom-like singing	Relatively little	Some nom-tom-like improv.	Minimal	Bolbant-like sargam
bolbant	Emphasized	Emphasized (less, recently)		Emphasized	Occasional	Occasional
boltan	Emphasized	Emphasized	Little	Emphasized	Emphasized	Emphasized, alap & elsewhere
sargam	None	A little, recently	Judicious	In alap & elsewhere		
tan	Descending sapat, melodic leaps, alankarik, wide range	Relatively slow, clarity emphasized	Sapat, melodic leaps	Rippling, roller-coaster shape		Variety emphasized
Miscellaneous	Slow-speed bara khyal for alap-type improv. Medium-speed bara khyal emphasizes rhythm more. Active musical relationship with accompanist is likely	All of ciz text used throughout improv. Wilful enunciation or 'mumbling' of text, for reasons of rhythm. Active musical relationship with accompanist is likely	Use of dynamics. Multiple types of improv. within one tala cycle	Large proportion of performance time on tans	Clear text, but mostly mukhda phrase. Vowels other than 'a' for sustained melody. Use of dynamics	All of ciz text used throughout improv. Text & sargam combined in one tala cycle

The parameters by which Table 10–1 is organized – vocal technique or quality, vocal range and ornamentation, choice of *ragas*, etc. – were derived from the sources cited in this study which describe particular *gharana* styles. Blank spaces in the table indicate that no particular statement need be made about that characteristic for that *gharana*. For vocal range, for example, it can be assumed that all *khyal* singers strive to sing within the requisite three registers (octaves), but Gwalior and Sahaswan *gharana* musicians are distinguished by making a special effort to encompass most of the full three octaves in their improvisation. Likewise, for ornamentation, it can be assumed that all *khyal* singers use ornamentation of various sorts, but Kirana singers are noted particularly for *kan*, a subtle oscillation within a pitch, and for the pulling slurs called *mind*. This table complements the description of the basic elements of *khyal* given in Chapter 2.

Because there are and have been so many musicians in each *gharana*, such a list of style characteristics consists entirely of gross generalizations. However, such generalizations provide a basis for comparisons and contrast. The contrast between some *gharana* styles is striking, Agra and Kirana perhaps the most so. The explanation for the co-existence of two such different styles as Agra and Kirana within the same performance genre is complex; while a thorough explanation would constitute another monograph, the temptation to suggest an explanation is too strong to resist. This hypothetical explanation involves the nature of the *gharana*s in which the styles originated, and also the factors of cultural value, musical value, and social status among musicians.

Since the sixteenth century in North India, singers of the vocal genre *dhrupad* have held the position of highest social status among musicians. The early members of the Agra *gharana* were *dhrupad* singers, and even when the *gharana* became noted for *khyal*, Agra *gharana* singers continued (until the present generations) to perform both *dhrupad* and *khyal*. This is not surprising, because *dhrupad* is the type of Hindustani art music which is accorded the highest cultural value; by continuing to perform *dhrupad*, the singers of the Agra *gharana* have continually asserted their claim to both the musical tradition of highest cultural value and the highest rank in the social sphere of musicians. *Dhrupad* (*alap-dhrupad*) is accorded the highest cultural value because it is the traditional repository of the element of Hindustani art music that is accorded the highest musical value: melody in general, and, specifically, knowledge of *raga*. (Students wanting to learn a *raga*, or to learn about *raga*, are told to study with a *dhrupad* singer.) *Dhrupad* singing also requires skill in rhythmic play.

It is said consistently about the Agra *gharana* style of *khyal* that it is 'close to *dhrupad*'. Some of the characteristics enumerated for Agra style in Table 10–1 elucidate that statement, and further pertinent discussion is found in Chapter 4. It is clear that the Agra *gharana* style has been changing constantly through time, and generalizations about the style should be qualified for different periods of time. It may have been in the generation of Faiyaz Khan that the Agra style of *khyal* came 'closer to *dhrupad*' than it was before, and it might have occurred in the following way.

When two different genres of music are sung in a performance, it is logical to assume that the purpose is to offer variety and contrast. It must have been necessary for Agra *gharana* *khyal* style to be clearly distinguishable from *dhrupad* in such circumstances. The lifetime of the great Faiyaz Khan saw the expansion of performance contexts into the public sphere. The esoteric *dhrupad* was not the type of music to which urban audiences were being exposed by the leaders of the movement; it was *khyal* and *thumri*, or regional songs, or *bhajan*, they were hearing from singers such as Vishnu Digambar Paluskar and Bade Ghulam Ali Khan and others. Seeing little audience interest in *dhrupad*, but unwilling to neglect his family's heritage, or being interested perhaps in educating his public audiences, it is possible that Faiyaz Khan began to restrict his singing of *dhrupad* to more cloistered performance contexts and to add to his 'public' performances of *khyal* the elements of *dhrupad* which many sources now attribute to Agra *gharana khyal* style in general – a long *alap* before the composition is performed, taking the classical form of *ragalap*. The singing of *nom-tom*-like improvisation in Agra style of *khyal* may also have originated with Faiyaz Khan as part of this process. The present generation of Agra singers does not appear to have maintained the practice of performing *dhrupad* along with *khyal*. This may be why the amount of intricate rhythmic play in their performances is less than that in the performance styles of previous generations. Nor is the long pre-*ciz alap* deemed a necessary component of *gharana* style by the present generation. The reasons for this are unclear. It could be personal preference; it could be that the cultural status of *dhrupad* is no longer so vital as to affect the musical content of Agra *gharana khyal* style. This may not threaten the high social status accorded to Agra singers among musicians, because they are now respected for the strength of the hereditary institution of *gharana* which they alone have maintained.

The same factors – cultural value, social status among musicians, and musical value – are significant for an explanation of Kirana *gharana khyal* style. The 'founders' of the Kirana style were members of a type of *gharana* which has been accorded low social status among musicians: they were from a family of accompanists, specifically players of the bowed-lute-type *sarangi*. Because the *sarangi* has been an accompanying instrument and, furthermore, has been associated with the musical ensemble for dancing girls in North India, the music played on it has traditionally been accorded low cultural value. In several places in this study the tension between *sarangi* players and singers of *khyal* has been mentioned. Since *khyal* is accompanied by *sarangi* players, they have had informal access to the musical knowledge of solo singers, and if *sarangi* players wished to elevate their status, the music of *khyal* singers was their means. It is the next logical and logistical step upward, both in terms of musical value and of social status.

While this might explain why Abdul Karim Khan and Abdul Wahid Khan became singers of *khyal*, it remains to consider why their *khyal* style was what it was. What did they choose to emphasize among the musical options available in *khyal*? They chose that aspect of music which is accorded the highest musical value – melody, *raga*. (The particular musical means by which they emphasized melody – vocal expressiveness, ornamentation such as *kan* and *mind* – are techniques which are related directly to their string tradition.) It is striking as well that the use of *sargam* (exegesis-like emphasis on melody, as if to prove a point) is highly cultivated by these artists. It is also striking, in the light of the hierarchy of musical values, that Kirana *gharana* singers use traditional musical material – traditional compositions, traditional *ragas* – as if to assert their place within tradition rather than to call attention to their departure from it.

The factors of social organization, cultural value, and musical value will continue to be powerful forces in the shaping of the classical vocal traditions of North India. There seems to have been a shift from group organization of the musical tradition to individuals asserting themselves in the growing 'star system'. The shift can be witnessed in the decline of hereditary family involvement and in the growing number of *khyaliyas* who prefer to combine aspects of several *gharana* musical styles. Such a shift could disturb the delicate balance between tradition and creativity which has characterized *khyal* as a genre, resulting either in conservatism or in more radical change than has taken place in North Indian music in several hundred years. But in India, even that has always been so.

Appendix: Selections on the cassette

SIDE A

*Selection 1   Narayan Rao Vyas
  (Ex. 3–12) Rag Gaur Malhar, Madhya laya Tintal
  Text: Jhuka [Jhuki] ād badariyā sāvan kī.
        Sāvana me umage jobanavā chāṅdi cale paradesa piyaravā; Sudhi na rahī ghara
        āvana kī.

        The clouds of the month of Sawan . . .
        In Sawan my youthful passion overflows, but my husband/lover has left and gone to
        a far land;
        he has not remembered to come home.

Selection 2   Irene Roy Chowdhury
    A   (Ex. 2–5a)   Rag Bageshri, Vilambit Ektal
                      Avarts 1–2
    Text: Kauna gata bhaī [lī morī re] piyā na pūche eka [huṅ] bāta.

            What has happened that my husband never asks about me?

    B   (Ex. 2–5b)   Pran Nath
                      Rag Bageshri, Vilambit Ektal
                      Avart 1
    Text: as Selection 2

*Selection 3   Abdul Wahid Khan
  (Ex. 7–5)   Rag Darbari Kanhra, Vilambit Jhumra tal
                Avarts 5–9
  Text: Gumānī, jāga.

        Wake up, and don't be angry with me.

*Selection 4   Bade Ghulam Ali Khan
  (Ex. 8–4)   Rag Malkauns, Vilambit Jhumra tal
                Avarts 15–16
  Text: Erī kaba āo sajana.

        Oh, when will you come, beloved?

281

*Selection 5   Gangubai Hangal
  (Ex. 7–1)   Rag Asavari, Madhya laya Tintal
          *Avart*s 18–20
  Text: Āye mātā Bhavānī.

> *Please come, mother Bhavani* [Parvati, consort of Lord Shiva].

*Selection 6   Kishore Amonkar
  (Ex. 6–3)   Rag Jaunpuri, Madhya laya Tintal
          Avart 31
  Text: Bāje jhanana pāyaliyā morī rājdulāre.
  Make your anklets jingle, my princess.

[Note: Her anklets have little bells attached which make the sound 'jhanana'. 'Rājdulāre' is a term of endearment for a young lady who is about to be married.]

*Selection 7   Kishore Amonkar
  (Ex. 6–4)   Rag Bageshri, Vilambit Tintal
          *Avart*s 26–7
  Text: Birahā na jāe.

> *The pain of separation will not go away.*

Selection 8   Krishnarao Pandit
  (Ex. 3–4)   Rag Desi, Madhya laya Tintal
          *Avart*s 46–7
  Text: Mhāre dere āo/āvojī mahārājā.
  Baja ke bīna [ke]. Bajāvojī rājā.

> *Please come to my door, oh maharaja.*
> *The bin is sounded. Please play, raja.*

*Selection 9   Nisar Hussein Khan
  (Ex. 5–3)   Rag Abhogi, Madhya laya Jhaptal
          *Avart*s 48–52
  Text: Jhanana āyo rī/re.

> *Come, with your anklets jingling.*

*Selection 10   Bade Ghulam Ali Khan
  (Ex. 8–1)   Rag Malkauns, Vilambit Jhumra tal
          *Avart*s 12–14
  Text: Erī kaba ā sajana.

> *Oh, when will you come, beloved?*

*Selection 11   Vinayak Rao Patwardhan
  (Ex. 3–10) Rag Hamir, Vilambit Ektal
          *Avart*s 18–19

Text: Karana cahū raghupati guna gāhā.
      Laghu mati mori charita avagāhā.

I want to sing the praises of Raghupati [Rama] but my mind is tiny and his deeds are vast.

*Selection 12 Vinayak Rao Patwardhan
  (Ex. 3–11) Rag Hamir, Vilambit Ektal
          Avarts 11–12
Text: as Selection 11

*Selection 13 Bade Ghulam Ali Khan
  (Ex. 8–2b) Rag Kaushi Dhani, Rupak tal
          Avarts 105–10
Text: He mana [and *sargam* syllables]

Oh, my heart . . .

*Selection 14 Amir Khan
  (Ex. 9–3) Rag Megh, Vilambit Jhumra tal
          Avarts 10–12
Text: Barakha ritu ā.

May the rainy season come.

Selection 15 Nisar Hussein Khan
  (Ex. 5–1) Rag Jaijaiwanti, Vilambit Ektal
          Avarts 7–8
Text: Vā kahāṅ kala ho, jinake piyā pardes gayo/gaye.

There is no rest/peace, for those whose lover has gone away.

*Selection 16 Kishore Amonkar
  (Ex. 6–5) Rag Pat Bihag, Madhya laya Tintal
          Avarts 20–3
Text: Maṅgala gāvo 'dhana dhana'.
      Āge bole: '. . . gala gā "dhana dhana". Maṅgala gā . . .'
      Āja more ghara ā.

Sing auspicious songs: 'dhana dhana'.
Say it again: 'Sing auspicious songs "dhana dhana". Sing auspicious songs . . .'
Come to my house today.

**Selection 17 Latafat Husain Khan
  (Ex. 4–8) Rag Miyan ki Todi, Vilambit laya
          Pre-*ciz alap*
Text: vocables

*Selection 18 Bhimsen Joshi
    (Ex. 7–2) Rag Lalit, Vilambit Ektal
             Avarts 16–17
    Text: Sovata sovata rī āṅkha khulī
           Jaba kahūna pāyo apanā
           Raina kā sapanā . . .

           From a deep sleep I woke all of a sudden and saw no husband [lit.: no one of my own] *in my bed.*
           My dream of the night . . .

*Selection 19 Dattatreya Vishnu Paluskar
    (Ex. 3–13) Rag Kamod, Drut Tintal
             Last 17 *avarts*
    Text: Mori nah lagana lāgi re . . .

           Because of my new love for you, my beloved . . .

Selection 20 Krishnarao Pandit
           Rag Desi, Madhya laya Tintal
    A (Ex. 3–1a)   *Avarts* 11–13
    B (Ex. 3–1b)   *Avarts* 88–9
    C (Ex. 3–1c)   *Avart* 41
    D (Ex. 3–1d)   *Avart* 52
    E (Ex. 3–1e)   *Avarts* 78–9
    Text: as Selection 8

Selection 21   Krishnarao Pandit
           Rag Desi, Madhya laya Tintal
    A (Ex. 3–2a)   *Avart* 22
    B (Ex. 3–2b)   *Avart* 26
    C (Ex. 3–2c)   *Avart* 34
    Text: as Selection 8

Selection 22   Krishnarao Pandit
           Rag Desi, Madhya laya Tintal
    A (Ex. 3–3a)   *Avarts* 42–4
    B (Ex. 3–3b)   *Avart* 65
    C (Ex. 3–3c)   *Avarts* 76–7
    Text: as Selection 8

Selection 23 Chandrakant Krishnarao Pandit
    (Ex. 3–5) Rag Bhairav, Madhya laya Tintal
             Avart 13
    Text: Koyala bo[le] . . .

           The cuckoo says . . .

Selection 24   Chandrakant Krishnarao Pandit
   (Ex. 3–6)   Rag Bhairav, Madhya laya Tintal
             Avarts 26–8
   Text: Piyā milana kī bārī.

      I have a chance to meet my husband.

Selection 25   Lakshman Krishnarao Pandit
   (Ex. 3–7)   Rag Kedar, Drut Tintal
             Avarts 69–71
   Text: Pāyala bā[jī] . . .

      Anklets jingle . . .

*Selection 26   Vinayak Rao Patwardhan
   (Ex. 3–8)   Rag Anandi Kedar, Vilambit Ektal
             Avarts 9–10
   Text: Udho tuma ho nikatavāsī . . .
        Je suriyā base Kāsī.

      Uddhava, you are his close companion . . .
      who lives in Kasi [Benares].

*Selection 27   Vinayak Rao Patwardhan
   (Ex. 3–9)   Rag Anandi Kedar, Vilambit Ektal
             Avart 21
   Text: as Selection 26

Selection 28   Faiyaz Khan
   (Ex. 4–1)   Rag Jaijaiwanti, Vilambit laya
             Pre-*ciz alap*: *nom-tom*
   Text: *nom-tom* syllables

Selection 29   Faiyaz Khan
   (Ex. 4–2)   Rag Jaijaiwanti, Vilambit laya
             Pre-*ciz alap*: *nom-tom*
   Text: *nom-tom* syllables

Selection 30   Faiyaz Khan
   (Ex. 4–3)   Rag Jaijaiwanti, Vilambit laya
             Pre-*ciz alap*: *nom-tom*
   Text: *nom-tom* syllables

Selection 31   Faiyaz Khan
   (Ex. 4–4)   Rag Jaijaiwanti, Madhya laya Ektal
             First *tan*s
   Text: Ā (*akar*)

Selection 32 Faiyaz Khan
(Ex. 4–5) Rag Jaijaiwanti, Madhya laya Ektal
Boltans
Text: Tihāre jiyā kī . . .
Your heart's feeling . . .

Selection 33 Faiyaz Khan
(Ex. 4–6) Rag Jaijaiwanti, Drut Tintal
Bolbant
Text: Sagarī raina me jāge . . .
Awake the whole night . . .

SIDE B

Selection 34 Sharafat Husain Khan
(Ex. 4–7) Rag Gara Kanhra, Vilambit Ektal
14th minute
Text: Bārama bāra vārī re mā . . .
Time and time again . . .

**Selection 35 Latafat Husain Khan
(Ex. 4–9) Rag Miyan ki Todi, Vilambit Ektal
Avarts 10–12
Text: Daiyā baṭh dūbhar bhaī.
Bharan na deta gagariyā.
Oh God, the path became difficult.
He [the naughty urchin Krishna] does not allow me to fill my pitcher.

**Selection 36 Latafat Husain Khan
Rag Miyan ki Todi, Vilambit Ektal
A (Ex. 4–10a) Avart 9–10
B (Ex. 4–10b) Avart 7–8
Text: as Selection 35

**Selection 37 Latafat Husain Khan
(Ex. 4–11) Rag Miyan ki Todi, Vilambit Ektal
Avart 22
Text: as Selection 35

Selection 38 Dipali Nag
(Ex. 4–12) Rag Lalit, Vilambit Ektal
Improvisation on sthai text
Text: Bhore hī āye. Tuma alakha jagāye.
You came early in the morning and uttered a blessing.

*Selection 39 Nisar Hussein Khan
                  Rag Abhogi, Madhya laya Jhaptal
                  Avarts 52–81, encompassing:
  (Ex. 5–2) *Avarts* 52–9 [*avarts* 60–9 not recorded]
  (Ex. 5–4) *Avarts* 78–81
  (Ex. 5–5) *Avarts* 70–6
  Text: Jhanana āyo rī/re.

      Come, with your anklets jingling.

Selection 40 Sharfaraz Hussein Khan
  (Ex. 5–6) Rag Chhayanat, Vilambit Ektal
            Avarts 16–18
  Text: Sugrīva Rāma kṛpā

      By the grace of Rama, Sugriva . . .
[Note: Since Sugriva is the name of a monkey-king in the *Ramayana* epic, the unclear portion of this text must refer to Sugriva's role in helping Rama to conquer Ravana.]

Selection 41 Sharfaraz Hussein Khan
  (Ex. 5–7) Rag Chhayanat, Vilambit Ektal
            Avart 26
  Text: as Selection 40

*Selection 42 Kishore Amonkar
  (Ex. 6–1) Rag Jaunpuri, Madhya laya Tintal
            Avarts 11–14
  Text: as Selection 6

*Selection 43 Kishore Amonkar
  (Ex. 6–2) Rag Jaunpuri, Madhya laya Tintal
            Avart 19
  Text: as Selection 6

*Selection 44 Bhimsen Joshi
  (Ex. 7–3) Rag Miyan ki Todi, Vilambit Ektal
            Avarts 13–17
Text: DAIYĀ BATH DŪBHAR bhai. MĖ kā laṅgaravā BHARANA NA DET gagariyā. Bihān tore saṅg kaise jāuṅ SAJANI. BICH māṅjh THĀDĀ SADARANG uchkaiya.

      Oh God! The path to the river is difficult to pass through. The urchin [Krishna] will not allow me to fill my pitcher.
      Oh friend, how can I accompany you to a desolate place when that naughty boy is standing in the middle of the path? Composed by Sadarang.
[Note: Joshi uses the capitalized words in various combinations to make phrases such as 'difficult path', 'friend, [he] does not allow [me]', 'to fill the path', 'Sadarang stood in the middle', '[Krishna] allows me/does not allow me'.]

*Selection 45 Bhimsen Joshi
  (Ex. 7–4) Rag Shudh Kalyan, Vilambit Ektal
            Avart 27
  Text: Tum bin, kaun?
        Without you, what?

*Selection 46 Abdul Wahid Khan
  (Ex. 7–6) Rag Darbari Kanhra, Vilambit Jhumra tal
            Avart 18
  Text: Gumānī, jāga.
        Wake up, and don't be angry with me.

*Selection 47 Hirabai Barodekar
  (Ex. 7–7) Rag Multani, Vilambit Ektal
            Avarts 10–12
  Text: Kavana desa gaye?
        To what country did he go?

*Selection 48 Hirabai Barodekar
  (Ex. 7–8) Rag Yaman, Vilambit Ektal
            Avarts 24–5
  Text: Sugara banā . . .
        Handsome bridegroom . . .

 Selection 49 Pran Nath
  (Ex. 7–9) Rag Bageshri, Vilambit Ektal
            Avarts 2–9
  Text: Kauna gata bhaī [lī]?
        What has happened?

*Selection 50 Bade Ghulam Ali Khan
  (Ex. 8–2a) Rag Kaushi Dhani, Rupak tal
            Avarts 57–62
  Text: He mana [and *sargam* syllables]
        Oh, my heart . . .

*Selection 51 Bade Ghulam Ali Khan
  (Ex. 8–3) Rag Gunkali, Madhya laya Tintal
            Avarts 26–31
  Text: E kāratā, purī karo mana kī āshā.
        O creator, you should fulfill the desires of my heart.

*Selection 52 Bade Ghulam Ali Khan
  (Ex. 8–5) Rag Malkauns, Drut Tintal
             End of *chota khyal*
  Text: Yahi bhed son [and *sargam* syllables]

     With this secret/mystery . . .

Selection 53 Nasir Ahmed Khan
  (Ex. 9–1) Rag Bageshri, Vilambit Ektal
             Avarts 6–8
  Text: Kauna gata bhaī?

     What has happened?

*Selection 54 Amir Khan
  (Ex. 9–2) Rag Megh, Vilambit Jhumra tal
             Avarts 2–4
  Text: Barakha ritu ā [āe/āye].

     May the rainy season come.

  * Reproduced with permission of The Gramophone Company of India Limited
** Reproduced with permission of Music India Limited

Recording quality for some selections is relatively poor because they were taken from broadcasts for study purposes only.

Discography

Recordings are listed by *gharana* in the order in which the *gharana*s are discussed in the book. Within each *gharana* they are listed in alphabetical order of singer's names: by first names of Muslim musicians (all of whose names end in Khan); and by the last name of Hindu musicians.

All selections are listed only by *raga* (bracketed words indicate a variant transliteration of the *raga* name used in the book). Performances of genres other than *khyal* are not specified in the list, but most of those listed are *khyal*. When there are more than three *raga*s listed for a long-play recording, the selections are *ciz*, probably reissued from older recordings.

Numbers in the form '69.3–XX' indicate the archival number assigned to recordings in the author's collection which are deposited in the Ethnomusicology Archive at the University of California, Los Angeles.

In the column 'Company and Recording No.', GCI indicates The Gramophone Company of India Limited, which belongs to the EMI group of companies; GCI is the manufacturer and distributor. This company has used several registered trademarks over the years, including HMV (His Master's Voice), Odeon, Regal, and Columbia.

Artist	Raga	Company and Recording No.
GWALIOR		
Paluskar, D. V.	Shri	GCI EALP 1263
	Lalat [Lalit]	GCI EALP 1295
	Bibhas	
	Bilaskhani Todi	
	Asawari [Asavari]	
	Goud [Gaur] Sarang	
	Hameer [Hamir]	
	Tilak Kamod	
	Kedar	
	Miyan ka [ki] Malhar	
	Malkauns	
	Kamod	GCI EALP 1366
	Bageshri Kanada [Kanhra]	
Early issue:	Deshkar	Columbia VE 1013
	Champak	
	Gaur Sarang	HMV N 36649
Pandit, Chandrakant Krishnarao	Bhairav	69.3–136
Pandit, Krishnarao Shankar	Todi	GCI ECSD 2453
	Hamir	
	Desi	69.3–152

Artist	*Raga*	Company and Recording No.
Pandit, Lakshman Krishnarao	Komal Re Asavari	69.3–74
	Bhimpalasi	69.3–77
	Kedar	69.3–78
Patwardhan, Vinayak Rao	Lalita Gauri	GCI EALP 1314
	Malgunji	
	Hameer [Hamir]	GCI ECLP 2766
	Anandi Kedar	
	Bhupali Todi	HMV 7 EPE 1227
Vyas, Narayan Rao	Gaur Malhar	GCI EALP 1314
	Malgunji (performed with	
	Vinayak Rao Patwardhan)	

AGRA

Aqeel Ahmed Khan	Puriya Kalyan	69.3–60
Faiyaz Khan	Nat Bihag	GCI EALP 1292
	Darbari	
	Jaunpuri	
	Lalit	
	Paraj	
	Ramkali	
	Sughrai	
	Todi	
	Bhankar	GCI EALP 1365
	Des [Desh]	
	Chhaya	Hindustan Records LH 4
	Nat Bihag	
	Kafi	
	Paraj	
	Jaijaiwanti	author's collection
Ghulam Ahmed Khan	Bageshri	69.3–92
Latafat Husain Khan	Patdeepki	GCI ECSD 2759
	Bageshwari [Bageshri]	
	Miyan ki Todi	Polydor 2392 018
	Gara Kanada [Kanhra]	
Nag, Dipali	Lalit	69.3–52
	Bilaskhani Todi	69.3–146
Sharafat Husain Khan	Gara	69.3–122
	Pancham Sohini	69.3–123
Vilayat Hussain Khan	Sohini Pancham	Columbia 7 EPE 1207
	Paraj	
	Bilawal	Columbia 7 EPE 1215
	Dhanashri	
Yunus Husain Khan	Sujani Malhar	Bärenreiter Musicaphon
		30 SL 2051

Artist	*Raga*	Company and Recording No.
	Lalita Gauri	69.3–76
	Shudh Sarang	69.3–133
	Hussaini Bhairav	69.3–145
SAHASWAN/RAMPUR		
Ghulam Taqi Khan	Deshkar	69.3–127
	Kamod	69.3–131
Mushtaq Hussein Khan	Gandhari	GCI ECLP 2538
	Mirabai ki Malhar	
	Kafi	
	Gunkari	GCI ECLP 2573
	Mahakni	
	Bihag	GCI ECLP 2608
	Barwa	author's collection
Nisar Hussein Khan	Abhogi	GCI ECLP 2260
	Gobardhan Todi	
	Chhayanat	HMV N 88215
	Malkauns	
	Jaijaiwanti	69.3–160
Sharfaraz Hussein Khan	Chhayanat	69.3–48
	Miyan ki Todi	69.3–104
Yajurvedi, Sulochana (Rampur)	Bilaskhani Todi	author's collection
ALLADIYA KHAN		
Amonkar, Kishore	Jounpuri [Jaunpuri]	GCI ECLP 2326
	Patabihag [Pat Bihag]	
	Bhoop [Bhup]	GCI ECSD 2702
	Bageshri	
Kerkar, Kesarbai	Lalat [Lalit]	GCI EALP 1278
	Todi	
	Kukubh Bilawal	
	Desi	
	Bhairavi	
	Lalita Gouri [Gauri]	
	Nat Kamod	
	Goud [Gaur] Malhar	
	Malkauns	
Early issues:	Malkauns	HMV HQ 2
	Maru Bihag	
	Durga	HMV HQ 4
	Nat Bihag	
	Multani	HMV P 10735

Artist	*Raga*	Company and Recording No.
Kurdikar, Moghubai	Multani	GCI ELRZ 17
	Purvi	
	Kedar	
	Sohoni [Sohani]	
	Jaijaiwanti	
	Nayaki Kanada [Kanhra]	
	Sudha	
	Bilawal	
	Shukla Bilawal	
	Hindol	
Mansur, Mallikarjun	Bahaduri Todi	GCI ECLP 2384
	Gaud [Gaur] Malhar	
	Jaunpuri	GCI ECSD 2402
	Jair Kalyan	
	Bihari	

KIRANA

Abdul Karim Khan	Bilawal	GCI 33 ECX 3251
	Tilang	
	Basant	
	Shudh Pilu	
	Sarpada	
	Gara	
	Malkauns	
	Bhairavi	
	Basant	GCI 33 ECX 3252
	Jogia [Jogiya]	
	Bhim Palas [Bhimpalasi]	
	Shankara	
	Dev Gandhar	
	Shudh Kalyan	
	Anand Bhairavi	
	Jhinjhoti	
	Lalit	GCI 33 ECX 3304
	Gujri [Gujari] Todi	
	Marwa	
	Mishra Zangula [Jangla]	
	Patdeep [Patdip]	
	Mishra Kafi	
	Abhogi Kanhra	
	Darbari Kanhra	
Early issues:	Jogiya	Columbia BEX 251
	Mishra Jangla	
	Jhinjhoti	Columbia BEX 258

Artist	*Raga*	Company and Recording No.
	Basant	
	Basant	Columbia BEX 259
	Bhairavi	
Abdul Wahid Khan	Patdeep [Patdip]	GCIECLP 2541
	Multani	
	Darbari Kanada [Kanhra]	
Barodekar, Hirabai	Multani	GCIECLP 2275
	Yaman	
	Basant Bahar	GCIECLP 2356
	Chandrakauns (performed with Saraswati Rane)	
Early issues:	Ahir Bhairav	Columbia SEDE 3306
	Puriya Kalyan	
	Deshkar	Columbia GE 8766
	Patdip	Columbia VE 5015
	Bhairavi	HMV 7 EPE 1205
	Shyam Kalyan	
	Ramkali	69.3–56
Hangal, Gangubai	Asavari	HMV 7 EPE 1225
	Chandrakauns	
	Abhogi	HMV 7 EPE 1232
	Yaman	
	Devgiri	HMV 7 EPE 1239
	Jaijaiwanti	
	Marwa	HMV N 36258
	Bhairav	
	Abhogi (Tansen Festival)	69.3–141
Joshi, Bhimsen	Miyan ki Todi	GCIEALP 1280
	Puria [Puriya] Dhanashri	
	Multani	GCIEALP 1321
	Yaman Kalyan	
	Chhaya	GCIEALP 1328
	Darbari	
	Chhaya Malhar	
	Suha Kanada [Kanhra]	
	Lalit Bhatiyar	GCIEASD 1501
	Kalashree [Kalashri]	
	Pooriya [Puriya]	GCIEASD 1513
	Durga	
	Gaur Sarang	GCIEASD 1515
	Brindabani Sarang	
	Miya [Miyan ki] Malhar	GCIECLP 2253
	Puriya Kalyan	
	Lalit	GCIECLP 2264

Artist	*Raga*	Company and Recording No.
	Shudh Kalyan	
	Malkauns	GCI ECLP 2276
	Maru Bihag	
	Komal Rishabh [Re]	
	Asavari Todi	GCI SMOAE 5010
	Marwa	
	Abhogi	HMV 7 EPE 1234
	Bhairavi	
Nath, Pran	Bhupali	Earth Groove SD 784
	Asavari	
	Shudh Sarang	69.3–85
	Bageshri	69.3–86
Roshanara Begum	Basant	GCI PCLP 1514
	Kedar	
	Shudh Kalyan	GCI PCLP 1530
	Shankara	

PATIALA

Bade Ghulam Ali Khan	Goonkali [Gunkali]	GCI EALP 1258
	Malkauns	
	Darbari Kanada [Kanhra]	GCI EALP 1265
	Kaushi Dhani	
	Shudh Sarang	GCI EALP 1364
	Megh Malhar	
	Gujari Todi	GCI MOAE 5004
	Desi Todi	
	Bhimpalasi	
	Kamod	
	Pahari	
	Kedar	
	Jaijaiwanti	
	Darbari	
	Adana	
	Malkauns	
	Paraj	
Early issues:	Jaijaiwanti	HMV N 36341
	Kedar	
	Desh	HMV N 36595
	Gujari Todi	
	Kamod	HMV N 36705
	Darbari	
	Paraj	Columbia VE 5049
	Malkauns	
	Adana	Columbia VE 5051

Artist	*Raga*	Company and Recording No.
Chowdhury, Irene Roy	Bageshri	69.3–83
	Komal Re Asavari	69.3–119
Munnawar Ali Khan	Bihag	GCI ECSD 2750
	Gujari Todi	
Sultana, Parveen	Salag [Salakh] Varali Todi	GCI ECSD 2480
	Lalita [Lalit]	
	Kusumi Kalyan	GCI ECSD 2731
	Mangal Bhairav	

INDIVIDUAL SINGERS

Amir Khan	Marwa	GCI EALP 1253
	Darbari Kanada [Kanhra]	
	Megh	GCI EASD 1331
	Lalit	
	Hansadhwani [Hamsadhwani]	GCI EASD 1357
	Malkauns	
Nasir Ahmed Khan	Miyan ki Todi	GCI ECSD 2496
(Delhi *gharana*)	Rageshwari	
	Mishra Kirvani	
	Marwa	69.3–79
	Bageshri	69.3–80
Thakur, Omkarnath	Desi Todi	GCI 33 ECX 3252
	Todi	
	Nilambri	
	Sughrai	
	Malkauns	
Early issue:	Shudh Kalyan	Columbia GE 3117
Verma, Manik	Jog-Kauns	GCI ECLP 2313
	Bhatiyar	
	Lalit	69.3–50
	Abhogi	69.3–51

Bibliography

Abul Fazli-i-'Allami 1977. *The Ā'īn-i Akbarī*. Translated from the original Persian by H. Blochmann, 1873. 2nd edition revised and edited by D. C. Phillott, 1927. New Delhi: Oriental Books Reprint Corporation [3rd edition repr. from 2nd]

Adyanthaya, R. P. 1965. *Melody Music of India and How to Learn it*. Mangalore: N. M. Adyanthaya

Agarwal, Meena 1970. Music in the Poetry of Surdas. *Saṅgīt* 4 (April) 30–3

Agarwala, Viney K. 1966. *Traditions and Trends in Indian Music*. Meerut: Rastogi and Co.

Ahmad, Aziz 1964. *Studies in Islamic Culture in the Indian Environment*. Oxford: Clarendon Press

Ahmed, Nazir 1954. The Lahjat-i-Sikandar Shahi, a Unique Book on Indian Music of the Time of Sikandar Shah. *Islamic Culture* 28:3 (July) 410–17

Aiyar, P. A. Sundaram 1961. Pandit Vishnu Digambar Paluskar, the Pioneer of the Renaissance of Indian Music. *Nāda Rūpa* 1:1, 100–3

Allen, J., T. Wolseley Haig and H. H. Dodwell 1945. *The Cambridge Shorter History of India*. Cambridge: Cambridge University Press

Ambardekar, G. J. and others 1961. *Commemoration Volume in Honour of Dr S. N. Ratanjankar*. Bombay: K. G. Ginde

Anonymous 1962. A Singer who would Not be Beaten: Bade Ghulam Ali Khan, One of the 'Greats'. *Statesman* ([August])

    1963. Delhi Gharana's Love for Kheyal, Sarangi. *Times of India* (September 18)

    1968. Bade Ghulam Ali Khan: Passing of a Maestro. *The Hindu* (April 26) 9

    1969. Maifil that Still Lingers. *Bhaskarbuwa Bakhale Birth-Centenary Souvenir*, ed. Dnyaneshwar Nadkarni. Bombay: Bhaskarbuwa Bakhale Centenary Samiti, 17, 19, 21

Arnold, T. W. 1927. India. *The Encyclopedia of Islam*, ed. H. A. R. Gibb and others. Leiden: E. J. Brill, vol. 2, pp. 478–93

Ashton, Roger 1967. Indian Music and Philosophy. *Journal of the Sangeet Natak Akademi* 5 (July–September) 68–77

Athavale, V. R. 1967. *Pandit Vishnu Digambar*. New Delhi: National Book Trust

    1976a. Khayal Singing and Bandish. *Journal of the Indian Musicological Society* 7:4 (December) 35–40

    1976b. The Source of Inspiration behind Pandit Paluskar's Contribution to Music. *Journal of the Indian Musicological Society* 7:1 (March) 14–21

Atiya Begum 1942. *Sangit of India: Classical Instrumental Music, Singing and Nâtch*. Bombay: Mallini Printing

Bajwa, Fauja Singh 1969. *Patiala and its Historical Surroundings*. Patiala: Punjabi University, 2nd edition

Bali, Harischandra n. d. *Bhāratīya Saṅgīt Vijñān*. Allahabad: Hindi Bhavan

Bandopadhyaya, Shripada 1958. *The Music of India*. Bombay: Taraporevala Sons and Co., 2nd edition, revised

Banerji, B. M. 1972. *Musiqi and Musiqar: Bio-data on Yunus Hussain Khan for Performance Purposes*. New Delhi [including an interview by S. R. Chatterji for *The Dateline Delhi* (October)]

Bansi, Rajendra Misra 1969. Kāvya aur Saṅgīt kā Pāraspirik Sambandh. *Saṅgīt* 1 (January) 38–9

Basham, Arthur L. 1954. *The Wonder that was India*. London: Sidgwick & Jackson

Berry, Wallace 1966. *Form in Music*. Englewood Cliffs, N.J.: Prentice-Hall

Bhagvat, Durga 1972. Kesarbai Kerkar. *Quarterly Journal of the National Centre for the Performing Arts* 1:1 (September) 5–7

Bhanu, Dharma 1955. Promotion of Music by the Turko–Afghan Rulers of India. *Islamic Culture* 29 (January) 9–31

Bhatkhande, Vishnu Narayan 1963. *Krāmik Pustak Mālikā*, ed. L. N. Garg. Hathras: Sangit Karyalaya, 2nd edition

  1966. *Smriti Granth* (Bhatkhande Commemoration Volume). Khairagarh: Indira Kala Sangeet Vishwavidyalaya

  1968. *Bhātkhande Saṅgīt Śāstra*. 4 vols. Hathras: Sangit Karyalaya, 2nd edition

Bhatta, Bishambhar Nath 1964. *Saṅgīt Kādambinī*. Hathras: Sangit Karyalaya, 4th edition

  1968. *Saṅgīt Archnā*. Hathras: Sangit Karyalaya, 5th edition

Bhattacharya, Sudhi Bhushan 1968. *Ethnomusicology and India*. Calcutta: Indian Publications

Bisht, Krishna 1978. *The Balanced Artist*. In *Program of the Silver Jubilee Celebration of Ustad Nasir Ahmed Khan Taan Samrat* (March 27) [2 pp.]

Blacking, John 1981. The Problem of 'Ethnic' Perceptions in the Semiotics of Music. In *The Sign in Music and Literature*, ed. Wendy Steiner. Austin: University of Texas Press, 184–94

Brahaspati, Acharya 1975. Mussalmans and Indian Music. *Journal of the Indian Musicological Society* 6:2 (June) 27–49

Brihaspati [Brahaspati], Kailash Chandra Deva 1959. Music and Research. *Sangeet Natak Akademi Bulletin* 13–14 (October) 28–31

  1963. *Saṅgīt Chintamani*. Hathras: Sangit Karyalaya

  1967a. Some Handicaps in India. *Indian Music Journal* 7 (April–May) 60–2

  1967b. Some Important Concepts: An Elucidation. *Indian Music Journal* 8 (October–November) 104–6

Brown, Michael H. (editor) 1940. *Gwalior Today*. Bombay: Times of India Press

Brown, Robert 1965. The Mrdanga: A Study of Drumming in South India. University of California at Los Angeles: unpublished Ph.D. dissertation

Chakravarti, S. C. 1966. Future of Khyal. *Bhāratīya Saṅgīt* 1:3 (February) 4–7

Chandra, Sarvesh 1979. The Gharana System of Teaching in Hindustani Music: A Critical Analysis. *Journal of the Indian Musicological Society* 10:3–4 (September–December) 31–3

Chaubey, S. K. 1958. *Musicians I Have Met*. Lucknow: Information Department, Uttar Pradesh

Chaudhary, Bimala Kanta Roy 1958. Mirh Khand. *Music Mirror* 1:5 (May) 10–13

Chaudhuri, Debrata 1966. Ustad Vilayat Hussain Khan. In *Homage to Vilayat Hussain Khan* [Program for memorial concerts, August 6–7]. New Delhi: Pran Piya Sangeet Samiti

Chopra, Pran Nath 1963. *Some Aspects of Society and Culture During the Mughal Age (1526–1707)*. Agra: Shiva Lal Agarwala & Co., 2nd edition

Choudhary, Birendra Kishore Roy 1955. Proper Use of Dhrupad. *Lakshya Sangeet* 2:1 (June)

  1973. The Senia Gharana of Rampur. *Journal of the Sangeet Natak Akademi* 29 (July–September) 5–8

Clements, Ernest 1912–13. *Introduction to the Study of Indian Music*. London. Repr. Allahabad: Kitab Mahal (n. d.)

Cohen, Jerry 1966. *An American Student and North Indian Music*. Benares: Benares Hindu University and University of Wisconsin College Year in India Program [published research report]

Coomaraswamy, Ananda K. 1968. *The Dance of Shiva*. New Delhi: Sagar Publications, revised edition

Daniélou, Alain 1951. Music of Faiyaz Khan. *The March of India* 3:3 (January–February) 56–7

Das, Akheranjan (Argus) 1954. Kirana Style of Singing. *Hindustan Standard*, Sunday Magazine, p. 111

Das, Chandrakant Lal 1958. Kirana in Hindustani Music. *Music Mirror* 1:5 (May) 46–8

De, S. K. 1963. *Sanskrit Poetics as a Study of Aesthetic*. Los Angeles: University of California Press

DeJong-Keesing, Elisabeth 1974. *Inayat Khan: A Biography*. The Hague: East-West Publications

Deodhar, B. R. 1966a. Art is Adventure. *Indian Music Journal* 6 (October–November) 51–2

  1966b. Evolution in Indian Music. In *Music East and West*. New Delhi: Indian Council for Cultural Relations, 16–21

  1972. *Gayanacharya Pandit Vishnu Digambar*. Bombay: Akhil Bharatiya Gandharva Mahavidyalaya Mandal (in Marathi)

  1973. Pandit Vishnu Digambar in his Younger Days. *Journal of the Indian Musicological Society* 4:2 (April–June) 21–51

1981. Aftab-e-Mousiki Ustad Fayyaz Khan (1881–1950). *Quarterly Journal of the National Centre for the Performing Arts* 10:1 (March) 27–32 (translated from the Marathi *Thor Sangitkar*)

Desai, Chaitanya 1969. The Origin and Development of Khayal. *Journal of the Music Academy* (Madras) 40, 147–182

Desai, G. S. 1968. Panditji: An Appreciation. In *Saṅgīt Marttand: Pandit Omkarnath Thakur Pratham Punyatithi Smārikā*. Varanasi: Benares Hindu University, 47–79

Deshpande, P. L. 1972. Vishnu Digambar Paluskar. *Quarterly Journal of the National Centre for the Performing Arts* 1:1 (September) 16–22

Deshpande, Vaman Hari 1963. Carl Seashore, Banis and Gharanas. *Nāda Rūpa* 2:2, 2–11

1972. The Alladiya Khan Gharana. *Quarterly Journal of the National Centre for the Performing Arts* 1:1 (September) 2–5

1973. *Indian Musical Traditions: An Aesthetic Study of the Gharanas in Hindustani Music.* Bombay: Popular Prakashan, first published in Marathi, 1961, as *Gharāndāj Gāyakī* (translated by S. H. Deshpande)

1974. Gāna Tapasvinī. *Sayakatha* (Bombay) 41:9 (July) 10–15 (in Marathi, trans. Sudhakar B. Joshi)

1979. *Ālāpini*. Bombay: Monj Prakashan Graha (in Marathi)

Deva, B. Chaitanya 1963. *Psychoacoustics of Music and Speech.* Madras: The Music Academy

1975. Tradition and Non-conformity in Indian Music. *Journal of the Indian Musicological Society* 6:4 (December) 27–30

1981. *The Music of India: A Scientific Study.* New Delhi: Munshiram Manoharlal Publishers Pvt. Ltd

Devanga, Tulsi Ram 1969. Kāvya Aur Sāhitya kā Pāraspirik Sambandh. *Saṅgīt* 1 (January) 33–8

Dimock, Edward C. 1967a. *In Praise of Krishna: Songs from the Bengali.* New York: Anchor Books

1967b. *Bengal Literature and History.* East Lansing, Michigan: Asian Studies Center, Michigan State University

Dixit, K. O. 1973. Khansaheb Abdul Karim Khan and the Kirana Gharana of Hindustani Music. *Quarterly Journal of the National Centre for the Performing Arts* 2:1 (March) 37–43

Doshi, A. V. 1964. Some Useful Hints. *Indian Music Journal* 2 (October–November) 41–4

Dubholia, Ram Charan 1969. Kāvya Saṅgīt Aur Uske Pranetā. *Saṅgīt* 1 (January) 50–6

Durga, S. A. K. 1978. *Voice Culture.* Special issue of the *Journal of the Indian Musicological Society.* 9:1–2 (March, June)

Elliot, Henry M. (editor) 1953. *A History of India as told by its Own Historians, edited and continued by John Dowson, vol.* 16: *The Muhammadan Period.* Calcutta: Susil Gupta, reprint

Erdman, Joan L. 1978. The Maharaja's Musicians: The Organization of Cultural Performance at Jaipur in the Nineteenth Century. In *American Studies in the Anthropology of India*, ed. Sylvia Vatuk. New Delhi: Manohar Publications, 342–67

Fox Strangways, A. H. 1967. *The Music of Hindustan.* Oxford: Clarendon Press, reprint (first published 1914)

Gajendragadkar, Kumari Nalini 1964. Classicism and Romanticism in Hindustani Music. *Journal of the Music Academy* (Madras) 35, 77–84

Gangoly, O. C. 1935. *Ragas and Raginis: A Pictorial and Iconographic Study of Indian Musical Modes based on Original Sources*, vol. I: Text. Bombay: Nalanda Publications

Garg, L. N. 1957. *Hamāre Saṅgīt Ratna.* Hathras: Sangit Karyalaya. 6 vols.

Geekie, Gordon 1980. The Study of Individual Carnatic Musicians. *Yearbook of the International Folk Music Council* 21, 84–9

Geeta, Mayor 1977. Siddeshwaridevi of Benares (1908–1977). *Quarterly Journal of the National Centre for the Performing Arts* 6:2 (June) 49–50

Ghosh, Nikhil 1968. *Fundamentals of Raga and Tala with a New System of Notation.* Bombay: Nikhil Ghosh.

Gilani, Malti 1969. Memorable Moments with my Guru. *The Illustrated Weekly of India* (April 27) 23, 57

Gosvami, O. 1957. *The Story of Indian Music.* Bombay: Asia Publishing House

Gupta, B. L. 1973. The Gwalior School of Music. *Journal of the Indian Musicological Society* 4:1 (March) 5–15

Gupta, Ushe 1960. *Hindī Ke Krshan Bhaktī Kālīn Sāhitya Meṅ Saṅgīt.* Lucknow: Lucknow University

Halim, A. 1945. Music and Musicians of Shah Jahan's Court. *Islamic Culture* 19:4 (October) 354–60

Hindustan Times 1968. Music . . . A New Vision of Eman (November 2)

    1969. Mansoor's Voice Control (February 9)

    1973. Entertaining Recital (Padmavati Shaligram) (March 22)

Hurie, Harriotte Cook 1980. A Comparative Study of Khyal Style: Pandit Omkarnath Thakur and his student Pandit B. R. Bhatt. Wesleyan University, Middletown, Conn.: unpublished M.A. thesis

Ibrahim Adil Shah II 1956. *Kitab-i-Nauras*, with introduction, notes and textual editing by Nasir Ahmad. New Delhi: Bharatiya Kala Kendra

Ikram, S. M. 1964. *Muslim Civilization in India*. New York: Columbia University Press

Imam, Hakim Mohammad Karam 1959a. Melody through the Centuries: A Chapter from Ma'danul Moosiqi, 1856. *Sangeet Natak Akademi Bulletin* 11–12 (April) 13–26, 33 (translated by Govind Vidyarthi)

    1959b. Effect of Ragas and Mannerism in Singing: A Chapter from Ma'danul Moosiqi, 1856. *Sangeet Natak Akademi Bulletin* 13–14 (October) 6–14 (translated by Govind Vidyarthi)

Indian Council for Cultural Relations 1966. *Music East and West*. New Delhi.

Indian Express 1968. [Lakshman Pandit's Khayals] (October 30)

    1969. Kishori at her Best (March 9)

    1971a. Gopal Misra Good in Patches (April 4)

    1971b. Gangubhai Hangal Creates Spell (April 13)

    1971c. Picnic Style Concert (April 14)

    1971d. Concert a Tame Affair (August 21)

    1971e. Music and Dance Festival Ends (August 28)

    1971f. Lively Recital by Padmavati Shaligram (October 12)

    1972a. Bright Shehnai Recital (March 8)

    1972b. Sharan Rani Excels (March 21)

    1972c. Yunus Hussain's Recital Good in Patches (March 27)

    1972d. Munnawar Ali in Fine Form (April 1)

    1973. Parveen Sultana Disappoints (August 18)

Interviews 1968–9. Pran Nath. July 1968–April 1969. Classes and daily singing lessons, Delhi

    1968–9. Sita Ram. October 1968–April 1969. Private *tabla* instruction, Delhi

    1969. Sunil Bose. New Delhi, March 27

    1969. M. R. Gautam. Benares, Uttar Pradesh, April 2

    1969. Vinay Chandra Maudgalya. New Delhi, February 26, March 8, March 12, March 24

    1969. Sumati Mutatkar. Delhi, March 25 [my adviser/teacher at Delhi University, July 1968–April 1969]

    1969. Amar Nath. New Delhi, March 19, March 20

    1969. Prem Lata Sharma. Benares, Uttar Pradesh, April

    1969. Vasant Thakur. New Delhi, March 15

    1970. Prem Lata Sharma. Rochester, New York, July 31–August 2

    1978. Urmila Shankar Bhargava. New Delhi, May 10

    1978. Irene Roy Chowdhury. New Delhi, May 16

    1978. Vinay Chandra Maudgalya. New Delhi, April 25, May 1, May 3

    1978. Munnawar Ali Khan. New Delhi, April 9, April 11

    1978. Dipali Nag. New Delhi, May 17

    1978. Nasir Ahmed Khan. New Delhi, April 25

    1978. Amar Nath. New Delhi, April 20, May 8

    1978. Lakshman Krishnarao Pandit. Delhi University, May 1

    1978. Shinglu. New Delhi, May 17

    1978. Dilip Chandra Vedi. New Delhi, April 21, May 3

    1978. Yunus Husain Khan. Delhi University, April 18, May 1

    1980. Hariotte Hurie. Middletown, Conn., August 25

Ivory, James (compiler) 1975. *Autobiography of a Princess*. New York: Harper & Row

Jairazbhoy, Nazir 1961. Svaraprastara in North Indian Classical Music. *Bulletin, School of Oriental and African Studies* (London) 24:2, 307–25

Jariwalla, Jayantilal S. 1973. *Abdul Karim Khan, the Man of the Times: Life and Art of a Great Musician.* Bombay: Balkrishnabuwa Kapileshwari

Jones, William and N. Augustus Willard 1962. *Music of India.* Calcutta: Susil Gupta, 2nd revised edition (first printed 1793, repr. 1834)

Joshi, D. T. 1976. Record liner notes for 'Ustad Abdul Wahid Khan: Great Master, Great Music' (GCI ECLP 2541)

Joshi, G. N. 1976. Khayal–Gayaki and its Presentation. *Journal of the Indian Musicological Society* 7:4 (December) 45–55

Joshi, Nirmala 1957. Wajidali Shah and the Music of his Time. *Sangeet Natak Akademi Bulletin* 6 (May) 36–8

    1959. Compositions of Ustad Zahoor Khan (Ramdass). *Sangeet Natak Akademi Bulletin* 13–14 (October) 15–18

Joshi, Umesh n. d. *Bhāratīya Saṅgīt Kā Itihās.* Ferozabad: Mansrovar Prakashan Mahal

Kapileshwari, Balkrishnabuwa 1972. *Saṅgīt Ratna Abdul Karimkhan Yaneha Gīvancharitra.* Bombay: Abdul Karimkhan Sangeet Prachar (in Marathi)

Kapoor, Bishan 1957. Aftabe Musiqi Ustad Faiyaz Khan. *The Hindustan Times Weekly* (February 24)

Karnani, Chetan 1976. *Listening to Hindustani Music.* Bombay: Orient Longman

Kaufmann, Walter 1959. The Forms of the Dhrupad and Khyal in Indian Art Music. *The Canadian Music Journal* 3:2 (Winter) 25–35

    1965. Rasa, Raga–Mala and Performance Times in North Indian Ragas. *Ethnomusicology* 9:3 (September) 272–91

    1968. *The Ragas of North India.* Bloomington, Indiana: Indiana University Press

Keay, F. E. 1960. *A History of Hindi Literature.* Calcutta: YMCA Publishing House, 3rd printing (first published 1920)

Keskar, B. V. 1967. *Indian Music: Problems and Prospects.* Bombay: Popular Prakashan

Khanna, Lalita 1972. Ustad Hafiz Ali Khan. *Quarterly Journal of the National Centre for the Performing Arts* 1:2 (December) 9–10

Kirana Society of Music 1966. Program, Society Inauguration Concerts (November 18 and 19)

Krishnaswamy, S. 1965. *Musical Instruments of India.* New Delhi: Publications Division, Ministry of Information and Broadcasting, Government of India

Lane-Poole, Stanley 1951. *Medieval India under Mohammedan Rule (A.D. 712–1764),* 2 vols. Calcutta: Susil Gupta, 2nd edition (first Indian edition)

Majumdar, R. C. 1957. *The History and Culture of the Indian People,* vol. 5: *The Struggle for Empire.* Bombay: Bharatiya Vidya Bhavan

Mangekar, Kamla 1964. Hirabai's Life is a Song. *Sunday Standard* (January 26)

Mathur, Raya Sahab Surja Narayna and Shankar Lal Mitra n. d. *Nad Ras.* Allahabad: Universal Press

Mattoo, Jiwan Lal 1953. Development of Indian Music–I. *Hindustan Times Magazine* (March)

    1960. Gharanas in Hindustani Gayaki. *Vishnu Digambar Jayanti Saṅgīt Samaroha.* New Delhi. (program notes, August 19–21) 61–7

Maudgalya, Vinay Chandra 1966. Ramakrishna Buwa Vaze. *Indian Music Journal* 6 (October–November) 28–9

    1967a. Rahimat Khan. *Indian Music Journal* 7 (April–May) 35–6

    1967b. Balakrishna Buwa. *Indian Music Journal* 8 (October–November) 95–6

    1968a. Bare Ghulam Ali Khan. *Indian Music Journal* 9 (April–May) 35–6

    1968b. Omkarnath Thakur. *Indian Music Journal* 9 (April–May) 32–4

Mehta, Rampalal 1969. *Āgrā Gharānā: Paramparā Gāyakī aur Chīzeṅ.* Baroda: Bharatiya Sangit-Nrtya-Natya Mahavidyalaya

Mehta, R. C. 1959. Melodic Tensions and Musical Aesthetics. *Journal of the Music Academy* (Madras) 30: 78–86

Mirza, Mohammad Wahid 1935. *The Life and Works of Amir Khusrau.* Calcutta: University of Calcutta

Misra, Susheela 1952. Ustad Mushtaq Hussain Khan: Link with a Great Musical Tradition. *The Illustrated Weekly of India* (October 26) 20

    1954. Profile of a Maestro: Bade Ghulam Ali Khan. *The Illustrated Weekly of India* (August 8) 50

    1969. Vocalist Nirmala Devi. *The Illustrated Weekly of India* (March 16) 35

1970a. The Khyal and the Common Man. *Hindustan Times* (January 7)

1970b. Gharanas Enrich Music in the North. *Hindustan Times* (January 14)

Misra, Uma 1962. *Kāvya aur Saṅgīt kā Pārasparik Sambandh*. Delhi: Delhi Pustak Sadan

Misra, Vidya Niwas (editor) 1965. *Modern Hindi Poetry: An Anthology*. Bloomington: Indiana University Press

Misra, Vishvanath Prasad (editor) 1952. *Ghananand Granthāvalī*. Benares: Vani-Vitan

Moheyeddin, K. 1955. Muslim Contribution to Indian Music. *Pakistan Review* (March) 33–5

Mukherjee, Bimal 1966. Influence of Khyal on Instrumental Music. *Bhāratīya Saṅgīt* 1:3 (February) 8–14

Mutatkar, Sumati 1965. What Silence Means to Music. *Bhāratīya Saṅgīt* 1:2 (November) 15–16

Nadkarni, Dnyaneshwar (editor) 1969. *Bhaskarbuwa Bakhale Birth-Centenary Souvenir*. Bombay: Bhaskarbuwa Bakhale Birth-Centenary Samiti

Nadkarni, Mohan D. 1948a. Contribution of Ustad Alladiya Khan to Art. *Bharat Jyoti*

1948b. A Great Exponent of Khyal: Sawai Gandharva. *Bharat Jyoti* (November 14)

Narayan, Ram and Neil Sorel 1980. *Indian Music in Performance: A Practical Introduction* [with cassette recording by Ram Narayan]. New York: New York University Press

National Herald (Saraswati) 1968a. Week's Music (Hindustani) (August 4)

1968b. Week's Music (Hindustani) (August 25)

Neelkant, K. 1964. Pandit Omkarnath Thakur. *Thought* (March 28) 16ff

Neog, Maheswar 1968. Classical Music in Assam. *Journal of the Sangeet Natak Akademi* 7 (January–March) 13–19

Neuman, Daniel M. 1977. The Social Organization of a Music Tradition: Hereditary Specialists in North India. *Ethnomusicology* 21:2 (May) 233–45

1978. Gharanas: The Rise of Musical 'Houses' in Delhi and Neighboring Cities. In *Eight Urban Musical Cultures*, ed. Bruno Nettl. Urbana: University of Illinois Press, 186–222

1980. *The Life of Music in North India: The Organization of an Artistic Tradition*. Detroit: Wayne State University Press

1981. Country Musicians and their City Cousins: The Social Organization of Music Transmissions in India. In Daniel Heartz and Bonnie Wade, eds., *Report of the Twelfth Congress [of the International Musicological Society]*, *Berkeley 1977*. Kassel: Bärenreiter, 603–8

Newspapers 1948. *Bharat Jyoti*. Bombay (Sunday edition of the *Bombay Free Press Journal*)

1968. *The Hindu*. Bombay

n. d. *Hindustan Standard*. New Delhi (closed in about 1959)

1968–70. *Hindustan Times*. New Delhi

1956–7. *Hindustan Times Weekly*. New Delhi

1961, 1968–9. *Illustrated Weekly of India*. New Delhi

1968. *National Herald*. New Delhi

1968–9. *Sunday Standard*. New Delhi (Sunday edition of the *Indian Express*)

1968–9. *The Statesman* and *The Sunday Statesman*. New Delhi

1954, 1968–71. *The Times of India*. New Delhi and Bombay

Pandit, Krishnarao Shankar 1969. Gwālior kī Gāyan Shailī. *Saṅgīt* 1 (January) 89

Pant, Chandra Shekhar 1961. Khyal Compositions from the Point of View of Poetry. In *Commemoration Volume in Honour of Dr S. N. Ratanjankar*. Bombay: K. G. Ginde, pp. 136–43

1966. Ustad Vilayat Hussain Khan: A Tribute. In *Homage to Vilayat Hussain Khan* [program for memorial concerts, August 6–7]. New Delhi: Pran Piya Sangeet Samiti

Patanjali, V. 1978. Two Pakistani Singers in Delhi: Nostalgia is Sweet Pain. *The Times of India* (April 23)

Patel, Alakananda 1979. Gharana Sammelan, Rang Bhavan, Bombay, February 23–27, 1979. *Quarterly Journal of the National Centre for the Performing Arts* 8:2 (June) 51–2

Pathak, R. C. (editor) 1965. *Bhargava's Standard Illustrated Dictionary of the Hindi Language*. Benares: Bhargava Book Depot, revised edition

Patwardhan [Patvardhan], V. N. 1960. *Rāg Vijñān*, 7 parts. Poona: Timalepar

1966. The Musician's Dilemma. *Indian Music Journal* 5 (April–May) 47–8

Pingle, Bhavanrao A. 1962. *History of Indian Music*. Calcutta: Susil Gupta, 3rd edition (first published 1894)

Popley, Herbert A. 1966. *The Music of India*. New Delhi: YMCA Publishing House, 3rd edition (first published 1921)

Powers, Harold 1958. The Background of the South Indian Raga-System. Princeton University: unpublished Ph.D. dissertation

1968. Omkarnath Thakur and V. N. Bhatkhande. In *Saṅgīt Marttand: Pandit Omkarnath Thakur Pratham Punyatithi Smārikā*, ed. G. S. Desai. Varanasi: Benares Hindu University, 44–6

1970. An Historical and Comparative Approach to the Classification of Ragas. *Selected Reports* 1:3. Los Angeles, California: Institute of Ethnomusicology, University of California, pp. 2–78

1979. Classical Music, Cultural Roots and Colonial Rule: An Indic Musicologist Looks at the Muslim World. *Asian Music* 12:1, 5–39

Prajnananda, A. 1965. *A Historical Study of Indian Music*. Calcutta: Anandadhara Prakasharn

Program Notes 1960. Bharatiya Kala Kendra. Music and Dance Recitals (March 1 and 2). New Delhi

1966. Kirana Society of Music. Inauguration Concerts (November 18 and 19). New Delhi

1968. 'Shane-e-Oudh', Kathak Dance Drama. Presented by the Kathak Kendra (August 19–21). New Delhi: Fine Arts Theatre

1978a. Shankar Lal Festival of Music. New Delhi

1978b. Silver Jubilee Celebration of Ustad Nasir Ahmed Khan Taan Samrat (March 27). New Delhi

Puchhavale, Rajabhaiya 1954. *Dhrupad-Dhamār Gāyan*. Gwalior: Ramchandra Sangit Pustak Bhandar

1959–60. *Tān Mālikā*, 2 parts. Gwalior: Ramchandra Sangit Pustak Bhandar

Qureshi, Regula 1981. Islamic Music in an Indian Environment: the Shi'a *Majlis*. *Ethnomusicology* 25:1, 41–71

Raghavan, V. 1957. The Popular and Classical in Music. *Journal of the Music Academy* (Madras) 28:100–6

Rahman, Fazlur 1966. *Islam*. London: Weidenfeld & Nicolson

Raja, C. Kunhan (translator) 1945. *Saṅgīta Ratnākara of Sarṅgadeva*. Madras: The Adyar Library

Rajam, N. 1968. Guruji – A Glimpse of his Greatness. In *Saṅgīt Marttand: Pandit Omkarnath Thakur Pratham Punyatithi Smārikā*, ed. G. S. Desai. Varanasi: Benares Hindu University, 53–6

Ram, Vani Bai 1962. *Glimpses of Indian Music*. Allahabad: Kitab Mahal.

Raman, A. S. 1971. She's 82 and still the Gracious Queen of Song. *The Sunday Standard* (September 12), Magazine Section: VI

Ranade, Ashok D. 1976a. Dr Kumargandharva: An Experiment Within the Tradition. *Journal of the Sangeet Natak Akademi* 42 (October–December) 5–14

1976b. Khayal-singing and Purity of Raga. *Journal of the Indian Musicological Society* 7:4 (December) 41–4

1981. Ustad Bade Ghulam Ali Khan (1901–1968). *Quarterly Journal of the National Centre for the Performing Arts* 10:2 (June) 17–21

Ranade, G. H. 1961. Some Thoughts about the Laya-Aspect of Modern Music. In *Commemoration Volume in Honour of Dr S. N. Ratanjankar*. Bombay: K. G. Ginde, 121–3

1967. Gayanacharya Pt. Anant Manohar Joshi. *Journal of the Sangeet Natak Akademi* 4 (March–April) 69–81

1969. Gayanacharya Pandit Mirashibuwa. *Journal of the Sangeet Natak Akademi* 14 (October–December) 50–64

Ranade, G. M. 1967. *Music in Maharashtra*. New Delhi: Maharashtra Information Centre

Ratanjankar, S. N. 1949. The Closed Forms of Hindusthani Music. *Journal of the Music Academy* (Madras) 20:78

1960. Gamakas in Hindustani Music. *Journal of the Music Academy* (Madras) 31:94–107

1961. Raga, its Meaning and Purpose. In *Commemoration Volume in Honour of Dr S. N. Ratanjankar*. Bombay: K. G. Ginde, 221–5

1965. The Old and the New. *Indian Music Journal* 4 (October–November) 43–8

1966. Musicians and Musical Terms: Allah Diya Khan. *Bhāratīya Saṅgīt* 1:3 (February) 27–31

1967. *Pandit Bhatkhande*. New Delhi: National Book Trust

Rawlinson, H. G. 1938. *India, A Short Cultural History*. New York: D. Appleton-Century Co.

Rizvi, Dolly 1968. *Great Musicians of India*. Bombay: IBH Publishing Company

Roolvink, R. and others 1958. *Historical Atlas of the Muslim People*. Cambridge, Mass.: Harvard University Press

Roy, Bimal 1955. Taana Ancient and Modern. *Lakshya Sangeet* 2:3 (December) 38–9

Sahukar, Mani 1943. *The Appeal in Indian Music*. Bombay: Thacker & Co.

Sambamoorthy, P. 1957. *Sruti Vadyas*. New Delhi: All Indian Handicrafts Board

    1958. *South Indian Music*. Madras: The Indian Music Publishing House, 6th edition

Sambamoorthy, P., P. V. Subramanian, and others 1971. AIR's Seminar on the Harmonium. *Journal of the Sangeet Natak Akademi* 20 (April–June) 5–29

Sangeet Natak Akademi 1968. *Who's Who of Indian Musicians*. New Delhi

Sanyal, Amiya Nath 1959. *Ragas and Raginis*. Calcutta: Orient Longmans Private Ltd

Sastri, K. Vasudev 1968. *Saṅgīt Sāstra*. Lucknow: Hindi Samiti

Saxena, S. K. 1955. D. V. Paluskar. *Thought* (November 5) 17

    1956a. The Late Pandit Bhaskar Rao Bua Bakhle. *Hindustan Times Weekly* (April 15)

    1956b. Ustad Bade Ghulam Ali Khan. *The Hindustan Times* (August 16) 7

    1960. Meaningful Terminology of Ancient Aesthetics. *Vishnu Digambar Jayanti Sangit Samaroha*. New Delhi (program notes, August 19–21)

    1966. Altaf Hussain Khan. *Journal of the Sangeet Natak Akademi* 2 (April) 92–104

    1970. The Fabric of Āmad: A Study of Form and Flow in Hindustani Music. *Journal of the Sangeet Natak Akademi* 16 (April–June) 38–44

    1974. Ustad Ameer Khan: The Man and His Art. *Journal of the Sangeet Natak Akademi* 31 (January–March) 5–12

Seeger, Charles 1960. On the Moods of a Music Logic. *Journal of the American Musicological Society* 13:1–3, 224–61

Shankar, Rajendar 1973. Ustad Allauddin Khan. *Journal of the Sangeet Natak Akademi* 29 (July–September) 9–16

Sharma, B. L. 1971. Contribution of Rajasthan to Indian Music. *Journal of the Indian Musicological Society* 2:2 (April–June) 32–47

Sharma, Bhagavat Sharan 1967. *Tāl Prakash*. Hathras: Sangit Karyalaya

Sharma, Patanjal Deva 1957. *Uttariya Saṅgīt Sāstra*. Delhi: Atma Ram & Sons

Sharma, Prem Lata 1963. European Aesthetics of Music and Indian Sangita Sastra. *Nāda Rūpa* 2:1, 39–90

    1965a. The Concept of Sthaya in Indian Sangitasastra. *Indian Music Journal* 3 (April–May) 29–35

    1965b. A Glossary of Sthayas. *Indian Music Journal* 4 (October–November) 33–41

    1966a. A Glossary of Sthayas: Part II. *Indian Music Journal* 5 (April–May) 29–38

    1966b. The Thumari. *Indian Music Journal* 6 (October–November) 39–40

    1969. Ragakalpadruma. *Indian Music Journal* 10 (Spring) 108–12

    1972 (translator and editor), *Sahasa Rasa*. New Delhi: Sangeet Natak Akademi

Shukla, Narendrarai N. 1966. Evolution in Hindustani Music. In *Music East and West*. New Delhi: Indian Council for Cultural Relations, pp. 32–7

    1971. Alladiya Khan – As I Knew Him. *Journal of the Indian Musicological Society* 2:3 (July–September) 14–25

Singh, Naina Ripjit 1964. *Mushtaq Hussain Khan*. New Delhi: Sangeet Natak Akademi

Singh, Thakur Jaideva 1961. The Evolution of Khyal. In *Commemoration Volume in Honour of Dr S. N. Ratanjankar*. Bombay: K. G. Ginde, pp. 127–32

    1965. The Evolution of Thumri. *Bhāratīya Saṅgīt* 1:2 (November) 7–11

    1974. Amir Khusrau. *Quarterly Journal of the National Centre for the Performing Arts* 3:4 (December) 7–14

Smith, Vincent A. 1919. *Akbar, The Great Mogul (1542–1605)*. Oxford: Clarendon Press, 2nd edition

    1923. *The Oxford History of India from the Earliest Times to the End of 1911*, continued to 1921 by S. M. Edwardes. Oxford: Clarendon Press, 2nd edition revised

Srimal, Pyarelal 1961. Bhāratīya Saṅgīt kī ek sarvotkrsht sharlīkhyāl. *Saṅgit Ank* 8 (August) 17–19, 21

Srinivas, P. B. 1978. Naseer Ahmed Khan: The Musician with the Magic Touch. Program, Silver Jubilee Celebration of Ustad Nasir Ahmed Khan Taan Samrat (March 27) 4–5

Srinivasan, R. and Alakh Niranjan 1959. Whither Indian Music? Need to Revive Pristine Glory. *The Times of India* (January 26)

Statesman 1964. Agra (January 21)

  1968a. [Review of Ishtiaq Hussein Khan AIR Concert, Delhi] (April 16)

  1970. L. K. Pandit Excels (December 21)

  1978. Shankarlal Festival Ends (April 10)

Stewart, Rebecca Maria 1965. An Examination of the Benares School of Tabla Performance. University of Hawaii: unpublished M.A. thesis

Sunday Standard 1972. Dependable Singer [Manik Verma] (March 5)

Sunday Statesman 1968. [Review of Bhimsen Joshi] (December 29), by 'Vigilante'

  1969a. An Excellent Vocal Recital [Mallikarjun Mansur] (February 9)

  1969b. Music [review of Nasir Ahmed Khan and others] (February 16)

Swarup, Bishan 1950. *Theory of Indian Music*. Allahabad: Swarup Brothers, 2nd edition revised (first published 1935)

Thakur, Vasant V. 1966. Faiyaz Khan. *Indian Music Journal* 6 (October–November) 30–1

Times of India 1962. A Great Exponent of Agra Gharana (May 19 or 20)

  1966. Yunus Hussain Khan Excels (November 14)

  1968a. Sulochana Yajurvedi's Fine Recital (October 1)

  1968b. Gangu Bai's Music is Pain Dissolved in Song (October 9)

  1968c. Lively Recital of Vocal Music (October 9)

  1968d. True Flavour of Tradition in Moitra's Recital (October 13, 14, 15, 16)

  1968e. Pran Nath's Keen Feeling for Design (October 14)

  1968f. Brilliant Recital by Laxman Pandit (October 30)

  1968g. Raag Rang Concert Opens on Tame Notes (October 29)

  1968h. Gangubhai Hangal's Star Performance at Festival (October 31)

  1968i. Soulful Singing by Mira Banerjee (October 31)

  1968j. Inspiring Recital by Lakshmanrao (November 29)

  1968k. Poor Tribute to Tansen's Memory (December [9])

  1969a. Exciting Recital by Malikarjun (February 8)

  1969b. Raag Rang Festival Concludes (February [9])

  1969c. Nasir Gives Entrancing Recital (February 25)

  1969d. A Moving Todi by Srinivasa Iyer (February 27)

  1969e. Kishore Amonkar Recital is Disappointing (October 11)

  1970a. Bismillah Excels, but Amir Khan Disappoints (April 20)

  1970b. Shuklaji's Vocal Recital – a Dream Come True (April 27)

  1970c. S. Gurav at his Best in Miyan Malhar (June 1)

  1970d. Pleasing Music Recital by Kamal Tambe (July 14)

  1970e. [Review of Latafat Husain Khan] (August 30)

  1970f. AIR's Loss is Listeners' Gain (November 22)

  1970g. Thrilling Marwa by Lakshmanrao (December 21)

  1971. Pleasing Recital by Lakshman (March 1)

  1978. An Unending Sitar Recital (April 10)

Trikha, S. N. 1967. *A Glimpse of Hindustani Music and Musicians* [illustrated]. New Delhi: S. N. Trikha

Van der Meer, Wim 1975. Cultural Evolution: A Case Study of Indian Music. *Journal of the Sangeet Natak Akademi* 35 (January–March) 49–65

  1980. *Hindustani Music in the 20th Century*. The Hague, Boston, London: Martinus Nijhoff Publishers

Vasant, Ram Charan Chubolia 1969. Kāvya Saṅgit aur uske Praṇetā. *Saṅgīt* 1 (January) 50–6

Vasistha, N. K. 1966. The Kirana Gharana. In Program for inaugural concerts of the Kirana Society of Music. New Delhi (November 18 and 19)

Vasudev, Uma 1958. Bade Ghulam Ali Khan. *The Illustrated Weekly of India* (September 21) 51

  1959. Gangubai Hangal. *The Illustrated Weekly of India* (May 31) 42

  1961. Vilayat Hussain Khan. *The Illustrated Weekly of India* (March 29) 51

  1964. Mushtaq Husain Khan. *The Illustrated Weekly of India* (September 20) 21

Vedi, Dilip Chandra 1969a. He Raised Us. In *Bhaskarbuwa Bakhale Birth-Centenary Souvenir*. ed. Dnyaneshwar Nadkarni. Bombay: Bhaskarbuwa Bakhale Centenary Samiti, 13, 15
    1969b. Incarnation of Musical Beauty. *Ibid.*, 7, 9, 11
    1969c. . . . They All Acclaim. *Ibid.*, 31–2
Vilayat Hussain Khan 1959. Saṅgītajñoṅ ke Samsmaran. New Delhi: Sangeet Natak Akademi
Vyasadeva, Krishnananda (compiler) 1842–9. *Saṅgīt Rāga-Kalpadrūma: Encyclopaedia of Indian Music*. Calcutta. Revised edition by Nagendra Nath Vasu, 1914, Calcutta: Bangiya Sahitya Parishad
Wade, Bonnie C. 1971. Khyāl: A Study of Hindustānī Classical Vocal Music, 2 vols. Ann Arbor, Mich.: University Microfilms
    1973. Chiz in Khyāl: The Traditional Composition in the Improvised Performance. *Ethnomusicology* 17:3 (September) 443–59
    1979. *Music in India: The Classical Traditions*. Englewood Cliffs, N.J.: Prentice-Hall, Inc.
Wadhera, Chandra Prakash 1953a. Music Notes: Delhi's Tribute to Faiyaz Khan. *Times of India* (November 8)
    [1953]b. Music Notes: Hirabai Barodekar, Master of Kirana Style. *Times of India*.
    1954a. Music Notes: Last Great Exponent of Delhi Garana. *Times of India* (May 9)
    1954b. Music Notes: Pandit Omkarnath Thakur. *Times of India* (May 16) 13
    1954c. Music Notes: The Kirana School and its Exponents. *Times of India* (July 11)
    1954d. Music Notes: Vilayat Hussain Khan, Veteran Vocalist. *Times of India* (July 18)
    1955. Music Notes: Behre Bua – A Profile. *Times of India*
    195[6]. Bade Ghulam Ali Khan – A Great Vocalist. *Times of India* (Spring)
    1957. Akademi Awards Winners. *Hindustan Times Weekly* (March 31)
    1975. (editor) *Festival '75: Women Music-Makers of India*. New Delhi: Kaladharmi
Willard, N. Augustus 1965. A Treatise on the Music of Hindoostan. In *Hindu Music from Various Authors*, compiled by Raja Sir Sourindro Mohun Tagore. Benares: Chowkhamba Sanskrit Series Office, 1–122
Yodh, Sadhuram N. 1978. Vilayat Hussain Khan of the Agra Gharana. *Journal of the India Musicological Society* 9:3 (September) 17–37

Index